The Common Worship Lectionary

The Common Worship Lectionary

A Scripture Commentary Year A

John Rogerson

and

Leslie Houlden

Published in Great Britain in 2001

Society for Promoting Christian Knowledge
36 Causton Street
London SW1P 4ST

British Library Cataloguing-in-Publication Data
A catalogue record for this book is available from the British Library

ISBN 978–0–281–05325–4

5 7 9 10 8 6 4

Typeset by Wilmaset Ltd, Birkenhead, Wirral
First printed in Great Britain by
The Cromwell Press, Trowbridge, Wiltshire
Subsequent printing in Great Britain by
Ashford Colour Press

Produced on paper from sustainable forests

Contents

Introduction

The purpose of this book is to offer a particular kind of help and stimulus to those who must address congregations and other groups where the Revised Common Lectionary is followed. We provide entries for all the Sunday readings for Year A and for the readings put down for a selection of major Holy Days.

The tone aims to be decently academic, not in the sense that readers are to feel led back to their earlier education, with examinations in the offing, but in the hope of helping them to read a passage in terms of its context and intentions. Of course it would be confusing, and is not possible in the space available, to give a full range of current ways of understanding a text, but the interpretation offered is meant to be neither eccentric nor shallow.

Given this kind of treatment, the entries are emphatically not designed to give instant sermon-fodder; rather, they offer one element in preparation. To it, the speaker will add pastoral experience and a sense of local need – and of course creative imagination. The underlying 'philosophy' of preaching is that, far from being an exegetical plod, it should be seen as, in effect, an art form, with its own special characteristics. The content is the gospel, and the resources and approaches are manifold – but always so that, by way of rhetorical art, hearts and minds are moved. Of course, sometimes a point from the kind of material given here may make a direct appearance in the spoken address, but that will be because it is a telling way of conveying a particular message.

This philosophy seems to downgrade expository preaching as once commonly practised and sometimes still found in (it is to be hoped) appropriate circumstances. But, despite the unparalleled number of opportunities now available for various kinds of formal biblical study, most congregations do not include many people able to slot in, at a moment's notice, to the world of a passage of Scripture that has just been read – at least, as that passage is currently discussed in the academy. Anyway, it is scarcely desirable that this should be the sermon's primary focus. It is an existential act of speech, offered to particular people, here and now.

A further factor is the character of modern biblical scholarship itself – with which the Christian community has always had a guarded relationship. One might say that it exists, for good or ill, and it takes forms that are sometimes informative, sometimes edifying, but often technical and seemingly remote from life and from modern issues. More seriously, it is widely believed to be inimical to faith, especially in the tendency of some of its historical judgements. It is no part of this book's task to enter into a defence or assessment of modern scholarship, and it is unlikely that those who suspect or reject such scholarship, more or less on principle, will be among those who use the book. In part, we simply take it as an inescapable feature of the current scene. But we do also see it as offering great opportunites for the understanding of the ancient writings that make up the Bible, as well as steering us away from modernizing subjectivism. Our attitude is positive. We also believe that the attempt to grasp the sense of Scripture more clearly is necessary if serious mistakes are not to be made in its use and if mere intuition is not to prevail. The preacher has a responsibility to the text in its own right and decisions to make about its style of relevance, perhaps only of an oblique kind.

Of course modern scholarship is vast in range and multiple in method. The writers of this book have sought to avoid one possible way of reacting to this situation, the method of bland generality. Rather, there has been an attempt to present some of the more stimulating approaches currently in use and to show them working out in practice. The attempt is not rigorously organized. Contributors have written as they thought appropriate to the particular case.

Perhaps the most striking development of recent decades has been to move away from constant attention to questions of mere historicity to an understanding of the minds, intentions and social setting of the numerous writers of Scripture, as well as to seek a grasp of the sheer literary 'flow' of what they wrote. Such approaches are more easily and fruitfully adopted in some writings than in others. Often, in the Old Testament especially, there is too little agreement about the dating or make-up of many of the books that finally emerged. In other cases, notably the Gospels, there is enough discernible homogeneity of mind to offer real illumination if we work along these lines. With the newly adopted sequential reading of one synoptic Gospel in course per year, there is every encouragement to help both preachers and congregations to enter into the thought-forms, ideas and spiritualities of each evangelist in turn – though of course weekly 'doses' of a few verses do not make sermons necessarily the best medium for the conveying of such understanding. (In this respect, liturgists and biblical scholars are not exactly working in tandem.) Our contributors, all experienced scholars and preachers are identified by initials. They do not conform to one particular method or school of biblical interpretation, and there has been no narrow editorial policy in this respect.

Contributors to the Old Testament readings are Richard Coggins and Rex Mason, in addition to contributions from the overall editor, John Rogerson. The New Testament contributions are from Charles Cousar, Ruth Edwards, John Fenton, Sophie Laws, Beverly Gaventa, David Horrell, John Muddiman and the overall editor, Leslie Houlden. The contributions from Charles Cousar and Beverly Gaventa have been included by kind permission of Westminster John Knox Press, and are taken from *Texts for Preaching, Year A*, ed. James D. Newsome. The author's initials are at the end of each entry.

The First Sunday of Advent

Isaiah 2.1–5; Romans 13.11–14; Matthew 24.36–44

Isaiah 2.1–5

Verse 1 is an editorial 'marker' to indicate that a new section of the book is beginning. With all its charges against leaders and people it begins here and ends (chs. 11—12) on a note of hope.

The oracle of vv. 2–4 occurs, with only a few variations, in Mic. 4.1–4. Editors have placed it well in both books. How fittingly here it follows the charges against rulers and people in 1.2–6, 10–17 and 21–23. The corrupt state of society revealed there no doubt fitted both the time of Isaiah in the eighth century and many another time afterwards. Yet, even there, the emphasis is not only on the sin of human beings but the grace of God (1.18–19, 25–26, 27–29).

Verses 2–4 represent a remarkable transformation of chauvinist nationalistic dreams of superiority to be found in some parts of the Old Testament (e.g. Pss. 48.1–8; 72.8–11; Isa. 49.22–26). Certainly, Zion/Jerusalem is seen as the centre of the world, but it is the religious centre of worship and revelation. Here the nations are no longer enemies whose defeat marks Israel's salvation but those who are attracted to the revelation of God's justice as that is embodied in a renewed Israel. In a real sense the promise that the Israelites would act as priests to the world is to be fulfilled (Exod. 19.5–6 and, slightly more chauvinistically, Isa. 61.5–6). However, little is said here of the agents by whom God would dispense the knowledge of his law and administer his justice between the nations. All the emphasis is on him alone.

War becomes a thing of the past, not because there are no longer disputes and clashes of interest between human beings, but because, acknowledging the supreme Lordship of the one God, their disputes are settled by the administration of his justice, exactly the kind of role the Davidic king had been supposed to exercise in the city (e.g. Jer. 22.2–3).

The increase in economic prosperity which the abandonment of arms in favour of agricultural production makes possible (v. 4) is rather like what has been called the 'Peace Dividend' of our own day which, it was hoped, the end of the cold war would make possible.

Two things render this oracle more than an optimistic 'pipe dream'. The first is that it depends, not primarily on human will and intention, but on the grace and power of God. The second is that it calls for faithfulness and obedience *now* (v. 5). For the God who will act is the God who walks with his people now, challenging them to find the reality of the future in the present, calling us, in the words of Heb. 6.18 'to seize the hope set before us'. RM

Romans 13.11–14

With its combination of early Christian eschatological expectation and ethical dualism, Rom. 13.11–14 may initially appear to present the preacher with more hazards than opportunities, especially on the First Sunday of Advent. A careful examination of this text, however, will more than repay the investment by revealing its connections with traditional themes of Advent.

Beginning with Rom. 13.1, Paul offers a series of ethical exhortations having to do with the need for mutual respect among believers, appropriate attitudes toward outsiders, and respect for the 'governing authorities'. This section of exhortations continues in 14.1—15.13, but at the beginning of ch. 14 Paul focuses more intently on conflicts within the Christian community. Rom. 13.11–14, then, marks an important transition within the ethical instructions as a whole.

The first words in the text have to do with time: it is time *now* to wake from sleep because 'salvation is nearer to us now than when we became believers'. Here we catch a glimpse of the dynamic character of Paul's understanding of salvation. Far from being a possession that human beings *acquire* – either by their own achievements or by God's grace – salvation is here personified; it is something that can come closer. In this text salvation is a metonymy, in which the single term stands for the whole of God's actions on behalf of humankind.

Salvation has come closer to us than 'when we became believers'. We might expect Paul to say simply, 'when we converted', but he reserves the traditional language of conversion for reference to Gentiles who 'convert' to belief in the one God (see e.g. 1 Thess. 1.9; cf. Gal. 4.9). Here, as elsewhere (cf. 1 Cor. 15.2, 11), he speaks of the beginning of faith simply as 'to believe'.

Out of context, we might take the references to time in v. 11 as simple markers of time. That is, time has passed since he began to believe. But the beginning of v. 12 announces that the passage of time is not a simple matter of 'marking time'. It is urgent: 'the night is far gone, the day is near.' The salvation that draws near does so, not with the measured pace of sand in a glass or even the beeps of a digital watch, but with the suddenness of an intruder whose schedule is known to no one.

Here the dualistic motif already present in v. 11's imagery of awakening from sleep becomes dominant. Paul contrasts night with day, darkness with light, evil behaviour (revelling, drunkenness, and so on) with that of those who have 'put on the Lord Jesus Christ'. Such dualistic imagery appears, of course, in a wide variety of religious traditions, including the writings of Paul's contemporaries at Qumran and in the community that produced the Fourth Gospel. Paul's contrast between 'darkness' and 'light' refers, here as elsewhere, to the contrast between the darkness of night and the welcome coming of day's light.

What makes this text difficult for interpreters is that Paul places these two concerns, eschatology and ethics, alongside each other without explicitly articulating what the relationship is between the two. Our initial impulse may be to assume that the eschatological reminder constitutes a warning about ethics. That is, behaviour that is not ruled by the light will eventuate in judgement and the wrath of God. For Paul, however, the eschaton is not a threat to employ in order to manipulate human behaviour. Nor does he present the eschaton as a reward for living 'in the light'. Instead, the nearness of the eschaton recalls for him not only an urgency regarding time but also the urgency of the Christian life. Conviction that salvation draws near is, for Paul, inextricably linked with altered behaviour, since the way we live always reflects our loyalties. Consistent with this expectation, he opens this section of ethical admonitions in 12.1–2 with a plea that the reasonable service of God consists in the offering of the 'body', that is, the entire person.

The ancient Christian connection between the first advent of Christ at his birth and the second at his return emerges forcefully in this reading from Romans, as it does in the reading from Matt. 24. Paul's initial words provide us with an important clue to the meaning of both advents: 'Besides this, you know what time it is ...' In the RSV the word 'hour' translates the Greek noun *kairos*, but it is better translated 'time' (NRSV) or 'season', since everything that Paul says in these short verses depends on knowing what time it is. In the same way, what is at stake in Advent is knowing what time it is, and this text challenges us to reflect on that 'time', perhaps in contrast to the ways in which we use our time or fret over our time during the season of Advent. BG

Matthew 24.36–44

Preaching on the second advent presents a challenge. Texts such as this one from Matthew's Gospel come from apocalyptic sections where highly symbolic language is used. On the one hand, to interpret the images literalistically or to refashion the biblical world view as if there were no gap between the first century and the twenty-first leads to absurd claims. Most sensitive readers of the text devoutly wish to avoid the excesses of those interpreters who discover in the biblical images specific timetables for the events of the end-time. On the other hand, if we demythologize the texts and ask only about their existential significance for the moment, we rob the early Christian witness of its hope in the fulfilling, consummating activity of God. The task is to listen carefully to the texts and allow the symbols to evoke the sense of urgency and expectancy at God's future.

Matthew 24.36–44 begins and ends with declarations that the hour of the Son of man's coming is unknown. The fact that even Jesus and the angels are not privy to the time of the second advent provides a sharp warning against speculation and an overeagerness to read the signs of the times. In fact, any claim to special insight about the future merely exposes human arrogance and pretence.

But there is also a positive word in the statement of the unknowableness of the hour. Readers are reminded that they live not as speculators guessing about the future nor as prospectors hunting for gold nuggets, but as those to whom a promise has been given. They count on the reliability of the promiser; they wager on the advent of the Son of man. It is not that the future is somehow mysteriously shrouded so that armchair apocalyptists must seek to break the secret code and discover when the end will be. A promise is less scientific; it allows considerable latitude. Since a promise does not depend on the natural possibilities inherent in the present, it may appear unrealistic by current standards. It may (and in fact the text says that it will) come as a surprise, something one cannot calculate. Nevertheless, those receiving the promise are bound to the future. They are oriented toward the outstanding fulfilment, and thus they watch.

Two vivid figures are set forth in this passage. One is Noah, who is strikingly contrasted with his surrounding society. His contemporaries were eating and drinking, marrying and giving their children in marriage, while he engaged in the incredible task of building a boat. They are not faulted for their gross sinfulness (as in Gen. 6.11–13). They simply assumed that business-as-usual would continue for ever. Their lives were composed of a seemingly endless series of repeated activities, leaving them neither time nor reason to face the future. Noah could hardly perceive what the future would be any more than they, but he acted on a word of God and built a boat. When the flood came, he entered the ark and they were swept away. The days of Noah brought separation.

The other figure is that of the householder who lacks vigilance in protecting the house. Because he fails to keep watch, the thief succeeds in breaking in and plundering the house. What Noah's contemporaries and the householder share in common is that 'they knew nothing' (24.39, 43). Unaware of any impending crisis, they were lulled into a false security by savouring the present to the detriment of a future-oriented existence. They failed to watch.

The readers, however, are commanded to be ready and to watch for the Son of man's coming. Three parables that follow in Matt. 24 and 25 (24.45–51; 25.1–13, 14–30) reinforce the exhortations, but also lead to a climactic, apocalyptic scene. There, in a vision depicting the actual coming of the Son of man, a judgement is rendered regarding those who have or have not tended to the hungry, the thirsty, the stranger, the naked, the sick, and the imprisoned (25.31–46). The judgement leaves no doubt as to what readiness and watchfulness entail.

As the Church observes the season of Advent and is pointed by the lectionary to texts that highlight waiting and watching, it is salutary to recall that what the Church currently awaits is not Christmas but the second advent. In one sense, the baby born in Bethlehem fulfils the promise of the Hebrew Scriptures; but in another sense, the baby becomes a promise of something more, the coming of the Son of man at an unknown hour. We no longer await the baby's birth. We await his return, his revelation as the Lord of heaven and earth, as the King-Judge, who renders judgement and sets right all that is twisted and distorted. Celebrating Christmas means renewing the promise and standing ready to welcome God's consummation. cc

The Second Sunday of Advent

Isaiah 11.1–10; Romans 15.4–13; Matthew 3.1–12

Isaiah 11.1–10

Isaiah 11.1–10 speaks of a king of the Davidic line who is so close to God that he is able to be the perfect intermediary for God's rule on the earth. This is made possible externally by the overthrow of Israel's oppressors by God (10.24–34) and internally by the king's endowment with the Spirit of God.

All kings of the Davidic line were regarded as endowed by this spirit to enable them rightly to administer God's justice (2 Sam. 23.2–5; Ps. 72.1–4), the latter psalm also stressing the link between such justice and God's blessing in the material world with peace among the nations (vv. 5–7, 16, 8–10). The question therefore arises as to whether this was originally a promise by the eighth-century prophet Isaiah concerning a king like Hezekiah or, perhaps more naturally, a later allusion to the end of the Davidic line when Jerusalem fell, predicting its miraculous renewal with the coming of a future 'Messiah'. The constant disappointment of actual historic Davidic kings, so clearly reflected by the editors of the books of Kings, must have led early to such hopes of a future 'ideal' king. Citation of these verses in Isa. 65.25 and Hab. 2.14 show how, whatever their origin, they sustained hopes in times of despair.

In the Old Testament the 'Spirit' of God is depicted as endowment for a particular task or office, whether that were for military prowess (Judg. 6.34), for artistic achievement (Exod. 31.3–5), for prophecy (2 Chron. 24.20) or, as here, for governing. Just as the Spirit-endowed prophet speaks as God speaks, so the ruler governs as God does. This gives him true discernment and insight (v. 2) born of an intimate relationship with God which is his chief delight (v. 3). Indeed, God-like qualities of character are so natural to him that they are like 'clothing' (v. 5). Thus he is not deceived by appearances or taken in by false reports (v. 3), nor does he favour unfairly the wealthy and powerful, but administers impartial justice to all (v. 4). Yet he also has the power to enforce his decisions; his word of decision is powerful and effective as a 'rod', an indispensable factor in maintaining justice.

Just as the rule of God, universally acknowledged, led to international peace (2.4) so it leads to idyllic unity in the realm of nature (vv. 6–9). After all, human sin had made its mark on the natural world (Gen. 3.17–19), and the thought of the restoration of the universal sovereignty of God inspires this poetical and symbolic picture of creation restored, a thought taken up by Paul (Rom. 8.19–25).

Verse 10 stresses the intermediary role of the future king as a 'sign' to all nations to find their true unity in the worship and knowledge of God. Some believed that calling was to be inherited by the whole community (Isa. 55.3–5). RM

Romans 15.4–13

In the later chapters of Romans Paul turns to exhortation and instruction: these verses form part of an extended section from 14.1—15.13 (based to some extent on 1 Cor. 8.1—11.1) in which Paul seeks to foster unity and harmony among different groups in the Roman congregations. These groups take different views on matters of diet, observance of special days, etc., some following Jewish customs in this regard, others not. Urging the members of the congregations to 'please their neighbour' and not themselves, Paul appeals to the example of Christ as the model for this self-giving other-regard, quoting from the Psalms to illustrate the way in which Christ has borne the burdens of others (15.2–3). This is the train of thought which leads into the lectionary reading, which cuts in at v. 4, where Paul reflects on the importance of the (Jewish) Scriptures as the repository of instruction and source of hope.

As the Scriptures reveal the saving purposes of God in Christ so, for Christians facing the prospect of suffering, they may be a source of encouragement, engendering endurance and hope, qualities Paul has already linked and reflected on in this letter (Rom. 5.4; 8.25). Indeed, ultimately, it is God who is the source of endurance, encouragement and hope (15.5, 13). However, these are hardly Paul's central concerns here; he is focused rather on his hope for harmony among the different and antagonistic groups within the church(es) of Rome. His chief appeal is for people to 'welcome one another' (15.7) and particularly for Jewish and Gentile Christians to come together in unity and harmony, despite their differences in matters of conduct. This specific concern – the unification of Jewish and Gentile believers – is evident throughout Romans, where Paul frequently stresses the equality of Jew and Gentile before God (though struggling also to affirm his sense of the special status of Israel: see e.g. Rom. 3.1–9; 9—11). Here the concern is clear in the way Paul declares that Christ came both for the Jews ('the circumcised') and for the Gentiles. The salvation available in Christ is a fulfilment of the promises made to the patriarchs of Israel and a message for the whole world, a fulfilment of Israel's heritage and Scriptures rather than an abrogation or rejection of them. Thus Paul underpins his point with a list of scriptural quotations, linked by the common occurrence of the keywords 'Gentiles' and 'people(s)'. Paul's vision is of one people offering praise to God – 'the Gentiles, with his people' (15.10) – and together finding joy, peace and hope in the Spirit. DH

Matthew 3.1–12

Matthew's first two chapters have explained by means of narrative what he thought Mark had meant when, in the opening words of his book, he had used the titles 'Christ' and 'Son of God'. Matthew now returns to his source and reproduces Mark's description of John the Baptist, not in identical words (he seldom does that) but with alterations, omissions and additions, all designed to retell the gospel story in the way that Matthew believes it should be done.

He signals the beginning and ending of this part of his book by means of an *inclusio*: putting identical words into the mouths of John and then Jesus, 'Repent, for the kingdom of heaven has come near' (3.2; 4.17). This is his version of Mark's 'The time is fulfilled, and the kingdom of God has come near' (Mark 1.15). ('Heaven' in Matthew is a common devout periphrasis for 'God'.)

Whereas Mark had attributed the whole of what seems to be a composite quotation to Isaiah, Matthew corrects this by omitting the words from Malachi (3.1) and concentrating on those from Isaiah (40.3). Both evangelists are using the Septuagint version of Isaiah which, appropriately, locates the one who cries in the wilderness (Hebrew – and the men of Qumran – read: 'Prepare in the wilderness the way of the Lord').

The Baptist is presented as both fulfilment and prophet of things still to come. He is Elijah returned from heaven (2 Kings 1.8; 2.11; Mal. 4.5; Ecclus. 48.10; see also Matt. 17.12f.) and gives warning of the coming day of the Lord, of God's judgement, of the one who is greater than himself, and (though this is only hinted at, v. 9) of the expansion of Israel to include the Gentiles. John's message is a brief summary (or 'pre-echo') of the message of Jesus, as Matthew will set it out in the rest of his book. So, just as he fills out Mark's very concise report of the words of Jesus, so he has also expanded the Marcan account of the Baptist's proclamation.

One feature of this passage, and indeed of Matthew's Gospel as a whole, is the emphasis on the need for repentance and good works, referred to by means of the metaphor of fruit and harvest. The coming of the time when God will rule the world provokes a crisis for the world's inhabitants, beginning with those with whom he has made his ancient covenants. They are not to think of themselves as exempt from judgement, nor are they (or others) to think that John's baptism (or Jesus') will of itself deliver them from the wrath to come. Good works are required and the lack of them will bring punishment; they are the only certain evidence of repentance.

The question is sometimes raised whether the historical figures, John the Baptist and Jesus, were dissimilar, one an ascetic and the other (as he is reputed as saying it was said of him), a glutton and a drinker (11.19). Here at least, Matthew seems to want to place them side by side, with identical statements concerning the coming of the kingdom and repentance, rather than to contrast them, as perhaps he does in 11.18f. The herald speaks as the one he proclaims. JF

The Third Sunday of Advent

Isaiah 35.1–10; James 5.7–10; Matthew 11.2–11

Isaiah 35.1–10

This magnificently poetic picture of the future salvation of God's people follows the account of the judgement of Edom in ch. 34, in which Edom is seen as a type of the enemies of God. Evil must be overcome before salvation can be experienced. The chapter contains many of the themes and much of the language and imagery of chs. 40–55, not surprisingly considering that they are separated only by the historical interlude of chs. 36–39. Second Isaiah's picture of salvation as deliverance from exile in Babylon has here been broadened to promise salvation from all conditions of human suffering and all 'Babylonish captivities of the people of God', of which the miraculous deliverance through the wilderness from bondage in Egypt was prototype and promise, supplying much of the imagery here.

The yawning desert separating all dispersed Jews from their land of promise will be miraculously made as fruitful as Lebanon with its forests and Sharon with its rich pasturage (cf. Ps. 104.16). Indeed the natural world will reflect the very character and nature of God as he bestows 'glory' and 'majesty' on it, the qualities he himself possesses and which he will reveal to his people (v. 2). The vision which Isaiah had in the temple will be fulfilled as 'the whole earth becomes full of his glory' (6.1–3).

It is such a vision and such a hope that form the basis for the encouragement given by the prophet to all who are in present despair. If it is true that people perish without a (prophetic) vision (Prov. 29.18) it is essential that God's messengers make God and his certain action the centre of their message (v. 4).

The result is that the mission of the Servant (Isa. 42.7; cf. 61.1–3) will find fulfilment as those who have been blind to the signs of God's presence, deaf to all encouragement to hope, and crippled from taking any constructive action will find the release of the newly saved (vv. 5–6). Their journey from despair to deliverance will be possible since the aridity of the desert will be transformed, as once the wilderness of Sinai provided manna and water, and the wild beasts who made it dangerous to travel will no longer terrify them (v. 7). The way across the desert promised by Second Isaiah (40.3–4) will be open to God's people, 'holy' since it leads to the temple in Zion and thus to worship of, and fellowship with, God (v. 8).

They will be the 'redeemed' of the Lord, those for whom God has acted as nearest kinsman in their need (Lev. 25.25–28) and whom he has 'ransomed' from the powers of evil on whom he has shown his vengeance (v. 4, cf. 34.8).

Matthew 11.5 and Luke 7.22 show how naturally the early Christian Church found a promise here, which was more fully to be realized in Jesus Christ. R M

James 5.7–10

This passage may initially recall Rom. 13.11–14, with its connection between apocalyptic expectation and ethical admonition, but the two passages actually reflect very different understandings of the 'coming of the Lord'. For Paul, that day, which he refers to simply as 'salvation', seems to be very close at hand and impinges on the present. James shows, apart from this passage, very little expectation of an immediate parousia, and seems to be introducing it to offer some specific ethical teaching, typical of the paraenesis that runs throughout the letter.

James 5.7–8 introduces and repeats the admonition of patience or endurance. 'Be patient, therefore, beloved, until the coming of the Lord.' Following the example of the farmer's patience, the admonition is restated: 'You also must be patient. Strengthen your hearts, for the coming of the Lord is near.' Taken on its own, without further comment, this admonition seems odd. How is it possible to be *patient* if the coming of the Lord is indeed at hand? The urgency that pervades the Son of man sayings in the Gospels or the eschatological language in Paul's letters is missing here. Why encourage patience in this situation?

The example of the farmer separates the two forms of the admonition and may shed light on this curious interpretation of the parousia: 'The farmer waits for the precious crop from the earth, being patient with it until it receives the early and the late rains.' Unlike the imagery of the 'thief in the night' (1 Thess. 5.2) or the 'stars ... falling from heaven' (Mark 13.25), which conjures up the unexpected, even the violent, this imagery invokes the farmer, who must wait for the regular, predictable cycle of Palestinian rains before the arrival of the harvest. For the author of James, the parousia has less to do with God's invasion of the world as it is than it does with the absolute reliability of God's promises. Like the farmer who relies on God to send the needed rain (Deut. 11.14; Jer. 5.24; Zech. 10.1), the faithful may and must rely on God. Patience derives from that certainty about God's protection.

James 5.9 makes concrete and specific the general exhortation to patience: 'Beloved, do not grumble against one another.' In the Septuagint this same verb (*stenazein*) characterizes the sighing of people who live in situations of oppression, whether as a result of their own sin or that of others (e.g. Exod. 2.23; 6.5; Isa. 59.11). Here it applies to the complaints believers may have against other believers; hence, the repetition of the word 'beloved' in the middle of the injunction heightens the scandal of believers engaging in wrongdoing against one another. With his negative view of those outside the church, James is characteristically unconcerned about 'grumbling' that may be directed toward the outside. Believers are not to grumble because 'the Judge is standing at the doors'.

We find in vv. 10–11 other examples of patience and endurance. The prophets are often cited for their suffering (e.g. Acts 7.51–52), but here they serve as examples also of patience. James 5.11 singles out the individual Job, who remained steadfast throughout great suffering. These examples suggest that the call for patience in this text does not arise from some general conviction about the virtue of patience.

Instead, the patience referred to is that of suffering people who know that God will vindicate them.

The larger context of this passage reinforces this conclusion. Throughout the letter James rails against those who lack integrity, whose actions do not convey the faith that they assert (1.22–27; 2.14–26). Just prior to our passage comes a warning to the rich about the judgement that will come upon them as a result of their mistreatment of others (5.1–6). The 'therefore' at the beginning of v. 7 connects our passage with what precedes it, suggesting that the patience called for is that of believers, even in situations of oppression and injustice.

For the letter of James, then, the advent of Jesus Christ calls for patience, even on the part of the oppressed and suffering. The patience that is called for, however, is not so much passive acquiescence to situations of oppression and injustice as it is active confidence in God, whose promise extends to human beings in every context and every situation. The advent of Jesus Christ, for this letter, also contains a theme of judgement. To say that 'the Judge is standing at the doors' is to recall that Jesus' advent brings with it the accountability of human beings before God. The letter of James reminds us that our accountability includes both our convictions and our actions. BG

Matthew 11.2–11

The Gospel reading for the Third Sunday of Advent returns to the figure of John the Baptist, but now in a far different setting from the reading of last Sunday. No longer in a wilderness preaching his message of judgement and calling for repentance, no longer the baptizer of and witness to Jesus as 'the one who is to come', John is now in prison. It is the first mention of John's confinement in Matthew, and only later do the readers learn that the arrest was occasioned by John's denunciation of Herod for his philandering with his sister-in-law. The narrator says that Herod really wanted to kill John, but withheld from doing so because the people took John to be a prophet (14.1–5).

In prison, however, John is troubled. Hearing about 'what the Messiah was doing', he sends disciples to Jesus to ask, 'Are you the one who is to come, or are we to wait for another?' What precipitates John's uncertainty? How does he move from being the vigorous preacher of repentance to being a questioning doubter? The text provides us with two possible explanations. One reason for his uncertainty could be his situation in prison. This is the explanation often picked up in sermons on the passage and developed psychologically, that is to say, John lies depressed and forgotten in his jail cell, and as his incarceration continues he becomes haunted with doubts. Out of his dejection and discouragement, he sends to question Jesus.

The text, however, offers another, more likely, explanation. In prison John hears about 'what the Messiah was doing', presumably those acts of healing and mercy depicted in Matt. 8–9. To a fierce denouncer of the sins of the people, the Messiah's primary task must be to carry out the final judgement, to see that the axe is laid to the root of the trees and to burn every tree that does not bear fruit (3.10–12). What sort of Messiah could Jesus be who teaches in the synagogues, preaches the gospel of the kingdom, and heals every disease and infirmity (9.35)? John seems uncertain, not because of his own plight but because of what Jesus is reputed to be doing. He is not turning out to be the kind of Messiah John expected.

John's question provides an occasion for Jesus to clarify who he is. In the language of two texts from Isaiah (35.5–6; 29.18–19), he invites John's messengers to report what they have seen, what in fact he is doing for the blind, the lame, the lepers, the deaf, the dead and the poor. His activity fulfils an expectation about the Messiah from the Scriptures. To be sure, there is judgement in Jesus' presence; the next few chapters of Matthew relate the various responses to him, many of which are negative and self-condemning. But his primary activity is the restoration of the needy and the giving of life to the lifeless. No wonder that John has doubts about the Messiah!

What John needs is a new understanding of who the Messiah in reality is, what sort of work the Messiah does, and with what sort of people he does it. Jesus acknowledges that such a new understanding may be hard to come by. He pronounces a beatitude on the person who takes no offence at him (11.6). Seeing and hearing that Jesus is preoccupied with people who have been marginalized by their situations, who can do little or nothing for themselves, may represent a threat to some and prevent their accepting Jesus as Messiah. Like John, they expect that the Messiah should be doing more about stopping crime and punishing criminals. They would prefer to wait for another in hopes of finding a leader more to their liking. Jesus alone, however, defines his own Messiahship.

From John's uncertainties the focus changes to Jesus' opinions about John. Three times the crowds are confronted with their eagerness to hear John ('What did you go out . . . to look at?' 'What then did you go out to see?' 'What then did you go out to see?'). He is a prophet, but more than a prophet. He fulfils a special role as the messenger who prepares the way of the Messiah (11.10; Mal. 3.1). There is no one born of woman who is greater than John, Jesus states. Superior accolades for this figure who occupies a distinctive place in the prophetic line-up! And yet, the one who is least in the kingdom of heaven is greater than John. The age of fulfilment toward which John points is so decisive that even Jesus' disciples (named and commissioned in the previous chapter of Matthew's Gospel), who understand and share his fulfilling activity, are greater than John. The comment is not made as a rebuke of John, but as an acknowledgement of the surpassing character of the new age dawning in the person of Jesus. It is an age in which disciples are still vulnerable to arrest and imprisonment (10.17–23), but also are charged and empowered to participate in the very messianic activity of Jesus (10.7–8). cc

The Fourth Sunday of Advent

Isaiah 7.10–16; Romans 1.1–7; Matthew 1.18–25

Isaiah 7.10–16

This describes an encounter between the prophet and King Ahaz following the earlier one recounted in vv. 1–9 relating to an attempt by Israel and Syria to force Ahaz into a defensive alliance against Assyria. His inclination was to appeal to Assyria for help, a course vigorously rejected by Isaiah. In this second interview the prophet promises Ahaz a 'sign', any sign, for nothing is beyond God's power whether as high as heaven or deep as Sheol (v. 11; cf. Ps. 139.7–8). Ahaz cloaks his lack of faith under a veneer of piety citing the spirit if not the letter of Deut. 6.16.

In interpreting the 'sign' of the birth of a child given the name 'Immanuel' (= 'God is with us', an often repeated credal statement from the temple worship, Ps. 46.7, 11) it is important to realize that *in the first instance* this was a sign for Ahaz in the eighth century BC. If some young, pregnant woman (whether one of the royal household, the prophet's wife or just any woman) had the faith and courage to call her child 'Immanuel', that faith would be vindicated within the two or three years it took the child to grow to an age of discernment (v. 16). Those who appeared to be threatening now would be shown for what they were. (We should note that it is the *name* of the child which is significant for Isaiah, not the manner of its birth. The use of another Hebrew word could have stressed unambiguously the virginity of the mother had that been intended.)

There is, in fact, a strange note of ambiguity running through the prophet's words. The news that 'God is among us' can be good or bad, according to what he finds when he comes (cf. Mic. 3.11). It is not clear whether the 'curds and honey' the child will eat refer to the rich diet of 'milk and honey' promised in Canaan (Exod. 3.8) or suggest a return to the nomadic fare of the wilderness. The promise that Ahaz and his people will know 'such days' as they have not known since the division of the kingdom (v. 17) leaves open the question whether they are to be such good or such bad days. A later reference to the threat from Assyria comes from someone who saw it as threat. God's 'rock' may be a rock of salvation or a rock of stumbling (28.16; cf. 8.14 and Luke 2.34–35). It depends on our response.

To say that this prophetic word applied *initially* to Ahaz in the eighth century BC is by no means to limit its relevance to its original context. The birth of a child can be a sign that God is 'with' his people in all their times of darkness and despair. Matthew's claim that this particular promise found fulfilment in the birth of Jesus (Matt. 1.22–23) has found echo in Christian faith and worship ever since. RM

Romans 1.1–7

The most obvious point of association between these opening lines of Romans and the other texts for this Sunday derives from Paul's reference in v. 3 to the Davidic descent of Jesus. Beyond that narrow connection, however, these verses announce the coming of the gospel of Jesus Christ, so that the assignment of this passage to Advent is far from arbitrary.

Romans 1.1–7 constitutes the most extensive salutation and greeting of any of Paul's letters. Because Paul had not yet been to Rome (see 1.13) he cannot rely on a personal relationship having already been established and needs to provide an introduction of himself (vv. 1, 5–6) and the gospel he proclaims (vv. 2–4). That these two are inseparable is made clear from the way in which they are introduced here.

The three phrases with which he identifies himself reiterate Paul's connection with the gospel. First he says that he is a 'servant of Jesus Christ' (NRSV). The Greek word *doulos* is more accurately rendered by the English 'slave' rather than 'servant', and the more forceful word 'slave' appropriately conveys Paul's sense of the compulsion under which he labours (cf. 1 Cor. 9.16). 'Called to be an apostle' reinforces the involuntary nature of Paul's labour; that is, he did not choose to be an apostle, but was chosen by God. 'Set apart for the gospel of God' both restates Paul's calling and introduces the gospel itself, which becomes the subject of vv. 2–4.

What Paul says first about the gospel is that God promised it 'through his prophets in the holy scriptures'. This early reference to Scripture will seem odd if we think of Roman Christians as primarily Gentile, but there are strong indications that Jewish Christians were also part of the Roman church (e.g. the discussion of the law in Rom. 7). More important, a recurrent issue in Romans is the faithfulness of God, and this early reference to the promises of Scripture introduces that issue by insisting on God's having kept God's promise.

In vv. 3–4 the gospel takes on content in the form of two assertions about Jesus Christ. First, he 'was descended from David according to the flesh'. Second, he 'was declared to be Son of God with power according to the spirit of holiness by resurrection from the dead'. Formally, the two assertions stand in parallel; the first describes Jesus 'according to the flesh' and the second 'according to the spirit'. There is no indication that the second assertion negates or deemphasizes the first. Both assertions are part of the gospel.

The first assertion locates Jesus firmly within the people of Israel and, indeed, within the royal line itself. Any Christian claim that Jesus was not really a Jew or ceased to be a Jew flounders on this statement that God's Son was from the house of David. This assertion also undermines the perennial Christian temptation to deny or denigrate the humanity of Christ, whom Paul clearly identifies as living 'according to the flesh' (cf. Rom. 9.5).

If we read the second assertion as a bit of systematic theology, it poses numerous problems. The suggestion that Jesus becomes 'Son of God' only at his resurrection contradicts the Gospels as well as the hymn Paul quotes in Phil. 2.5–11, and consequently commentators scurry to resolve the difficulties. What these attempts sometimes miss is the richness that emerges from the varying early Christian interpretations about the point at which Jesus is the Christ (e.g. at the baptism in Mark? At the conception in Luke and Matthew? At creation in John?). Attempts to resolve the conflicts also overlook the parallel between the two assertions. Paul's is not a systematic attempt to describe the point at which Jesus *became* the Christ. Verse 4 is, rather, a statement about the triumph of God as it breaks through in the resurrection of Jesus Christ.

Verse 5 moves from this recitation of the gospel *in nuce* back to the apostolic task. It is through Jesus Christ that Paul and his co-workers attempt to bring about the 'obedience of faith' among all nations. This peculiar phrase appears again in 16.26 and nowhere else in Paul's letters. It may be a subtle way of forging a compromise between those Christians (both Jew and Gentile) who emphasize the need for obedience to the law and those Christians (both Jew and Gentile) who emphasize the significance of faith alone. To speak of the obedience of faith, or the obedience that stems from faith, is to enable both groups (or the several groups that may have existed) to hear their own claim and also that of their brothers and sisters.

Verses 6 and 7 bring the salutation and greeting to a close in a way customary for Paul. It is important to note, however, that this greeting involves the statement that believers in Rome are called. Not only apostles, but also 'ordinary' believers receive their faith as a calling from God. BG

Matthew 1.18–25

Matthew begins the narrative chosen for this last Sunday in Advent with the declaration, 'Now the birth of Jesus the Messiah took place in this way' (1.18). But as the verses unfold, it becomes apparent that Matthew is not so much concerned with Jesus' birth as with his conception and naming. The birth is finally reported in the last verse of the chapter, but simply to signal the termination of the period of sexual abstinence between Mary and Joseph (1.25). The circumstances surrounding the conception of Jesus and the names given this special baby, however, serve to identify who he is and what he is to do.

The *conception* is described from the perspective of Joseph, this righteous man who repeatedly obeys the counsel of the messenger sent by God (1.20, 24; 2.13–15, 19–21, 22). When Mary discovers she is pregnant, we are told nothing of the conversation she had with Joseph, intriguing as that interchange may have been. Instead, we are informed that on hearing the news Joseph determines to handle the matter in as discreet and honourable a manner as possible, until he learns in a dream that the baby is not the result of human activity at all, but of the Holy Spirit.

Through this interesting and somewhat allusive account, two very clear affirmations are made about Jesus. First, the conception is the work of God. Jesus is the product of a fresh, new divine act, startling and heretofore unheard of. While there may have been tales of such unusual births in ancient literature, the long list of characters enumerated in Matthew's genealogy (1.1–17) contains none with a beginning like this. Jesus is not simply one more name like all the rest. From his very conception, this child is distinctive, unique. He is more than the accumulated best of his ancestors. The developing narrative tells how he acts distinctively as the agent of the divine Spirit and how he manifests uniquely the power of God.

Second, the stress on Mary's virginity serves to tie the conception and birth of Jesus to the Septuagint text of Isa. 7.14. Matthew obviously wants to make clear to his readers that neither Joseph nor any other male was Jesus' biological father. Joseph's own suspicions are satisfied by the word of the messenger, and the narrator goes out of his way to remove any suspicions the reader might have about Joseph's part in the conception. 'He had no marital relations with her until she had borne a son' (1.25). There may be some attempt here to respond to charges made in or to Matthew's community that Mary was an adulteress and Jesus an illegitimate child (such rumours undoubtedly circulated on other settings; cf. John 8.41). The virginal conception is not to be thought of as disreputable or embarrassing. But more important than this denial, the virginal conception signals the beginning of the fulfilment of God's saving purposes. This fresh, new act of God ushers in an age, long expected and hoped for, yet in a fashion so unusual that it could hardly be anticipated. The sign of Ahaz is finally revealed, but in a way that neither Ahaz nor Isaiah could ever have dreamed.

If the conception calls attention to Jesus' special place in history, so also does his *naming*. Joseph, acting the part of the legal father, is directed by the messenger to call the child Jesus, and in case non-Jewish readers miss the significance of the name, the narrator adds an interpretation, 'for he will save his people from their sins' (1.21). The explanation, together with the title 'Messiah' used earlier for Jesus (1.16), alerts us to the peculiar role the infant is to play throughout his ministry and especially in his death and resurrection – the Messiah who heals divided selves and reconciles to God those estranged and alienated (see 9.1–8; 26.28). No ordinary figure this baby is to be, but one who does what only God can do.

This explanation of Jesus' name serves an important function, particularly in light of the narrative Matthew provides us. It is Matthew's Jesus who directs us to turn the other cheek and go the extra mile (5.39–41), to be perfect as the Heavenly Father is perfect (5.48), not to lay up treasures on earth (6.19), to avoid anxiety about basic physical needs and seek the kingdom first (6.25–33). When reading selections of Matthew's account in isolation, it is easy to become overwhelmed by the demands of the gospel and wonder whether one's shortcomings and failures can ever be transcended. But at the outset, before the demands are made, we are told that the Jesus who makes such demands is the one to 'save his people from their sins'. Wherever the name of Jesus appears, there is the assurance of divine forgiveness.

But the text gives the baby another name – Emmanuel, again given special stress by being translated, 'God is with us'. It is not so much a name as a title, derived from the citation of Isa. 7.14. But it functions in the narrative as an important description of who Jesus is as he engages in his ministry (Matt. 17.17; 18.20; 26.29). Wherever Jesus is, God is there, present with the people of faith. Of particular significance is the conclusion of the Gospel, where Jesus declares as part of his commission to the disciples, 'I am with you always, to the end of the age' (28.20).

Jesus' story is bracketed by these two declarations of the divine presence – Emmanuel. He is no mere figure of the past, contained by the space of three decades, localized in places like Bethlehem, Nazareth, Galilee and Judea. Jesus is the presence of God, accompanying the Church in its mission, energizing its teaching and pioneering its efforts to make disciples of all nations. CC

Christmas Day and Evening of Christmas Eve

Set I
Isaiah 9.2–7; Titus 2.11–14; Luke 2.1–14 (15–20)

Isaiah 9.2–7

This passage illustrates how God's word in Scripture can prove relevant at different times, and in very varied circumstances. The many parallels to the 'royal psalms' show that this passage could have been used at the coronation of any of the Davidic kings. Such an occasion was seen as the dawn of a bright new epoch (v. 2, cf. 2 Sam. 23.4; Ps. 110.3). The joy of hope the occasion brought, like the joy of harvest or the division of the spoils of war (v. 3) finds echo in 1 Kings 1.39–40; Ps. 132.9. The overthrow of national enemies (vv. 4–5), the responsibility of the king (1 Sam. 8.19–20), is assured because of the promise of God to his 'son' (Pss. 2.8–9; 89.23). Indeed, at his accession the king was 'born', given birth as a son by God (v. 6, cf. Ps. 2.7). As Egyptian pharaohs at their accession were given a number of titles, so the king here is given four. He will govern in divinely given wisdom of counsel; he will be a god-like warrior; he will be a 'father' to the nation for a long period and, by his military prowess and just rule (v. 7) he will establish conditions of 'peace', that is both security from the nation's enemies and all that makes for fullness of life (cf. Ps. 72.1–4, 8–11, 16). Indeed, such conditions will endure 'for ever' (v. 7, cf. Ps. 72.5), as conventional a wish as 'O king, live for ever'.

This passage may, therefore, consist of a number of very general themes from the royal worship of the pre-exilic Jerusalem temple. Yet Isaiah may have composed it particularly for the accession of Hezekiah to the throne, in which case the 'darkness' and distress of the later part of ch. 8 (see especially v. 32, cf. 9.2) would have referred to the ravages caused by the Assyrians under Tiglath-Pileser III. Yet such times of darkness often returned. Job uses the same word as that in v. 2 to describe the darkness of the underworld and the despair of death (Job 10.21–22). Again and again the people of God would have felt the need for the birth of a great deliverer who would fill the conventional phrases of the enthronement ceremonies with new and real meaning, especially when the Davidic line proved a failure and came to an end. A passage like this would furnish 'messianic' hopes for the Jewish people after the exile. And Christians found in the birth, life, death and resurrection of Jesus the perfect fulfilment of all that is merely promised in this passage (Matt. 4.15–16). Nevertheless, at each level it reinforces the truth that, only when the king's sovereign rights are acknowledged, can people know the blessings of his reign.

The promise rests on God's 'zeal'. The word can denote the 'ardent' love of a lover

(Song of Sol. 8.6) and God's burning concern for the well-being of his people (Zech. 1.14). RM

Titus 2.11–14

This passage is one of a small number of more doctrinal interludes in the largely pastoral, ethical and organizational topics that occupy the greater part of the Pastoral Epistles. This proportioning of the theological and practical themes is one factor that leads us to think of these writings as coming from the post-Pauline church world of the late first or early second century: practical concerns were now even more pressing for the Christian communities, and so was the need to find ways of developing cohesion in holding to basic Christian beliefs that could be succinctly stated.

It is hard to think of a more succinct statement of those beliefs than that presented here, with its mixture of doctrine and, immediately, its moral implications. And (v. 15) all is to be propagated with authority, the arrangements for which are of major importance for this writer, in the closely interwoven spheres of Church and household (1.5–9; 2.1–10; cf. 1 Tim. 3).

Nevertheless, despite the community concerns, the vision remains universal ('salvation to all', v. 11), even if God's practical goal has an Israel-like quality – the creation of a purified people (v. 14).

The vocabulary in which the doctrine is couched owes something to Scripture and something to the wider religious terminology of the day. 'Has appeared' (v. 11) and 'manifestation' (v. 13) belong to the same family of words: *epiphaneia* conjures up the drama of a visit by the deified emperor, with its excitement and hope of tangible benefits. All the more so with Christ. This idea of his appearance (however expressed) had tended to be associated with the hope of his return, but now the two statements refer to the first and the second comings, as if in balance. They are the brackets within which Christian life is lived.

'Saviour', though a scriptural word, is also characteristic of the imperial cult. It is a favourite with this writer to refer to both God and Christ. The translation of v. 13, it has to be said, presents problems. That commonly given ('our great God and Saviour, Jesus Christ'), which seems to affirm Christ's divinity, would be unique in this (and probably, in fact, any other New Testament) writer, and it is hard to imagine quite what might have been in his mind (he is not the most daring of theologians) – unless the context is indeed that of other cults, and Jesus Christ is being affirmed as *our* deity and saviour (as opposed to those worshipped by others): he, and he alone, is the centre of our full devotion. Less dramatically, the translation could and perhaps should be: 'the glory of the great God and of our saviour Jesus Christ'. It is God who sent Jesus as a supreme act of 'grace' (v. 11); and the writer's perspective appears plainly in 1 Tim. 2.5. LH

Luke 2.1–14 (15–20)

This passage, so beautifully crafted in Luke's narrative, certainly counts among the most familiar passages in the Bible. Dramatizations of the Christmas story as well as repeated readings make it a well-known text. People who know little or nothing about the Christian faith know about the shepherds and the angelic chorus. For that reason, the text presents a challenge to the preacher to hear and declare a fresh word that probes the familiar and yet moves beyond it.

What immediately emerges from the early portion of this story is the political context in which the birth of Jesus is recounted. We are told that Emperor Augustus had ordered an enrolment and that Quirinius was governor of Syria. Despite the problems surrounding the historical accuracy of this beginning (dealt with in most commentaries), the narrative setting cannot be ignored. It is not against the background of the reign of Herod, the local ruler who is known for his heavy-handed and brutal ways, that the story of Jesus' birth is told (as in Matthew's Gospel), but against the background of the Roman Empire.

The Emperor Octavian was a prominent figure, who solidified the somewhat divided loyalties of the various regions of the empire and ushered in the famous Pax Romana. In 27 BC, the Roman senate gave him the title 'the August One'. Poets wrote of his peaceful ideals and anticipated that his reign would signal a golden age based on virtue. Ancient monuments even ascribed to him the title 'saviour'. He represented a high and hopeful moment in Roman history.

Luke gives Octavian his familiar title and recognizes his authority by noting that 'all the world' (actually the Roman Empire) is encompassed by his decree. Often in ancient times the demand for a census evoked rebellion and opposition, but Luke records a dutiful response: 'All went to their own towns to be registered.' The mention of Augustus not only provides an indispensable time reference to help readers date the events that are being narrated, but also enables Luke to explain how Mary and Joseph, who lived in Nazareth, had a baby born in Bethlehem.

The introduction, however, provides a much more important function than this. It sets the stage for the birth of one who is Saviour, Christ the Lord. Octavian is not pictured as an evil, oppressive tyrant, a bloody beast 'uttering haughty and blasphemous words' (Rev. 13.5). The Roman state in Luke's narrative simply does not represent the enemy against which Christians must fight. The backdrop for Jesus' birth is rather a relatively humane and stable structure, the best of ancient governments, which led to dreams of a peaceful era and aspirations of a new and wonderful age. The decades between the time of Jesus' birth and the time of Luke's narrative, however, exposed the failed hopes and the doused aspirations. Octavian is succeeded by caesars who turn the imperial dreams into nightmares.

Against the horizon of disillusionment, we read of the birth of another ruler, from the lineage of David, whose meagre beginnings, on the surface, do not compare with the promise and hope of Augustus. All the world obeys the caesar, but Jesus' parents are rejected and relegated to a cattle stall. Yet the birth of Jesus is good news for all the people, ensuring a new and lasting promise of peace and goodwill.

The narrative does not present us with a confrontation between Augustus and Jesus, but with a contrast between vain expectations and true hope, between the disappointment that follows misplaced anticipations and the energy born of a divine promise, between the imposing but short-lived power of Caesar's rule and the humble manifestation of the eternal dominion of God, between the peace of Rome and the peace of Christ. The titles for Jesus, found later in the narrative (Luke 2.11) – Saviour, Christ and Lord – stand out starkly against the claims made for Augustus, and in the ensuing story become titles interpreted in fresh and surprising ways.

The setting for Luke's birth narrative clarifies for us the distinction between false hopes and true ones. Relatively humane, stable structures that contribute to the well-being of others often tend to promise more than they can deliver. Their very positive nature becomes seductive and generates impossible expectations. In contrast, Jesus is the anchor for reliable hope, for dependable promises, for anticipations that are more than fulfilled. CC

Set II
Isaiah 62.6–12; Titus 3.4–7; Luke 2.(1–7), 8–20

Isaiah 62.6–12

It is usually thought that chs. 56—66 come from the time shortly after some had returned from the Babylonian exile and were addressing the tasks of rebuilding city, temple and national life so poignantly mirrored in the book of Haggai. Some of the great promises of return in chs. 40—55 had, therefore, been fulfilled, but the reality fell painfully short of the kind of pictures of salvation promised there. So the words and imagery of chs. 40—55 are used a great deal in these chapters to reassure them and renew those hopes.

In the light of v. 1 it is probably the prophet and his circle who are called upon for such an active ministry of intercession in vv. 6–7. The idea of the prophet as 'watchman', looking, like the sentry on the walls of a besieged city, for the first signs of deliverance and proclaiming news to the people, is a familiar one (e.g. Ezek. 3.17; Isa. 21.6–12; 52.8, cf. 2 Sam. 18.24–27). Here the prophet calls for a more strenuous response to the situation than a resigned 'How long, O Lord?' It brings us face to face with the mystery of God's self-limitation in calling for active human participation in the accomplishment of his work, in both deeds and, as here, in prayer.

The response from God is as emphatic as could be imagined, reinforcing the promise of deliverance from the crippling economic hardship which comes from political subservience with an oath of the most solemn nature (vv. 8–9). The promise envisages the restoration of worship in the rebuilt temple as they praise God and know fellowship with him there (v. 9). The same link between economic prosperity and the centrality of God among them in the rebuilt temple is made by Haggai (Hag. 2.4–9).

Again active human participation is called for in a clear allusion to the promise of 40.3–5 that God would miraculously make a highway by which his exiled people could return home (v. 10). Here prophet and people are called on to make all ready for the great things God is going to do in their midst. Presumably, what is in mind is being ready by repentance and faith and doing all in their power to rebuild a new community. Again the mystery of divine sovereignty which yet makes use of human cooperation is stressed.

The promise of that divine sovereign initiative is that God himself will be present in power and grace among his people (he himself is described as their 'salvation' in v. 11). To know him *is* salvation, yet he always brings his 'reward' and 'recompense' with him, v. 11, cf. 40.10. Among the 'rewards' of fellowship with him is the giving of a new nature ('name', v. 12, cf. v. 2). His people will have been 'redeemed' from their bondage by their divine kinsman (cf. Lev. 25.25–28); they will be God's people because he has 'sought' them (cf. Ezek. 34.11–16) and they will live as God's chosen bride (cf. v. 4, and Eph 5.25–27). RM

Titus 3.4–7

Like the other virtually formulaic, brief doctrinal passages in the Pastoral Epistles, these verses are a concise statement of basic Christian faith. Many of the characteristic words of these writings are here: 'appeared', 'saved', 'saviour'. Therefore much that was said about 2.11–14 (see p. 18) is equally relevant here.

But there is in these verses, in this surely post-Pauline writing, rather more Pauline vocabulary than in the other passage: notably in v. 7, where we are reminded of the language of Rom. 5.1f.; 8.17. Equally Pauline is the putting of the contrast between righteous works and God's mercy (v. 5). However, the linking of the mercy of God and baptism is unique. And this is the only reference to baptism in the Pastoral Epistles, perhaps rather surprisingly in view of their interest in the practicalities of Christian life.

'Rebirth' is not used elsewhere in the New Testament explicitly in relation to baptism, though a parallel idea of the utterly transformative meaning of the rite occurs in Romans 6.4, and in the closer parallel in John 3. It is akin to Paul's sense of Christ's coming as giving a new creation. The link between baptism and the Spirit is common early Christian teaching: cf. 1 Cor. 12.13 and numerous passages in Acts. The rite is far more than one's initiation into Christianity or the Church in a purely formal sense: it is a making new – an entry to the life of the new age, in the here and now. The Spirit is a recognized symptom of the presence already of the new state of affairs to which both Jewish and Christian hope looked and which Christian faith saw as now available as the fruit of Christ's saving life and death. It is one of the most powerful verbal means used in early Christianity to express the experience of radical newness and strength of fulfilment which were major features of the Christian community. LH

Luke 2.(1–7) 8–20

The birth of Jesus is the centre of Christmas. What one learns about Jesus from the narratives that relate his birth comes, however, from the actions and words of the other characters of Christmas – in Luke, from the shepherds, the angelic messenger, the heavenly chorus, the mysterious bystanders (2.18), and Mary; in Matthew, from repeated angelic messengers, Joseph, the wise men, Herod, the chief priests and scribes. Nowhere is that more evident than in the Lucan story, where a bare statement of the birth of Jesus is followed by the intriguing account of the nameless shepherds. They are traced from their location in the field tending their flock through their visit to Bethlehem and back to where they originated. From their actions and their interactions with the angelic messenger and the heavenly host, we learn about the character and significance of Jesus' birth.

We first meet the shepherds doing what shepherds are supposed to be doing – tending their flocks. They no doubt remind Luke's readers of the shepherding done once in these same regions by Jesus' famous ancestor, David. The routineness of these shepherds' lives is abruptly interrupted by the appearance of the angelic messenger. Their world, circumscribed at night by the wandering of the sheep, is exploded by the awesome presence of this one who brings news of Jesus' birth. The manifestation of the divine glory, the shepherds' fright, the announcement of the messenger disrupt their order and uniformity and set them on a journey to hear and see earth-changing events.

Three things we note about the intrusive announcement of the messenger. First, the good news includes great joy for 'all the people'. It is not merely the shepherds' small world that is changed by the word of Jesus' birth, but it is Israel's world. While Luke sets the story of the birth in the context of the Roman Empire (2.1–2), he has a primary interest in the destiny of Israel and 'the falling and the rising of many' for whom this baby is set (v. 34). Jesus' relevance for the world, in fact, begins in the city of David as the fulfilment of Jewish expectations. It includes the acceptance of Jewish traditions (vv. 21, 22–40, 41–52), and only from this very particular origin does its universal character emerge.

Second, the announcement focuses on three astounding titles this baby is to carry – Saviour, Messiah and Lord. 'Saviour' has meaning in the narrative because original readers would recognize that the exalted Emperor Augustus had borne such a title. Unfortunately, the eager anticipations for a brighter, more peaceful day stirred by his rule were long since dashed by the brutality and weakness of his successors. Now a true and promise-fulfilling Saviour appears. 'Messiah' (or 'Christ') reminds us of Israel's hope for the anointed figure and God's grand design that he will inaugurate. 'Lord', interestingly, occurs four times in our passage, and in the other three instances is used for God (2.9 [twice], 15). It is inescapable in such a context, then, that divine associations be attached to Jesus (in v. 11).

Third, the angelic announcement designates the sign that will assure the shepherds that they have found 'a Saviour, who is the Messiah, the Lord'. But such a strange sign! Hardly fitting for one bearing such honoured titles! The babe 'wrapped in bands of cloth and lying in a manger', however, is only the beginning of the story of God's unusual ways in accomplishing the divine rule. Not by might or coercive tactics, but in submission and humbleness, Jesus fulfils his vocation.

Perhaps it is the perplexity caused by such a menial sign for such an exalted baby that evokes the immediate confirmation of the heavenly chorus, who join the angelic messenger in a doxology. God is praised for the birth of this child because the birth begins God's reign of peace on earth. The creatures of the heavenly world, in a context of praise, announce God's good plans for this world.

Having heard the heavenly witnesses, the shepherds now decide to go to Bethlehem and 'see' this revelation. Like other disciples who abruptly leave fishing boats and tax tables, they go 'with haste'. We are not told what happened to the flocks, apparently left in the fields. The shepherds' old world has been shattered by the appearance of the messenger, and now they are in search of a new one, one centred in the event that has occurred in Bethlehem.

When the shepherds find Mary, Joseph and Jesus, the narrator records that they report the message that had been made known to them about the baby. To whom did they give their report? To Mary and Joseph? Perhaps. Perhaps the shepherds in responding to the angelic messenger in fact become a confirmation to Mary and Joseph of the significance of this baby so unusually born. But there must have been a wider audience for the shepherds' report too, since 'all who heard it' were astonished – not believing or thoughtful or adoring, just 'amazed'. Apparently nothing spurred them to ask questions or pursue the matter further. In contrast, Mary clings to what has happened. She continues to ponder the events and the words (the Greek word is inclusive of both) of the shepherds' visit.

Finally, the shepherds go back to where they came from, apparently back to fields and to flocks, but not back to business as usual. What was told them by the angelic messenger has been confirmed. They have heard and seen for themselves. Their old world is gone, replaced by a new world. Whatever the structure and order of life before, their world now is centred in the praise and glorifying of God. The nights in the field will never be the same. CC

Set III
Isaiah 52.7–10; Hebrews 1.1–4 (5–12); John 1.1–14

Isaiah 52.7–10

The prophet predicts the certainty of coming deliverance for God's people in a graphic poem depicting the arrival of the messenger bearing news of victory to a besieged and beleaguered city. To share the suspense which precedes it and the intoxicating sense of relief which follows it we need only to read of David and his people anxiously waiting for news from the battlefield (2 Sam. 18.24–28).

First comes the single messenger, running from Babylon, the place of Israel's defeat and misery, appearing over the 'mountains', i.e. the Mount of Olives. At a distance it is impossible to say whether he brings good news or bad. Until he comes within hailing distance it is like watching a doctor coming in to tell us the result of a medical examination. Then the body language and shout tell that the news is good, victory has been gained (cf. 2 Sam. 18.28). God's victorious kingship over hostile forces has been established. The faith and hope expressed in their worship (Pss. 96.10; 97.1; 99.1) has been realized in fact.

Now the city watchmen take up the good news of the messenger (v. 8). In place of anxious hope they have now seen for themselves evidence of victory. 'Eye to eye' they see God returning to his city and his people, just as Job, who had 'heard of God with the hearing of the ear' could say 'but now my eye sees you' (Job 42.5).

The song of salvation, begun as the messenger's solo, then swollen by the concerted shouts of the watchmen, is taken up by the whole chorus of God's people. They are apostrophized as 'the waste places of Jerusalem' (v. 9) because they live in the ruins of their former buildings and among the shattered disillusionment of their former hopes. When God comes as saviour it is the 'waste places' of human suffering, sin and despair that are the first to be so transformed that they become the scene of praise and joy. The promise of the prophet that God would 'comfort' his people (40.1) has been fulfilled, and he has shown that, in their need and failure, they are still 'his' people as he takes on the role of nearest relative and 'redeems' them from their slavery (cf. Lev. 25.25–28).

God has taken his arm from his mantle and acted in power on behalf of his oppressed people (v. 10, cf. Ezek. 4.7). And this is no introverted, domestic matter within the small family of Israel only, but is accomplished on a universal scale. It is because he is the only God of all the earth, victorious over all other powers, that God can redeem his people and fulfil his purposes for all the nations through them (v. 10).

All is of God. Effective messengers and watchmen serve their people best by speaking of God and what he has achieved. R M

Hebrews 1.1–4 (5–12)

The document known as the Epistle to the Hebrews opens with none of the address and greetings that characterize the Pauline letters, but with a polished and highly rhetorical statement of the person and work of Christ; more like the text for a sermon or the proposition for an argument. Ideas are introduced that will be expounded later in the epistle: the continuity between the old and the new, as in chs. 11—12.1; the sacrificial work of Christ and his exaltation to heaven, as in chs. 8—10. God has spoken through 'a Son', and in 2.10–14 the author will describe him as a son among many brethren, fully identified with them. He will clearly affirm Jesus' humanity, but here at the outset needs to express the deeper significance of that individual human life. There are obvious comparisons to be made with the Prologue to the Gospel of John and both authors draw on the language of wisdom, as in Prov. 8; here most closely echoing Wisdom of Solomon 7.26.

Scholars disagree as to whether 'wisdom' in Jewish tradition was understood as a heavenly being, present with God at creation as his agent, or as a personification: a way of talking about the creative work of God himself; but here it hardly matters, for whatever is meant by the wisdom of God is now seen in the person of Christ.

The opening statement is followed by a series, or catena, of quotations, loosely linked by verbal echoes in a manner familiar in Jewish exegesis, and all taken to demonstrate the Son's superiority to angels. There is no need to employ the conspiracy theory of interpretation and to suspect a veiled attack on a contemporary deviant group who held Christ to be an angel, of whom there is no evidence at all. All the texts are ones that may have been used as messianic texts in Judaism and came early into Christian use, and so would have been familiar to the readers. There is some suggestion later in the epistle that the author was dealing with an educated audience who were, however, failing to grow in their faith (5.11–14). They need to be 'stretched' to explore the meanings of familiar texts, and the exposition of such texts as Ps. 110.4 will shape the course of his later argument. SL

John 1.1–14

(See Second Sunday of Christmas, pp. 32–33.)

The First Sunday of Christmas

Isaiah 63.7–9; Hebrews 2.10–18; Matthew 2.13–23

Isaiah 63.7–9

It is important to see this splendid passage in its context. It introduces a prayer which ends at 64.12, a prayer of a type found frequently in the Psalter, described by scholars as 'community laments'. Such prayers represent the cry to God on behalf of the people in times of national distress. Often they begin, as here, by recollection of God's past mercies; include an acknowledgement of the sin which has merited their suffering, but end with a plea for God's merciful deliverance nevertheless. Examples may be found in Pss. 40 and 89. Not only does this extended passage echo the form and nature of such psalms but includes many of their expressions. It thus shows how a people's worship can be a real help to them in times of need.

The prophet begins by 'calling to remembrance' the 'mercies' of the Lord. The Hebrew word *hesedh* is a covenant term meaning God's loyalty to all his covenant promises, and its plural form both begins and ends this verse. Like his 'praises', i.e. those deeds which are 'praiseworthy', they are plural because they have been repeated and renewed over and over again throughout their history.

Such covenant love began with their very election by God as his people (v. 8, cf. Lev. 26.12) who adopted them as his own 'children' (cf. Hos. 11.1). He hoped they would respond to such love by being faithful to him, a hope time and again disappointed (Deut. 32.6; Isa.1.2). Yet still he did not abandon them but continued with them and delivered them (v. 9, and cf. vv. 10–11, which follow).

'In all their affliction he was afflicted' (AV, RSV, retained by NIV) is a much loved translation expressing a profound theological truth of the Old and, even more, the New Testament. The Hebrew presents difficulties, however, giving rise to various possible renderings: 'In their affliction he became their saviour. It was no angel or messenger but his presence which saved them', or 'In all their affliction he was afflicted and the angel of his presence saved them'. (Such apparent inconsistencies are due to uncertainty about how the lines are thought to scan and to one short Hebrew word which can mean either 'no' or 'his'.)

None of these alters the great truth expressed here, however, that God himself comes with his people into all their suffering, even that caused by their own sin, and seeks to 'redeem' them (cf. the NEB rendering of Hos. 2.14). This truth of his 'presence' is stressed by the use of the phrase 'his face saved them' in v. 9, cf. Exod. 33.14–15.

It is this same theological truth which becomes the basis for the prayer of utter abandonment to God and trust in him which is to follow in 63.15—64.12. RM

Hebrews 2.10–18

As we continue into the Christmas season, Hebrews continues to emphasize to us the full humanity of Jesus. His use of the personal name is itself a reminder of this. Jesus shares to the full the nature of those with whom he belongs, in the human family; the family that owes its existence to the creator God and so calls him Father, as Jesus did, and taught us to do with him in the Lord's Prayer. Jesus' membership of that family means sharing in the common experiences of human nature: suffering, death, fear and temptation. Sharing in physical, bodily humanity – flesh and blood – is not enough, for human body, mind and emotions are not separable. Jesus was not, as some of the early fathers of the Church seemed to suggest, an impassible divine being walking around in a human body. Jesus will not only die, he will share the *fear* of death; he will not only suffer; he will feel suffering as *testing* or tempting him. The author's analysis rings true: it is not the physical fact of death that haunts and enslaves, it is the fear of it as the unknown, as the inevitable end that casts its shadow backward into life and mocks it as ephemeral; it is not physical pain and suffering alone that are hard to bear, but their effects on our sense of ourselves: what can we bear, are we diminished, will we cry out against God?

Jesus' suffering and death, even in these wider dimensions, are not only, however, a measure of his identification with humanity: they are an essential part of the work of salvation; and in these few verses, the author provides three models of what salvation means. First, it is exemplary. As Jesus shares in common humanity, and in it passes through suffering to glory, he paves the way for others to follow him: he is the trail-blazer, the pioneer. Second, salvation means the defeat of the hostile power of evil: the devil as the angel of death. This is the 'Christus Victor' model, popular in early medieval art and theology. Third, the death of Jesus is sacrificial, for Jesus is the great high priest who is fully identified with those whom he represents, and so is able to offer the only sacrifice for sin that can ever be effective: the sacrifice of himself which, because of that identification, can avail for all humanity. It is this last model that this author will explore most extensively in the succeeding chapters of the epistle, but at the outset he makes it clear that there is no one exclusive and normative way of expressing the saving work of God in Christ.

It is worth noting that the Old Testament quotations that the author uses to express Jesus' relationship to those other children, his brothers and sisters, are both drawn from passages which were soon established in Christian use: the first is from the 'passion psalm', Ps. 22, and the second from Isa. 8, following the 'Immanuel' prophecy. His readers are likely to have recognized this, and made connections that we, less familiar with their (and our) Scriptures, might miss. SL

Matthew 2.13–23

This is the final section of Matthew's birth and infancy narrative (chs. 1 and 2). It is highly Matthean in many respects; for example, the word he uses for 'dream' (six times in his Gospel, three of them in this passage), occurs nowhere else in the New

Testament. The word translated 'leave' or 'go away' comes 14 times in the New Testament, ten of which are in Matthew (three of them here, vv. 13, 14, 22). There are also three examples of Matthew's characteristic formula-quotations; and Matthew alone, of all the New Testament writers, refers to Jeremiah by name (v. 17; cf. 16.14; 27.9). The themes that run through this passage are also characteristically Matthean: the wickedness of a Jewish king, and the providence and intervention of God. The result of all this is that it is impossible to say with certainty to what extent Matthew is dependent on a source at this point; he may himself be the author of the legend that he reports.

Threats to the life of a saviour or hero soon after birth were almost universal in the literature of the ancient world; the most obvious parallel to this passage is the early life of Moses, to which Matthew seems to refer in v. 20 (see Exod. 4.19, and note the plural, 'those who were seeking the child's life', where we would have expected the singular, i.e. Herod). For another instance in the New Testament of a threat to a child who will be a ruler, see Rev. 12.4.

Matthew believes that Jesus is God's Son, miraculously conceived and destined for the highest office under God: he will judge the world on the last day (e.g. 7.21–23; 16.27; 25.31–46). His life had been prophesied by God through the prophets, and this included his healings (cf. 8.17) and his teaching in parables (cf. 13.35), his death and burial. Jesus, therefore, had to be preserved from the usual threat of destruction, just as Moses had been; but whereas Moses fled from Egypt to Midian, Jesus was taken from Israel to Egypt; what had been the place of danger was now the place of safety; and the destruction is located now among God's people, as Matthew shows so frequently (e.g. 27.25). Moreover, both Jesus and Matthew's readers are victims of the same persecution; see 5.11f.; 10.16ff.

These verses highlight the difference between the evangelist's world and ours. He is, almost certainly, a first-century Jewish teacher who has become a follower of Jesus and holds office in a church largely composed of others who have converted from Judaism. The quotations from Hosea and Jeremiah, and the final quotation in v. 23 (the source of which is disputed and obscure – it is not to be found plainly in Scripture and may be a verbal play) would have been more persuasive to them than they are to us, who find them detached from their original contexts. Nevertheless, Matthew's confidence in God and faith in Jesus, expressed here in ways that are likely to strike us as foreign and antique, are not entirely irrelevant: as Matthew found, it is necessary for those who believe in a good and loving providence to include some account of the existence of evil and of the tragedies that happen, bafflingly, to holy innocents. JF

The Second Sunday of Christmas

Jeremiah 31.7–14 or Ecclesiasticus 24.1–12; Ephesians 1.3–14; John 1.(1–9), 10–18

Jeremiah 31.7–14

These are probably not the words of the prophet Jeremiah, but the work of a disciple whose outlook was similar to that of the author of Isa. 40—55. They were probably composed towards the end of the Babylonian exile, which lasted from 597 to 540 BC, and were meant as a comfort and challenge to those in exile. Where they were spoken/written and precisely to whom they were addressed is uncertain.

The opening words are either a command to the people to lead into the prayer 'Save, O Lord, your people', or, more likely, a declaration that God's victory is already accomplished, in which case a preferable translation would be 'the Lord has saved his people' (SO NEB, REB).

God affirms that he is about to bring the exiles home, no matter how far away they might be. It is noteworthy that explicit mention is made of precisely those groups who would find the journey, mostly on foot, of some thousand miles (if only Babylon is envisaged) most arduous and forbidding: the blind, the lame, pregnant women and those giving birth. Their journey will be made possible because God will provide an even path (rather than a straight path) which is well provisioned with water. Behind this language is the image of the shepherd leading his flock, finding the best pasture, and paying particular attention to its weakest members (cf. Ezek. 43.16).

The description of the life of the returned community in Jerusalem is one which draws on those images that most adequately express a perfect existence in the harsh world of subsistence farming. 'Life shall become like a watered garden' (cf. the description of paradise in Gen. 2.10), and those things that sustain the necessities of life (grain, wine, oil, flocks and herds) will be abundantly blessed. The dancing of young women and the rejoicing of young and old men symbolize the peace (i.e. the lack of danger from enemies) that Jerusalem will enjoy.

Was this prophecy fulfilled? The answer must be 'no'. The actual restoration after 540 BC was nothing like what is envisaged here. Will it be fulfilled? The answer must again be 'no', at any rate at the level of its details, which concern the restoration of a peasant and not an industrial or technological society. What, then, is the value of the passage? Its value is that it is a sublime expression of the compassion of God: a God who, because he regards his people as his very offspring, can never be indifferent to their plight and their sufferings; a God who, because he has scattered, will gather his people. Then why has he scattered, or allowed his people to be scattered? The parent image partly answers this question. How can children grow up if they are always to be under parental control? The good news is that God will never give up on his people – including ourselves. JR

Ecclesiasticus 24.1–12

This poem, in which personified Wisdom speaks in the first person, draws upon other parts of the Old Testament, most notably Gen. 1 and Prov. 8.22–36; but it also contains original ideas. The opening introduction (vv. 1–2) sets the scene for Wisdom's oration. There is a twofold scenario. In v. 2 she is standing in the divine assembly, surrounded by God's angels and his heavenly armies (the stars). In v. 1 she is speaking to 'her people', i.e. Israel. How she combines these two stances is explained by the two parts of the passage.

The first part of Wisdom's speech in vv. 3–6 describes her privileged position in relation to God and the created order. That she 'came forth from the mouth of the Most High' has made Jewish interpretation identify her with the Law (Torah), and Christian interpretation identify her with the Logos (cf. John 1.1). 'Mist' in v. 3 translates the Greek, whereas the Hebrew version discovered in Cairo in the 1890s has a word meaning 'dark cloud'. This takes us closer to Gen. 1 as does the Hebrew word rendered as 'abyss' in v. 5, the same word translated as 'deep' in Gen. 1.2. The idea of 'covering the earth' in v. 3 is also similar to the spirit of God hovering over the waters in Gen. 1.2. Combined with allusions to the Genesis creation narrative is one from the exodus and wilderness wanderings traditions. The 'pillar of cloud' in v. 4 alludes to the symbol of the divine presence at Exod. 13.21 and elsewhere. The word 'alone' in v. 5 is important, because it excludes other deities from the governance of the universe and firmly anchors Greek ideas of wisdom (Sophia) into Israel's monotheistic faith.

The second part of the poem describes how universal Wisdom entered into a special relationship with Israel and Jerusalem. The idea that God chose Israel as the particular nation for which he would care is found in Deut. 32.8–9. Here, he cares for Israel through his surrogate, Wisdom. Initially, Wisdom is represented as ranging over the whole universe seeking a resting place (v. 7; and cf. again the hovering spirit of God in Gen. 1.2) until God commands her to go to Israel (the Jacob of v. 8) and Jerusalem. Three times in vv. 7–8 come words based upon the Hebrew verb *shakan*: 'where should I abide?', 'place for my tent', 'make your dwelling'. In later Judaism this verb is used for the noun *shekinah* denoting the divine presence, while in John 1.14 'dwelt among us' (*eskénosen*) uses the Greek verb that usually renders the Hebrew *shakan*, including here in the Septuagint. Thus does the poem nobly express the transcendence and imminence of the divine principle, embodied for Jews in the Law (Torah) and for Christians in the incarnation. JR

Ephesians 1.3–14

Paul customarily opens his letters with an expression of thanksgiving for God's action in the lives of the congregation he addresses. Ephesians, which was probably written by a disciple of Paul rather than by Paul himself, not only continues that practice but expands it. Virtually the whole of chs. 1—3 is taken up with expressions of praise and thanksgiving. Eph. 1.3 introduces this dominant mood of doxology with an ascription of praise to God for God's gifts to humankind. Since the word 'blessing' in Greek can refer both to an act of thanksgiving or praise and to an act of bestowing some gift on another, the play on the word in this verse sets the tone for what follows: God is to be blessed for God's blessings. The extent of these blessings comes to expression in the phrase 'every spiritual blessing in the heavenly places'. God's goodness takes every conceivable form.

Verses 4–14 detail the form of God's blessings and focus on God's choosing of the elect. First, the author points to the agelessness of God's election: 'He chose us in Christ before the foundation of the world.' This bit of eloquence need not be turned into a literal proposition about God's act of election. Instead, the author asserts that God's choosing has no beginning. Just as it is impossible to identify the beginning of God's Christ (John 1.1), so it is impossible to conceive of a time when God did not choose on behalf of humankind.

God's election creates a people who are 'holy and blameless before him'. Verse 5 elaborates this characterization of God's people. They become God's children through Jesus Christ, but always what happens is 'according to the good pleasure of his will'. Everything that has occurred comes as a result of God's will and results in 'the praise of his glorious grace that he freely bestowed on us in the Beloved'. In the face of God's eternal choice on behalf of humankind, in the face of God's revelation of his Son, Jesus Christ, in the face of God's grace, the only appropriate response is one of praise (v. 6).

Verses 7–14 continue the exposition of God's gifts to humankind – redemption, forgiveness, wisdom, faith. The exposition culminates with repeated references to the inheritance believers receive through Christ (vv. 11, 14). That inheritance carries with it the responsibility already articulated in v. 6, which is to praise God's glory. Primary among the Christian's responsibilities is the giving of praise to God. With v. 15, the writer moves from this general expression of thanksgiving for God's actions on behalf of humankind to particular expressions of thanks relevant to his context. He constantly keeps the Ephesians in his prayers, asking for them 'a spirit of wisdom and of revelation as you come to know [God]' (v. 17). The prayer continues in v. 18 with the petition that believers might be enlightened so that they know the hope to which they have been called and the riches that are part of God's inheritance. This mood of doxology continues throughout ch. 2 and most of ch. 3, as the author celebrates the nature of God's action in Christ Jesus.

For Christians in the West, these words may have an alien and perhaps even an exotic tone. They run counter to at least two of our most deeply held values. First, these verses insist over and over again that humankind is utterly dependent on God. To assert that God creates, God destines, God wills, God reveals, God accomplishes God's own plan means that human beings, in and of themselves, accomplish nothing. This assault on the Western sense of independence and autonomy poses not only a challenge, but also a significant opportunity for preaching.

The second way in which this text cuts against the grain of Christianity in a modern context derives from its insistence on the obligation to praise God. Our thoroughgoing pragmatism inclines us to respond to the claim that God has acted on our behalf with the question, 'What are we to *do?*' If we stand in God's debt, then we understand ourselves to be obligated to pay back the amount owed. The text, however, stipulates no repayment, for the debt can never be paid. Instead, the exhortation is to give God thanks and praise. To our way of thinking, this is no response at all, and yet it is fundamental to our existence as God's creatures. The reading of Ephesians should prompt us to recall the words of the Westminster Larger Catechism, that the chief end of human life is 'to glorify God, and fully to enjoy him for ever'. BG

John I.(1–9), 10–18

Beyond the sentimentality and romance of Christmas, we encounter in the baby born at Bethlehem, so the passage tells us, nothing less than God's decision to become human.

One notable feature of the Prologue to the Fourth Gospel is the prominence of visual language (a particularly relevant feature for the Epiphany season). 'Light' and 'glory' are terms associated with the Word, and 'seeing' (alongside 'receiving' and 'believing') is the verb used for the perception of faith. Even before a statement of the incarnation, we read that the life found in the Word illuminates human experience, that the light continually shines in the darkness, and that the darkness has neither understood nor succeeded in extinguishing the light. (The Greek verb in 1.5 translated in the NRSV as 'overcome' has a double meaning: 'comprehend' and 'seize with hostile intent.' Perhaps an appropriate English word retaining the ambiguity would be 'grasp', or 'apprehend'.)

The mention of John the Baptist, who is a kind of lesser luminary or reflected light (5.35) and is contrasted with the true light, signals the movement from a pre-incarnate lumination to the historic advent of the light in Jesus. It is in this context that we understand that the coming of the light into the world 'enlightens everyone' (1.9). This universal reference has sometimes been taken to refer to the ancient notion that every individual possesses a spark of the divine, a measure of a universal conscience. The function of religion (any religion?) is to nurture the inextinguishable spark until it glows with understanding, so the argument goes. But such a reading hardly coheres with the evangelist's use of the image of light throughout the Gospel. Jesus claims in a specific way to be the light of the world (8.12), without whom people grope in the darkness (12.35). The coming of the light entails judgement, because it discloses that people prefer darkness to light (3.19). What seems to be implied in the Prologue is that all people, whether they believe it or not, live in a world illuminated by the light just as they live in a world created by the Word. What they are called to do is to trust the light, to walk in it, and thereby to become children of light (12.36).

Whether as a bolt of lightning in a dark sky, or as a distant beam toward which one moves, or as a dawn that chases the night, what light does is to push back darkness. The Prologue, however, gives no hint that the light has totally banished the darkness, that life now is a perpetual day. In fact, the story John tells reiterates the powerful opposition of the darkness in the ministry of Jesus and beyond. But the promise of the Prologue is that the darkness, despite its best efforts, including even a crucifixion, has not put out the light.

The last paragraph of the prologue has to be understood in terms of the many references to the book of Exodus, which it reflects. In a sense its background is the statement that 'no one has ever seen God' (1.18). Though in fact there are places in the Hebrew Bible where people 'see' God (e.g. Exod. 24.9–11; Isa. 6.1), the statement seems to recall the occasion where Moses, eager to behold the divine glory, is not allowed to view the face of God, only God's backside (Exod. 33.23). In contrast, now God is seen in 'the only Son'.

Furthermore, the seeing of the divine glory is made possible by the incarnation of the Word, who 'tabernacled among us'. The Greek verb translated in the NRSV (John 1.14) as 'lived' more specifically means 'tented' or 'tabernacled', and recalls the theme of God's dwelling with Israel, in the tabernacle of the wilderness wanderings and the temple at Jerusalem. In the humanity of Jesus, the Christian community has beheld the very divine glory Moses wished to see, that unique and specific presence of God that hovered over the tabernacle as a cloud by day and a fire by night.

Terms like 'light' and 'glory' tend toward abstractions and become very difficult to communicate in concrete language to a contemporary congregation. What, then, does it mean to 'see' God, to behold the divine glory? Two other words repeated in the Prologue help in the translation: grace and truth. To behold God is to be a recipient of wave after wave of the divine generosity (grace) and to experience God's faithfulness to the ancient promises (truth). 'Seeing' includes but goes beyond mere sense perception; it has to do with becoming children of God, with discovering the divine benevolence and reliability. Revelation in the Fourth Gospel has a strongly soteriological cast (17.3). CC

6th Jan or preceding Sunday

The Epiphany

Isaiah 60.1–6; Ephesians 3.1–12; Matthew 2.1–12

Isaiah 60.1–6

This passage introduces a section (chs. 60—62, and especially 60.1–22) that announces the good news of deliverance for stricken Israel. The imperatives 'arise', 'shine', are feminine singular and so it is 'Zion' which is addressed, that is the community whose life is centred on the still poor and unreconstructed city. The future action of God is announced in a series of 'prophetic perfects'. It is seen as so certain that it can be described as having happened already.

They are to 'rise' from the lethargy of despair and to 'shine', but with the reflected light of God for it is his 'glory', that is, his manifested presence, which is 'rising' on them, ushering in a new age as the rising sun brings a new day. Three times in vv. 1 and 2 the words 'on you' are repeated, emphasizing that it is these very defeated, fearful people who are being summoned to reflect the light of God who comes among them, just as Moses' face shone with the reflected glory of God (Exod. 34.29–35, cf. 2 Cor. 3.18).

By contrast, the other nations are still in deep darkness (v. 2a). This might be an allusion to the 'darkness' which covered the face of the earth before God said 'Let there be light' at creation (Gen. 1.2–3). More likely, however, it is recalling the exodus story when God's presence ensured the Israelites had light by which to travel while the pursuing Egyptians were frustrated by darkness (Exod. 10.21–23). So, attracted by what they see of the miracle transforming Zion, these Gentile nations come to seek the source of that light for themselves (v. 3) so fulfilling the original promise to Abraham that 'all the families of the earth' would be blessed through him (Gen. 12.1–3).

Nor do these nations come empty-handed. They bring back all the dispersed Israelite exiles whom they have taken away captive (v. 4), a sight destined to bring such joy that, when the people see it, they will be radiant with the light of God's presence and power (v. 5, cf. Ps. 34.5, the only other instance of this word in the Old Testament) and their hearts will be enlarged to accommodate all their joy.

Further, the prophet pictures caravans of camels trekking across the desert bearing rich gifts of gold and frankincense, just as the Queen of Sheba brought tribute to Solomon, having heard of his great reputation (1 Kings 10.1–2). This inspired a continuing hope for the Davidic king (Ps. 72.15). Verse 6 here has probably also influenced the account in Matthew's Gospel of the coming of the wise men from the east bearing gifts (Matt. 2.1–11).

If all this sounds the note of nationalist chauvinism we have at least to remember that the Gentiles are attracted, not by Israel's splendour, but by the degree to which they reflect God's splendour (cf. Matt. 5.16). Further, the nations are envisaged as coming, not as servants of Israel, but as fellow worshippers in the temple (v. 6). RM

Ephesians 3.1–12

Following the first two chapters of Ephesians, with their extensive thanksgiving to God, in 3.1 the author takes up Paul's ministry in the context of God's mystery. Verses 1–3 characterize Paul's calling as his 'commission'. Verses 4–6 elaborate on the nature of God's mystery that is now revealed, and this section provides the most obvious entrance into a discussion of the Epiphany. In vv. 7–9, the focus is once again on Paul's ministry concerning that mystery, and in vv. 10–12 it is on the ministry of the Church as a whole.

The opening statement breaks off awkwardly after the identification of Paul as 'a prisoner for Christ Jesus for the sake of you Gentiles'. Verse 2 verifies Paul's calling as prisoner on behalf of the Gentiles by referring to the gift of God's grace that bestowed on him a 'commission' on behalf of Gentiles. Verse 3 makes specific the nature of this gift of grace, in that the mystery became known to Paul through revelation. In common with all believers, Paul's knowledge of God's action comes to him solely through God's own free gift.

Verse 4 returns to the term 'mystery', which is initially described only as a 'mystery of Christ'. The newness of the revelation of this mystery emerges in v. 5, which emphasizes that only in the present time has the mystery been revealed. This assertion stands in tension with statements elsewhere in the Pauline corpus regarding the witness of the prophets to God's action in Jesus Christ (e.g. Rom. 1.2; 16.26). What the author celebrates is the present revelation of God's mystery, and the contrast with the past helps to emphasize that fact but should not become a critique or rejection of past generations. Similarly, the second part of v. 5 identifies the 'holy apostles and prophets' as recipients of revelation, not because revelation confines itself to those individuals but because of their central role in proclamation.

Verse 6 identifies the 'mystery of Christ': 'the Gentiles have become fellow heirs, members of the same body, and sharers in the promise in Christ Jesus through the gospel'. Given the previous few verses, we might anticipate that the 'mystery' refers to the mystery of Jesus' advent. For this letter, however, the 'mystery of Christ' has a very specific connotation, namely, the inclusion of the Gentiles. Each word identifying the Gentiles in v. 6 begins with the prefix *syn*, 'together', emphasizing the oneness created through the mystery. We might convey this phrase in English as 'heirs together, a body together, sharers together'. For the writer of Ephesians, central to the 'mystery of Christ' is the oneness of Jew and Gentile.

The emphasis here on the social dimension of the gospel, the unification of human beings, needs specific attention. Certainly Ephesians does not limit the mystery to its social component, as if the only characteristic of the gospel is its impact on human relations. The extensive praise of God and of Jesus Christ in chs. 1 and 2 prevents us from reductionism. Nevertheless, here the radical oneness of Jew and Gentile who become one new humanity (2.15) becomes a necessary ingredient in the larger reconciliation of humankind to God (2.16). Any separation between 'vertical' and 'horizontal' dimensions of faith here stand exposed as inadequate.

Verses 7–9 return us to Paul's role with respect to the gospel. He, despite his own standing as 'the very least of all the saints', receives the gift of preaching among the Gentiles and, indeed, among all people (v. 9). Proclamation of the gospel comes not from Paul and his fellow apostles alone, however. Verse 10 identifies the role of the whole Church in proclamation. The Church, both through its verbal proclamation and through its actions, makes known God's wisdom. Here that wisdom is addressed to 'the rulers and authorities in the heavenly places'. The gospel addresses not only human beings but all of God's creation.

Verses 11–12 affirm once again the purpose of God in the proclamation of Paul and of the Church. God's purpose has its final goal in Christ Jesus our Lord, 'in whom we have access to God in boldness and confidence through faith in him'. These last terms connote more in Greek than the English translations can convey. To speak 'boldly' (*parrēsia*) is to speak without regard for the consequences, and to have 'access' (*prosagōgē*) is to have, through Jesus Christ, a means of drawing near to God. In other words, the revelation, or epiphany, of Jesus Christ carries with it both the obligation of proclaiming the gospel and the strength needed for carrying out that obligation. BG

Matthew 2.1–12

The Book of Common Prayer explained Epiphany as the manifestation of Christ to the Gentiles, and this is certainly how Matthew understood his story of the wise men. He never describes them explicitly as Gentiles, but the way in which they are presented by Matthew indicates that this is how he meant them to be understood. Thus they ask where the child is who has been born king of the Jews, in contrast with the Jewish chief priests and scribes, who know the answer from the Scriptures; they say 'king of the Jews', whereas Jews usually referred to themselves as Israelites. Notice that Herod rephrases their title with 'the Messiah'.

The story presents a contrast between Gentile 'wise men' (astrologers, whom Matthew surely values as among the intellectual elite of their day, a plus mark for the Christian cause) worshipping the true king and a Jewish false king seeking his apparent rival's death. Antitheses of this kind are characteristic of Matthew's Gospel: destruction–life; wheat–weeds; good servants–bad servants; etc.

There is another point which confirms this view of the wise men. Matthew seems to have arranged his whole book as a diptych, with the beginning matching the end; e.g. God is with us (1.23) and I am with you always (28.20). Similarly, the coming of Gentiles in ch. 2 is matched at the end by the command to make disciples of all the nations (*ethnè*, Gentiles). In one of the very few healing stories that Matthew adds to what he had received from Mark, the contrast is made between the faith of a Gentile and the faithlessness of Israel, and between the final salvation of Gentiles and the damnation of Jews (8.5–13).

The presence of this theme in Matthew's Gospel is extraordinary, and calls for some explanation. The book as a whole seems to come from a church or churches where the law of Moses was still regarded as authoritative (5.17–20). We might therefore have assumed that these 'Jewish-Christians' would have disapproved of a mission to Gentiles. Moreover, the Gospel does contain the prohibition, 'Go nowhere among the Gentiles' (10.5f.). The Twelve are to preach to Israel, and to Israel alone (perhaps, however, just for the present, during Jesus' lifetime, with 28.20 providing for the rest of time). There remains, however, something of a puzzle about how Matthew quite held these two attitudes together; and we can also note his use from time to time of 'Gentiles' as a term of abuse or at least as an expression of superiority: 5.47; 6.32; 18.17: is that just an unthinking and unregenerate reflex?

Perhaps, like Paul, he was convinced of the rightness of preaching to Gentiles, by the bare fact that they had received the Spirit. And, also like Paul, by the fact that Jews, on the whole, were less likely to become Christian believers than Gentiles were. Perhaps, even as a Jew, he was on the 'liberal' wing that saw a positive future in God's purposes for at least some Gentiles.

Whatever the reason for it, Matthew's book contains both a high belief in the Jewish elements of Christianity and a conviction that these are to be made available to those who were not physically descended from Abraham. Though Jesus himself had few contacts with Gentiles, Matthew, like Paul before him, and like Luke and John later, believed that the mission to the Gentiles was according to the will of God. For him this must have been in many ways a costly belief to hold. JF

The Baptism of Christ

(The First Sunday of Epiphany)

Isaiah 42.1–9; Acts 10.34–43; Matthew 3.13–17

Isaiah 42.1–9

This passage contains (in vv. 1–4) the first of the passages in chs. 40—55 that have been called 'servant songs'. However, it is a great mistake to isolate such passages from their context in the section as a whole.

God is the speaker, describing his 'servant', the title given in the Old Testament to such heroes as Abraham, Moses and David whom God chooses for particular tasks. He 'grasps' him, supporting him in his task, and endows him with his Spirit, seen as the essential equipment to undertake any work for God (e.g. Bezaleel, Exod. 31.2–3; Samson, Judg. 13.25; the king, Isa. 11.2, and prophets, Ezek. 2.2).

The servant's mission is no domestic one confined to Israel, but universal in its scope, to 'bring forth justice for the *nations*' (v. 1) who wait for this just rule (v. 4). The word 'justice' is related to the verb 'to judge' and means, in effect, 'a way of life based on God's teaching and judgements'. It is used by Manoah who asks the angel who predicts the birth of Samson what the boy's 'justice' is to be (Judg. 13.12), meaning, 'By what rule of life are we to bring him up?' By establishing God's law throughout the world the servant will bring about 'justice' for all nations.

Unlike ancient powerful rulers who sent heralds before them proclaiming their greatness (let alone the 'PR' people of celebrities today) he will not draw attention to himself but work quietly and gently. Gentleness is not to be confused with weakness, however. Just as he will not snap off the damaged reed or snuff out the burning wick (v. 3) neither will he be 'snapped off' or 'snuffed out' (v. 4).

Verse 5 announces God as the creator of the whole world and the arbiter of all peoples. That is why he has called his 'servant' for this universal mission (v. 6). Just as the rainbow was a sign of God's covenant with all peoples, and circumcision a sign of his covenant with Israel, so the servant is a sign of his covenant purpose for the nations. They are to be a source of light, the reflected light of God himself (cf. 60.1–3). The results will be as liberating as sight to the blind and deliverance for the prisoner.

In 41.8–9 Israel is addressed as God's specially called 'servant'. These chapters reveal God's purpose to reveal himself to all peoples by his great redemption of Israel (cf. 49.5–6). In context, therefore, the 'servant' is intended by God to be Israel. Yet aspects of this 'servanthood' can be seen in the ideal king and in the prophets who embody this ministry to Israel when they proved unworthy (e.g. Isa. 61.1–4).

In the same way, Jesus saw himself, or was seen, to embody in his own life and ministry all that Israel was meant to be as servant, but so often failed to be (e.g. Luke 2.29–32). R M

Acts 10.34–43

This sermon of Peter's stands near the climax of the story of the conversion of Cornelius. Peter, who has protested against the notion that he might violate the boundaries of the food laws (see 10.9–16), has been summoned to the home of Cornelius. Since God has directly told Peter to cooperate with the summons, he has done so (vv. 19–20). Upon arriving at Cornelius's home, Peter hears Cornelius explain that God had instructed him to send for Peter. In the face of this accumulating evidence that God has accepted Cornelius, Peter can no longer protest. The sermon opens with Peter's proclamation of the impartiality of God: 'In every nation anyone who fears him and does what is right is acceptable to him' (v. 35).

Verse 36, then, begins a recitation of the Christian kerygma. The opening words, 'You know', seem oddly matched to the story context, since the whole point of the sermon is that Cornelius and his household do *not* know what has happened. Probably these words address Luke's own audience, which would know what was to follow. Peter's first statement summarizes the Christ-event as 'the message he sent to the people of Israel, preaching peace by Jesus Christ'. Even at this late point in the story, Peter's resistance to the radical inclusion of the gospel shows through, as he identifies the gospel's audience here solely with Israel.

The 'message' of this good news was proclaimed throughout Judea, but it started in Galilee 'after the baptism that John announced'. As in Acts 1.22, Luke carefully refers to the baptism of John, not quite saying that John baptized Jesus. This conforms to the Lukan Gospel, in which John the Baptist is already in prison when Jesus is baptized (Luke 3.18–22). Presumably Luke regarded a direct statement about John's baptizing of Jesus as somehow making him subservient to John. Whatever the reason for this distinction, Luke still ties the beginning of Jesus' ministry firmly with John the Baptist. Indeed, the Lucan infancy narrative couples the two and their work.

Verse 38 summarizes the public ministry of Jesus. First, God anointed him with the Holy Spirit and with power. Jesus does not act of his own accord or out of his own strength. He is God's agent. As such, he 'went about doing good and healing all who were oppressed by the devil'. Consistent with the Gospels, the healings Jesus carried out are here portrayed as an assault on the power of the devil, not simply errands of mercy.

In the simplest terms, vv. 39–40 summarize the death and resurrection of Jesus. Following his resurrection, Jesus appeared to his disciples who 'ate and drank with him'. This bit of information not only recalls the powerful Emmaus road scene in Luke 24 but appropriately refers to Jesus' practice of table fellowship, a practice that is at the heart of the controversy over the inclusion of Gentiles in the fledgeling church (see Acts 11.3). The appearance of the risen Lord culminates with his commandment to proclaim the gospel.

Punctuating these terse statements of the Christian kerygma is a second set of statements that has to do with the witness of the apostles. Following the summary of Jesus' ministry comes the first statement that 'we are witnesses to all that he did' (v. 39). Jesus' appearances were to those who had been chosen as witnesses (v. 41), and he commanded them to testify (*martyrein*, 'witness'). The sermon itself concludes with yet another reference to witness, this time the witness of the prophets.

The theme of witnessing dominates the book of Acts and is in no way limited to this passage. Its function in this passage, however, is important. Peter and his colleagues go to Cornelius as witnesses of the risen Lord, but events that take place in Cornelius's household make them witnesses yet again. Immediately following our passage, while Peter is still speaking, the Holy Spirit comes on Cornelius and his household. Peter, who is forced to pronounce that Cornelius may *also* be baptized with water, becomes now a nearly passive witness of God's intention that the Gentiles become a part of the Christian community.

In one sense, this passage has virtually nothing to do with our commemoration of the baptism of Jesus. Only by stretching v. 37 can we arrive at a reference, however allusive, to the actual baptism of Jesus by John the Baptist. In a deeper sense, however, this passage has everything to do with recalling the baptism of Jesus, for that baptism carries with it the promise of the gift of the Holy Spirit (see Luke 3.16), a promise that is richly fulfilled in the baptism of the Gentile Cornelius. BG

Matthew 3.13–17

In the West, unlike the East, Epiphany was kept mainly as the celebration of the coming of Gentile wise men to Bethlehem. A change occurred in 1955, however, when the status of the feast in the Roman Catholic Church was reduced: the octave and the vigil were abolished, and the first Sunday after Epiphany was made the feast of the Baptism of Christ (see *Oxford Dictionary of the Christian Church* under Epiphany). We can only speculate as to the reason why this happened; was it, perhaps, that it was now recognized that the story of the wise men and the star was legendary, whereas the baptism of Jesus by John was believed to be far more solidly factual?

The contemporary attitude to these two incidents is the reverse of what was thought about them in the ancient world. Then, the baptism was embarrassing, but the wise men were highly popular.

In John's Gospel, for example, it is never said, in so many words, that Jesus was baptized by John. In Luke, the statement is made *en passant* in a subordinate clause, and the impression given that John was in prison before it, somehow, happened. It is Matthew who introduces the dialogue between the Baptist and Jesus. The words 'fulfil' and 'righteousness' are characteristic of Matthew, and they stand in this Gospel as the first words of Jesus, providing the reader with the Lord's own summary of his vocation. Even in Mark, the earliest account of the baptism that we have, the climax of the story is the voice from heaven, God's declaration of the true identity of Jesus, to Jesus himself (contrast Matthew's 'This is my Son' with Mark's 'You are my Son'), and thus also to Mark's readers, as if overhearing God's voice.

The baptism was an embarrassment because it raised the problem, why was one who was without sin baptized for the forgiveness of sins (Mark 1.4, a phrase that Matthew omits at this point in his Gospel, cf. 26.28)?

But now that our interests are far more in questions of history, the event becomes a rich source of information. It passes the test: if it was embarrassing, it must have happened; why would it have been invented?

The Baptist is always reported as baptizing in the Jordan, the frontier of the Promised Land, originally crossed on dry ground (Josh. 3.17). Now they must immerse themselves in it, in order to enter the new age, the time when God will rule.

Christianity began as a breakaway movement from an apocalyptic sect the leader of which was John the Baptist (a perspective hinted at, oddly, in the Gospel of John 1.35f.). Jesus' attitude to him is recorded by Matthew (11.11): no one has arisen greater than he. JF

The Second Sunday of Epiphany

Isaiah 49.1–7; I Corinthians 1.1–9; John 1.29–42

Isaiah 49.1–7

In this, the second of the four 'servant songs' in chs. 40—55, the servant speaks of his calling, his training and his mission in the first person. Like most of the prophets he stresses that he is not 'doing this off his own bat' but because of the direct call of God who singled him out for this task from even before his birth (cf. Jer. 1.5). In the same way it could be said that Israel was called from 'before its birth' since it was God's election that made a people of Abraham's descendants (Gen. 12.2; Josh. 24.3). It is God also who 'names' those who are his (Isa. 62.2).

As for all effective servants of God public ministry was preceded (and, doubtless, accompanied) by a period of quiet preparation and training as a warrior prepares and carefully preserves his weapons. The 'word' of God is a powerful agent by which he accomplishes his purposes, as at creation when God said, 'Let there be . . .' and all came into being, and as delivered to the prophets (Jer. 23.29).

For all the difficulties it raises in interpretation of this passage there is no good textual ground for rejecting the identification of the 'servant' with 'Israel' (v. 3). The context of these chapters as a whole makes it clear that God proposes to reveal himself to the nations through his great work with his people, Israel (e.g. 43.8–13). In a real sense, therefore, the speaker here is identifying himself with his people as a whole.

Yet, perhaps as part of the training of God's servant, it seems necessary that he must prove himself faithful even through apparent failure and disillusionment. It is through such experiences that the reality of God's presence and power to deliver are found at a deeper level (v. 4). Through personal experience the prophet finds the answer for his disheartened generation (cf. Isa. 40.27).

Verses 5–6 raise the problem of the servant's identity in its most acute form. How can 'Israel' have a mission *to* Israel? Even if, as is just possible, the Hebrew is read to mean that it is God who raises up Jacob, tension remains. The calling is to Israel, as a whole. But, so often, groups and individuals have to keep the torch of a community's destiny and calling alive. It is in such a sense that the prophet, perhaps, saw his own role, and how we can think of Jesus faithfully and completely fulfilling in himself the role of the servant. The role of the 'true Israel' is to enable 'Israel' to become and remain true to its calling.

Yet, the mission must never become introspective. The true goal is not the life of the people of God in and of themselves. They exist, not for themselves, but for the whole world whom God proposes to reach through them (v. 6). It is when his people are true to their God-destined role that others fall in worship before him (v. 7). RM

I Corinthians I.I–9

Because Paul follows a standard format in the openings of his letters, the preacher may experience a strong temptation to skip past these lines and into the 'meat' of the letter itself. This temptation needs to be resisted, however, since the salutations and thanksgivings reflect some of Paul's most fundamental theological convictions and also provide clues to major topics of the letter.

In the opening lines of 1 Corinthians one theological conviction that emerges is that of calling. The first word with which Paul identifies himself is the word 'called'. By the will of God, Paul was called as an apostle. Calling belongs not only to what we might term 'professional church leaders', however. Already in v. 2 Paul speaks of Christians in Corinth as those who are 'called to be saints' and who in turn 'call on the name of our Lord Jesus Christ'. That this designation is no mere nod in the direction of the laity emerges in 1 Cor. 1.26 and 7.17–24, where Paul uses the language of vocation to describe God's summons of persons to obedience. For Paul each and every Christian is such because of God's calling.

As in other letters, the thanksgiving (vv. 4–9) identifies ways in which Paul is grateful for this particular community of believers. He thanks God for God's grace, specifically for the gift of 'speech and knowledge of every kind'. The Corinthians lack no 'spiritual gift'. These words sound odd if we know the discussions that lie ahead in this letter, where it is precisely the Corinthians' knowledge and gifts that provoke Paul's wrath. A suspicious first reading of the thanksgiving might lead us to conclude that these words carry an ironic tone, but they are in fact guarded and carefully chosen. The thanksgiving, after all, addresses God and thanks God for these gifts – not for the accomplishments of the Corinthians. The question that dominates part of the letter is not whether the Corinthians have the gifts, but how they interpret them and how they use them.

Debate about the origin of the difficulties at Corinth continues unabated. Whatever had occurred there, Henry Joel Cadbury's description of the Corinthians as 'overconverted' seems apt. Their enthusiasm led at least some of them (perhaps those from the higher social strata) to conclude that they had already arrived at the fullness of Christian life. Nothing more could be added to them (see e.g. 1 Cor. 4.8f.). Paul responds to this situation throughout the letter, but one element in his response appears already in vv. 7–8, 'you are not lacking in any spiritual gift as you wait for the revealing of our Lord Jesus Christ. He will also strengthen you to the end, so that you may be blameless on the day of our Lord Jesus Christ.' In common with all Christians, one task of the Corinthians is to *wait*. The ultimate revealing or apocalypse of Jesus Christ lies in the future, not in the past. Only when God has completed that apocalypse can believers expect their own completion, their own 'arrival'. The reference to a future judgement ('the day of our Lord Jesus Christ') underscores the fact that the Corinthians are not yet to regard themselves as perfected or mature. That decision will come.

Another element in Paul's response to the 'overconversion' of the Corinthians comes in v. 9: 'You were called into the fellowship of his Son, Jesus Christ our

Lord.' The vocation of the Christian is a vocation to 'fellowship' (Greek, *koinōnia*). In contrast to the factionalism that appears to plague the Christian church in Corinth, Paul asserts the commonality of believers. Over and over in this letter he will insist that considerations about the community as a whole outweigh the prerogatives of individuals or small groups (see e.g. 10.23–30). The reason for this insistence lies not in the inherent good of the group, but in the fact that the fellowship is that of 'his son, Jesus Christ our Lord'. Because all members of the community belong to the God who has called them in Jesus Christ, the community merits upbuilding.

While it is a kind of table of contents for the remainder of the letter, 1 Cor. 1.1–9 has far more than merely pragmatic significance for contemporary Christians. The insistence on the calling of all Christians challenges our professionalism, which threatens to treat the laity as qualitatively different from the ordained. If all Christians are called, although to differing tasks (as emerges in the body image of 1 Cor. 12), then the gospel's most radical claims intrude into the lives of every believer. Finally, if all Christians are called, they enter alike into a community that requires full participation. BG

John 1.29–42

Most people recognize that John's Prologue (1.1–18) forms an introduction to his Gospel. It presents Jesus as the eternal Word – God's agent in creation and God's communication to humanity, the bringer of light and life – made flesh. What is not always appreciated is that the rest of ch. 1 is also introductory. Ostensibly we move from *meditation* on Jesus in the light of eternity to *historical narrative*, marked off by clear indications of time (e.g. v. 29, 'the next day'). In fact, John is giving us a further preview of his understanding of Jesus through a series of 'testimonies'. Different people bear witness to Jesus, and their testimony involves christological confessions, e.g. of Jesus as 'Lamb of God' (vv. 29, 36), 'Messiah' (v. 41), 'Son of God' and 'King of Israel' (v. 49).

A key figure is John the Baptist. Our author gives no account of Jesus' baptism by John (contrast Matt. 3.13–17; Mark 1.9–11; Luke 3.21–22). Does he take it for granted, or is he deliberately suppressing it? The effect of the omission is to focus attention on the Baptist's role as a *witness* to Jesus. In early days some people may have thought that the Baptist actually was the messiah. John is keen to emphasize his subordinate role, as the one who prepared the way for Jesus. At the same time John the Baptist is presented as spiritually perceptive. He sees the Spirit descend on Jesus like a dove. He points to Jesus as the one who will baptize with the Holy Spirit. He testifies to Jesus as both 'Lamb of God' and 'Son of God' (or God's 'Chosen One' – the MSS in v. 34 vary). John's Gospel insists that the Baptist was *a* light but not *the* light; the bridegroom's friend, but not the bridegroom (1.8; 3.28–30; 5.35).

Some scholars have conjectured that Jesus himself was once a follower of the Baptist. That is speculative: what is clear is that John describes some of Jesus' disciples as having first followed the Baptist. One of these is Andrew. In contrast to the other Gospels, where Jesus calls the two brothers from their fishing, in John's Gospel Andrew takes the initiative in following Jesus, recognising him as Messiah, and finding his brother. Seeking out a teacher and finding a fellow-learner is a rabbinic pattern of discipleship. It is only later that we learn that it is not Andrew who has chosen Jesus, but Jesus who has chosen him (15.16).

The passage is a splendid example of John's 'narrative christology', in which he uses story and dialogue to unfold the mystery of Jesus' identity. RE

The Third Sunday of Epiphany

Isaiah 9.1–4; I Corinthians 1.10–18; Matthew 4.12–23

Isaiah 9.1–4

These verses are the opening part of the so-called dynastic oracle that celebrates the child that is born and the son that is given (Isa. 9.6). The oracle's presence in truncated form among the readings for this Sunday is because vv. 1–2 are quoted in the gospel for the day, at Matthew 4.15–16.

Isaiah 9.1 has a particular geographical and historical reference. In 734/3 BC the Assyrian King Tiglath-Pileser III conquered most of the northern kingdom, Israel, turning the annexed territory into the three districts of Du'ru, Gala'azu and Magidu corresponding to 'the way of the sea', 'the land beyond Jordan' and 'Galilee of the nations' of our text. A crucial question of translation and interpretation is whether 'in the latter time he will make glorious' is correct. If it is, then there is a contrast between what the Assyrian king did, and what God will shortly do. He will set free those parts of Israel that became Assyrian provinces. However, a different view is implied in the NEB where the former and latter times become the first and second invaders, and 'will make glorious' becomes 'has dealt heavily with'. This rendering makes v. 1 a wholly sombre introduction to the promise or affirmation that those who were once in darkness are, or will be, in light.

The reference to the 'day of Midian' in v. 4 introduces ideas from 'holy war'. This is a set of ideas and language found especially, although not exclusively, in Joshua and Judges, according to which Israel's battles, which they could not possibly have won on their own, are won for them by God, on condition that they remain faithful to him. The battle of Midian is recorded in Judg. 7.15–23. Gideon defeats the Midianites with a group of only 300 men, carrying out God's instructions. What begins, then, in Isa. 9 as an earthy statement about geography and history moves into a visionary statement about God's ultimate victory, drawing upon language which is not related to the real world. In practice, God did not assist tiny Israel to defeat mighty empires such as Assyria, and language that implies that he did or will must be seen as the expressions of hope that God's kingdom will ultimately defeat evil. If Matthew was able to use v. 3, he was certainly not able to use the warfare language of vv. 3 and 4. In the New Testament the language of holy war gives way to the language of suffering and redemptive love. JR

I Corinthians 1.10–18

Far from being abstract treatises of systematic theology, Paul's letters provide us with parts of the ongoing conversations between Paul and various early Christian communities. This text, which opens the body of 1 Corinthians, makes the conversational character of the letter apparent. From persons he identifies only as 'Chloe's people', Paul has received disturbing news about the behaviour of Christians at Corinth. Presumably these agents, perhaps even slaves, of a prominent woman at Corinth have brought Paul a report about the church at Corinth that differs from the report contained in the congregation's own letter (see 1 Cor. 7.1).

The matter reported to Paul by Chloe's people becomes a major pastoral issue in this letter – namely, the presence at Corinth of dissension within the Christian community. The nature of this dissension remains a matter of debate, but Paul's reference to various leaders ('I belong to Paul', 'I belong to Apollos', and so forth) suggests that factions have aligned themselves around key personalities and their teachings.

Because it is so easy for us to see the folly of those Corinthians who may have identified themselves with one or another Christian leader, we risk falling into a cheap moralizing of this text by identifying too quickly with Paul's point and distancing ourselves from the actions of the Corinthians. The irony of such a reading of the passage is that we fail to see the extent to which we ourselves participate in, even encourage, similar behaviour. Whether in the local congregation or at the denominational level or in our reading of contemporary theology, church leaders especially fall prey to the temptation to identify with a leader or a cause that is penultimate to the gospel itself. Do we see ourselves as aligned with, for example, social activists or the evangelicals, traditionalists or feminists, denominational leaders or local figures?

Paul's response to such dissension and the theological problems behind it constitutes the bulk of the first four chapters of 1 Corinthians, but our text provides clear indications of what the nature of his response will be. The rhetorical questions of v. 13 imply a sharp criticism of any devotion to a Christian leader that compromises the central identification of the believer with Jesus Christ. The answer to the question, 'Has Christ been divided?' is obviously no, but the behaviour of the Corinthians suggests that they believe Christ may indeed be divided into special-interest groups. The seemingly absurd questions, 'Was Paul crucified for you? Or were you baptized in the name of Paul?' point up the equal absurdity of identifying oneself with a Christian leader rather than with Christ.

Standing behind these questions is the unspoken assumption that dissension among Christians is inappropriate because they have in common the Lordship of Jesus Christ. It is not Paul or Apollos or Cephas who was crucified or in whose name believers were baptized. The very notion that Christians would identify themselves in terms of their teachers or their favourite preachers rather than in terms of Jesus Christ seems ludicrous on the face of it. The introductory verse in our passage confirms this reading of Paul's response. Paul launches his appeal 'by the name of our Lord Jesus Christ'. Far from being a mere slogan, this statement grounds all that follows in the single reality of Jesus Christ.

At first glance Paul's point may seem obvious. What else would Christians find to be their unifying centre except their faith in Jesus Christ? But there are, always, alternative reasons for urging unity. For example, Paul might have urged unity as a pragmatic good: the evangelistic task of the congregations in Corinth required them to have a 'united front' or the stability of the Christian community depended on their unity. Indeed, these very elements emerge later in the letter (see e.g. 1. Cor. 14.16–17), but they are constantly grounded in the theological claim that the church's unity stems from its centre, Jesus Christ. The pragmatic need for unity has its origin in the theological unity of the Church.

Paul's call for unity may be heard as a threat to diversity of viewpoints and opinions, but that is because we confuse unity with uniformity. Later in this same letter, Paul will defend the plurality of judgements about whether Christians may eat what has been sacrificed to idols (1 Cor. 8) and yet call for care in practice so that the unity of the Church and the faith of its members are not damaged. In a similar way, when Paul discusses the gifts of the Spirit and their place in worship, he acknowledges the diversity of gifts, but only as they come from the one Lord, Jesus Christ (1 Cor. 12.4–11). Unity in faith does not mean uniformity in thought and practice. BG

Matthew 4.12–23

Religious texts generally increase in length as time goes by, and this is one explanation of the relationship between Matthew and Mark. Matthew's account of the temptation of Jesus (4.1–11, which will be the gospel for the First Sunday of Lent) expands Mark's brief statement (1.13), and similarly Mark's reference to Galilee as the place where Jesus' preaching began (Mark 1.14) is enlarged by Matthew, partly by the addition of the formula-quotation from Isa. 9.1f. Jesus 'must' begin his work in Galilee because that was what God had foretold through the prophet. (And note that it already carries a hint of a future mission to Gentiles.)

Somewhat against his usual practice, Matthew abbreviates Mark's account of the preaching of Jesus, repeating now what he had earlier put into the mouth of the Baptist (3.2), the two heralds of the kingdom seen as working in tandem. The emphasis is thus concentrated on two matters: repentance, and the imminence of the coming of the time when God (= heaven) will rule, the latter being the reason for the former ('for' = 'because', v. 17).

Matthew then takes the next paragraph in his source (Mark 1.16–20), the account of the calls of Simon and Andrew, James and John, and reproduces them largely in identical words, but making the two incidents more closely parallel than they had been in Mark.

Comparisons have been made with the story of Elijah's call of Elisha in 1 Kings 19.19–21; in both passages, the pupil does not choose his teacher (as was customary in the case of rabbis and their disciples); charismatic teachers chose their colleagues or followers. But there is a difference between the 1 Kings model and the New Testament: there is no time for a farewell party; both pairs of brothers follow Jesus immediately (contrast Luke 5.27–32).

The brothers are to assist Jesus in the work that he has come to do, and this is described by the analogy of fishing. The metaphor is unusual, perhaps even unprecedented (though the use of it in an 'end-time' context is sometimes seen as set down in a passage like Ezek. 47.10). There is something slightly inappropriate about it: how can salvation from judgement on the last day be compared with killing fish? As in some of the other recorded sayings of Jesus, where there is the same roughness, it may be that what is being recorded still has the element of being 'off the cuff'.

Usually, Matthew puts verbs in Mark that are in the historical present into a past tense (i.e. 'says' becomes 'said'); but here the reverse is the case: 'Jesus said', in Mark 1.17, becomes 'Jesus says' in Matt. 4.19 (in the Greek); what he said when he called people to follow him in the past, he still says in the present. Then, as now, the initiative always lies with him. We did not choose him. JF

The Fourth Sunday of Epiphany

I Kings 17.8–16; I Corinthians 1.18–31; John 2.1–11

I Kings 17.8–16

Zarephath is identified with modern Sarafand, situated on the coast road between Tyre and Sidon in Lebanon. Because of its position on an important route, the village is often mentioned in extra-biblical sources from the thirteenth century onwards.

Two main themes are recorded in the story. The first is that generosity and loyalty to God are more likely to be found outside Israel than within it. The second is that God uses human generosity and creativity to fulfil his purposes. The journey of Elijah away from Israel and into foreign territory is said to be at the command of God, who has also appointed a widow to feed him during the severe drought. Yet the woman herself appears to have no inkling of this divine commission. Elijah comes upon her looking for firewood outside the village, and he asks for a drink of water, presumably from a nearby well that has not yet dried up. She responds with the customary hospitality to a travel-stained stranger, but when he asks for food as well, she indicates how little she has for herself and her son, let alone for a stranger. Her oath 'as the Lord *your* God lives' is best meant to identify her as someone who has faith in or respect for the God of Israel while being fully aware that, as a foreigner, she is an outsider. Nevertheless this outsider, in contrast to the Israelite King Ahab later in the story, is willing to trust the prophet's word. She depletes her supply of provisions in response to the promise that rain will fall before her meal and oil run out.

The terse, matter-of-fact narrative leaves open how her supplies lasted out. It may imply that, miraculously, the jar of meal and the jug of oil were somehow replenished. Such miracles, quite outside modern experience and thus problematic to modern readers, are attributed elsewhere to Elijah and Elisha. The narrative can also be read to imply that careful rationing of resources enabled the woman to eke out what she had until the rains came. In this case, her statement that she is about to prepare a very last meal for her son and herself must be taken as an exaggeration.

The narrative presents us with a foreign woman who is a model of faith and trust as well as of resourceful action. In this regard she resembles the Moabitess Ruth and the Canaanite harlot of Jericho, Rahab, who harbours Joshua's spies in Josh. 2.1–14. These passages express the conviction that God fulfils his purposes through the risk-taking and resourceful action of unexpected people, especially those who do not belong to the household of faith. JR

I Corinthians 1.18–31

In this remarkable passage Paul asserts that the cross of Jesus Christ reveals the power of God. While for Christians some 20 centuries removed from Paul, and accustomed to the cross as a symbol in churches and even in jewellery, this assertion may seem inoffensive, it must have struck some of Paul's contemporaries as the ravings of a madman. The cross was, in fact, the antithesis of power – except as it revealed the power of the Roman Empire to crush those regarded as its opponents. Even so, this humiliating death was reserved for slaves, criminals, social outcasts – those who were deemed to be outside the boundaries of ordinary human society. Only the powerless died on the cross.

Yet Paul, who knew these brutal facts of crucifixion and its victims far better than we do, nevertheless asserts that the cross reveals God's power. God chose this act of foolishness because the world was unable to recognize God's wisdom (vv. 19–21). Instead of meeting the expectations of the world, either Jew or Greek, God offers the good news of 'Christ crucified', good news in the form of a scandal. Even so, God's foolishness is wiser than human wisdom. The cross is the point at which the conflict between God's ways and human ways is revealed to be irreconcilable; human wisdom is utterly bankrupt.

Alongside this assertion that the cross is God's power and God's wisdom (v. 24) runs the recognition that not everyone 'sees' the cross in this way. It is those 'who are being saved', in contrast to 'those who are perishing', who are able to see God's power in the crucifixion. The precise expression 'who are being saved' is important because it touches on the way in which salvation occurs: human beings do not save themselves, they are the recipients of God's salvation; and salvation is not a past event but a continuous one ('being saved').

Those who are being saved are those whom God has 'called', as Paul asserts in vv. 26–31. This passage serves as an extended illustration, based on the experience of the Corinthians, of the point Paul has been making in vv. 18–25. Paul asks the Corinthians to consider their own calling: 'Not many of you were wise by human standards, not many were powerful, not many were of noble birth.' Interpreters have often understood this verse to mean that early Christians came almost exclusively from the poor and uneducated elements of society, but Paul's statement, as well as the rest of the letter, indicates that indeed *some* of the Corinthians were from the ranks of the well-established. The point Paul is after is not primarily social, but theological: God did not choose you because you deserved to be chosen. God chose those who are undeserving, by the world's logic, in order to confound the logic of the world. The Corinthians, then, may look to their own experience to see that God does not act by human rules.

Later in this letter, Paul hints (not always subtly) that the Corinthians are boasting in their own accomplishments. They have achieved honour because of their wisdom (e.g. 4.8–13); in the gospel they have been freed from restrictive rules and regulations (5.1–3). Throughout the present passage Paul urges a different understanding of boasting, namely, the only boasting that belongs to a Christian is boasting in the cross. The only boasting rightly done is boasting in what God has given believers through Jesus Christ (1.31). Boasting in human wisdom and power is rejected, for it is precisely human wisdom and power that bring about the crucifixion of Jesus Christ and are thereby revealed to be utterly bankrupt.

It may strike us as curious, at first glance, that Paul does not interject in this passage a reference to the resurrection. Surely it is the resurrection rather than the crucifixion that reveals God's true power. In ch. 15, he does explain how the resurrection guarantees God's final triumph over all other powers, but here, in ch. 1, the resurrection is carefully, perhaps even intentionally, omitted. There may be two reasons for this omission. First, Paul understands that the Corinthians, with their emphasis on their own wisdom and their own spiritual gifts, needed to understand that the gospel is not about human accomplishments and being a Christian does not mean that one has already arrived at a life of glory. By issuing this forceful reminder about the centrality of the cross Paul places the entire Christian life in the context of the cross itself. Second, a central theological issue is at stake here – namely, the place of the cross in Christian faith. For Paul this is not merely a persuasive step through which he can bring the Corinthians over to his side. The cross, for Paul, is not a human error that God corrected through the resurrection or an embarrassment to be overcome. It is, instead, the point at which God's own and God's wholly other wisdom and will are revealed. BG

John 2.1–11

John calls the great deeds of Jesus 'signs', directing our attention to their inner meaning, beyond their role as mere 'wonders'. So, in this Gospel, 'sign' is almost always a positive word (but see 4.48 where it is linked to 'wonders' in its disparaging sense, typical of the other Gospels). Here is the first of the succession of signs that occupy much of chs. 2—12 (which C. H. Dodd called John's 'Book of Signs'); and then the passion is perhaps to be seen as the greatest of all, to which, in various ways, the rest point. Here, that hint of the passion is to be found in the final verse: Jesus shows forth his 'glory', his God-given splendour that is seen in its highest degree in his death by crucifixion (e.g. 13.31f.).

We are given this story to read at this season of Epiphany, by centuries-old association, as a result of v. 11: Jesus 'manifested' his glory; and surely because of its theme of the widening of God's bounteous provision beyond the confines of Judaism (water), into the headier reaches of the new salvation in and through Jesus (wine). As in the scene at the cross (19.25–27), perhaps the (unnamed) mother of Jesus signifies Israel, from which Jesus springs (as indeed, therefore, does 'salvation', 4.42), even as he then transcends it. This transcending of old Israel explains what (despite various attempts at mollifying) remains the harsh candour of v. 4: in this Gospel particularly, the place of the old dispensation rarely avoids negativity; for Jesus, we remember, has in truth been at work from the very start (1.1–3). Hence, the 'glory' (i.e. his true nature and role in all its radiance) that Jesus displays here in this action is one with that which believers continue to 'behold' (1.14). He is 'light', and the light of glory is there to be seen, though of course not all perceive (v. 10). So the faith that is evoked (in the disciples, v. 11) by this act is not at all the cheap product of sheer amazement at so much wine so miraculously produced (the quantity is huge – like the abundance of grace in 1.16 (cf. v. 17) and of bread in 6.1–14: God's saving generosity is without bounds). It is rather the faith that binds his own to him and brings them into the new dispensation – whose character is woven into them in the supper discourse of chs. 13—17, words achieving life. In the Christian mystery, newness is always to the fore and the sense of it must not be lost. In the hierarchy of the signs, this, worked on inanimate matter rather than a human being, is sometimes seen as the 'lowest' (with the raising of Lazarus in ch. 11 as the topmost); but it contains in fact the whole gospel message, in its own idiom and manner. LH

The Presentation of Christ

(2 February)

Malachi 3.1–5; Hebrews 2.14–18; Luke 2.22–40

Malachi 3.1–5

The book of Malachi, evidently dating from the late fourth century BC, was written or compiled within a society that contained sorcerers, adulterers, perjurers, and corrupt employers and landowners (cf. v. 5). This state of affairs, together with other unsatisfactory conditions, produces a series of charges and counter charges in the book, as God and the people engage in a dialogue of questions and answers. The passage in 3.1–5 is best seen as God's reply to what immediately precedes (2.17), where God takes objection to the view that he approves of, or is powerless to deal with, evil-doers.

The Hebrew of 'I am sending' implies that something is about to happen. A messenger or angel (the same word in Hebrew) will precede the coming of God to his temple. The function of the messenger is unclear. If it is to prepare the people for the divine coming, then why will it be necessary for God to refine and judge (vv. 2–5)? Perhaps the messenger's function will be to warn the people of the imminence of the divine judgement. At any rate, the divine coming will be painful for those who experience it. People may desire God, but will they be able to endure his judgement?

This judgement will begin with the temple and its worship (v. 3), with the place that ought to know better because it supposedly exists to mediate between the people and God; the place where the experts in prayer, sacrifice and holiness are supposed to be found. The judgement will then pass to the social sphere. A religion in which the cult is acceptable but which tolerates social injustice is an abomination to the Old Testament prophets. True religion is neither an acceptable cult without social justice nor social justice without a worthy cult. The two must go together because they belong together. People who fear God but are indifferent to their fellow human beings, especially those most socially disadvantaged, do not really fear God. People who are only humanitarian workers fail to recognize that the deepest instincts of human sympathy and compassion are God-given.

Although this reading is selected to go with the gospel story of Christ's presentation in the temple 40 days after his birth (cf. Lev. 12.2–8) it is arguably the story of the cleansing of the temple (Mark 11.15–18) that comes closest to a fulfilment of this prophecy in the ministry of Jesus. JR

Hebrews 2.14–18

No writer in the NT was more dedicated to the sense of Jesus' identification with the human race, 'his brothers and sisters in every respect', than the author of Hebrews. In chapter 1, using a barrage of Scripture quotations, he had established his heavenly status as God's Son, occupying the role of God's 'wisdom' and above the angels, seated at God's right hand. But then the writer had shifted his gaze – to Jesus who, in the role foretold in Psalm 8, had become (to take the words in a convenient sense that the Greek version could bear) 'for a little while' below the angels, a human among humans (2.7). (In the Hebrew, the sense was spatial, not temporal.)

Yet in that place, he had a task that was unique: he was to bring 'many sons to glory', by being 'the pioneer of their salvation' (2.10) – an image found also in Acts 3.15 and 5.31. Again, scriptural texts demonstrated that Wagnerian hero-role: Ps. 22.22 and Isa. 8.17–18. It is made plain that his position in relation to the angels, temporarily put aside, was now incidental. Instead, his significance related to human beings, specifically 'the descendants of Abraham': this writing functions, it now emerges, within Jewish horizons, however wide some of its language.

The leadership role of Jesus prompts the first appearance of the image or analogy that comes to dominate the later chapters: that of the high priest who, human as he is, has the role of making 'expiation for the sins of the people', above all on the Day of Atonement. Whether the actual high priests of Jerusalem saw themselves quite thus is another question; here, it is their very identity with everybody else, in temptation and suffering, that qualifies them to perform their vital and sacred task. Humility and leadership are not incompatible. LH

Luke 2.22–40

The narratives in Luke 1—2 evoke the atmosphere and world of old Israel, sometimes (as in the echoes of Sarah in the aged Elizabeth and in the near repeat of Hannah's song from 1 Sam. 2 in the Magnificat) very old Israel indeed. It is a literary old Israel, for Luke writes here in the style and vocabulary of the Septuagint. The evocation occurs also in the depiction of the characters – not just Elizabeth and Mary, but Zechariah and the rest; in the dominant temple scenario, and indeed in the nature of the episodes themselves. We are to understand that, new and decisive in God's purposes as Jesus is, he is no novelty or bolt from the blue. Even if his saving significance is for all, Israel can still be seen as 'thy people' (v. 32).

Simeon and Anna (Luke works in pairs of persons throughout these chapters) are typical of the venerable holy sages of Israel, and their great age ratifies their wisdom and their power to speak God's truth. And as through all Luke's history, they are Spirit-led. Paralleling Zechariah in relation to John, Simeon reminds us of Eli in relation to Samuel and Anna of Judith in the second-century BC tale of piety. Both are obscure figures, exemplifying the divine favouring of the poor and simple, as the Magnificat said. (In the figure of Anna, Luke may also have an eye on the status of Christian widows in his own day, as described and regulated in 1 Tim. 5.) They are in effect oracular persons, and Simeon's words are almost a catena of scriptural allusions. All this is more important to Luke than the precise details of the ritual which the parents of Jesus carry out and in fact he has not wholly understood the law's requirements. The 'presentation' of a new firstborn carried no visit to the temple and was distinct from the mother's 'purification' which entailed sacrifice: it is the latter which Luke is really describing.

It is hard to know whether Luke is keen to show Jesus as rooted in scriptural validation for reasons of doctrine (God's work is uninterrupted from start to finish) or, also perhaps, for reasons connected with his church situation in the later first century, when Jewish Christians were becoming more plainly a minority and needed reassurance, perhaps in the face of some Gentile-Christian intolerance: it is a message of balance and reconciliation that Acts is at pains to reiterate, notably in the council of Acts 15.

All the same, as the annunciation story and the shepherds' vision have already made clear, Jesus is the focus of faith and hope: the one who brings 'salvation', a word resonant for Jews and pagans alike, and virtually confined to Luke among the evangelists. Yet the child's purpose will only be carried out through suffering which Simeon also foresees. The suffering will also devastate Mary: in the image in v. 35 we have one more example of how Luke is the true originator of what would eventually flower as Marian devotion. LH

The Fifth Sunday of Epiphany

Isaiah 58.1–9a (9b–12); I Corinthians 2.1–12 (13–16); Matthew 5.13–20

Isaiah 58.1–9a (9b–12)

At the heart of this passage is the complaint of the people in v. 3a that God is failing to act in their present distress. Verses 1–2 state God's call to the prophet to go to the heart of their need – their sin. He is to speak with the vehemence and urgency that is the hallmark of all authentic prophecy (for the voice like a trumpet, cf. Hos. 8.1, and for the task of showing the people their true need, cf. Mic. 3.8).

In this case the clarity and insistence are all the more necessary because the people are armour-plated in a complacency built on the fervour of their religious and devotional activity (vv. 2–3). The fact that only fasting is mentioned and not sacrifices suggests that the temple is not yet rebuilt (cf. v. 12). Probably this dates the oracle early after the return in 538 BC, before the rebuilding instigated by Haggai and Zechariah in 520 BC.

Fasting was practised in times of crisis and was regarded as a sign of humility before God and dependence on him in times of crisis (cf. Joel. 1.14; Jer. 36.9). It appears to have been constantly repeated during the time of the exile, for people came to Jerusalem to ask if they should continue this practice of 'many years' now that Zechariah assures them the new age is dawning (Zech. 7.3).

The prophet gives two reasons why their fasting is ineffectual. The first is that it is self-regarding (v. 3). The words may mean that they are more concerned with their own business interests than the rights of others but, possibly, that they have been looking more for religious 'kicks' than true relationship with God.

The second is that it is a cloak for their failure to live in the way God requires (cf. Isa. 1.10–17). Verses 3b–4 describe their internecine strife and their exploitation of those dependent on them.

Verses 6–8 contain one of the finest descriptions of true religion to be found anywhere in the Old Testament. The practice of fasting is not rejected, but a true spirit behind it is expressed only when it is backed by concern for 'doing' righteousness (cf. v. 2), especially for the poor and 'little people' of society.

It is when they truly express such an attitude towards God (a relationship always affecting and being affected by the attitude shown towards other people) that God will arise as light for them (cf. 60.1) and heal them (cf. 57.18–19). Indeed, their need is for inner healing rather than change of circumstances. For then, even as they travel like Israel earlier through their own wilderness, they will find God's presence guiding them just as their fathers did (v. 8, cf. Exod. 14.19–20). Restoration is promised in the expansion of vv. 9b–12 but, meanwhile, it is those who keep faith in the dark times who are the real 'builders' of any community (v. 12). RM

I Corinthians 2.1–12 (13–16)

The art of persuasion surrounds us. From slick advertising campaigns to telephone salespersons to political posturing, the tactics of persuasion for a variety of causes and in an expanding array of media are an often unwelcome factor of contemporary life. The question inevitably arises: which of these tactics is appropriate for the promotion of the Christian gospel and how may they be employed with integrity? Is any medium appropriate for the Christian message? What is gained by employing the tactics of advertising for the Church? What is lost by clinging to the media of past generations?

While these questions do not find an easy answer in Paul's comments in 1 Cor. 2, contemporary preachers may take some comfort from the limited correspondence between Paul's situation and their own. In this passage, a central issue is the difference between – the conflict between – human wisdom and divine wisdom. The opening lines, vv. 1–5, have to do with the use of human wisdom as a means of persuasion on behalf of the gospel. Recalling his initial preaching at Corinth, Paul insists that he did not employ 'lofty words or wisdom'. Rhetoric, the art of persuasion that was highly developed and highly prized in Paul's era, did not become for him a means of proclaiming the gospel.

Since Paul's letters in fact betray his acquaintance with standard rhetorical devices, we may look on his assertions here with considerable scepticism. The point he makes, however, has little to do with whether or not Paul drew on the rhetorical arts. What he is after here is the way in which faith comes into existence. Faith comes, not from elegant speech or from the wisdom of human beings, but from God alone. The right object of belief is not human achievement (in whatever form), but the crucified Christ. This same conviction comes to expression in the notion of the sixteenth-century reformers that faith stems from faith. Faith is not a response to persuasion, whatever form that persuasion might take; it is a gift of God.

Again in this text, as in 1 Cor. 1.18–31, Paul summarizes the content of his preaching as 'Jesus Christ, and him crucified'. Not only does Paul eschew the effectiveness of ordinary means of persuasion, but he identifies his preaching with that feature of the gospel that most offends and scandalizes human wisdom. Faith in response to this gospel must indeed be based 'not on human wisdom but on the power of God' (v. 5).

The second part of this passage, vv. 6–12, appears to contradict the first. While Paul does not preach wisdom, there is a wisdom to be imparted among the more mature in faith. The contradiction, of course, is apparent rather than real, for the wisdom Paul does not employ is 'human wisdom', wisdom that stems from the reasoning of human beings who believe themselves to be the sole arbiters of what is wise and good. The wisdom Paul is able to share with the mature stems, on the other hand, from God and concerns God's plan for humankind. Christians come to their awareness of God's wisdom by means of the gift of the Spirit of God (v. 10). The seemingly convoluted discussion about the Spirit in vv. 11–13 is less an analysis of the workings of the Spirit than a confession that only through God's initiative could this insight be granted to human beings. Human beings do not work their way to knowledge of the Spirit or in any other way merit that particular form of wisdom; God's Spirit conveys it as a gift. It would be a serious mistake to read into this passage the existence of a class of special Christians who have earned their access to a secret knowledge about God. Paul's point is that the Spirit gives this wisdom, in the Spirit's own time, to those who are able to understand.

Sometimes Christians see in this passage, together with the end of 1 Cor. 1, the legitimation of a kind of Christian anti-intellectualism. Paul's words about the wrongheadedness of human wisdom serve to endorse the notion that Christians should use their hearts but not their heads. The problems with that sort of reading are several and serious. First, as we have seen, the passage itself is not about reason or wisdom *as such*, but about human wisdom and God's wisdom; or better, about human wisdom as it sets itself over against and independent from God's wisdom. Second, within the text itself as elsewhere in his letters, Paul actively uses his own mental powers in order to make the case that he wants to make; Paul uses his head, in other words. Third, the conclusion Paul draws is not that the brain is a dangerous thing and much to be avoided, but that it, like all other human assets, must be acknowledged as a gift of God. The use of the human intellect is indeed to be commended, with the stipulation only that it be used in service of God's power and God's glory. BG

Matthew 5.13–20

The disciples have been told in the Beatitudes what it means to be a follower of Jesus. One thing is clear: their way is different from that of the majority. Hence the parables of contrast: salt and earth, light and darkness.

The final paragraph in today's gospel (vv. 17–20) explains what it is that constitutes the difference between Jesus and his followers on the one hand, and the world on the other (in the immediate case, the Jews of the author's environment): Jesus teaches a righteousness that exceeds even that of the scribes and Pharisees. The will of the Father (a characteristic Matthean expression, 6.10; 7.21; 12.50; 18.14; 21.31; 26.42) is perfection (5.48); there are no limits to what is required of them. This is the salt that retains its saltiness and the light that gives light to all in the house. And it must be, and will be, apparent to everybody. There is no contradiction between 5.16 and 6.1–18 (the commands to conceal righteousness from others): what people will see is those who do not want praise and honour now; they hope for it only from God when the new age comes and God judges the world. Those who see this will give glory to God, not to those who seek it for themselves.

In Mark, the first public act of Jesus was the exorcism in the synagogue, with the (programmatic) cry of the unclean spirit, 'You have come to destroy us' (Mark 1.21–28, REB margin). In Matthew, on the other hand, the first main event is a speech rather than a miracle, and the speech demonstrates that Jesus has not come to destroy, but to fulfil the law and the prophets; he does this by providing his followers with a more rigorous interpretation of the Law, which exceeds that of the teachers in the synagogue.

Does this mean that Matthew and those for whom he was writing kept the whole of the Mosaic Law? It is highly likely that there were people, still in the second century, who understood Matthew's Gospel in this way. Irenaeus (*c.* 130–*c.* 200), Bishop of Lyons, refers to Ebionites who would have no other Gospel than Matthew, probably for this reason. And this may be the reason why Jesus is presented in Matthew in general as less critical of the Law than was the case in Mark (e.g. Matthew omits Mark 7.19: 'Thus he declared all foods clean'; and Matt. 22.40 replaces Mark 12.32–34).

Part of the attractiveness of Matthew's Gospel is the refusal to compromise. What God requires is total obedience; this is what the Law and the prophets demand and it is the way to love God and the neighbour (22.40); this is what it means to be perfect (5.48), and it is the one condition for entering into eternal life (19.16–22).

There is something both powerful and appealing, though also highly disturbing, about this – which is not to be found in the Preacher, for example: 'Do not be over-righteous and do not be over-wise. Why should you destroy yourself?' (Eccles. 7.16). But without it, nothing much will ever be done, in Church or state or society. Is it just a brute fact that fanatics are people we need? J F

The Sixth Sunday of Epiphany

Deuteronomy 30.15–20 or Ecclesiasticus 15.15–20; I Corinthians 3.1–9; Matthew 5.21–37

Deuteronomy 30.15–20

Deuteronomy 28 to 30 form a conclusion to the legal section of the book (chs.12—26) and are concerned to set before hearers/readers the logical conclusion that follows from the laws: that they can be obeyed or ignored. The set passage presents at least three difficulties. The first is that it seems to be pure 'justification by works'. Obedience to God will bring prosperity. The second difficulty is the opposite of the first. Not only will disobedience entail divine disfavour; it will bring down curses upon the disobedient. Is the wish to avoid curses an adequate reason for serving God? Will it not lead to a grudging and half-hearted religion? The third difficulty is that life in general and many passages of the Old Testament disprove any simplistic correlation between doing good and enjoying prosperity. The psalms are full of complaints about the prosperity of the wicked!

These problems can be partly, but not wholly, explained in terms of the kind of material that Deuteronomy and our passage are. They are based upon vassal treaties which defined the relationship between powerful kings and their subject nations in the ancient Near East of the seventh century BC. The treaties set out the obligations (laws) of the subjects to the king, demanded absolute loyalty, and threatened severe reprisals if this loyalty was broken. Gods were invoked as witnesses to the agreement between the parties (cf. v. 19, where heaven and earth are called on as witnesses). The deuteronomic legislators utilized the vassal treaty form to articulate a covenant between God and the people of Judah, using the literary device of an address of Moses to the people as they were about to enter the promised land.

In defence of the passage it can be said that the fact that there is no automatic, or necessarily demonstrable, link between goodness and a material prosperity does not mean that no attempt should be made to obey God and seek his way. If we hope for a better world it will be one in which evil will be corrected and punished in the way it deserves. Further, if we seek God's way in a world in which goodness is not automatically rewarded, we do so not for the reward but because of the intrinsic value of God's laws. In Deuteronomy, there are laws designed to promote compassion towards the needy and to articulate what I call 'structures of grace'. Obedience to God's ways is then no grudging service designed to avoid punishment. It is a creative and loving service which can justifiably be called 'life'. JR

Ecclesiasticus 15.15–20

The verses that precede this excerpt describe how those who keep the Law (Torah) will obtain Wisdom, who, personified, will then joyfully receive and sustain her devotees. She is described as a mother and a virgin bride who will stand by those she has received. She will not be available to fools and sinners.

These sentiments are the necessary prelude to vv. 15–20, which urge hearers/readers to observe the commandments and to be thus embraced by Wisdom. The opening line 'if you choose, you can keep the commandments' is not a pelagian-type belief that humans are capable of perfection, but a matter-of-fact statement that hearers/readers can choose what way of life they will follow: either one of obedience to or neglect of the Law (Torah).

However, there is also a realistic hesitancy in what precedes the excerpt. The writer envisages people responding that they have failed to keep the commandments and they have blamed God for creating humans with a propensity for doing wrong (cf. vv. 11–12). The robust response is that God must not be blamed for human failure. The excerpt deflects such objections by affirming God's wisdom and all-seeing power (v. 18). He will have no truck with wickedness; and it lies in everyone's power to chose either the way of life or death.

Modern readers can be forgiven for thinking that this is too simplistic, and perhaps a reflection of the author's privileged position as a comparatively wealthy intellectual who could look down upon those who worked with their hands (cf. Ecclus. 38.25–34). The passage is too individualistic, and takes no account of the structural evil which, as much in the ancient world as in today's world, did not enable moral decisions to be taken on a level playing field, but often entailed a choice between a greater and a lesser evil.

If the excerpt is to have any relevance to today's readers/hearers it must be in terms of an invitation not to isolated decisions about right and wrong, but to embrace a particular way of life in the course of which many mistakes may be made. In this case, the verses that precede the excerpt, and describe the relationship between Wisdom and her devotees in personal terms, will assume particular importance. JR

I Corinthians 3.1–9

Having just written about the activity of the Spirit of God among believers, and especially about those who are spiritual (1 Cor. 2.14–16), in this passage Paul uses the distinction between 'spiritual people' and 'people of the flesh' to illuminate the divisiveness at Corinth. His opposition between the spiritual and the fleshly catches our attention immediately, for we associate that opposition with the extremely negative attitude toward the human body that influenced parts of the Church in its early centuries. What Paul articulates, however, is not a rejection of the body for the spirit, but an understanding of what makes for maturity in the Christian community. Very often, in fact, Paul uses the term 'flesh' (*sarx* in Greek) in a quite neutral way, simply to refer to human beings in their finite existence. For example, Rom. 1.3 states that Jesus Christ 'descended from David according to the flesh', which means simply that Jesus is physically a descendant of David. When Paul writes about being ruled by the flesh or dominated by its way of thinking, however, he refers not to an inherently evil flesh but to the flawed perspectives that characterize human values and human decisions. For example, in 2 Cor. 1.17, Paul asks the rhetorical question, 'Do I make my plans according to ordinary human standards?' (literally, 'according to the flesh'), a question that suggests that the standards of the flesh are flawed and transient. In our passage, to be 'spiritual people' does not mean to ignore or suppress the needs of the body, but to be guided by the Spirit of God as distinct from the standards of the world apart from God.

In his description of the Corinthians as 'people of the flesh' or 'infants in Christ', Paul employs the image of feeding them with milk, as mothers feed their babies. Paul initially fed the Corinthians with milk, with a form of the gospel they could understand. Even now, when they ought to be ready for more serious nourishment, they are unable to receive it because they remain infants. The evidence Paul produces in order to justify his claim that the Corinthians are still infants is their jealousy and quarrelling, especially quarrelling over the relative importance of particular Christian leaders, such as Paul and Apollos.

The imagery Paul uses here for his relationship with the Corinthians merits some reflection on Paul's understanding of his apostolic work. Although it is customary to think of Paul in paternal – even paternalistic – terms, language about feeding infants milk is almost necessarily maternal imagery. After all, Paul wrote long before the advent of infant formula and baby bottles, when mothers or wet nurses were the only ones who could feed young babies! This use of maternal imagery, together with other such images in Gal. 4.19 and 1 Thess. 2.7, provokes some reconsideration of the notion that Paul thinks of himself in exclusively paternal terms. Particularly because Paul applies to himself maternal roles that are patently impossible, these passages reflect an understanding that the apostle is also one who nurtures as a mother nurtures.

With the second half of the text (vv. 5–9), the imagery shifts from that of nurturing human life to that of nurturing plants, as Paul develops his objection to divisiveness within the Corinthian church over loyalties to various Christian leaders. Although any form of divisiveness reflects the immaturity of believers, quarrels about the merits of Paul and Apollos reflect a misunderstanding of the nature of Christian growth. Neither Paul's role, that of planting or initiating the church at Corinth, nor Apollos's role, that of watering or watching over the church, makes the church grow. The growth itself comes from God alone. Paul and Apollos are not figures to be regarded with awe or to be compared with each other; they are simply servants of God with a common purpose and a common responsibility.

The final verse in the passage appears, at first glance, to establish a great contrast between Paul and Apollos on the one hand and the Corinthian church on the other: '*We* are God's servants . . . *you* are God's field, God's building' (emphases added). Paul does clearly understand that his task sets him apart, although not above, the Corinthians, and he is not afraid of that responsibility. What is more important than the contrast between Paul (and Apollos) and the Corinthians is their common standing before God: 'We are *God*'s servants . . . you are *God*'s field, *God*'s building' (emphasis added). No matter what the respective roles of Paul,

Apollos, and the Corinthians, they all belong to God and derive their importance from that fact alone. Here is an understanding of ministry and the Christian life as a whole that assesses all contributions not as reflections of individual talent or labour, but as part of service to God. BG

Matthew 5.21–37

The commentators on Matthew's Gospel who are best informed about first-century AD Judaism (or indeed Judaism of any other century) warn us against a mistake that it is all too easy to make when this passage is being discussed. It has, for example, been common to speak of this section of Matthew (5.20–48) as 'the Antitheses', implying that there is a contrast and opposition between what had been said in the law (in the Old Testament) and what Jesus taught in the Sermon on the Mount.

It is unfortunate that recent versions of the New Testament have continued to translate Matthew's Greek as '*But* I say to you' (NRSV) or '*But* what I tell you is this' (REB), in vv. 22, 28, 31, 34, 39, 44. The word that Matthew uses need mean no more than 'and'; there are other words in Greek if contrast or antithesis is intended. Jesus is explaining the law, not correcting it.

The commandments with which each of these paragraphs begins – against murder, adultery, breaking oaths, excessive retaliation, discriminating between neighbour and enemy – are either quotations from the law or regarded as such. They would be thought of as words of God; 'it was said' could mean, 'it was said by God' (a passive verb being used as a devout periphrasis). Matthew did not mean that what Jesus said contradicted what God had said in the beginning. The paragraph in Matthew immediately before this section (5.17–19) explicitly rules out any such interpretation of 5.21–48. Jesus did not abolish the law or the prophets.

Another mistake in the discussion of this passage (5.21–48) is to refer to adherence to the law as 'legalism', the letter rather than the spirit of God's revelation (which is itself a misuse of Romans 7.6). Matthew wrote that Jesus had said that everything in the law and the prophets hangs on the two commands, to love God and to love your neighbour (22.34–40); and this was an insight that had already been arrived at within Judaism, before and apart from Jesus, as Mark (12.32f.) and Luke (10.25–28) both knew. Legalism, adherence to rules, being satisfied with a minimal and merely formal obedience, is no more characteristic of Judaism than it is of Christianity, or any other religion.

Nor is it the case that Matthew believed that Judaism was concerned with laws but Jesus with attitudes and motives that could not be expressed in rules. At the end of his book, Matthew represents Jesus as saying: 'Teach them to obey everything that I have commanded you' (28.20), an instruction modelled on sayings in the Old Testament addressed to Moses (Exod. 7.2; Deut. 6.1). For Matthew, Jesus is the new Moses.

God's requirement is perfection (5.48, which sums up the teaching of this whole section, beginning at 5.20). It must be so. Anything less would be unbearable. JF

The Seventh Sunday of Epiphany

Leviticus 19.1–2, 9–18; I Corinthians 3.10–11, 16–23; Matthew 5.38–48

Leviticus 19.1–2, 9–18

Since at least as early as the fourth-century Jewish interpretation of Lev. 19, it has been recognized that the chapter contains most or all of the ten commandments. Following the Anglican and Reformed numbering of the commandments (as opposed to the Catholic and Lutheran numbering) they come in the following order: V (honour mother and father) v. 3, IV (keep the sabbath(s)) v. 3, II (make no idol) v. 4, I (I am the Lord your God) v. 4, VIII (do not steal) v. 11, III (do not profane God's name) v. 12, VI (do not murder) v. 16, IX (do not bear false witness) v. 16, X (do not covet) v. 18, VII (do not commit adultery) v. 29. While not every identification is convincing (are X and VII really present?) the similarities are sufficiently striking for it to have been argued that Lev. 19 either contains an independent version of ten (or more) commandments, or that it is an interpretation of the ten commandments as well as of other passages in Exod. 21—23 and Deuteronomy.

Critical scholarship inclines to the latter view because of the dating of Leviticus and its so-called holiness code (chs. 19—25) to the post-exilic period. Whatever its date, a comparison with the ten commandments in Exod. 20 and Deut. 5 is illuminating. In their traditional form, the ten commandments are addressed to a landowning, slave-owning group, and thus have been accused, rightly or wrongly, of representing the interests of a ruling class. No such charge can be brought against Lev. 19. Not only are there specific provisions to provide materially for the poor by deliberately not harvesting everything (vv. 9–10), the commandment not to steal is repeated in v. 13 and expanded into an injunction not to hold back a day-worker's wages until morning, i.e. to pay him as soon as the working day has ended.

The climax of the chapter comes in the words about loving one's neighbour as oneself (v. 18). How do these words relate to the rest of the chapter, and what is the scope of the term 'neighbour'? Recent scholarship suggests that v. 18 is an interpretation of Exod. 23.4 'if you see your enemy's ox or his ass going astray, you shall bring it back to him' and that what is being commanded in Leviticus is therefore love of one's enemy. As to the scope of 'neighbour', it has been argued that this must include at least the alien mentioned in vv. 10 and 33–34. The alien, or stranger (Hebrew *ger*) could be an Israelite estranged from his family or village or it could include a foreigner. This inclusiveness is well brought out in Martin Buber's rendering: 'Be loving to your fellow man, as to one who is just like you.' The whole chapter, with its mixture of religious and moral injunctions adds a new dimension to what it means for God and his people to be 'holy'. JR

I Corinthians 3.10–11, 16–23

Students of Paul often find his swift changes of metaphor frustrating. In 1 Cor. 3.9, Paul abruptly shifts from a metaphor of planting to one of building – 'You are God's field, God's building' – and in our passage he carries that new metaphor through, ignoring the earlier descriptions of himself and his follow workers as tillers of the field. This change does not simply vary the language for the sake of maintaining the reader's interest. Indeed, this particular change allows Paul to introduce the theme of judgement, a theme far easier to explore in the case of a building than in the case of a farmer. The quality of a building depends directly on the work of the labourers, but who can fault the farmer if crops fail for lack of rain?

Whether or not the shift of imagery is intentional, the theme of judgement enters the letter in our passage, a theme that is surprisingly absent from the Pauline letters. In 3.10–15, it is the builders, Paul and his colleagues, who are susceptible to judgement for the quality of their work. In 3.16–18, judgement threatens anyone who might destroy the temple of God, that is, the Church. What stands out here is the conviction that the Church is itself so important that anyone whose behaviour constitutes a threat to it stands in jeopardy of God's own judgement. The language in vv. 13–15 about the 'Day' and about 'fire' demonstrates the gravity with which this judgement should be regarded.

The metaphor of building also allows Paul to speak of the community as God's temple. Often vv. 16–17 are read in connection with individuals; that is, 'Each one of you is God's temple and God's Spirit dwells in you personally.' That kind of interpretation leads to an overemphasis on the individual and the individual's personal relationship to God. What that interpretation overlooks is the fact that the 'you' in both verses is plural, not singular, so that we might translate 'You are together God's temple ... God's Spirit dwells in you together.' Paul and his co-workers have built a building, a temple, out of a *group* of people, and the plural pronoun reflects that fact.

Carrying that plural through the reading of v. 17 is equally important. Consistent with the context, in which an individual's actions may either contribute to or threaten the life of the community, the destruction of the temple of God to which Paul refers is some action that threatens the life of the community. Elsewhere in this letter Paul speaks about the human body as belonging to God and about the need to live in conformity with that understanding (1 Cor. 6.12–20), but here it is not the individual but the community that stands in the foreground of discussion. The importance of the community emerges in the threat of destruction against one who would destroy 'God's temple'.

The theme of boasting, which Paul introduces in v. 18, at first glance appears to be an abrupt intrusion into the theme of building that has dominated vv. 10–17. The unstated premise behind the transition is that boasting in one's own wisdom lies at the root of the threat to the temple, the community. This concern about boasting recalls the discussion in 1 Cor. 1.18–31 about the nature of wisdom and the appropriate and inappropriate bases for boasting.

Paul reintroduces the theme of boasting with a caution about self-deception (v. 18). Like those who evaluate the crucified Jesus by the human standards of power or wisdom (1 Cor. 1.22), those who trust in themselves deceive only themselves. Verses 19–20 of our lection reinforce this point by recalling 1 Cor. 1.20–21 and by the use of quotations from the Hebrew Bible: God's wisdom is such that human wisdom turns to foolishness by contrast. Boasting about human wisdom or about human leaders reveals a shortsightedness about God's own wisdom.

More important, boasting in human leaders demonstrates a lack of confidence in God. Verses 21b–23, with their powerful assertion that 'all things' belong to believers, underscore the power of God to care for humankind. Believers may trust that all things belong to them *because* they in turn belong to Christ and Christ to God. Dividing allegiance among various Christian leaders is pointless, because it neglects the obvious fact that all human beings live within, and only within, the grasp of God.

The transitional character of this text may make it a daunting text for preaching. It both summarizes the comments Paul has been making since 1 Cor. 2.5 about the responsibilities of Christian leaders and returns to earlier points about the nature of human and divine wisdom, making it difficult to articulate a single central concern. On the other hand, each of the three themes that emerge – the responsibility of Christian leaders for their work, the necessity of upbuilding the Christian community as a whole, and the need for confidence in God – may prove to be both timely and provocative. BG

Matthew 5.38–48

The gospel reading for this Sunday continues the series of consecutive lessons from Matt. 5. Any of the lessons isolated from the context can read like a horrendous burden laid on the backs of disciples, who must exhibit a righteousness that exceeds that of the scribes and Pharisees (5.20). It is critical to keep the lessons firmly anchored in the setting in Matthew shaped by the confirmation of the voice from heaven that Jesus is God's Son (3.17), by Jesus' own announcement of the imminent advent of God's reign (4.17), by the gathering of a community of followers (4.18–22), and by the demonstration of Jesus' power over disease (4.23–24). A radically new era in God's relations with the human community has been inaugurated, and in the Sermon on the Mount Jesus clarifies the nature of the new era, how it entails a reversal of values and undoubtedly evokes opposition. The lesson for today focuses on the two final antitheses established between Jesus' teaching and the teaching of the law, culminating in the command to be perfect 'as your heavenly Father is perfect' (5.48).

The fifth antithesis (5.38–42) is concerned with the law of retaliation, which appears several times in the Hebrew scriptures (Exod. 21.24–25; Lev. 24.19–20; Deut. 19.21). Over against the law (which originally seems to have been intended to restrain excessive punishments), Jesus cites four examples of behaviour that totally subvert the system of retaliation and depict unheard-of, unrealistic reactions to injustices. The first three involve the forgoing of legal redress – for the insult of a slap in the face, for litigation over a poor person's cloak, for the Roman soldier's demand that his burdens be carried. The fourth example touches on a religious obligation, almsgiving.

Strikingly, Jesus does not adjust the law of retaliation to make it more humane – 20 years in prison instead of capital punishment for brutal murders. It is not the improvement of this world's system that he is about, but the vision of a new world, the depicting of human conduct that becomes the sign of God's rule of peace and justice.

As with many of the statements of Jesus in Matt. 5, these are uncompromising and shocking. Misunderstood, they can be easily dismissed as utopian. When taken legalistically and made the standard for community life, they have rarely been productive. They are limited in scope and extreme in their specificity. Though given in the form of legal ordinances, they represent the language of the poet. They describe very unnatural responses, and in effect assail the consciousness of the reader, forcing the contemplation of something other than business as usual in a blemished, defective world where courts of law are demanded and generosity is measured. These statements prod the imagination. Like the Beatitudes, they provoke reflection on a God whose values and commitments seem strange and who promises a brand-new starting point in human relationships.

The sixth and final antithesis (5.43–48) makes an appeal somewhat different from the other five. The statement 'and hate your enemy' is not found in the Hebrew Scriptures, nor in rabbinic literature. It is apparently a deduction drawn from the command to love one's neighbour, when the neighbour is limited to being a fellow Israelite. In any case, Jesus expands the circle to include specifically one's enemies.

Is this demand of Jesus unreasonable? In one sense, yes. Loving enemies is not the natural thing to do and can hardly be made the crowning expression of human love. It is not immediately translatable into political or social strategy. But the appeal to love one's enemies is not made on the ground that it is the reasonable or expedient thing to do (that is, by doing so, you might convert your enemies or at least create a better world), but rather because it reflects the character of God. The common gifts of divine grace are indiscriminate, and they become both model and stimulus for children of the Heavenly Father. Loving one's enemies may turn out to be of little practical worth and hardly prudent, but it creates signs of God's unconditional love for human beings for their own sake.

The concluding injunction to be perfect as God is perfect is a call to consistency of thought and deed, integrity of word and action, that reflects the divine pattern. Moral perfection that tiptoes around evil and avoids any taint or stain is hardly what is implied. Instead, 'perfect' (*teleios*) has to do with wholeness and authenticity of relationships, genuine relationships that manifest the hidden but actual rule of God. Such relationships, which in terms of behaviour show themselves in extravagant moves toward reconciliation, new attitudes between males and females, simple truth-telling, outrageous expressions of generosity, and the distinctive care of one's foes, begin to flesh out the higher righteousness essential to the rule of God. The very pointedness of the rhetoric jolts the imagination to project unheard-of expressions of obedience to the 'perfect' God. cc

The Second Sunday Before Lent

Genesis 1.1—2.3; Romans 8.18–25; Matthew 6.25–34

Genesis 1.1—2.3

See Trinity Sunday p. 159.

Romans 8.18–25

In Rom. 8 Paul contrasts life 'according to the flesh' with life 'according to the Spirit'. The former leads only to death whereas the latter promises life and peace. Since Christians have received the Spirit, they have an obligation to live according to the Spirit, and thus to reap the harvest of life. Paul's flesh/spirit contrast, together with his exhortation to 'put to death the deeds of the body' (v. 13), has understandably contributed to a tradition which denigrates the physical body and regards all 'bodily' actions – especially sexual ones – as somehow dirty. Paul should probably be understood, however, not as opposing all that is physical, or natural, but as contrasting life under the power of sin with life empowered by the Spirit of God, a life which is not a form of slavery but of sonship (cf. Gal. 3.23—4.7). This status as a son of God is bestowed and confirmed by the 'Spirit of adoption', the Spirit that enables the Christian to cry to God in the language of familial intimacy, 'Abba, father' (v. 15). It is the word 'sons' (*huioi*) that Paul uses in vv. 14 and 19 (and in Gal. 3.26 and 4.5–6) but he switches to 'children' (*tekna*) in vv. 16, 17 and 21. This indicates that he includes both male and female Christians in the category of sons/ children of God, though there may be some significance in affirming that they are *all* sons: they all participate fully in the 'son-status' made possible by their first-born brother, Jesus (Rom. 8.29) and all are equally heirs, co-inheritors with Christ of all that God has promised, as long as they also share in Christ's sufferings.

This mention of suffering and inheritance leads Paul to reflections on the contrast between present hardship and future glory. While this theme is present elsewhere in Paul's writings, it is only here that we find Paul's notion of the whole creation subjected to futility and slavery to decay, groaning in labour-pains and straining to see the revelation of God's sons. The hope of redemption is not only for humanity; the whole creation looks for its liberation and its time to share in the freedom of God's children. This inspiring language hardly offers a developed environmental ethic, but it surely provides some foundations on which one may be built. Paul's vision here challenges any version of the gospel that restricts its focus to the salvation of human beings, and challenges Christians who work to further the cause of human liberation to consider also the wider canvas of the freedom of creation.

It is not only creation that groans, but Christians groan too, as they await their adoption as sons (there is something of the Pauline tension between 'already and not yet' evident in the expressions of vv. 15 and 23), and the redemption of their *bodies* (v. 23) – so the body is ultimately redeemed, and not denigrated! This, of course, is a matter of hope (on which see e.g. the reading for the Third Sunday of Lent), which by its very nature involves patient expectation of something not yet seen. DH

Matthew 6.25–34

It is hard to think of a passage in the Gospels that is more familiar as a piece of attractively heart-warming teaching or easier to grasp, and explanatory commentary may only spoil its effect. In fact, a number of matters have been the subject of scholarly comment in recent years, most of them too detailed for consideration for our present purpose: though it is of some interest that the word translated 'worry about', which dominates the passage, may carry the nuance 'make effort'. And in Luke's version of the passage, we have 'seek' in the parallel to v. 31 (Luke 12.29). If this accent is right, then the thrust of the passage is less on what one should 'worry' about, with its overtones of neuroticism, than on where one puts one's effort or drive: on the material necessities of life or rather on the kingdom. Matthew himself uses *zeteō*, 'seek' (here translated 'strive for') in vv. 32 and 33.

More broadly, in the context of the Sermon on the Mount as a whole, it may be that we should see 5.21—7.12 as the extended working out of the greater 'righteousness' (Matthew's favourite word for God's required way of life that belongs to the kingdom, v. 33) enjoined in 5.20. (Then the rest of ch. 7 comments on 5.17–19, with its endorsement of the foundation laws bequeathed through Moses; so 5.17–20 is the 'text' for the rest of the Sermon, expounded chiastically.) If this is so, then our present passage deals with the basic direction of one's energies and efforts: not towards the basic necessities, but the kingdom of God.

It is of course a highly unfashionable message, all the more so, surely, in the subsistence culture in which Jesus and his early followers mostly lived. It conveys something of the heady atmosphere that could animate early Christian communities, including that of Matthew, who may sometimes seem to be dominated by more prosaic judgemental and disciplinary concerns.

All the same, the message here has old scriptural prototypes and echoes Jewish 'wisdom' teaching (and, according to some critics, shows the influence of the priorities of Cynic philosophers of the period). One may recall for example Ps. 37.11: 'The meek shall possess the land and delight themselves in abundant prosperity.' Compare already 5.4; and note v. 33 – it is a matter of priorities in one's striving, with loving trust in God as their heart, not of the asceticism of self-deprivation. We must be careful in expounding Matthew's idea of virtue: it does not coincide with that of many later Christian ascetics. The final verse echoes the petition for bread in the Lord's Prayer (6.11) and the general Matthean concern for the present as the time for our obedience. And our danger, in Matthew, is always to be imperfect in trust (v. 30): you are not faith*less*, but you could do better than at present. This is teaching from a bracing but encouraging pastor. LH

The Sunday Next Before Lent

Exodus 24.12–18; 2 Peter 1.16–21; Matthew 17.1–9

Exodus 24.12–18

This passage contains two immediate difficulties, one of context and one of detailed interpretation. The difficulty of context is that chs. 20—23 have already detailed the ten commandments and the so-called Book of the Covenant that God gave to Moses, and Moses has already written all these words down (Exod. 24.4) and has used them as the basis for making a covenant between God and the people (24.5–8). What, therefore, is the purpose of the tables of stone (v. 12) that God has written? The particular difficulty is contained in the words 'I will give you the tablets of stone, with the law and the commandment' (v. 12) which are an attempt to translate a baffling piece of Hebrew.

The contextual difficulty is solved by source criticism. On the assumption that the narrative of Exodus can be divided into two or more sources, our passage can be seen as a continuation of material in ch. 19. It therefore represents an alternative version of Moses going up the mountain to receive God's law. Indeed, our passage itself may be composite, since it states three times that Moses went up the mountain (vv. 13, 15, 18). The particular problem of v. 12 is that, according to tradition elsewhere in the Old Testament (Deut. 10.4), the tables of stone contained only the ten commandments; and this is how the matter has been subsequently represented in art. What were the 'law and commandment' that God wrote, and where did he write them? Jewish tradition understood the Hebrew to mean 'I will give you the tablets of stone, namely, the law and the commandment', arguing that the ten commandments implicitly contained all the other divine laws. The easiest critical solution is to regard the phrase 'with the law and the commandment', which breaks all rules of Hebrew syntax, as a later gloss.

The theological function of the passage, taken in its canonical form, is to emphasize the importance and divine origin of the commandments given to Israel. Features from the ancient Near East help to do this. The laws of Hammurabi picture the king receiving the laws from the sun god Shamash, while the stone tablets have been linked to copies of treaties that were deposited in local sanctuaries as a record of the agreement between kings and subject peoples. The gravity of the law and of its divine origin is further reinforced by the time spent by Moses in the divine presence – 40 days and 40 nights. JR

2 Peter 1.16–21

Among the most mysterious stories about the life of Jesus, the transfiguration eludes simple description or moralizing. Even if he describes Peter and others as 'eyewitnesses' of the transfiguration, the author of 2 Peter refers to it primarily as something that is heard: 'He received honour and glory when that voice was conveyed to him . . . We ourselves heard this voice come from heaven.' For this author, the transfiguration gains its significance from what is heard and from those who hear it and become the leaders of the early Church. By contrast, the Synoptic Gospels call attention to what is seen – the face of Jesus that shines 'like the sun', the whiteness of his clothing, the appearance of Moses and Elijah, the cloud that comes upon them (Matt. 17.1–5).

In the context of 2 Peter, the significance of the transfiguration is christological, eschatological and ecclesiological. The transfiguration has christological significance, just as it does in the Synoptics, by virtue of the pronouncement, 'This is my Son, my Beloved, with whom I am well pleased.' However, in our passage the transfiguration is further identified as the point at which Jesus 'received honour and glory from God the Father when that voice was conveyed to him'. It would be a mistake to connect this with the questions that later informed the development of the creeds, such as when Jesus became Christ, concluding that for the author of 2 Peter, Jesus only becomes Christ at the transfiguration. Most New Testament writers are not preoccupied with that kind of question. Instead, the text is a positive assertion about the transfiguration as a moment when Jesus is exalted.

In this passage, the significance of the transfiguration is also eschatological. While the Synoptic accounts of this event connect Jesus with Moses and Elijah, and hence connect it with the fulfilment of past promises to Israel, in 2 Peter the transfiguration points forward. In 1.16 the writer insists that Jesus' coming (*parousia* in the Greek) is not a myth, but a fact. He then demonstrates the reliability of the expectation of Jesus' return by recalling the transfiguration. Just as Jesus was seen then in honour and glory, so his coming is also assured.

The eschatological character of the transfiguration emerges explicitly in 1.19, with the assertion that it is 'a lamp shining in a dark place, until the day dawns and the morning star rises in your hearts'. The transfiguration here becomes a promise that the glory of Jesus will again be seen when he returns. To a society accustomed to abundant light at any time and at the flick of a switch, the metaphor of light and darkness loses much of its strength. For a first-century audience, however, the metaphor would have been familiar and powerful. To wait through the night for the coming of the morning star (see also Rev. 2.28) is one thing; to wait with the comfort of a lamp – a reminder of the promised light to come and, at the same time, a real help in the darkness – is another altogether. The transfiguration, in this interpretation, is a source of Christian confidence; the glory of Jesus witnessed in the transfiguration promises the glory of all God's creation in the day to come. By virtue of that confidence, Christians live hopefully in the present, by the lamp of the transfiguration.

In addition to its christological and eschatological significance, the author of 2 Peter sees an ecclesiological importance in the transfiguration. Because the letter responds to a situation in which other Christian teachers and preachers have been interpreting the gospel in very different and unacceptable ways ('waterless springs and mists driven by a storm', 2.17), the author seeks to ground the authority of

Peter in the life of Jesus. The claim to have witnessed the transfiguration is made in v. 16 and repeated in v. 18. In fact, in v. 18 the personal pronoun 'we' (*hymeis*) appears, making the reference to the eyewitnesses emphatic.

In this context, the statements of vv. 20 and 21 regarding prophecy have to do with the authority of the author and his teaching over against the author's opponents. The point being made is that real prophecy (such as the prophecy inherent in the transfiguration) comes from God and not simply from human interpretation. Since Peter witnessed the transfiguration, clearly a divine act, he and his teaching may be regarded as authentic prophecy. Those who attack him, however, are not true prophets, because their message comes from within themselves rather than from God. Taken out of context, of course, vv. 20 and 21 lend themselves to the notion that the interpretation of Scripture can itself be somehow divorced from human thought processes and can rely on the direct intervention of God. The apologetic intent of these verses becomes clear at the beginning of ch. 2, which takes up the problem of the 'false teachers' directly. BG

Matthew 17.1–9

The transfiguration, like the walking on the water, is one of the few passages in the Synoptic Gospels before the resurrection where belief in Jesus as a supernatural, otherworldly being shines through or momentarily overshadows the otherwise down-to-earth story of his life.

Matthew follows the sequence, also preserved in Mark and Luke, that places the incident just after the confession of Peter at Caesarea Philippi. The precise time lapse is noted 'after six days'; it may mean simply 'about a week later' (cf. Luke 9.28) though readers sensitive to the Old Testament typology of this passage would pick up an allusion to the six days during which the luminous cloud of God's glory rested on the top of Mount Sinai before the giving of the law (Exod. 24.16). As in Mark, Jesus takes with him the inner circle of three disciples who also figure as his closest confidants elsewhere (cf. 20.20; 26.37; cf. also Exod. 24.9). It is pointless to speculate about the geographical location implied; for the 'high mountain' is a literary, transcendent motif. Jesus preached his first sermon from a mountain top (5.1), and will issue the great commission from one at 28.16; if the mountain requires a name, it could be called the heavenly Zion (cf. Gal. 4.26).

The word 'transfigured' (17.2) means literally 'changed shape', but unlike the more startling 'metamorphoses' of Greco-Roman mythology recounted by the Roman poet Ovid, the implication here is that Jesus remained recognizably the same, only bathed in a celestial light. Mark in parallel had emphasized the change in Jesus' clothing; Matthew adds the reference to the illumination also of his face (cf. Exod. 34.29f.), to enhance the Mosaic parallelism. Similarly where Mark had spoken of 'Elijah with Moses', Matthew reverses the order, giving priority to Moses. The two figures – how they were visually identifiable as such is not explained – are probably intended to represent the law and the prophets, i.e. they provide scriptural testimony to the Messiah. Similarly, the heavenly voice attests that he is God's beloved Son (Gen. 22.2) on whom his favour rests (Isa. 42.1), and to whom Israel must listen (Deut. 18.15) as Moses' successor and superior.

Mark had characterized Peter's proposal to construct three booths as yet another example of the blindness of the disciples: typically Matthew removes the implication. There is probably here an allusion to the Jewish Feast of Booths (Tabernacles) that commemorated the wilderness wandering, led by the pillars of light and cloud, both of which also appear in this fulfilment of the exodus story. Matthew postpones Mark's reference to the disciples' panic ('fear') till after the pronouncement from heaven, where it becomes reverential awe (cf. 'they fell on their faces' 17.6), a common Matthean motif.

The origin of the transfiguration story is obscure: it may have developed out of an actual visionary experience on Jesus' part; or have started as a resurrection appearance, relocated to an earlier point in the ministry to function as a prophecy of what was to come (cf. 17.9). In literary terms, if Mark's account functioned as a kind of 'heavenly baptism' complementing the earthly baptism by John the returning Elijah, for Matthew the incident is a presentation in narrative form of the fulfilment of the Mosaic covenant through the even greater glory that shines from the face of Christ (see 2 Cor. 3.7f. esp. v. 18 and cf. 2 Cor. 4.6). JM

Ash Wednesday

Joel 2.1–2, 12–17 or Isaiah 58.1–12; 2 Corinthians 5.20b—6.10;
Matthew 6.1–6, 16–21 or John 8.1–11

Joel 2.1–2, 12–17

The book of Joel appears to have been occasioned by a devastating plague of locusts round about the year 400 BC. These locusts and the havoc they have wrought are explicitly described in 1.4–7, one effect of the plague being that some of the regular offerings in the temple have been interrupted (1.13). While ch. 1 describes the threat to the land of Judah, ch. 2 envisages the plague approaching Jerusalem itself. The city is put on a war footing with the blowing of the trumpet, and the sky darkened by the dense cloud of the flying locusts, seems to be a portent of the coming day of the Lord (v. 2), an event that prophetic tradition had come to associate with judgement. Just as the locusts were unstoppable by any human agency, so nothing could forestall the day of the Lord.

In the verses omitted from the reading (vv. 3–11) the oncoming unnatural army is described in vivid and terrifying poetic images, leading to frightened reactions from heaven and earth, and sun, moon and stars (v. 10). Such phenomena elsewhere accompany descriptions of God's coming in judgement, and the army of locusts is seen as one commanded by God (v. 11).

In the face of this terror, God offers respite. If the people return to God, if they proclaim a solemn fast, and if they pray to God to spare them, he may alter their fortunes for good. The book, from 2.18 onwards, implies that the times of prayer and fasting have been noted by God, who now promises his blessing on the land.

This material prompts two questions. Was the plague averted as a result of the prayer and fasting? If it was, did the people remain faithful once the danger was over, or was theirs a temporary piety prompted more by the instinct of self-preservation than a genuine desire for repentance?

The closest point of contact between the text and modern readers lies in the fact that, when confronted by overwhelming forces of nature, humankind becomes aware of its limitations and seeks help from the divine. If we can learn to live our lives as what we really are – creatures with limits to our strength, our intellect and, ultimately to our lives – we may be able to achieve the kind of genuine dependence upon God that is not generated solely by emergencies, special occasions or self-interest. JR

Isaiah 58.1–12

See Fifth Sunday of Epiphany p. 57.

2 Corinthians 5.20b—6.10

Contemporary Christians sometimes look back to the early days in the Church's life with rose-tinted glasses. That period seems to have been inhabited by believers who were filled with zeal, who knew the necessity of evangelism, who had the advantages of a new and innocent faith. Read with care, Paul's letters reveal another side to the story, one in which there are conflicts, struggles and misunderstandings. In the present passage, Paul pleads with baptized Christians, people whom he elsewhere characterizes as being 'in Christ' and belonging to the 'body of Christ', to become reconciled to God. The need for reconciliation is inherent in the Christian faith – it is not a symptom of degeneracy in the latter days of the Church's life.

Set against the other texts assigned for Ash Wednesday (e.g. Ps. 51) and other reflections on the need for reconciliation between God and humankind, 2 Cor. 5 sounds a distinctive note. Here human beings do not cry out to God for forgiveness and reconciliation, for it is God who seeks reconciliation. In the sending of Jesus Christ, God acts to reconcile the world to God (5.20a). Paul characterizes the gospel itself as God's making an appeal to human beings to be reconciled to God (5.20; 6.1). Consistent with Paul's comments elsewhere (Rom. 1.18–32), the point he makes here is that it is not God who must be appeased because of human actions; but human beings, who have turned away from God in rebellion, must accept God's appeal and be reconciled. Even in the face of the intransigence of human sin, it is God who takes the initiative to correct the situation; human beings have only to receive God's appeal.

The urgency of the appeal for this reception comes to the fore in 6.1–2. Without accepting God's reconciliation, the Corinthians will have accepted 'the grace of God in vain'. Moreover, the right time for this reconciliation is now: 'Now is the acceptable time; see, now is the day of salvation!' This comment about time lays before the Corinthians the eschatological claim of the gospel. As in 5.16 ('from now on'), Paul insists that the Christ-event makes this appeal urgent. There is also, however, a very specific urgency that affects the Corinthian community. It is time – or past time – for them to lay aside their differences and hear in full the reconciling plea of God made through the apostles. Time is 'at hand' (NRSV 'near'), both for the created order as a whole and for the Corinthians in particular.

Throughout the text, Paul asserts that it is God who brings about this reconciliation, but he also points to the role of Christ. God reconciles the world 'in Christ', that is, by means of Christ. Specifically, God 'made him to be sin who knew no sin' (5.21). To say that Christ 'knew no sin', consistent with Paul's understanding of sin as a state of rebelliousness against God, means that Christ was obedient to God, that Christ submitted to God's will. That God 'made him to be sin' suggests, in keeping with Rom. 8.3 and Gal. 3.13, that Christ's death on the cross had redemptive significance. Through it human beings are enabled to 'become the righteousness of God' (2 Cor. 5.21b); in Christ's death the reconciling act of God becomes concrete.

Paul's eloquent plea for reconciliation stands connected to comments on the ministry that he and his co-workers are exercising among the Corinthians. Throughout this entire portion of the letter (1.1—7.16), in fact, the focus is on both the nature of the gospel and the nature of the Christian ministry. That dual focus exists not simply because Paul is once more defending himself against his critics (although he certainly is defending himself!), but because the ministry can be understood rightly only where the gospel itself is understood rightly. Paul's ministry, like his gospel, has to do with reconciling human beings to God. In 6.3–10 he expands on that role, insisting that he and his colleagues have taken every measure that might enhance the faith and growth of believers in Corinth. Ironically, he begins his itemization of the things that commend him with a list of things that would certainly not impress many readers of a resumé or letter of recommendation – afflictions, hardships, calamities, beatings, imprisonments ... For those who see the gospel as a means of being delivered *from* difficulties rather than *into* difficulties, Paul's commendation of the ministry will have a very negative sound. As earlier in the letter, he insists on the contrast between how the apostles are viewed by the world and how they stand before God. If the world, with its standards of measure, regards them as impostors, unknown, dying, punished, those assessments matter not at all. Before God, the apostles know that they are in fact true, well-known, alive and rejoicing.

This aspect of the passage makes powerful grist for reflection for those engaged in Christian ministry today, but it is equally relevant for all Christians, especially on Ash Wednesday. The reconciliation God brings about in Jesus Christ obliges not only ordained ministers but all Christians to proclaim the outrageous, universal, reconciling love of God. BG

Matthew 6.1–6, 16–21

It was perhaps not very respectful towards the author of this Gospel to omit from this lection the Lord's Prayer that is at its centre, but at least we can be led to focus on a particular aspect of Matthew's teaching, here and elsewhere: his use of financial language in his exposition of the good news. That use is down-to-earth: for example, the noun 'reward' (coming four times in our passage) can mean payment for work done, and the corresponding verb can mean to pay workers for what they have done (e.g. 20.8, where both words occur). In the whole section, 6.1–21, Matthew presents Jesus as an accountant advising clients to invest in long-term securities rather than in those that mature sooner, and to do without interest payments in the meantime.

For all our love of money – or perhaps because of it and of our feelings of guilt about it – we find this way of thinking embarrassing when it is applied to God. Should not our love for him be pure? ('Not with the hope of gaining aught, not seeking a reward ...') Matthew appears not to have thought so. His characteristic emphasis on reward can be seen by comparing the frequency with which he and the other evangelists use the noun: Matthew 10 times, Mark once, Luke three times, John once. He has created problems for moral theologians.

But there is another aspect of Matthew's language that must be borne in mind. In

vv. 4, 6 and 18, he refers to God as 'your Father' (see also 7.7–11). God's rewards are presents; there is no need to think of them as payments for work done. In Matthew, the language of commerce gives way to that of family. We are not employees in a faceless business, but sons and daughters of a father. It is a sad fact that 'paternalism' became a term of abuse in the late nineteenth century. No New Testament writer calls God 'father' more than Matthew, normally with a possessive 'my', 'your' or 'our'.

Matthew believed that to love God was the greatest and first commandment (22.34–40). There is some evidence that in Judaism at the time of Jesus there were reckoned to be three pious acts through which one fulfilled this command: almsgiving, prayer and fasting (see, e.g. Tobit 12.8). If they are performed in order to acquire a good reputation in the sight of others, then they lose their reality as deeds of love *for God*. Matthew is very clear on this aspect of the matter. But there is more to it than that. If they are done in order to receive payment from God, they cease to be acts *of love* for God. There is a saying from the Jewish fathers: be not like servants who serve the master on condition of receiving a gift, but be like servants who serve the master not on condition of receiving. It is entirely the result of God's love that he repays according to their work (Ps. 62.12, quoted, in its darker aspect, at Matt. 16.27; see also 20.1–16).

Matthew has not, therefore, transferred the language of payments and earnings to the relationship between God and his family without transforming it. It is a happy fact that God's love for his creatures expresses itself in gifts, embarrassing though we find such excessive generosity. J F

John 8.1–11

It is dispiriting (but perhaps not wholly surprising) that this passage has traditionally been known as 'the pericope concerning *adultery*', when so many readers have been glad to find it the story about Jesus' generous forgiveness and his shaming of the censorious. It has indeed been the comfort of sinners and the banner of the liberally minded, even though there are always those to wag a cautionary finger with the final words: 'go, and do not sin again'. But from a pastoral point of view, it has been a prime model, leaving its mark notably on the practice of sacramental confession. And, in another dimension, who can forget, once having seen it, Guercino's picture in the Dulwich Picture Gallery, with the look of piteous contempt on the face of Jesus as he confronts the woman's tormentors? As the word goes, it says it all.

From a more academic point of view, however, the story is remarkable for a quite different reason. It is unique in the Gospel tradition in being demonstrably an example of what form criticism has seen as the earlier stage of all the stories. It truly is a floater and came to rest in this location in the Gospel of John only late and, as it were, by accident. The oldest manuscripts do not have it at all, while others put it after 7.36, and still others place it at various locations in the Gospel of Luke. Indeed, it has often been felt that in ethos and tendency this is a Luke-type story, with its loving generosity of spirit. It certainly has no Johannine 'feel'.

Yet if its floating character presses us to dub this story apocryphal, that seems unsatisfactory, for it has none of the magical features which tend to characterize those episodes from the life of Jesus to be found in the later apocryphal Gospels. Quite the contrary: it is among the most believable (as well as welcome) episodes in the entire canon. It is not surprising that critics have put forward the case for its authenticity as a genuine memory from Jesus' life. After all, if Jesus' teaching and behaviour left a special mark, must it not have been precisely for striking, generous and unusual acts of this kind? It was an inspired move that the designers of the lectionary gave it to be read on Ash Wednesday.

Guercino also painted a picture of the scene in the garden on Easter Day. He used the same man as model and dressed him in the same clothes. I do not know whether he was making a deliberate point about the identity, the sameness, of Jesus across all divides of time, place and state; but in any case we can ponder the point. And in another way, the presence of this story in the still-read canon (even by the skin of its teeth – it might so easily have slipped into oblivion) speaks of the eternal freshness of the truth of its winning message. LH

The First Sunday of Lent

Genesis 2.15–17, 3.1–7; Romans 5.12–19; Matthew 4.1–11

Genesis 2.15–17, 3.1–7

This passage is full of puns and *doubles entendres*; for example, there is a pun in the Hebrew on the words for 'crafty' as applied to the serpent and 'naked' as applied to the human couple. The *doubles entendres* take us deeper, however.

On the face of it, God lies when he says that the humans will die if they eat from tree of the knowledge of good and evil. The serpent tells the truth; for when the humans do eat, they do not die but gain new knowledge. But would the humans have lived for ever if they had not eaten the fruit? This seems to be implied, and leads to two possible scenarios. Either the humans will live for ever without the knowledge of good and evil, or they will grow older and die if they do have this knowledge. This is the connection with sexual awareness and procreation; for if the knowledge of good and evil limits the length of individual human lives, the human race will soon die out without procreation. The possibility that has to be avoided is that the humans will both have knowledge of good and evil and live for ever, which is why later in the story they are driven from the garden and away from the tree of life.

What would be best for humankind? Everlasting life without knowledge of good and evil, or limited life with this knowledge? Both conditions have advantages and disadvantages, which is why the passage has sometimes been read as a 'fall upwards' – an account of a necessary stage of human intellectual development.

However, it is necessary to go deeper still. Attainment of the knowledge of good and evil makes humankind like God and, as far as we know, endows humanity with an awareness possessed by no other creature. But although humanity may be *like* God in this respect, this does not mean that humanity is able to cope with good and evil. On the contrary, the immediate result of this new-found knowledge as the Genesis narrative proceeds is strife between the man and woman, the subordination of the latter to the former, and the catalogue of human wrongdoing in Gen. 4 that culminates in God's decision to destroy the world with the universal flood.

Whatever may be the origin and nature of good and evil, only the eternal God, and certainly not limited humankind, can bring it to a resolution. God did not lie, after all. JR

Romans 5.12–19

In exploring the nature of life in Christ for those justified by faith, Paul turns to compare and contrast the impact on humanity of Adam and Christ. There is a typological relationship between these two figures, a relationship Paul depicts else-where by naming Christ as 'the last Adam' (1 Cor. 15.45). Here Adam is described as 'a type of the one to come' (v. 14). The figures are parallel in that their deeds affect all humanity; somehow humanity is bound up in the actions of these two men. Paul seems to view both Adam and Christ as representative, even corporate figures, 'in' whom people live: the sphere of life in Adam is one of sin and death, that in Christ is one of eternal life, peace and reconciliation with God.

The effect of Adam's sin was that sin and death entered the world, affecting all humanity, an idea also found in Jewish writings roughly contemporary with Paul (e.g. Wisd. 2.23–24; Syriac Apocalypse of Baruch 23.4; 54.15). Sin is almost personi-fied as a malevolent power here (cf. Rom. 7.8–11): like some kind of malicious virus (4 Ezra 3.22 describes it as a 'disease'), it found its way into the human race through the moment of Adam's disobedience. Only with the law, according to Paul, can sin be 'counted' (v. 13; cf. 4.15.: 'where there is no law there is no trans-gression'), yet even so, once the 'disease' had entered humanity through Adam, death reigned from then on, even in the time before the giving of the law through Moses. Thus *all* of humanity is, because of Adam, under the power of sin and the sentence of death. Paul's thinking here may be difficult for us to appreciate, but it raised certain difficulties for Paul too. One such difficulty concerns the law: if sin is only counted when the law appears then how far are God and God's law therefore implicated in the problem of sin? (Paul confronts this issue in Rom. 7.7–12; see also Rom. 5.20; Gal. 3.19.)

Paul's main concern here, however, is to compare and contrast the impact of Adam's disobedience and Christ's obedience, and the key phrase is 'how much more . . .' (vv. 15, 17). The focus is on how much greater, how much more sure are the positive effects of Christ's act of righteousness compared with the effects of Adam's sin. Adam's trespass brought judgement, condemnation, death; Christ's act of righteousness brought an abundance of God's grace, a free gift, righteousness and life. This raises an interesting theological issue. What does Paul mean when he says that Christ's act will lead to life for 'all' (v. 18)? (Notice how Paul parallels either 'many . . . many' [vv. 15, 19], or 'all . . . all' [v. 18] in comparing the impact of Adam's and Christ's actions on humanity.) If Paul considers the impact of Christ's act to be greater than that of Adam's, then can its scope be any less universal? Certainly Paul never spells out such a universalist doctrine, and indeed can depict a clear contrast between those who are being saved and those who are perishing (1 Cor. 1.18), but one can argue that the logic of his theology, at least here (and in the similar statement in 1 Cor. 15.22), pushes in that direction. DH

Matthew 4.1–11

Matthew is following the order of events that he found in his chief source, Mark: the Baptist and his preaching, the baptism of Jesus, and his temptation in the wilderness, were all in Mark in the same sequence as in Matthew. What is different in Matthew's account is that it is longer than Mark's; there is more about the Baptist's preaching, more about the baptism, and a much longer account of the temptations (now in the plural, and with 11 verses rather than Mark's one).

The story of the temptations here is closely parallel to that in Luke (4.1–13), the main difference between the two being the order of the second and third episodes. (We may note that Matthew ended his Gospel on a mountain, as here, and Luke ended his in the temple, as in his temptations.) The temptations – in a wilderness – fit well with Matthew's Mosaic typology in ch. 2 and in chs. 5—7, where Jesus gives his exposition of the Law on a mountain that is reminiscent of Sinai.

This raises the far more difficult question concerning the kind of story that Matthew is writing: is it in essence Jesus' own account of his experiences in the wilderness, or is it a narrative composed by someone else (Matthew or a predecessor) to explain the life (and death) of Jesus as his obedience to the will of God, in contrast with the disobedience of Israel in the wilderness? Where should we place it in a range from biography to Jewish-style midrash? In any case, Matthew has decided to expand Mark's bare (and, to him, sufficient) statement that Jesus was 'tested', like Israel of old. It is typical of him to answer our questions: so, tell us, how exactly was he tempted?

The Gospels do not provide much evidence that Jesus spoke of his experiences to his disciples: perhaps the saying about Satan falling from heaven is the most plausible (Luke 10.18). On the other hand, accounts of disputes between rabbis who quote texts against each other, and in one case between Satan and Abraham, are found in Jewish writings.

The replies of Jesus to Satan are all from Deuteronomy (8.3; 6.16; 6.13), and refer to the 40 years in the wilderness between the exodus and the entry into the promised land, marked by the 'tempting' or testing of God, the manna and the golden calf. One of Matthew's most frequently expressed beliefs was that Jesus and his life and death were the fulfilment of God's promises in Scripture. Where Matthew found Mark had no information on a topic, he believed that Scripture could supply it, giving backing and warrant.

The purpose of the passage is to explain Jesus' rejection of the temptation to depart from God's will, a purpose he maintained steadfastly: see 16.23; 26.53; 27.40–44. Jesus wins through where Israel had failed. JF

The Second Sunday of Lent

Genesis 12.1–4a; Romans 4.1–5, 13–17; John 3.1–17

Genesis 12.1–4a

See Proper 5 p. 174.

Romans 4.1–5, 13–17

Having spoken of the justification or righteousness which comes through Christ to all who believe, Paul turns to a crucial test case: what did Abraham, forefather of the Jewish people, discover concerning righteousness? Paul argues that Abraham's status as righteous was not something he gained on the basis of works, but something he received by faith as a gift from God, the one who 'justifies the ungodly'. (It is important to be aware that the Greek verb translated 'to justify' belongs to the same word group as the words translated 'righteous' and 'righteousness', a close link obscured in English translations. E. P. Sanders has therefore suggested using the verb 'to righteous', akin to the Old English verb 'to rightwise'.)

The lectionary reading omits a section of the argument crucial for Paul's purposes in Romans. It concerns the question whether Abraham's status as righteous can be shared only by the circumcised (Jews) or also by the uncircumcised (Gentiles). On the simple basis that Gen. 15.6 (where Abraham is declared righteous) precedes Gen. 17.9–14 (where circumcision is commanded as sign of the covenant) Paul maintains that the status of 'righteous by faith' is for all who share Abraham's faith, uncircumcised and circumcised alike, for both Jew and Gentile.

Paul's intentions in presenting this interpretation of the Abraham story (for a different interpretation, see Jas. 2.21–24) become clearer in vv. 13–17. He wants to show that Abraham's inheritance is for all who have faith and not only for those who have the law (vv. 14–15). Paul is negative here about the law – it is a source of 'wrath' – but positive elsewhere (e.g. Rom. 7.12; 13.8–10). Recent discussion has led many interpreters to conclude that Paul's concern here is not to draw some contrast between those who seek to earn salvation by doing good works and those who simply accept it by faith, but rather with the definition of the people of God. Are the descendants of Abraham, the inheritors of his promise, demarcated by adherence to the Jewish law, i.e. identified as Jews? If so, then any Gentile converts to Christ should adopt the marks of obedience to that law, including circumcision, a logical position which was argued by some of Paul's opponents (cf. Gal. 5.1–12). Paul is convinced, on the contrary, that both Jew and Gentile belong to God's people through faith in Christ, without the need for Gentiles to become Jews. He thus portrays Abraham here as the father of all who have faith – both Jew and Gentile – and quotes the Scriptures to support the idea of Abraham as the father of many nations, and not just one. The people of God are defined, for Paul, by faith in *Christ* (a difference from Abraham's faith which Paul does not comment on) and not by adherence to the Jewish law. DH

John 3.1–17

The fourth evangelist loves to relate how different people meet with Jesus and react to him. John uses their conversations with Jesus to communicate theological ideas by majoring on a particular image or theme. The dialogues often take a stereotypical form: Jesus makes an ambiguous statement; the interlocutor misunderstands it; Jesus clarifies or expands his original statement. The Nicodemus episode is an outstanding example of this technique, and it leads into some of John's most profound religious teaching.

Nicodemus is a member of the Jerusalem Sanhedrin (v. 1) – the Jewish male 'establishment'. He is quite sympathetically drawn, being respectful towards Jesus, and recognizing him as a teacher from God. Yet Jesus deals almost harshly with him, chiding him for not understanding his enigmatic pronouncements. Even when Jesus 'clarifies' his meaning (vv. 5–8), much remains mysterious. One hardly blames Nicodemus for asking, 'How can these things be?' Then Nicodemus fades out of the picture, and the evangelist develops his great message of salvation, that God so loved the world that he gave his only Son (v. 16). He also alludes enigmatically to Jesus' divine origin, as the descending and ascending Son of man, and to his 'lifting up' (vv. 13f.; cf. Num. 21.9).

This passage falls into two main sections, the dialogue with Nicodemus (vv. 1–10) and theological reflections on it (vv. 11–17). In the first part, interest centres on the image of being 'born anew' (which can mean either 'be born again' or 'be born from above', i.e. from God). Does this refer to a spiritual experience of cleansing and renewal (cf. Ps. 51.1f., 10f.; Ezek. 36.25f.), or to Christian baptism? At the story level, one would expect the meaning to be something that Nicodemus, as a learned Jew, could grasp; but since John writes from a post-Easter perspective, an allusion to the Christian sacrament is also possible. What happens to those who fail to be 'born anew'? Perhaps we should be wary of interpreting Jesus' statements too rigidly (compare Matt. 18.3; Mark 10.15; Luke 18.17).

Can Nicodemus say something to us in our faith-journey? Some think that he represents those of inadequate faith (cf. his coming 'by night', and the stern words following the end of our reading, vv. 19–21). But is he not also an example of those on the road to a fuller faith (cf. 7.50f.; 19.39)?

The second section (vv. 11–17) raises the question of what it means for God to *give* his Son, so that believers may have life. Why was Jesus' atoning death necessary? Does it replace Jewish animal sacrifices (cf. Hebrews)? Is there an allusion to Abraham's attempted sacrifice of Isaac (Gen. 22.12)? How does John's understanding of Jesus' death compare with Paul's (e.g. Rom. 5.6–8; 8.6–8)? Some people find

the idea that God should want Jesus to die abhorrent. Are there other ways of understanding Jesus' self-giving? We may take comfort from the emphasis in this passage
on God's love and positive salvific purpose. RE

The Third Sunday of Lent

Exodus 17.1–7; Romans 5.1–11; John 4.5–42

Exodus 17.1–7

The Massah and Meribah incident (the Hebrew place names mean 'test' and 'strife' respectively) is deeply embedded in the Old Testament devotional tradition, to judge from references to it in Pss. 81, 95 and 106, as well as other parts of the Pentateuch. This is because it records the ultimate test of God's patience in the words 'Is the Lord among us or not?'

It seems incredible that this question should have been asked. Those responsible had witnessed the plagues in Egypt, had been set free from slavery, had been delivered from Pharaoh's army at the Red Sea, and had been fed in the wilderness by the provision of quails (Exod. 16.13) and manna (Exod. 16.14–15, 31). Yet here they are complaining about their situation because they lack water, and doubting whether God is actually on their side. However, even miraculous satisfaction of their need for water brings no relief. In Exodus as we now have it, there is a further apostasy in the making of the golden calf (Exod. 32), while further complaints of the people against God and their condition in the wilderness are recorded in Num. 11 and 20.

What is important about the wilderness wanderings narratives is that they are foundation narratives; stories that set out the nature of the chosen people in the same way that the opening chapters of Genesis describe the nature of the world and its inhabitants. The picture that these narratives present of the generation that was actually delivered from slavery (not their children or grandchildren) is typical of the realistically self-critical self-portrait of the chosen people in the Old Testament.

Theologically, the passage makes three points. First, any religion based upon divine 'signs and wonders' is liable to be superficial and to leave its adherents always wanting more. It can become a self-centred religion in which God's function is satisfying his worshippers' needs. Second, God's way of redeeming humankind involves working through precisely the kind of people portrayed in the narrative, as well as their modern equivalents in the form of today's churches. Third, anyone who is called to lead God's people runs the risk of falling foul of their ingratitude. Moses fears for his life in this passage and elsewhere. He is not the last leader of God's people or part of it to exclaim 'What should I do with this people?' JR

Romans 5.1–11

Summarizing in a few words the essence of the preceding chapters ('being justified then by faith'), Paul now moves on to the consequences that flow from this. Its first result is peace with God, an end to hostility and alienation, an escape from the wrath of God. We may find talk of God's wrath difficult, but that is where Paul begins in explaining his gospel (Rom. 1.18f.) and here he assures his readers that they will be saved 'from the wrath' (v. 9; cf. 1 Thess. 1.10). Christ has provided a means of access, an entrance-way to stand in the grace of God, from where believers can boast, according to Paul, in their hope of the glory of God (by which he probably means the hope of sharing, at the end, in the glory which belongs to God, when God's children enter into the glory which awaits them: cf. Rom. 8.18–21). This hope, one of the triad of essential Christian qualities (1 Cor. 13.13), is not merely a matter of waiting, but brings a new perspective to the present. Paul can urge his readers to join him in 'boasting' in tribulations (cf. his own lists of hardships in 1 Cor. 4.9–13; 2 Cor. 6.4–10; 11.23–29), since these sufferings produce endurance, endurance produces character (the sense here is of one who has stood the test), and character hope. This theme of rejoicing in tribulations is common in early Christian teaching (cf. Jas. 1.2–4; 1 Pet. 1.6–7). The hope which such hardships serve to cultivate looks to the future but arises from experience in the here and now: future fulfilment is guaranteed by the present experience of the love of God, brought to the Christian by the Holy Spirit (v. 5).

This love of God is demonstrated in Christ's dying on behalf of humanity, dying for the ungodly, who were unable to save themselves. Paul illustrates how unusual and striking this is, though the background to his comments in v. 7 is not altogether clear. He evidently regards it as highly unlikely for anyone to die voluntarily on behalf of a 'righteous' or 'just' (*dikaios*) person, though he appears to find it more plausible to imagine someone dying for a 'good' (*agathos*) person. Perhaps Paul has in view here a benefactor or patron, an *agathos*, for whom loyal clients might give their lives. But the main point is clear: Christ died for 'sinners', going beyond the expectations of any normal pattern of voluntary self-sacrifice.

Verses 9 and 10 follow a similar pattern: 'if . . . then how much more . . .' The basic thought seems to be that if we have been justified and reconciled to God by the *death* of Christ, how much more will we be 'saved', brought to share in the glory of God, by his resurrection *life*. The death of Christ served to reconcile former enemies to God (precisely *how* is less easy to see: cf. e.g. Rom. 3.24–25); his resurrection provides the basis for new life 'in Christ', which Paul will go on to discuss. Notable here is the repeated mention of reconciliation (three times in vv. 10–11), which elsewhere too lies at the heart of Paul's gospel (2 Cor. 5.18–20). DH

John 4.5–42

Today's gospel tells how a Samaritan woman came to faith. It is elaborately constructed and exceptionally rich in theological ideas. In vv. 5–15, interest centres on Jesus' offer of 'living water' to the woman. We puzzle over whether he means physical, fresh water (as the woman supposes) or spiritual, life-bringing water (cf. Jer. 17.13b). Next Jesus refers to the woman's marital situation, about which he seems to know supernaturally (v. 18). She recognizes him as a prophet, and asks about the proper place to worship God. Jesus' reply, as often, goes beyond the formal question to say something radical: the time is coming when true worshippers will worship the Father in spirit and truth (v. 23). The woman wonders if Jesus could be the Messiah (whom the Samaritans called the *Taheb*, 'he who returns' or 'restores'). Jesus makes an astonishing act of self-disclosure, 'I am he' (v. 26).

The disciples return and are surprised to see Jesus talking with a woman. She rushes off to tell the townsfolk about her amazing encounter, while Jesus talks enigmatically about sowing and harvest – symbols of mission and kingdom (vv. 27–38). The episode concludes with many Samaritans coming to faith through the woman's testimony; they flock to hear Jesus, acclaiming him 'the Saviour of the world' (v. 42).

The story is narrated with vigour and realism. Yet it raises many questions. Did Jesus historically teach in Samaria, or is John seeking to 'validate' later Christian mission there (cf. Acts 8.14–25)?. Is the meeting at a *well* just circumstantial detail, or is it intended to recall the patriarchal narratives where similar meetings are a prelude to marriage (cf. Gen. 24.10–67; 29.1–30; Exod. 2.15–22)? Some scholars even speak of Jesus *wooing* the woman at the well! But this is hardly a hidden romance, even if the 'wooing' is interpreted as leading the woman from idolatry (symbolized by her five husbands) to acknowledgement of the true God.

More helpfully this episode may be seen as a counterpart to the story of Nicodemus (John 3.1–17). In both stories an individual encounters Jesus; in both, we have the favourite Johannine device of ambiguous statement, followed by misunderstanding and clarification. But instead of a Jewish male teacher, meeting Jesus by night, we have a Samaritan woman, carrying out her regular domestic duty, meeting him at noon. Her character is more developed than Nicodemus': she is practical (v. 11); trusting and enthusiastic (v. 15); impetuous and prone to exaggeration (vv. 28f.). But she is also theologically aware, perceptive and persistent (vv. 19f., 25, 29b). Her story ends very differently from Nicodemus' in ch. 3. Whereas there he just faded out of the picture, she successfully brings people to Jesus. John surely intends her as some kind of example.

This episode demonstrates the inclusiveness of the Christian message and, possibly, John's interest in women's potential for ministry. It is also about growth in faith, christology, 'realized' eschatology, mission, worship and the nature of God. RE

The Fourth Sunday of Lent

I Samuel 16.1–13; Ephesians 5.8–14; John 9.1–41

I Samuel 16.1–13

In history, as far as we can reconstruct it, David seems to have been an independent freebooter who temporarily allied himself to Saul against the Philistines, who then opposed Saul, and finally deserted to the Philistines when he could no longer avoid capture by Saul. Samuel was the leader of prophetic groups fanatically loyal to the God of Israel, groups to which Saul may also once have belonged (cf. 1 Sam. 10.12). Samuel's backing of David over against Saul may have resulted from a growing conviction that Saul could not ultimately defeat the Philistines, whereas David might be able to do so.

None of this turbulent background is apparent in the present passage, which is narrated from the divine perspective. Saul has been a false start, perhaps a necessary false start; but the time has now come to implement a new phase in the story of the chosen people. Whereas, humanly speaking, we would say that David became king by the exercise of his outstanding bravery and skill as a warrior, theologically, the narratives say that he was chosen and anointed by God. This is because God is ultimately in charge of the destiny of his people, and comes to their rescue when they are in danger of annihilation.

The section on Samuel's anointing of David rules out, of course, any suggestion that Samuel was exercising his own shrewd judgement. The tall Eliab is ruled out by God (possibly an allusion to Saul's commanding height in 1 Sam. 10.23) while the one chosen is a mere, but beautiful, lad who looks after the sheep. The choice of David, not for any proven ability, but because God 'looks on the heart' (v. 7) is a further way in which the narrative makes clear that it is God's initiative and endowment that will aid his people in their hour of need.

But if God looks on the heart, did he not see David's adultery with Bathsheba and his technical murder of her husband Uriah? Did he not see the incest, fratricide and rebellion that would become rife in David's family (2 Sam. 10.11–18)? Perhaps God did see these things and yet still chose David. It is part of the honesty of the Old Testament that it makes no attempt to whitewash God's ideal king; which means that God may also be able to choose and work today through flawed churches and their flawed members. JR

Ephesians 5.8–14

The symbolism of light and darkness is so natural and so common that in a way it scarcely requires comment. However, it is important to note that in Jewish and

Christian, as distinct from much Hellenistic usage, its associations tend to move swiftly from the existential to the moral, from being to doing. Our passage is no exception; and we may compare the opposition in the Dead Sea Scrolls of the sons of light and the sons of darkness, and the discipline of the community that ensues.

Here, a special feature is that the context in view may well be baptismal, itself carrying implications for way of life as well as for existence. The suggestion has been made that Ephesians as a whole is, if not exactly a liturgy for baptism, then perhaps written with the setting of baptism in mind: much of it is certainly about the new life in contrast to the old. This present passage is one of the strongest indications of such an association. It places former conduct in the sharpest opposition to that now required of the Christian believer, the pervasive ethical theme of the second half of Ephesians. And (to pursue the liturgical suggestion) v. 14 appears to be a quotation from a known formula of praise or exhortation, or else it is a kind of cry or slogan. If that is so, it stands alongside Phil. 2.6–11, Col. 1.15–20, and the numerous 'hymns' in the Revelation of John. Moreover, the passage, in its own way, reflects the association of baptism with resurrection that is familiar from other Pauline writings, most strikingly in Rom. 6.1–11 (and see Col. 3.1–4 for a comparable direct ethical linkage). Here, however, as generally in Ephesians, the bond between Christ and the believer is seen less in terms of the latter's profound incorporation into him and into his dying and rising, than of his powerful effect upon the believer, the child of light – who in v. 8 is nevertheless identified with light itself: 'you are light in the Lord'. It was left to the Fourth Gospel to identify Christ with light (8.12; 9.5), the sole source of his people's and the world's life and good (cf. 1.4f.). LH

John 9.1–41

In the healing of the man born blind we see John's narrative art at its most brilliant. After a brief introduction (vv. 1–5), the story falls into seven parts, each a miniature drama, fraught with irony and theological nuance: (1) the healing of the man (vv. 6f.); (2) the man and his neighbours (vv. 8–12); (3) the man interrogated by the Pharisees (vv. 13–17); (4) his parents interrogated (vv. 18–23); (5) the man interrogated a second time (vv. 24–34); (6) Jesus and the newly-sighted man (vv. 35–38); (7) Jesus and the Pharisees (vv. 39–41).

Remarkably, Jesus is 'off the scene' for some 27 verses, whereas the man is almost constantly 'on-stage'. His words comprise around one-quarter of the chapter. He must be important for John's theology. So what does he stand for, and how should we read his story?

The healed man moves from physical blindness to sight, and from spiritual darkness to enlightenment. Observe how his faith develops: he initially describes his healer as 'the man called Jesus' (v. 11); then he recognizes him as 'a prophet' (v. 17), sent from God (v. 33); finally he confesses him as 'Son of man' (or 'Son of God', v. 38). Contrast the Jewish leaders, who move from apparent enlightenment to darkness or spiritual blindness. Most obviously the healed man serves as a paradigm of strong and courageous faith. His story can be paralleled by other healings in Jesus' historic ministry, which excite opposition from Jewish religious leaders.

More subtly it can be seen as reflecting the experience of the Johannine community *c.* 85–100 A D. We hear (v. 22) that the Jews had already agreed to expel from the synagogue any who confessed Jesus as Messiah. This is most unlikely to have happened in Jesus' own lifetime, but became a reality when a new clause (known as the *birkath ha-minim*) was added to the synagogue prayers, effectively declaring accursed heretics and *noserim* (? = Nazaraeans). It has been argued that the man born blind represents Jews prepared to declare openly their Christian faith, while his parents represent 'crypto-Christians', afraid to declare their true identity. Although widely accepted, this interpretation remains conjectural.

The drama can also be read at a third level, as exemplifying the conflict between the creative, healing power of light, represented by Jesus, and the dark, destructive forces of evil, symbolized by 'the Jews' and 'the Pharisees'. Thus it develops themes heralded in the Prologue and chs. 7—8: Jesus, as the 'light come into the world', divides humanity into those who joyfully accept him and those who obstinately reject him.

Some readers may find elements in this story problematic. Few can now feel happy about the way John uses 'the Jews' to refer to unbelievers. Even the blind man's cure, seen as moving from darkness to light, raises questions about attitudes to those with disabilities. Jesus rejects the notion that the man might have sinned in the womb, or be suffering for his parents' sin. Yet one wonders at the idea that a person might be born blind *in order that* God's works could be revealed. We should read v. 3 not as theodicy but as pointing to Jesus' whole purpose. R E

Mothering Sunday

Exodus 2.1–10 or 1 Samuel 1.20–28; 2 Corinthians 1.3–7 or Colossians 3.12–17;
Luke 2.33–35 or John 19.25b–27

Exodus 2.1–10

The name 'Moses' is probably part of an Egyptian name, as found in the name of Pharaoh Thutmose(s), and connected with the verb *msy* 'to be born' and the noun *mes* 'child'. It is remarkable that the greatest founder of the Israelite nation should have a partly Egyptian name, and it suggests that Moses is not an invented figure.

In the present passage, however, the Egyptian name has been forgotten, even if Moses' Egyptian origins have not. The end of the story, in which Moses' name is explained as 'I drew him out of the water' depends on the similarity of the name Moses (Hebrew *moshê*) and the Hebrew verb *mashah* 'to draw (out)'. A further implication is that the story of Moses' preservation (the passage must be set in the context of the pharaoh's order that all Hebrew baby boys must be killed) belongs more to the realm of folk tale than that of fact. Stories from elsewhere in the world about the miraculous preservation of a future ruler while a child have been cited, including the close parallel relating to Sargon of Akkad, whose mother laid him in a basket of rushes.

But if it is correct to see the story as an instance of the genre of the miraculous deliverance of the future ruler when a child, what must not be overlooked is the realistic and resourceful human female side of the story. The bonds between the mother and her child, and between the child and his sister, are so strong that they lead to bold and imaginative action. Moreover, such is the nature of human sympathy, especially that evoked by a helpless baby, that when the pharaoh's daughter discovers the child, she deliberately overlooks the facts both that he is 'foreign' and that helping the child will involve disobeying her father's expressed decree. Far more instances of brave and self-sacrificing action by mothers on behalf of their own and other children must exist than parallels to the story of the delivered future ruler!

The function of this passage in the story of Moses is to explain how the future deliverer of the Israelite nation grew up in the Egyptian court. Its deeper message is that God works through the emotions and the determined and resourceful action of women, especially mothers. JR

1 Samuel 1.20–28

Motherhood and childhood as understood today in the West is a comparatively modern invention. In ancient Israel, as in the rest of the ancient world, women were expected, along with tackling arduous routine daily tasks such as fetching water, to bear as many children as possible, preferably males. They could expect to be constantly pregnant and childbearing and rearing from the time of their marriage, at 13 or 14, until they were around 40.

A barren woman was an economic liability as well as a failure in the eyes of her family and society. Perhaps the reason why Elkanah had two wives (1 Sam. 1.2) was because he could not afford economically and for social reasons to have one wife who bore him no children. Peninnah may therefore have been a second wife, who was married when Hannah produced no offspring. The tender way in which Hannah's husband treated her (1 Sam. 1.5, 8) needs also to be understood against the harsh realities of life in ancient Israel.

The birth of the son to Hannah, therefore, did more than remove a social stigma. Although we are not told whether Hannah had other children after the birth of Samuel, the possibility must be entertained.

Hannah's decision to dedicate her precious son to the service of God at Shiloh indicates how heavy the burden of her barrenness had been, and how important to her its ending was. She probably suckled her son, as was normal, for two or three years before bringing him to Shiloh, years that she would have relished in the circumstances. The offerings that accompanied the bringing of the child to Shiloh were lavish. A three-year-old bull would be an especially valuable animal.

The purpose of the narrative is to prepare readers for the remarkable career that the boy born in response to the divine answering of prayer will have. Modern readers will sympathize with pressures placed upon Hannah to conform to the social and economic expectations of women of her day. Such pressures are not unknown in today's world, where people are not accepted for what they are, but for how they measure up to norms of career, motherhood or physical beauty. God, fortunately, sees things differently. JR

2 Corinthians 1.3–7

In literary form, the passage follows a convention of the time, normal in Paul's writings, whereby a letter's opening greeting is followed by some form of thanksgiving. Here (alone, but see 1 Pet. 1.3f. and the dubiously Pauline Eph. 1.3f.), he uses a Jewish variant: a 'blessing' (*berakah*) – 'Blessed be God who . . .'

The content is dominated by two groups of words, which engage in an elaborate, interwoven dance: comfort or encourage, encouragement (*parakaleo, paraklēsis*); and affliction, suffer, sufferings (*thlibō, thlipsis, paschō, pathēmata*). The effect is clearest if the passage is read aloud, as, certainly, it was meant to be. The very repetition would have made it memorable. The first group is one of Paul's favourites (65 occurrences, but chiefly in this letter); note especially the link with the Spirit in 2 Cor. 13.13. As the Gospel of John shows, the theme and the linkage caught on (via the related *paraklētos*). In Paul himself, it is a powerful word, to which the English 'comfort' scarcely does justice.

'Affliction' and 'sufferings' make the natural counterweight. And of course the pattern corresponds to the fundamental one of death-resurrection, founded in the pattern of Christ, that is so pervasive in Paul (see, e.g. 4.7—5.5). And God, father of Jesus, is praised for the assurance that comfort (encouragement, strengthening) will prevail. As the pattern is that of Christ, so it is also ours, for we live 'in him'. What is more, the life and its pattern are mutual, with Paul on the one hand and his converts on the other as partners to the roots of their existence. In relation to this Christian community, Paul had ample reason to hold on doggedly to this fact of life. L H

Colossians 3.12–17

The two final chapters of Colossians (like the latter parts of other Pauline letters) are largely devoted to moral teaching. Here, following the establishing of a doctrinal base in the 'risen' standing of Christian people and a list of vices which are, therefore, to be 'put to death' (v. 5), and then a statement, akin to others in Paul, of the multi-ethnic, multi-status composition of the community for whom 'Christ is all' (v. 11), we have an uncomplicated list of virtues, of the kind common in the literature of the time. Again, the list contains few surprises and is comparable to passages else-where. There are also few exegetical difficulties, and the passage invites reflection rather than head-scratching.

All the same, it is important to note the presence of a number of well-known features. The previous verses drew the familiar contrast between the new way of life and the old: 'in these you once walked' (v. 7), and put the whole ethical instruction in an eschatological perspective: because of the prevalence of vice (sex, greed and idolatry), 'the wrath of God is coming' (v. 6).

Now the contrary virtues are headed by humility and its dependent social quality of forgiveness, which has God's forgiveness as its driving motive (cf. the Lord's Prayer). But love is the head of the moral pyramid, as in all the Gospels, as well as in Paul himself.

Then we have a practical note, referring to actual practice at Christian meetings: teaching, admonition and (in a reference virtually identical to Eph. 5.19–20, and therefore important in discussions of the connection between the two writings) music. Little can be said with certainty about the hymns referred to, though the New Testament is studded with possible examples, not least Col. 1.15–20 (see also Phil. 2.6–11; Eph. 5.14; and numerous passages in the Revelation of John). For the context of their use, 1 Cor. 14 provides the most vivid evidence. It must remain open whether 'the word of Christ' (v. 16) refers to something as precise as the tradition of his teaching and whether the giving of thanks (v. 17) refers to something as formal as the Eucharist: whether it does or not, the words 'to the Father through him' give a succinct statement of the structure and point of later eucharistic prayer. L H

Luke 2.33–35

For the passage from which this is a brief extract, see p. 55. It is a detail which, though pregnant and moving, is easily passed over in the flow of Luke's Gospel. It is a vignette, whose place in Christian life and imagination lay ahead, in the Middle Ages and since, and in the artistic and devotional tradition rather than the academic; also more Catholic than Protestant. It is one of the roots of Marian devotion, in particular that which centres on Mary as the suffering mother, forever alongside her Son, with his death implicitly yet cryptically foretold from the start by Simeon, and her involvement at the end and afterwards foreshadowed in these ominous words.

Their significance for Luke and his narrative remains mysterious. In one sense, however, this is not so: Luke is the effective founder of the 'cult' (however understood) of Mary; the first Christian writer to make her a Christian heroine, with a clear and emphatic role (yet almost in her own right) in the coming of Jesus. But this particular aspect, that is, her being associated with Jesus' suffering, now foreshadowed for the first time, is new. It is hard not to read it without the interposing of innumerable medieval and renaissance paintings of Mary's place in the dying of Jesus and its aftermath. This is already (but surely anachronistically?) the Mary of the *pietà*.

If however we stick to Luke's own context, there is more to be said, or at any rate there is an adjustment of perspective. Simeon, prophet-like, utters two oracles, first the Nunc Dimittis, with its general assurance of universal salvation now at hand, and now, in vv. 34–35, a more specific statement of Jesus' own part and his mother's association with his fate. The word rendered 'thoughts' is usually used, in the New Testament, in a pejorative sense: it is judgement that Jesus will bring, the 'fall' as well as the 'rise' of 'many in Israel'. He will be the instrument of God's sundering of his people into the genuine and the false, a common idea in apocalyptic and not here elaborated. It is in line with the frequent quoting of Isa. 6.9, making intelligible the rejection of Jesus by his own people. The passage occurs significantly, in relation to Paul's apostolate, in Acts 28.26. So the theme can be said to bracket Luke's work as a whole. The reference to the sword is obscure – despite numerous attempts to interpret it down the centuries. In any case, with its centring on death and division, this is a sobering reading for the normally rather cheerful atmosphere of Mothering Sunday, though even so it has its own realism. LH

John 19.25b–27

Since early days Christians have been touched by Jesus' tender love for his mother as he hangs dying on the cross. Traditionally in the words, 'Woman, behold your son', he is seen as commending his mother to the care of the disciple whom he specially loves, knowing that he – her firstborn – can no longer provide for her. In fact, this passage is about much more than this. Jesus is creating a new relationship: Mary is given a new 'son', and the beloved disciple a new 'mother'.

Many questions have been raised about this passage. Why does John alone mention the beloved disciple at the cross? According to Mark, when Jesus was arrested, all the (male) disciples 'forsook him and fled'. Only women watched Jesus' crucifixion, looking on 'from afar' (Mark 15.40). Would the Romans have permitted Mary to come near enough to hear Jesus' words? Does John envisage two, three or four women present? (Probably four.) Why do John and Mark have only one name in common (Mary Magdalene)? These questions are helpfully discussed by Raymond Brown in his massive book *The Death of the Messiah* (New York: Double-day, 1994). For the evangelists, the women who follow Jesus to the cross, and are first at his tomb on Easter morning, seem to be models of loyalty and faithfulness (though the silence of the women in Mark 16.8 remains a mystery).

Mary is not mentioned by name; Jesus simply addresses her as 'woman' (cf. John 2.4). Nor is 'the disciple whom Jesus loved' named; it is only church tradition which identifies this figure with the apostle John. This curious 'anonymity', com-bined with the Fourth Gospel's love of deeper meanings, has led scholars to suggest allegorical or symbolic interpretations. One suggestion is that in these verses the dying Jesus is creating a new family – a new community. The 'woman' Mary has been interpreted as the Church, the 'mother' of believers. The beloved disciple is often seen as representing the ideal follower(s) of Jesus. Some see the scene as representing Jesus' natural family, hitherto unbelievers (cf. John 7.5), becoming part of his spiritual family. Others see Mary as representing Israel, or rather part of Israel, coming to faith in Christ.

This is a difficult text on which to preach for Mothering Sunday, when our thoughts are turned to families, and gratitude to our parents (especially mothers). If we stress Jesus' love for his mother, we rely on our pious sense of what must have been the case. If we interpret this text symbolically of Israel and the Church it may seem irrelevant to the occasion, and even anti-Jewish. Although Jesus in the Gospels enjoins respect and care for parents (Mark 7.10), he does little to support traditional 'family values' (see John 2.4; Mark 3.31–35; Luke 2.49; 11.27f.); rather he stresses the priority of discipleship over family ties (e.g. Matt. 10.37; Mark 10.29; Luke 14.26). Maybe we could focus imaginatively on Mary and what it must have been like for her to be the mother of Jesus. RE

The Fifth Sunday of Lent

(Passiontide begins)

Ezekiel 37.1–14; Romans 8.6–11; John 11.1–45

Ezekiel 37.1–14

Although notions of life after death were rudimentary in sixth-century Israel, for a person not to be properly buried at death was considered to be a calamity. An individual's shallow grave was thought to be connected with Sheol, or the grave to which all the dead went, where they then existed in a shadowy, even lifeless way. People denied even this decency were more unfortunate; in a sense their lives had not been allowed to be completed.

These shared notions are the necessary background to Ezekiel's vision of the valley of dry bones. What he sees is evidently the aftermath of the battle, whose slain have been left unburied. Their flesh has been picked off by animals or carrion birds, leaving only the bones, which have become quite dry in the heat of the sun. A more hopeless scene could not be depicted, which is why the prophet gives the only possible human answer to the question 'Can these bones live?' which is, in effect, only you, God, know the answer to this question. The rest of the vision needs little elucidation, as the bones are reconnected, covered with skin and finally reanimated. The scattered, dried-up bones become a company of living individuals.

The passage is an excellent illustration of the different senses of the Hebrew word *ruach*, which is translated here as breath (v. 6), wind(s) (v. 9) and spirit (v. 14). Although in Gen. 2.7 a different Hebrew word (*neshamah*) is used for the breath that God breathes into Adam, Ezek. 37 well illustrates the Old Testament view that the difference between a living person and a dead one is that the former breathes (i.e. has *ruach*, breath) and that this phenomenon is to be related to the power of the wind, which humans cannot control, but which can have such obvious effects in the physical world. From this it is a short step to the idea of the Spirit of God as empowering individuals to do brave or noble deeds, or activities such as justice, music or artistic creation.

It has been plausibly questioned whether the application of the vision to exiled Israel (vv. 11–14) is a later expansion of the vision. The idea of bringing people from their graves does not exactly correspond with bringing to life unburied and scattered bones; and bringing people back to their land (v. 12) is no part of the vision. Whatever the original meaning of the vision, it was certainly appropriate for the restoration of Israel from exile; but that was within the world of human history. The original vision may have an eschatological dimension, that is, it may look forward to a new creation of humanity, one wrought by God after human action has produced the misery and hopelessness of a valley of dry bones. JR

Romans 8.6–11

The opening lines of Rom. 8 provide a needed transition from chs. 6 and 7, with their discussion of the relationship between the gospel of Jesus Christ, on the one hand, and the present order dominated by sin and even by the law, on the other. Chapter 8 looks forward to God's final triumph and assures believers that no struggle can separate them from God. In 8.1–11, Paul reviews what he has said earlier in the letter: the gospel of Jesus Christ has freed human beings from sin and death.

In this paragraph, Paul also introduces some new terms that will play a prominent role in this chapter. He talks about two kinds of people, those who 'live according to the flesh' and those who 'live according to the Spirit'. Since the dichotomy between flesh and spirit later in the Church's life results in a very negative assessment of the human body, and since some Christian ascetics and Gnostics did see Paul as a champion of their viewpoints, it is only natural that Paul has been held responsible for introducing that negative view of the body into Christian thought. The words 'flesh' and 'spirit' cause some to think that Paul is talking about two different parts of a human being, the flesh and the spirit, an unseen part that has to do with feeling and perceiving. What makes the problem of interpretation more complex is that sometimes Paul does use these words in just these ways. In Rom. 9.5, for example, he speaks of the Messiah coming from Israel 'according to the flesh', referring to Jesus' physical origins, and 1 Cor. 2.11 speaks of the spirit that knows what is within a person.

When Paul refers to 'liv[ing] according to the flesh' and 'liv[ing] according to the Spirit', however, he juxtaposes not two parts of the person but *two ways of living*. Living according to the flesh, then, does not necessarily mean living a life of gluttony or indolence or vanity – a life subservient to the demands of the body. Instead, it means living in a way that is shaped by, controlled by, the values and standards of the world in rebellion against God. What Paul refers to here is not a list of bad behaviours but what we would call a mindset, and it is a mindset that daily makes its way in the world apart from the recognition of its creator.

Paul contrasts this way of living with living according to the Spirit. Paul's comments about this manner of living are brief and elusive. As elsewhere when he describes the Christian life, Paul avoids offering the kind of strict guidelines that can too readily be subverted into rules and regulations. Here he simply says that living according to the Spirit is to have one's mind set on the Spirit; it means life and peace.

Having read this contrast between living in the flesh and living in the Spirit, pragmatic readers will inevitably begin to assess themselves and cast a sideways glance at the neighbours. Who stands where? What yardstick will allow an accurate evaluation of where people are? Another response, again shaped by the concern for practical action, is to conclude that Paul wants his readers to choose. He offers the proverbial fork in the road.

A careful reading of the passage reveals the short-sightedness of these questions. Paul both challenges premature conclusions about life in the Spirit and offers a positive statement of the Spirit's work. First, the Spirit does not belong to any human being. The Spirit is always *God's* spirit, never a possession to be acquired. God *gives* the Spirit. If even Jesus did not raise himself from the dead but was raised by the Spirit of God, then no human being can earn the Spirit or even choose it. It is always and forever a gift of the one sovereign and powerful God. To those Christians who would assert their own authority to correctness by means of their spiritual gifts, Paul sounds a powerful word of correction.

Second, the gift of the Spirit is a gift of empowerment. Paul does not have in view here the public and flashy spiritual gifts of speaking in tongues or performing healing, but the power of the Spirit to give life itself. It is the Spirit, after all, who enables human beings to leave behind the reign of the flesh – the reign that answers all questions by means of the world's answers – and to freely live in conformity to Christ. It is the Spirit who enables human beings to see the world's riches and power as mere entrapment and to see the foolishness of a crucified Messiah as life-giving power. For those Christians who find even the word 'Spirit' distasteful and slightly embarrassing, this passage forces the awareness that the gifts of the Spirit are not optional to the Christian faith.

Third, the Spirit's gifts belong not only to the present but to the future, as v. 11 makes abundantly clear: 'If the Spirit of him who raised Jesus from the dead dwells in you, he who raised Christ from the dead will give life to your mortal bodies also through his Spirit that dwells in you.' The Spirit of God secures the promise that life in the Spirit belongs not to this age alone. God's resurrection of Jesus from the dead means that God will grant that same life to human beings, to their 'mortal bodies'. Even the power of death cannot ultimately defeat God's Spirit. BG

John 11.1–45

The raising of Lazarus forms the climax of John's series of miraculous 'signs' narrated in chs. 2—11. The impressive restoration to life of a man whose body was already decaying in the tomb is generally seen as foreshadowing Jesus' own resurrection (though there are important differences). It does, however, raise acutely the question of John's historical accuracy. It is unparalleled in the Synoptics, and cannot convincingly be rationalized. Rather than speculate on what lies behind the story, it may be more helpful to reflect on its significance for John's theology and the life of the Church. First and foremost, it demonstrates Jesus as the giver of life (cf. 5.21, 28), offering hope of resurrection to Christian believers. At a more subtle level, it reflects on the nature of faith, as Jesus dialogues with a series of persons – the disciples, Martha, Mary and 'the Jews'.

Verses 1–6 locate the scene at Bethany (near Jerusalem) and introduce the chief characters. The prominence of the women is striking. Lazarus is described by his relationship to his sisters, rather than the women being defined by their male relative. In a remarkable 'prolepsis', Mary is identified as the woman who will anoint Jesus (cf. 12.3). Next John describes the reactions of Jesus and the disciples to the news of Lazarus' illness (vv. 7–16). His delay at going to the help of his friend is puzzling.

It is not through lack of compassion (note v. 5), but rather so that he may use the miracle to glorify God. The (male) disciples at this point are hardly models of faith: they are fearful about what will happen if Jesus returns to Jerusalem, though Thomas is prepared to die with him.

Verses 17–27 describe Jesus' encounter with Martha at the tomb. Martha's faith is at first expressed diffidently (v. 21), and then with confidence, 'I believe that you are the Christ, the Son of God, the one coming into the world' (v. 27). While some have criticized her 'confession' as inadequate, it is as full as Peter's (Mark 8.29 par.), and deserves commemoration as much as his. Note the Gospel's declared purpose in 20.30f.

We move to Jesus' relationship with Mary and 'the Jews' (vv. 28–37). Mary goes quickly to meet Jesus, and prostrates herself before him; but her only words are the same as Martha's first statement. 'The Jews' similarly look back to what might have happened (there is a hint of faith in their reference to the blind man).

The miracle is described in vv. 38–44. Lazarus' body has been wrapped in bandages, with a separate head-cloth. He emerges from the tomb still bound (contrast Jesus' resurrection). Our final verse describes the faith of many of the Jews who had been with Mary. However, John goes on to tell how other Jews inform on Jesus to the Pharisees, leading to a plot to kill him (vv. 45–53). The positive depiction of Martha and Mary in this episode has led some scholars to suppose that John's community was especially open to female leadership. RE

Palm Sunday

(Liturgy of the Passion)

Isaiah 50.4–9a; Philippians 2.5–11; Matthew 26.14—27.66 or Matthew 27.11–54

Isaiah 50.4–9a

Although the word 'servant' does not appear in this passage, its close similarity to 49.1–6 has led most to see it as the third of the so-called 'servant songs'. It is the most intensely personal and individual of them all. While in the others the servant could well depict 'Israel' in one way or another, as well, perhaps, as an individual or group who see themselves as embodying the calling of 'servant Israel', this seems like the outpouring of someone who sees himself in the prophetic tradition of such figures as Jeremiah, called, through many setbacks and much persecution, to summon 'servant Israel' to fulfil their true destiny. One commentator entitled this passage 'the Gethsemane of the Servant'.

Among the strongly individualistic features are the repeated mention of parts of the body – tongue, ears, back, cheeks, beard and face – a forceful reminder that God uses real human beings for his purposes. His word always has to become 'flesh'.

Before he can teach others the servant has himself to be 'taught', a word which appears twice in v. 4. It can come to mean 'those who have been instructed' and who are therefore 'skilled' or 'learned' (see, in various ways, NRSV, NEB, REB, NIV). Yet the verse speaks of daily listening to God and receiving his word, so that the second use of it is indubitably passive. Anyone who speaks for God and who hopes to teach others must be a lifelong and perpetual learner themselves. Only then are they able to perform God's purposes in human lives, such as sustaining those who are 'weary', God's own mission (cf. Isa. 40.30–31).

The sense of failure expressed in 49.4 is now reinforced by open and physical opposition (vv. 5–6), whether from fellow-Israelites because of his conviction that God has purposes for foreigners (for an opposed point of view see 45.9–13), or from Babylonian officials for his conviction that their power would wane (e.g. 43.14).

Yet, just as faithfulness through failure was a necessary prerequisite for the discharge of his mission (49.5–6), so persecution is an inescapable part of the 'learning' process for God's servant. Through such experiences his own faith is renewed as, in a courtroom metaphor, he becomes convinced that God will not desert him. He will be given the strength necessary for his task, his 'face set like flint' (v. 7, cf. Ezek. 3.8–9). Taught by God through his constantly renewed communion with him and by experience of his strength through persecution and rejection, he sees his mission in its true perspective. It is God's purpose that, ultimately, shall prevail (vv. 8–9). It is a lesson that was also learned by Paul through similar persecution (Rom. 8.31). RM

Philippians 2.5–11

It is usually held that though Paul's purpose in the wider passage is to urge the virtue of humility, these verses represent a separable unit, theological in character. Over the past 80 years in particular, it has become common to see them as an early Christian hymn, probably antedating Paul's use of it here in what may be his last extant letter. It may be seen to fall most naturally into three strophes (concerning Christ's pre-existent status, his self-abasement to earthly life and to death, and his subsequent exaltation to universal lordship). Thus, the passage may be taken as perhaps the oldest summary statement of Christian faith available to us, certainly in anything like poetic or imaginative form. If that is right, then its 'advanced character', in the common assessment of doctrinal terms, is all the more striking; for it seems to state a christological doctrine that is of the same order and ambitious profundity as that of the Johannine prologue.

There is dispute over the most likely sources of parts of the doctrine here stated and almost every word has its difficulties. It may be that Jesus is seen in terms of an amalgam of not wholly consistent Jewish images, with both speculation about Adam and 'wisdom' theology (like that in the Wisdom of Solomon) being prime contributors. The overall doctrine is of both the comprehensiveness of Jesus' significance and the cosmic scope of his achievement. In that way, the words are a striking example of that early Christian manner of laying hold of every possible Jewish idea and symbol and applying them to Jesus.

The final verses are the least problematic, appearing to draw on Isa. 45.23 and Ps. 110.1, that most common of all early Christian proof-texts, backing the idea of Jesus as 'lord', yet to God's glory. The background of the first part (vv. 6–8) is less clear, but the model for Jesus may best be seen as Adam; only, unlike him, Jesus accepts willingly his allotted place in God's purpose (no grasping at or retaining of equality with God), and even accepts the degradation of the cross. The two 'moves' in Jesus' drama are expressed with great vividness, even theatricality, and there is no missing the strength of the claims being made for Christ, though it is doubtful whether the 'form' of God in v. 6 carries, in context, the idea of 'divinity'; it is probably derived from the Gen. 1 picture of man as made in the image of God. So Jesus is seen as succeeding where Adam (and all of us, his progeny) failed – a doctrine used by Paul in Rom. 5 and 1 Cor. 15. Even if the comparison is less with Adam than with 'wisdom' as developed in Jewish thought, the picture is no less striking and the teaching no less powerful in its claim: Jesus' place is, for always, by God's side, his co-regent. All the more remarkable then is his foray into the world where death awaited him; and all the stronger his claim on allegiance and worship. L H

Matthew 26.14—27.66

On this Sunday, when the whole passion narrative is solemnly recited, according to a custom that may well go back to the early days of the Church, it is not normal to preach a sermon as well. The immediacy and pathos of this drama are allowed to speak for themselves. The following comments are, therefore, an attempt to raise awareness about the appropriate 'tone' of the liturgy itself.

Although the reading begins at 26.14, the preceding section (vv. 1–13), containing the anointing at Bethany should not be ignored, for it is integral to the proclamation of the gospel (see v. 13). The atmosphere of deadly conspiracy in the palace of the High Priest contrasts sharply with the perfumed devotion in the house of Simon. The lowly Messiah here receives his sacred anointing not from a prophet of Israel but from a woman, and not as his authorization to rule but as the warrant for death and burial. Love's beautiful expense highlights the mercenary ugliness of a friend's betrayal (v. 15).

Matthew's passion follows Mark's quite faithfully, but with a few major additions: the death of Judas (27.2–10); Pilate's wife's dream and his hand-washing (27.18–24); the resurrection of the saints (27.52–53); and the sealing of the tomb (27.62–66). In each case, an anti-Judaic motive seems to be at work, arising no doubt from Matthew's contemporary situation of conflict with the synagogue. Thus, Judas may epitomize the false disciple, whose very name evokes Judaea as the destined place of Messiah's rejection (23.37). Pilate and his wife become witnesses for Jesus' innocence, and show that the Jews are really to blame. The 'saints' here could be identified as those who will rise up at the judgement to condemn this generation (see Matt. 12.41–42). And the sealed tomb answers the slander current 'among the Jews to this day' (28.15) that the disciples stole the body.

However, we should be careful not to overstate the polemic. Judas' remorse, return of the blood money, and suicide (an action not necessarily dishonourable in the first-century world) cannot but evoke in the reader a certain pity (contrast the gruesome alternative of Acts 1.18–19). The governor's vain attempt to wash his hands of the affair is a clear dereliction of duty, and the corresponding cry of the crowd, 'His blood be on us and on our children' (27.25), is not, as it has been taken to be, a permanent indictment of the Jews but a poignant prophecy of the suffering which the next generation ('our children') will have to face in the war with Rome. The resurrection of the saints is likely, more positively, to be an illustration of the theological principle, 'His death meant life for others'; and the sealing of the tomb exposes all parties to the cover-up in an equally bad light. There is, admittedly, much in Matthew's passion, which, unless handled with sensitivity, can still fuel a latent anti-Semitism in Gentile Christian congregations.

So, the basic emphasis of the early kerygma from which the passion narratives grew needs to be remembered at this point: 'He died for *our* sins, in accordance with the scriptures' (1 Cor. 15.3). His death was caused by that universal human sinfulness that knows no boundaries of race, colour or religion; and far from replacing Israel's inheritance of faith, it finally fulfilled it. JM

Maundy Thursday

Exodus 12.1–4 (5–10), 11–14; I Corinthians 11.23–26; John 13.1–17, 31b–35

Exodus 12.1–4 (5–10), 11–14

The account of the institution of the Passover raises at least three difficulties for modern readers. The first is why it was necessary for the blood daubed on the doorposts to be a sign to God, indicating which houses should not be afflicted by the firstborn plague. After all, elsewhere in the plagues narratives God was able to exempt the Israelites from plagues that affected the Egyptians (cf. Exod. 9.22–26), so why was it not possible for the final plague? The second difficulty is the moral one of believing in a God who apparently puts to death the innocent children of the whole people, when only its ruler is in dispute with Israel. It needs further to be noted that there is a tension in the prescriptions between daubing the blood, which is essential in the Egyptian context, and consuming the lamb, which becomes the central part of the rite after the deuteronomic reform (cf. Deut. 16.1–8).

In order to explain these difficulties various theories of the origin of the rites have been proposed, such as that the blood of a lamb was daubed on their tents by herdsmen moving from winter to spring pasturage, in order to ward off misfortune; or the death of the firstborn has been explained in terms of the custom of dedicating all firstborn male humans and animals to God (cf. Exod. 13.1). It has also been pointed out that, whatever its origins, the Passover became connected with the barley harvest, at which unleavened bread marked the transition from bread made with the old grain to that made with the new.

Little of this will be of assistance to modern congregations and preachers, and a certain amount of idealizing will be unavoidable if the passage is to be used creatively. A possible starting point is the deuteronomistic observance (Deut. 16.1–8), in which the emphasis is placed upon sharing the meal in remembrance of deliverance which has affected those in every subsequent generation. This deliverance was as much political as spiritual, in that it freed people from slavery. Such deliverance was not achieved without cost and struggle, and it is an unfortunate fact of life that the innocent, including children, are caught up in and become the victims of human strife. However, the redemption of Israel from slavery is intended to bring benefits to all the nations, including Egypt. If Israel is not a light to the nations in the manner in which it establishes and practises mercy and compassion among its citizens, the Egyptians will have paid a heavy price in vain; and the Old Testament, in its narratives of the wilderness wanderings is unsparing in its condemnation of the attitude of the very generation that was freed from slavery. The path of redemption is never easy, as the whole passage indicates. JR

I Corinthians 11.23–26

These lines concerning the sharing of bread and wine are so familiar to most Christian ministers that the act of reading the text may seem superfluous. As the 'words of institution' they are known by heart and can be recited verbatim. And, indeed, that intimate knowledge of this passage is consistent with the way in which Paul introduces it. When he writes, 'For I received from the Lord what I also handed on to you', he uses technical language for the transmission of tradition, and the Church's intimate knowledge of this passage continues that understanding of it.

The tradition itself contains the simple and direct words that connect the ordinary sharing of bread and wine with the death of Jesus and its significance for humankind. The bread signifies the body of Jesus, broken in death. The cup signifies the blood of Jesus, poured out in death. Through that death comes a new covenant, and through participation in the meal comes the remembrance of Jesus. The word remembrance (*anamnēsis*) appears in both the statement regarding the bread and the statement regarding the wine, suggesting that the Lord's Supper is vitally connected with the Church's memory of Jesus. What the exact nature of that remembrance is becomes clearer in 1 Cor. 11.26.

With v. 26 Paul no longer cites the traditional words of Jesus, but offers his own interpretation of the Supper: 'For as often as you eat this bread and drink the cup, you proclaim the Lord's death until he comes.' Two crucial points emerge here. First, Paul asserts that the very act of the meal *is* an act of proclamation. In the celebration of the Lord's Supper itself, the Church engages in the preaching of the gospel. Protestant exegetes, uncomfortable with the omission of the verbal act of proclamation in this passage, long rejected this point by attempting to argue that Paul means that preaching *accompanies* every celebration of the Supper. If understood that way, however, the verse simply tells the Corinthians what they already know (preaching accompanies the meal) and adds nothing at all to the passage. Verse 26, in fact, culminates Paul's discussion of the meal by explaining its significance. The Lord's Supper is not just another meal, the eating of which is a matter of indifference; this celebration is itself a proclamation of the gospel of Jesus Christ.

The second point Paul makes in this verse comes in the final words, 'You proclaim the Lord's death until he comes.' The Lord's Supper is a very particular kind of proclamation – a proclamation of Jesus' death. A different kind of celebration, perhaps a celebration of Jesus' miracle of multiplying the bread and the fish, might proclaim Jesus' life and teaching. Even the Lord's Supper might be understood as a celebration of the person of Jesus as a divine messenger. Building on the words of institution with their emphasis on the coming death of Jesus, Paul forcefully articulates his view that the Lord's Supper proclaims Jesus' death. Unless the final phrase, 'until he comes', merely denotes the time at which celebration of the Lord's Supper will come to an end ('you keep proclaiming in this way until Jesus returns'), what it does is to convey the eschatological context in which the Church lives and works. The Church proclaims Jesus' *death* within the context of a confident expectation that he will come again in God's final triumph.

In this passage Paul has a very sharp point to make with Christians at Corinth, who are preoccupied with factions, with competing claims about the gospel, and with what appear to be class struggles. Paul's comments about their celebration of the Lord's Supper do not make the situation entirely clear to us, but it appears that they have followed the customs of the day, according to which the hosts of the meal served the choicer foods to their social peers and the less desirable foods to Christians of lower social or economic status. The activity of eating and drinking, and the struggle over that activity, have dominated the celebration of the meal. Paul's response to that situation is to recall forcefully the nature of the Lord's Supper. This is not another social occasion. It is *in and of itself* the proclamation of Jesus' death. Because it is a proclamation, Christians must treat it as such. Whatever conflicts there are about eating and drinking, they belong outside and apart from this occasion.

As earlier in the letter, Paul emphasizes the proclamation of Jesus' death as central to the gospel itself (see 1 Cor. 1.18–25; 2.1–2). Over against the Corinthians' apparent conviction of their own triumph over death, their own accomplishments and spiritual power, Paul asserts the weakness of Jesus, whose faithfulness to God led to his death, and Paul insists that the Church lives in the tension between that death and the ultimate triumph of the resurrection.

In the context of the Church's observance of Maundy Thursday, this passage recalls again the death of Jesus. That recollection is no mere commemoration, as occurs with the recollection of an anniversary or a birthday. The remembrance, especially in the Lord's Supper, serves to proclaim the death of Jesus Christ once again, as the Church continues to live between that death and God's final triumph. BG

John 13.1–17, 31b–35

Maundy Thursday derives its name from Latin *mandatum*, 'command', referring to the 'new commandment' given by Jesus at the Last Supper. The command to love is rooted in Old Testament teaching (cf. Deut. 6.4f.; Lev. 19.18), texts combined by Jesus in his famous 'summary' of the Law (Mark 12.29–31 par.). In the Johannine writings this teaching is given new impetus as it is grounded in Christ's own love for his disciples, and the Father's love for the Son and for all who obey his word (cf. John 13.34f.; 14.21; 15.9–13; 1 John 4.7–21). It is especially poignant that Jesus gives this command after washing the disciples' feet as an example of humility and love, and before giving up his life for others.

The footwashing is unique to John's Gospel, and there has been much speculation why it replaces Jesus' sharing of the bread and the cup in John's narrative of the Last Supper. The evangelist must have included it because it was important to him and perhaps his community. What does it mean for him?

Most obviously Jesus washes the disciples' feet as an example of humble service. In the ancient world, where people walked the fields and dusty streets in open sandals or with bare feet, footwashing was a normal preliminary before meals. Washing someone else's feet was a menial task, done by 'inferiors' for 'superiors'. It was performed for guests by slaves (usually women), by children for parents, wives for husbands, and sometimes by devoted students for their teachers. It was unheard of for a teacher to wash his pupils' feet. Yet this is what Jesus does, as an 'acted parable' or visual aid, to show those closest to him that their role must be not that of 'lords', but of servants. The teaching is exactly the same as given in Luke's narrative of the Last Supper (22.27), when Jesus rebukes his disciples for disputing over who is the greatest with the words, 'I am among you as one who serves (*ho diakonōn*)'.

Yet the footwashing in John is more than a moral example. It comes at a turning point in the Gospel, as the evangelist moves from his account of Jesus' self-revelation through 'signs' and personal encounters to his 'hour', when the time has come for him to be 'glorified' (cf. 13.1, 31f.). The verbs which John uses to describe Jesus' laying aside his garments and resuming them are the same distinctive terms as were earlier used for his laying down his life on the cross and taking it up in resurrection (10.11, 15, 17f.). The footwashing illustrates Jesus' loving 'his own' to the end and prefigures his death: cf. Mark 10.45, 'the Son of Man came not to be served but to serve, and to give his life a ransom for many'. Like Peter, we have to learn to accept Christ's 'washing' of our feet, so that we may share in his work of service and reconciliation. Do we have here a neglected sacrament? R E

Good Friday

Isaiah 52.13—53.12; Hebrews 10.16–25 or Hebrews 4.14–16; 5.7–9; John 18.1—19.42

Isaiah 52.13—53.12

This final 'servant song' is undoubtedly one of the greatest passages in the Old Testament and yet, with its densely packed thought and highly symbolic poetic language and imagery, one of the most difficult to interpret. The text presents many difficulties, perhaps evidence of the problems scribes and others have found in understanding it in the course of its transmission. Commentaries discuss these in detail. Yet the grand sweep of thought is clear, speaking in the sublimest language of the deepest mysteries of God's dealings with human beings.

It opens (52.13–15) and closes (53.11b–12) with words of God about his servant. The body of the song is spoken by an unidentified group in the first person plural commenting on the action rather like the chorus in a Greek tragedy. Like the psalms of lament and prophetic passages, especially in Jeremiah, it depicts the servant's suffering, yet contains assurance of God's triumphant vindication of him.

God's opening words about his servant (52.13–15, cf. 42.1) and closing speech (53.11b–12) confirm that his role will be to bring surprised joy to the nations. Indeed, by his 'knowledge' (which he gains from his own relationship with God, cf. 50.4) he will, like a sacrificial victim, cover their sins and bring them into a right relationship with God. Thus his ministry will be triumphantly vindicated as he believed (50.8–9).

The human speakers describe the suffering of the servant which so disfigured him (53.1–3); realize that he suffered as a sacrificial victim for their sins which they now freely confess (vv. 4–6); speak of his suffering and death (vv. 7–9), but, finally, see his vindication by God (vv. 10–11a.).

Who are these speakers? They may be the Gentile kings now telling of that which before they had never heard or known (52.13b). In that case the 'suffering servant' must be Israel, who suffered innocently at their hands. Yet, by his glorious redemption of his 'servant' Israel, God has so revealed his glory that all nations come to recognize and know him (43.8–13). Or the speakers may be fellow Israelites who, having failed in their mission to be God's witness to the nations, need someone or some group who, by their faithfulness to God and suffering for his sake, bring them back to an awareness of him. In their renewed recognition of God and relationship with him the servant's ministry is vindicated.

As poetry and profound theology the symbol of the 'suffering servant' can operate at many levels, finding, as Christians believe, its supreme embodiment in Jesus. What it does show is the extraordinary power of vicarious suffering. Just as we are born into life by the pain of our mothers, advance to understanding by the dedication of our teachers, and appreciate music, literature and art through the gifts of others, so God's love reaches us through those who are ready to pay the price of being its agents. R M

Hebrews 10.16–25

Hebrews is composed of an alternation of exegetical passages, often worked out with skill and ingenuity, followed by consequent ('therefore', v. 19) exhortation, sometimes, as here, developing the scriptural material in new, but characteristic ways. The theme of the new covenant, familiar from the words over the cup at the Last Supper, appears in the suggestive text in Jer. 31.31–34, which has been quoted in full in 8.8–12 and provides a leitmotif for chs. 8—10. There, the focus was on the word 'covenant', with its dual sense as the treaty-like bond between God and his people, and a will which only comes into force with the testator's death (see the word-play in 9.15f. – not easy to render into English). Here, it is on the more pervasive concern of this writer: the removal of sin, once by means of endlessly repeated animal sacrifices, now by the once-for-all death of Jesus.

By the time he wrote (surely after A D 70), the offering of beasts in the Jerusalem temple had ceased – in any case, he shows no interest in the rituals in practice, only in the provisions he finds in the Pentateuch. In that sense, his method is bookish. These he exploits here – yet further: this has been his subject from ch. 8. Detail after liturgical detail has been taken up and shown to be absorbed or fulfilled in some aspect of the death of Jesus, who occupies the roles of both high priest and victim in the ritual of the Day of Atonement. It is fruitless to seek tidy logic here. The pattern works by a concentration of images, even more than Johannine in its intensity. The symbolism of the entry into the Holy of Holies, seen as the counterpart of heaven, leads to a movement straight from Jesus' death to his heavenly arrival (cf. 12.2); there is no room in this scheme for his resurrection.

Then, our share in this great result awaits us, assured by the purifying water, presumably in baptism, here seen as the counterpart of liturgical purificatory washings in the old Law. Finally, there is a practical note: Christians must meet together, at least for the sake of mutual encouragement, as the future consummation approaches. S L

Hebrews 4.14–16; 5.7–9

As at Christmas, so on Good Friday a passage from Hebrews serves to affirm the full humanity of Jesus: like us in weakness, in temptation and in despair. The reference to Jesus' 'loud crying and tears' cannot fail to recall the gospel story of Gethsemane, especially in the Lucan version which emphasizes Jesus' mental and physical anguish. His prayer was to the God who was able to save him from death, and the author states firmly that 'he was heard' – yet he died. It was not that his prayer went unheard: prayer can be answered by 'no' as well as 'yes'; but here the author probably means us to understand that Jesus' prayer was answered with the assurance that this death was not only inevitable but necessary; an answer that Jesus accepted: 'thy will be done'. Jesus was heard because of his *eulabeia*, a word the English versions find difficult to translate in this context (e.g. 'godly fear', RSV, and 'reverent submission', NRSV). It has to do with awe in the presence of God, not naked human fear, and reflects the fact that Jesus faced his suffering in prayer. There is a similar problem with the translation of the first clause of the following verse: some translations opt for the concessive 'Although he was a Son ...' so that the process of learning obedience seems a contradiction of Jesus' real role and status but a part of his emptying himself of his divinity; but it could be read as causative: it is precisely *because* Jesus is son among many children of God (2.10–14), and fully human, that obedience through suffering is his lot. (The same ambiguity is found in the 'christological hymn' of Phil. 2.) Again: he 'learned obedience' can be understood as describing how Jesus, through the repeated experience of testing learned how to obey, or that he learned obedience in the sense of discovering the full extent of the demand, what it really means to obey. And so he was made 'perfect': a term frequent in and characteristic of Hebrews, with connotations of completeness and so effectiveness. Because both Jesus' identification with humanity and his obedience to God were complete, they effect salvation, enabling us to approach the throne of God as Jesus did, and find it the source of mercy and grace in time of need. He is the great high priest, fully identified with those whom he represents, offering the only fully effective sacrifice, the sacrifice of himself, and so opening up access to God. SL

John 18.1—19.42

The four evangelists describe the story of Jesus' passion in different ways. Each has episodes or details lacking in the others, and each his own theological slant. Whereas Mark stresses Jesus' humanity and suffering, culminating in his great cry of dereliction from the cross, 'My God, my God, why have you forsaken me?' (15.34), in Luke Jesus dies calmly, fully trusting in God: 'Father, into your hands I commend my spirit' (23.46). Matthew alone mentions the legions of angels that Jesus could have called to his aid (26.53).

John's special emphasis is on the *kingship* of Jesus, and his 'autonomy' throughout his arrest, 'trials', mocking and crucifixion. John has no account of the 'agony in the garden', nor of Judas' kiss of betrayal. Jesus identifies himself to those who had come to arrest him with the words, '*Egō eimi*' ('I am [he]'), and his opponents all fall to the ground in awe. Jesus himself tells them to let his followers go free. He carries his own cross.

In the dialogue with Pilate Jesus' true kingship is a recurrent theme: Jesus makes it clear that he was born to be king, but that his kingship is not 'of this world'. Both Pilate (18.39; cf. 19.14) and the crowd (19.3) refer to him as 'King of the Jews', and Jesus dies with these words affixed to the cross – words which Pilate refuses to change, in spite of protests. Throughout all this runs the irony that what Jesus is called in mockery he is in reality, 'the King of Israel' (cf. 1.49) – and much more!

Most remarkable of all is perhaps Jesus' final 'word' from the cross, 'It is accomplished' (19.30): he has completed the work that God gave him to do.

Behind all four passion narratives lies the theme of fulfilment of Scripture, sometimes explicit (e.g. Mark 14.27; John 19.24, 37), sometimes implicit. In 19.28 Jesus' words 'I thirst' may allude to Ps. 22.15; cf. Ps. 69.21. Many commentators note the irony that the source of 'living water' (4.14; 7.37) now needs to be given a drink. But Jesus' 'thirst' in John is probably more than physical (this is not to minimize his agony). Jesus' 'food' was to do the will of him who sent him (4.34); now he has to drink the 'cup' the Father has given him (18.11).

After his death, blood and water flow from Jesus' side (in John alone). Some interpret this as showing that Jesus truly had died (perhaps from a rupture of the heart, which can produce such apparent effects); more probably the blood and water symbolize the spiritual cleansing and new life effected for believers through Jesus' death. The unbroken bones, the hyssop (19.29), and the flow of blood all point to a sacrificial understanding of Jesus' death (cf. 1.29, 36). Only John describes the role of Nicodemus in anointing Jesus' body. The huge quantities of myrrh and aloes (19.39) perhaps hint at a *royal* burial. RE

Easter Day

Acts 10.34–43 or Jeremiah 31.1–6; Colossians 3.1–4; John 20.1–18 or Matthew 28.1–10

Acts 10.34–43

Peter's speech to the gathering at the house of Cornelius has roughly the same contents as the other major speeches by Peter in the early chapters of Acts, and indeed that by Paul in Acts 13 (though its reference to Jesus going about 'doing good', v. 38, is unique). This similarity of pattern has led to at least two not wholly consistent conclusions: that the speeches represent a standard pattern of Christian missionary preaching in the early decades, a pattern which may even be seen as one of the ancestors of the later baptismal creeds (a connection with the rite is discernible in some of the Acts episodes, including this one, v. 47f.); and that they are so similar (and the likelihood of shorthand records so remote) that, probably like all the Acts speeches, they are Lucan compositions, whatever they may or may not owe to memory and tradition – so following the practice of writers of the day. This second idea can be strengthened: the speeches are imbued with peculiarly Lucan themes and patterns, the present example being no exception. Note the universal scope of the message (v. 34), though its roots are in Israel (v. 36); the perception of Jesus as a doer of good, a fine description of especially Luke's characterization of Jesus; the post-resurrection meals with the chosen witnesses (v. 41, cf. Luke 24.35); the command to preach (v. 42, cf. Luke 24.48; Acts 1.8); Jesus as future judge (v. 42; Luke 21.36). The speeches contain what Luke saw as the core of the faith.

Cornelius is important as representing a real step forward in the mission. As promised in Acts 1.8, the preaching began in Judea, then moved to Samaria. But Cornelius is a Gentile, though one who is 'devout' and fears God (v. 2). He is one of a number of such people in Acts – a group for whose existence in at least some of the cities of the empire there is now other evidence and who may seem to be natural subjects for successful Christian evangelism: Gentiles who frequented the synagogue and valued its religious and moral teaching, but for whom conversion to Judaism seemed a step too far. Such people were perhaps social misfits of one kind or another (recent immigrants, upwardly mobile freedmen, independent-minded women, cf. Lydia in 16.14), and to whom the blessings of the Christian message may well have been both intelligible (for its roots in Judaism and in Scripture) and peculiarly attractive. It offered a spiritual home. With Cornelius the centurion (he invites comparison, like other Acts characters, with one in Luke's Gospel, the centurion in 7.1–10), the mission is on the verge of the wider move to the (fully) Gentile world. That will occupy Paul and others from chs. 13—20, and indeed implicitly to the end of the book, where Paul carries on the work even from his place of rather loose custody in Rome, 'openly and unhindered'. LH

Jeremiah 31.1–6

These words probably derive from a member of the Jeremiah school, either during the exile or the post-exilic period. Verse 2 is probably a reference to the exodus and wilderness wanderings, and to Israel's desire for 'rest' in the promised land. In this case, 'long ago' (so NEB) would be a better translation in context than 'from far away'. The 'appearance' of God to Israel 'long ago' would be an allusion to the giving of the Law at Mount Sinai.

All that was in the distant past; but in the meantime and ever since, God has loved his people with a love that will reach to eternity. The rendering 'I have continued my faithfulness' does not do full justice to the Hebrew, which speaks literally of God pulling or drawing Israel along with, or on account of, his unfailing love. NIV 'I have drawn you with loving-kindness' gets closer to the Hebrew than most other modern translations.

The affirmation that ever since the foundational event of the exodus, wilderness wanderings and the law-giving at Mount Sinai God has been guiding his people (drawing them along) becomes the basis of the promises that occupy the latter verses of the passage. A restoration of all Israel is envisaged, so that the land will be as it was ideally after the settlement in the promised land, and when the land and its people had rest from their enemies. The significance of planting and enjoying the fruit is that no enemies will disrupt the agricultural processes on which people's welfare depends. Dancing is also a symbol of peace, while the summons to those in Ephraim (in the old northern kingdom) to go up to Zion (the capital of the southern kingdom) indicates that the old enmities between north and south no longer exist.

The opening verse declares that, in that time, the Lord will be the God of all the families of Israel. He has, of course, been that all the time, especially as he has constantly been drawing Israel along in his unfailing mercy. From the point of view of those exiled or who faced injustice and persecution in Israel, this was not always apparent. The passage thus looks forward to a future time of revelation, when what has always been true will become apparent – that God has been loving his people with an everlasting love. This discovery will lead to joy and dancing. JR

Colossians 3.1–4

The passage is an encapsulation of a pattern of belief and teaching which, in various of its aspects, is not confined to this writing – or indeed to Paul, from whose hand (or perhaps from whose 'school') it comes.

In the first place, it takes a high view of the status of believers in the light of Christ's resurrection, a view more typical of the Fourth Gospel (e.g. John 5.24; 11.25). Paul gets close to it in Rom. 6.11, but in v. 5 had taken a lower view of the outcome of baptism: it was the start of a process, leading to resurrection, rather than the attaining, now, of the new risen life. 1 Cor. 15 sides firmly with the 'unfinished' view of our present situation, probably in the face of enthusiasts whose conviction was more in line with the leading note of our present passage. It depends whether you focus on the greatness of what God has already done for those who adhere to Christ or have a stronger sense of what, for all that greatness, remains in store.

In fact, even here the future orientation, basic to most forms of early Christianity and part of its Jewish inheritance, is real enough. Christ will return and the Christians' part in that triumph ('in glory') is assured (v. 4). In the meantime, there can be a sense of unreality about continued life in this world: whatever the appearances, the believers' 'true' location is 'in God', 'hidden with Christ'. Here we have the idiom of apocalyptic, only the envisaged future is in this case rooted in the past event, Christ's resurrection – that determines its character. And, from the other side, the resurrection can be seen as an anticipation of the end which will surely come and in whose fruits one's share is assured.

Yet this is not a doctrine of mindless euphoria, with no regard to the realities of life. Indeed, the new status carries with it the imperative: 'seek the things that are above' (v. 1) – and the passage leads on immediately to an exposition of the moral qualities that are to be rejected and those that are to be embraced. The Christian community must live out its 'risen' status in practical terms.

The modern reader is likely to sense in this passage, as indeed in so much of the New Testament, the presence of what is now seen as a sectarian style of religion and of the Christians' self-perception. There is a question how far and by what means faith can be both strong and deep on the one hand, rooted in the difference God has made, and on the other hand truly and responsibly engaged with the plain realities of the world. LH

John 20.1–18

Today's gospel tells one of the best-loved resurrection stories. It is carefully constructed, beginning with Mary Magdalene's arrival at the tomb (vv. 1f.). Next, two male disciples discover the empty grave-clothes: one 'sees and believes' (vv. 3–10). They both go home. Then we return to Mary at the tomb (vv. 11–18).

John's account shares many elements with the other Gospels. In all, the first people to visit the grave are women (though their number and names vary). They find the stone rolled back, and see an angel/angels (or a man/men in white). There are, however, differences. In Mark, the women run off and tell nobody (16.8; the following verses are an addition). In Matthew, but not Luke, Jesus appears to the women and they cling to his feet (28.9). Some texts of Luke 24.12 have Peter go to the tomb, but only John has Peter and the 'beloved disciple' run there together. The 'beloved disciple' appears to be a model of faith (but why does he just return home with Peter?).

In 20.1, 11–18, John focuses on just one woman at the tomb. Mary comes while it is still dark. It has been suggested that the darkness may symbolize the disciples' desolation. In the course of our narrative she moves from bewilderment to faith. At first she stands outside the tomb, weeping. Even after the angels have spoken to her, she still assumes the body has been removed. She takes Jesus for the gardener, surmising that he was responsible for its removal (what an irony!). But when he addresses her by name (cf. 10.3, 14), she recognizes him as her 'Teacher'. After he tells her of his ascent to the Father, she acknowledges him as 'Lord'. Entrusted with his message for his 'brothers' (the disciples), she truly becomes the *apostola apostolorum*.

John's account is so personal and moving that it is tempting simply to let it warm our hearts. Yet thinking people are bound to ask 'What really happened?' The resurrection is not the sort of event that can be verified from historical evidence, and the Gospel-writers themselves seem to understand it differently. Luke, with his descriptions of Jesus eating with the disciples (24.30, 41–44), stresses its seeming physicality. Matthew, with his great earthquake and opening of the tombs (27.52–54; 28.2) heightens the miraculous. John's attitude is more ambiguous. Is his careful description of the grave-clothes and napkin (v. 7) designed merely to show that the body had not been stolen (robbers would not have left them folded)? Or does John want us to understand that the risen Jesus passed *through* them (cf. his passing through closed doors in 20.19)?

We are not likely ever (in this world) to discover exactly what took place. The main point is that the first Christians firmly believed that something stupendous happened. God vindicated Jesus. Witnesses saw him alive (cf. 1 Cor. 15.5–8). The disciples were transformed and the Church was born. Can we share in their gladness and trust, and let the risen Christ transform our lives? RE

Matthew 28.1–10

The starting point for grasping what Matthew intended here is Mark 16.1–8, the story that he had inherited and now modifies. Unless one could appreciate, theologically and spiritually, Mark's allusive and apparently unrounded-off narrative, ending so abruptly, one was bound to be tempted to try to make 'improvements'.

The changes here are all along familiar Matthean lines, bringing clarity and firmness of outline, and dealing with difficulties that readers might feel. Thus, Mark's 'they said nothing to anyone' (16.8) – raising the questions: So did they then disobey the young man's instruction? And how then did the message of the empty tomb get about? – is dropped and contradicted: v. 8. What is more, Jesus actually appears to the women, whereas in Mark they had only the message. Verses 9–10 merely repeat what precedes, and are surely Matthew's work, fixing things, so there may be no doubt. Thereby, Matthew makes us face the question where 'resurrection faith' should truly reside. We may note too that the women (two, unlike Mark's three) go not to anoint the body of Jesus, but only to observe (cf. 27.61). So they witness what then happens and can report on the astounding event before their eyes.

In this, with problems of his own day in view, Matthew countered Jewish stories that what lay behind the Christians' claims was a grave-snatch by the disciples. Not so, says Matthew, there was a guard, who had a terrifying experience, at the hands of an angel, brilliant in appearance (gone is Mark's 'young man', wholly unalarming in himself, though awesome in his message); and later we read of the soldiers being bribed to tell the required lie.

This is then the first narrative of what became the standard, confident Easter story, which Luke and John develop, each in his own way, with his own resources and ways of seeing things: fear and joy (not Mark's pure fear) are the proper reactions. The apocryphal Gospel of Peter developed Matthew further to tell of Jesus actually emerging from the tomb: by comparison, Matthew is reticent. Where is faith if there is so much demonstration? LH

The Second Sunday of Easter

Exodus 14.10–31; 15.20–21 or Acts 2.14a, 22–32; I Peter 1.3–9; John 20.19–31

Exodus 14.10–31; 15.20–21

Where the sea was that the Israelites crossed and what exactly happened are questions that cannot be answered. This has not deterred commentators from attempting answers, however, even though the outcomes have often been less than satisfactory. Take, for example, the suggestion that the wind that held back the sea and dried the seabed was an actual wind that the Israelites were able to take advantage of. Even if we have never personally experienced hurricanes, we shall have seen sufficient evidence on television of their effect to know that a wind strong enough to part the sea would have been devastating for any humans and animals anywhere near it. Another, more plausible, suggestion is that the Israelites took advantage of tidal conditions to cross a strip of land at Lake Sirbonis not unlike the causeways at Lindisfarne or Mont St Michel, and that the incoming tide then swept away the pursuing Egyptians.

Most attempts to find a natural explanation for the Red Sea crossing only make it abundantly clear that the narrative as we have it goes out of its way to emphasize the supernatural. Further, similarities between Exod. 14 and 'holy war' narratives in books such as Joshua and Judges have been pointed out. Typical features of such narratives are the command not to be afraid (v. 13, cf. Josh. 10.25), the promise that God will accomplish the victory, and the fact that Israel's contribution to the outcome is little or nothing. Also, it is God who throws the enemy into panic (v. 24, cf. Josh. 10.10; Judg. 4.15).

What this means is that Exod. 14 is similar to narratives in Joshua and Judges and elsewhere, that present God as a God of war fighting on behalf of his people, and giving them victories that involve the deaths of their enemies. That this is a problem for modern readers goes without saying; but several points need to be made. First, narratives of this kind belong to rhetoric rather than reality and have parallels with other literature in the ancient Near East. Second, such narratives belong to later rather than earlier strata of the Old Testament. They are not evidence for primitive or barbaric practices in an early state of Israelite development, but functioned story-wise in the way that the violence contained in modern literature, film and television function in modern society. Third, a human race that has perpetrated the horrors of the wars of the twentieth century cannot afford to be morally superior. The purpose of Exod. 14 is to say, however problematically, that Israel owes its existence and freedom entirely to God. That it also includes a strong statement of the people's unwillingness to believe that this is possible, that slavery is preferable to freedom, should also not be overlooked. JR

Acts 2.14a, 22–32

Peter's speech at Pentecost, following the astonishing feat of trans-lingual comprehension of the Spirit-fired apostles' words, began (vv. 17–21) with a scriptural explanation of what had just occurred: it fulfilled Joel's prophecy of just such a day. Now the speech moves to its central message: a homiletically presented account of Jesus' deeds of power, his wicked execution and his resurrection, a fact to which Peter and his fellow-apostles can testify (cf. Luke 24.36f.). We may note that there is no reference here to Jesus' teaching: these speeches in Acts stick to the bare bones of what must be preached and grasped.

The speech is addressed to Jews, and appropriately its central message is backed by Scripture, whose true meaning has only become clear in the light of what has now occurred in the career of Jesus. Paul, in his brief quasi-credal formula in 1 Cor. 15.3f., says Jesus was raised 'according to the Scriptures' but, in the nature of the passage, does not tell us what passages were in mind. Here we have what was surely taken as one of the crucial testimonies to the resurrection, Ps. 16.8–11. It was read, as we should expect, as the work of David, seen as having prophetic charisma, whose messianic successor and descendant Jesus was. The psalm lent itself to Christian exegesis, which Peter supplies: at long last its meaning was plain. Luke doubtless saw this as among the passages of Scripture that Jesus had expounded to his disciples after his resurrection; in that sense, the exegesis had his authority (Luke 24.27, 44–47). The psalm gives us a valuable insight into how at least some early Christians saw 'the resurrection' and gives content to the mysteriousness of that deed. As we should expect, and as Luke, in common with the other main New Testament writers, is at pains to show, not only the resurrection, but the death of Jesus was in accord with God's 'plan and foreknowledge'. Luke has no intellectual interest in puzzles over how then human responsibility comes into the matter; though indeed (for pastoral reasons urgent in his own situation where Jewish and Gentile Christians must cohere?) he regularly exculpates those directly involved – they acted in ignorance (3.17; 13.27), as indeed the dying Jesus had said as he forgave them (Luke 23.34). At the same time, Luke repeats what was becoming more and more the Christian version of events: that Pilate ('those outside the law', i.e. Gentiles) was the dupe and tool of the Jews, here lumped together in the manner of Matthew (23.25) and John (with such devastating later consequences), for all Luke's toning down.

There is, finally, a general issue that affects all the great public preaching stories in Acts: was this really the manner in which early Christian evangelism took place? There is no sign of it in Paul (poor speaker that he tells us he was). Is it not more likely to have been a matter of informal networking? And is the model perhaps the Gospels' picture of Jesus' preaching to the crowds, and may it not be right to see here the beginnings of the sense of the early days as a golden age? LH

I Peter 1.3–9

The first readers of this epistle have been addressed as 'exiles of the dispersion' living in Asia Minor, and so are separated by time and space from the foundation events of the Christian gospel. Unlike the apostle Peter, they did not witness the resurrection of Jesus; but like him they wait to witness Christ's future revelation. They may be said to epitomize Christians on 'Low Sunday', when Easter is past and it is not clear what should happen next! Their faith is in an unseen Jesus: but it is not a faith that merely affirms him in the past and expects him in the future, but a faith that includes the love of Jesus in the present. In this syntactically complex but resounding opening passage, the author explains what it is like to live 'between the times'. It is a time full of hope and expectation for the future, for an assured inheritance and a salvation already prepared, but it is also a time in which the past and the future colour present experience. By the resurrection of Jesus, the readers have already been 'born again'; a metaphor for Christian life not common in the New Testament, but characteristic of this author, as in 1.23 and 2.2, and developed in John 3. They already live the new life; and though their final inheritance of salvation is still to be revealed, they are already receiving the salvation of their souls. Not future hope alone, then, but present experience sustains the readers through their current trials. It will become clear as the epistle proceeds that these are not the acute trials of active persecution – though this may come – but the humdrum, every-day pressure of outsiders' curiosity, suspicion and mockery (2.15; 3.14–16). The author will encourage them to see this situation as an opportunity to bear witness, gently but resolutely giving an account of their faith. His readers are exiles in a more than literal sense: they are the people of God in an alien world, and the people of the new age living in the present. Their confidence, however, in what they already possess gives them cause to bless God, to rejoice, and to demonstrate their faith. SL

John 20.19–31

The resurrection appearances in the Gospels serve two main functions: first, they witness to the fact that Jesus is alive; and second, they enable the risen Christ to instruct and commission the disciples. Today's gospel describes two separate appearances of Jesus, followed by a brief conclusion to the Gospel (ch. 21 is believed by most scholars to be an appendix).

In vv. 19–23 Jesus appears to the assembled disciples in a house on Easter Day itself. Functionally, this corresponds to the appearance described in Luke 24.36–49. Jesus greets the disciples, identifies himself to them, and equips them for mission. There are striking links with John's supper discourses. There, Jesus promised to 'come' to the disciples (14.18), which is what he now does (20.19). He said he was giving his 'peace' to them (14.27); he does so now (20.19f.). In his 'high-priestly' prayer he spoke (proleptically) of his sending them out (17.18), he does so now authoritatively (20.21).

Of particular interest is his 'breathing' on them in fulfilment of his promise to send them the Holy Spirit or paraclete (20.22). The 'insufflation' (as it is often called) is a creative and effective act of symbolism, reminiscent of Gen. 2.7 where the Lord creates humankind and breathes into Adam the breath of life (cf. Ezek. 37.9; in the

Greek text the same verb, *emphysaō*, is used in all three passages). While some have seen this as only a foretaste of what is to happen at Pentecost, this can hardly be anything other than the Johannine *equivalent of* Pentecost. There is absolutely no need to read John with Lucan spectacles and to presuppose that this dramatic gift of the Spirit is merely a preliminary to an event fifty days later.

The commission which accompanies the insufflation parallels the 'great commission' in Matt. 28.18–20, and that narrated indirectly in Luke 24.47. What is surprising is the strong focus on the forgiveness and retention of sins, without any mention of preaching or baptizing. The saying recalls Matt. 16.19 and 18.18, and may ultimately derive from Isa. 22.22. While some have seen this as conveying 'power' to one group within the Church (e.g. bishops and priests) to declare sins forgiven, more probably it should be seen as addressed to the disciples as representatives of the whole ecclesial community.

Verses 24f. prepare the reader for the fact that Thomas was not present on this occasion. The appearance a week later is unique to John's Gospel. Theologically its main function is to illustrate the nature of resurrection faith. Thomas says that he will believe only when he can see and touch Jesus' wounds. Yet when Jesus invites Thomas to touch him, he acknowledges Jesus as his 'Lord and God' without this physical assurance. The blessing that follows on those who have not seen and yet have faith is for all future believers. Has Thomas outshone even the 'beloved disciple' in his faith? RE

The Third Sunday of Easter

Zephaniah 3.14–20 or Acts 2.14a, 36–41; I Peter I.17–23; Luke 24.13–35

Zephaniah 3.14–20

The prophet Zephaniah is generally assumed to have been active in the early part of the reign of Josiah (640–609; cf. Zeph. 1.1). His prophecies in chs. 1 and 2 and beginning of ch. 3 speak of the coming day of the Lord and the judgement that will bring, not only upon Judah and Jerusalem, but also upon surrounding peoples such as those in Gaza, Ashkelon, Moab and Ammon. At 3.8 the mood changes to one of future promise; and although it is possible that Zephaniah is responsible for some of the material in 3.8–20, the concluding verses, especially from v. 16, seem to presuppose the situation of the Babylonian exile, with its language about dealing with Jerusalem's oppressors, gathering its people and bringing them home.

Verses 14–15 have been likened to language that could have been used at a coronation. The hopes and expectations that such an occasion would arouse are related, however, not to an earthly king but to the presence of God among his people, among them not for judgement (as in the opening chapters of Zephaniah) but for salvation. The theme of God being with, or in the midst of his people is a powerful one in the Old Testament (cf. Ps. 46. 5, 7, 11). The name Emmanuel – God with us – (cf. Isa. 7.14) is an important instance.

In vv. 16–17, 'holy war' themes appear, in the command to Jerusalem not to fear (cf. the notes on the Second Sunday of Easter), and in the description of God as a warrior who gives victory. Another important theme that is present is the idea that the exile brought shame and reproach upon the people in the eyes of the other nations and, by implication, upon the God of Israel. This situation will be reversed. Israel will receive renown and praise from the other nations when God ends its captivity and restores its fortunes.

However, it would be wrong to read the passage purely in military terms. No doubt the fortunes of war, and matters such as victory and defeat, were important to the Old Testament writers; but the prophetic tradition is not interested in Israel for its own sake, but as the people that will enable the nations to desire and embrace God's rule of justice and peace. The eirenic promises of restoration imply the prior punishment, judgement and purification, so strongly stated in the preceding chapters. JR

Acts 2.14a, 36–41

These are the final words of Peter's speech at Pentecost to the multi-lingual Jerusalem crowd of pilgrims. It is the first of Luke's series of kerygmatic pieces in Acts, and its effect is dramatic – no less than 3,000 converts. The preaching of Jesus as Lord and Messiah, so immediate in its effect, must be followed by baptism. Paul is our earliest witness (e.g. 1 Cor. 1.13–17; Rom. 6.3–11) to baptism as the rite of entry into the Christian community; and Matthew wrote at the end of his Gospel that Jesus enjoined it (28.19). Luke, however, is the first Christian writer to describe how it worked (or had worked). But, typically, and unlike Paul in Rom. 6, he never gives us a theology of baptism – except to say that it is done 'in the name' of Jesus Christ, perhaps meaning that the one baptized is, as it were, transferred to Jesus' ownership. Luke never gives any hint of the source of the rite. It was probably taken from Jewish practice, but quite how and where and why remains obscure. For Luke it is established practice and here is how it began in Christian use.

Nevertheless, for the modern reader Luke is not altogether tidy in his picturing of baptism. Here, it follows the outpouring of the Spirit, as also in Acts 10. But in Acts 8 (in Samaria), in an order more congenial to what became standard practice, baptism precedes the Spirit's gift, as also in the rather special (but are all these cases in Acts 'special'?) case of the followers of John the Baptist in 19.1–6. And as for the fruit of baptism? It is not, as in Paul, 'life in Christ', but forgiveness of sins and the gift of the Spirit (v. 38) – though of what then happens to these people we hear not a word.

Much ink has been spilt on v. 36: is this a primitive doctrine, to the effect that only at his exaltation did Jesus become 'Lord and Messiah'? That great early Christian proof-text, Ps. 110.1, might be taken to say as much (v. 35). If so, it may be a sign of the genuinely early character of Peter's speech, even perhaps what he preached that day (albeit, we take it, not in Greek). But is this how Luke's mind went? For him, Jesus has been Messiah from his conception and birth, and 'the Lord' is used of Jesus in his lifetime with unusual frequency. We may suppose that he saw no inconsistency in the statement here: Jesus is Lord and Messiah from start to finish. L H

1 Peter 1.17–23

The dramatic stories in the early chapters of Acts give the impression that joining up with the Christian community in its formative stages was an easy matter. Even if the authorities in Jerusalem did interfere occasionally, they posed little real danger. By contrast, becoming a Christian meant an enthusiastic welcome, the sharing of property, and the joyous confidence in the resurrected Lord. This romantic picture does not work for much of Acts, however, and it fades quickly when we read other parts of the New Testament.

The author of 1 Peter describes the Christians to whom he writes as 'exiles', a word that is often understood to refer in an entirely metaphorical sense to the fact that believers are no longer at home in this world. They are exiles who really have their home in heaven. Recent study of 1 Peter, however, raises up another dimension of its language of exile. John Elliott (*A Home for the Homeless*; Philadelphia: Fortress Press, 1981, 21–58) contends that the audience of this text consists of people who actually occupy the social and political fringes of their society, and who have found that the Christian faith has caused them more social tension rather than less. The letter seeks to offer them a new community as a social and religious centre, and the language of the household occupies a central place in that strategy.

In this particular passage, these exiles are admonished to 'live in reverent fear'. A wide variety of biblical texts present fear as an appropriate response to human awareness of divine activity. The fear encouraged here corresponds more nearly to awe than to terror, as is evidenced by the comments that surround this admonition. The God whom believers are to 'fear' is the one who judges all people impartially (1 Pet. 1.17); that is, this God may be relied on to do justice to every human being. Moreover, this God has already acted to save human beings from their own futile lives, has raised Jesus from the dead, and has given human beings every reason for trust. This God merits awe and reverence.

As the writer describes, in vv. 18–21, the actions of God through Christ, the implication is that these actions took place on behalf of the Christian community: 'You were ransomed', 'for your sake', 'you have come to trust in God'. If the original audience of this letter in fact consisted of people who were socially and politically marginalized, these assertions offer them confidence and hope. While they may have no place in the world around them as it is ordinarily understood, they know that God has already acted on their behalf and that their real place is secure. Without an awareness of that particular historical context, of course, Christians have felt justified in reading such passages as indicating that God acted exclusively for their own benefit. In that way, the text becomes a licence for asserting a kind of Christian possession of God rather than a word of assurance to the displaced and dispossessed.

The final lines of this passage introduce once more the notion that Christians have been born again. Because this language occupies an important place not only in 1 Peter but also in some segments of contemporary Christianity, it merits further attention. To some Christians, being 'born again' is a personal, even private, experience. It becomes a way of talking about an individual's relationship with God, or even about a particular incident of conversion. The phrase is also associated largely with the realm of spiritual experience more than with ethical behaviour.

What comes through clearly in this text, as elsewhere in the New Testament, is that being 'born again' means far more than simply having a private religious experience. Verse 22 admonishes believers to 'love one another deeply from the heart'. This notion of mutual love within the community is closely related to the household imagery that comes to the fore again in 1 Peter 2. Here, however, the emphasis is on living in a manner consistent with the gospel itself. New birth necessarily involves more than new mental processes or new spiritual awareness – it means new life, new action.

While this new birth is intensely personal, in that it involves individual human beings who find their lives radically changed by the gospel, it also involves an intensely social dimension. Those who experience the new birth *belong* to one another in a profound and unrelenting way. These newborns are not members of disparate family units, each of which may take its own infant and go home. They belong to one another, as surely as they belong to the God who grants them this new birth.

That it is God who grants this new birth is obvious, yet often overlooked: 'You have been born anew, not of perishable but of imperishable seed, through the living and enduring word of God.' Understandable and justified enthusiasm about being 'born again' occasionally leads to the impression that those who are 'born again' somehow accomplished this deed on their own, or at least that they had a significant role to play. Here, as elsewhere, the biblical word is that, as God alone creates life, God alone can claim responsibility for newness of life. The only word human beings may appropriately offer is one of doxology. BG

Luke 24.13–35

This story of Jesus' journey with the two disciples on their way to Emmaus is told with consummate skill. It deftly recapitulates Luke's narrative of Jesus (24.19–24), draws together a number of prominent themes developed in the Gospel, and announces that the self-revelation of the risen Messiah comes through the interpretation of the Scriptures and the breaking of bread. In essence the story relates how the Church encounters Jesus and learns to see him as someone other than merely a strange fellow traveller.

Readers come to this passage as people who already know that Jesus is risen. There is no secret about the resurrection to be disclosed to them. Instead, what they discover is a story of how disbelief is dispelled, how two deeply involved disciples are able to move beyond the tradition about Jesus to an experience of personal recognition. Early in the passage we learn that the two fail to perceive that it is Jesus who comes to walk with them because 'their eyes were kept from recognizing him' (24.16). God apparently has temporarily blinded them. Toward the end of the account we read that 'their eyes were opened, and they recognized him' (24.31). The story relates what happens in moving from blindness to sight, from disbelief to confession, from sadness to delight.

Two actions of Jesus lead Cleopas and his companion to recognize him. First, Jesus interprets for them the Jewish Scriptures. Though they can recount the story of the empty tomb from the women and from the disciples who confirm the women's statement, this is not enough. The tradition must be viewed through the lens of Scripture. In Jesus' death and resurrection the long story of God's purpose for Israel finds its culmination. The resurrection is not just a miracle of a revived corpse. In it the plan and reign of God are fulfilled.

What emerges in the story is a paradoxical relationship between the risen Jesus and the Jewish Scriptures. On the one hand, it takes the risen Jesus to explain the meaning of the text. He is the critical interpreter, who teaches the Church how to read the Scriptures and how to discern there God's intentions. Only in light of Easter does the divine story make sense. On the other hand, an understanding of the Scriptures is critical to recognizing who Jesus is and to grasping the import of what he has done. His death and resurrection are to be seen in a perspective broader than trials before Pilate and Herod, Roman gallows, and the empty tomb. One has to go back to Moses and the prophets to get the full picture.

Second, Jesus breaks bread with the two companions. The language of 24.30 recalls the account of the feeding of the multitudes (9.16) and the last supper with the disciples (22.19), making the allusion to the Lord's Supper inescapable (especially since the day is Sunday; see 24.13). The experience of eating precipitates recognition. In both 24.31 ('their eyes were opened') and 24.35 ('he had been made known to them'), however, the passive voice is used. Recognition does not come mechanically, nor is it the end product of an intellectual or existential search by the seeker. It is the gift of God, a self-revelation by which God honours promises made long ago to the covenant people.

The interpretation of the Scriptures and the breaking of bread appropriately go together. The rhythm of 24.30–32 (table fellowship, recognition, remembrance of Jesus' opening the text) indicates the interrelatedness of the two. In both, Jesus is understood as Messiah (24.26) and confessed as Lord (24.34).

The concluding scene at Jerusalem pictures a gathering of the Eleven and their friends and the two who had walked to Emmaus, each confessing the risen Jesus and relating their experiences of recognition. The Church is composed of those who have been led beyond disbelief to faith by the gracious revelation of God. Their repeated telling of and listening to the foundational story empowers them in anticipation of their mission to all the nations, a mission to begin here at Jerusalem (24.47).

In addition to being an account of recognition, this story also reflects several other themes important to Luke's telling of the story of Jesus: (a) the necessity of Jesus' death (9.22; 18.31–33; 24.44–46); (b) the confirmation of the women's witness (24.1–11, 22–24); (c) Jesus as the great prophet (7.16, 39; 9.8, 19; Acts 3.22); (d) the importance of hospitality to strangers (Gen. 18.1–15; Heb. 13.2). cc

The Fourth Sunday of Easter

Genesis 7 or Acts 2.42–47; I Peter 2.19–25; John 10.1–10

Genesis 7

Within the narrative structure of Gen. 1—11 the story of the flood is important because it is the dividing line between the original creation of Gen. 1 and the creation of our experience, in Gen. 9. The former creation is a vegetarian creation, as indicated by Gen. 1.30, that is to say, it is a world without 'nature red in tooth and claw', apart from one destructive element: the human race.

The flood as described in Gen. 7 is an undoing of creation. Creation in the Old Testament is a matter of order, of the restraining and ordering of forces which, when unleashed, can overwhelm and destroy the world. Thus the references to the fountains of the deep bursting forth and the windows of heaven being opened (v. 11) indicate that God has relaxed the forces that restrain the destructive power of nature (cf. Job 38.8, 10–11 'who shut in the sea with doors ... and prescribed bounds for it ... and said "Thus far shall you come" ').

Part of the order of creation is also the moral order, and the Old Testament is clear that the disruption of the moral order can affect the natural order; which is why God brings the flood upon the earth; to destroy the destructive creature, humanity, whose evil undermines the created order.

Noah and his family and the animals that enter the ark are the nucleus of a new world in the post-flood era. We are not told in what respect Noah is righteous; but the fact that he is, and that God can use this righteousness to preserve the human race that otherwise deserves extinction, is an important theme in the passage.

The story of the flood is one that provokes many reactions, from those who contend that Leonard Woolley found evidence of a flood at Ur (he did not; what he found had been caused by wind!) to those who are ever looking for, and claiming to have found, the ark.

Since 1872 it has been known that the biblical story of the flood is only one of numerous such stories from the ancient Near East, whose heroes are known variously as Ziasudra, Atra-hasis and Ut-napishtim. Flooding in the Tigris-Euphrates region of ancient Mesopotamia could have devastating results; whether there was a universal flood is less likely. Who would survive to tell us about it? Comparison with the other ancient flood stories shows how much more profound the one contained in the Old Testament is, as part of the larger narrative of Gen. 1—11, which boldly asserts both that God is the creator of the world, and that the world he originally made, the vegetarian world, is not the world of our experience. JR

Acts 2.42–47

It is easy to play down this passage as giving an edifying but idealized picture of the early developments in what Luke saw as the seminal Christian community in Jerusalem. The *Revised Common Lectionary* seems almost to collude with the sceptical tendency by paraphrasing v. 41 as telling us of the baptism of 'many' (i.e. anything between 'not very many' and 'a great many'!). In fact Luke was specific – and startling: about 3,000, no less.

It is fair indeed to accept that the whole Pentecost narrative is what we should call an idealization; but the word fails to capture either Luke's motivation or his meaning. And questions that occur to modern scriptural literalists simply fall away before a Lucan blank look: questions such as, What then happened to these 3,000 new Christians, or the 5,000 in Acts 4.4 (or, for that matter, the 'great many of the priests' in 6.7 and the 'tens of thousands' in 21.20)? It is as irrelevant to enquire into their subsequent role in church life or their effect on Jerusalem society as it is to enquire about the 5,000 who ate the Lord's salutary bread in the Gospel or indeed the later devotional life of Zacchaeus or Jairus' daughter. The meaning of the stories is to be sought along other lines – and Lucan lines at that.

The Pentecost story is certainly born out of enthusiasm – all of Acts is, in effect, a success story, under the hand of God, and even apparent setbacks like Paul's imprisonment turn to evangelistic gold (28.30f.). This is a diet of encouragement, offered to Christians living in bleaker or more humdrum times. The tools used are scriptural and also familiar Lucan themes; notably here, as elsewhere in Acts, the bread-breaking already fixed, beautifully, in our minds by the Emmaus story in Luke 24, as well as the Gospel feeding and the Last Supper. It would be anachronistic for us to ask Luke to tell us whether these meals were 'ordinary' or 'religious' acts. They are all wonderful events experienced in the company of the Lord.

The temple motif is, as before in Luke's Gospel and Acts, referred to without difficulty: he wants us to feel no disjunction between Israel and Church. All is under God's drive to save his own (v. 47).

Of course we have no evidence to put alongside what Luke tells us here. Paul's letters, windows into congregations 20 years later, no doubt give a more realistic picture, warts and all. But Luke knows how church life ought to be: for example, it should be under proper supervision, here that of the apostles, who begin to don that episcopal role that history has confirmed for them.

Community of property is not otherwise attested, but with generosity to the needy, we are probably in touch with what remained a major factor in the Church's power to attract and eventually its triumph in the Empire. LH

1 Peter 2.19–25

Although this reading begins with 1 Peter 2.19, even a glance at the context reveals that it addresses slaves and that complementary admonitions to wives and to husbands follow in 3.1–7. The seemingly innocuous claim that believers should follow Christ's example of suffering and patience takes on an entirely different tone in view of the fact that the particular group being called to suffering and patience consists of slaves (2.18). Since one knows the way in which these ethical injunctions have been employed in the Church's life, this text may promote acute embarrassment, shame and outrage. The temptation to select another text for preaching lies near at hand.

A closer examination of this entire section of the letter may cast a different and, indeed, radical light on the admonitions in vv. 18–25. Certain anomalies about this household code (the set of admonitions to members of a household) call for attention. Unlike other New Testament examples of the household code, this one *begins* with admonition to slaves. In Eph. 5—6, for example, the code addresses first wives and husbands, then children and parents, and finally slaves and their masters (cf. Col. 3.18—4.1; 1 Tim. 5.1—6.2; Titus 2.1–10). First Peter does not include the admonition to owners that normally stands in parallel to the admonition to slaves.

The substance of the ethical admonition in this passage is striking, because what slaves are encouraged to do here duplicates what all believers are called to do elsewhere in 1 Peter. If slaves suffer unjustly, so apparently does the entire audience of the letter (1.6–7; 2.12). Chapter 3.13–22 repeats the claim of 2.19–25 that believers are to be willing to suffer on behalf of the good and that Christ provides an example of just such suffering. The substance of this admonition, then, is in no way unique to slaves or incumbent on them alone.

Another unusual feature of this admonition is that the word 'slaves' in v. 18 translates the Greek word *oiketai*, rather than the more usual *doulos*. While *doulos* refers to slaves in a general sense, *oiketai*, used only rarely in the New Testament, specifically refers to slaves within the household. Given 1 Peter's emphasis on the household of God, the appearance of *oiketai* rather than *doulos* can scarcely be accidental, and surely recalls the household motif. If all believers are part of God's new household, a household that offers protection from a threatening world and solidarity within, the *oiketai* occupy an important place within that household.

The best explanation of the various anomalies in this household code comes from John Elliott, who argues that the *oiketai* in 1 Peter stand as paradigms for the way in which all members of the household should conduct themselves (*A Home for the Homeless*; Philadelphia: Fortress Press, 1981). In fact, all believers are slaves, in that they belong to God (2.16) and to the new household created through the gospel of Jesus Christ (2.2–10). In this new household, there are no 'masters' or 'owners' to address, since all alike are slaves. All believers are liable to suffer unjustly and may endure that suffering because they know that they follow Christ in so doing. The 'example' of Jesus provides a model for all believers (2.21–24). All believers have been returned to their Shepherd (2.25).

By reversing the usual order of the household code, placing the admonition to slaves before that to wives and husbands, 1 Peter also demonstrates the way in which the gospel overturns the hierarchy of the conventional household. Slaves are not, in this new household, the last and the least, to be treated merely as an afterthought. They occupy first place, because their *involuntary* submission to human masters has been transformed into a *paradigmatic* submission to God, who is the only appropriate master of the new household.

There is no easy way for contemporary preachers to employ the language of this passage, since it is imperative to avoid anything that even appears to soften or legitimize or romanticize the brutal facts of human slavery. On the other hand, particularly in a context that understands faith to be one option among a vast array of options, this lection's reminder that the gospel involves real submission carries a potent, and highly unpopular, message.

The relentless christological appeal of the passage bears home the message that Christians are always to be the obedient slaves of God, just as was Christ. The passage drives away at the unjust suffering of Christ. Verse 21 introduces this motif and the notion that Christ provides an example for believers. The example becomes very specific in the lines that follow. Verse 22 applies to Christ a quotation from Isa. 53.9 about the suffering servant, who is accused without reason. Verse 23 expands the motif by insisting that Christ did not repay the evil done to him. Verses 24–25 recall the result of Christ's suffering for humanity. This repetition serves to make the nature of Christ's suffering undeniably clear.

Throughout this passage, Christ becomes the example in whose steps believers are called to follow. Here the example of Christ is urged, not in the sometimes trivial way that asks what Jesus would say or what Jesus would do, but as the first and foremost among the slaves of God's household. BG

John 10.1–10

The image of Jesus as a shepherd has always appealed to the popular imagination. It was established early as a theme in Christian art, and is still a great favourite. One reason for its appeal is its connotations of nurturing and caring (cf. the Synoptic parable of the shepherd who seeks his strayed sheep: Matt. 18.12–14; Luke 15.3–7).

John treats the shepherd theme in a complex discourse, divided into sections by the reactions of Jesus' listeners, Jewish religious leaders. Shepherd imagery dominates the whole of 10.1–21, continuing in 10.22–39 (set at the midwinter Feast of the Dedication). The context is polemical: the shepherd discourse follows immediately after the healing of the man born blind, where the Jewish leaders are depicted very negatively, and it concludes with 'the Jews' seeking to stone Jesus, accusing him of blasphemy.

The passage selected for our gospel begins with a solemn warning about 'thieves' and 'robbers' who enter the sheepfold by stealth. They are contrasted with the one who enters by the door (NRSV: 'gate'), who is recognized by the doorkeeper and the sheep. Commentators puzzle over who, or what, is intended by the door, the doorkeeper and the intruders. However, attention soon focuses on the shepherd himself and his intimate relation to his flock. In contrast to 'strangers', he knows them by name and they know him. John adds that Jesus' hearers (presumably Pharisees, cf. 9.40) did not realize that Jesus' words applied to them (v. 6).

So Jesus continues (vv. 7–10), this time identifying himself with the 'door of the sheep'. The image of door may be less immediately appealing than John's other word-pictures. But imagine the door as open (cf. Rev. 4.1), and yourself a prisoner: your reactions would be different. The 'door' is a means of access, sometimes associated with entry to heaven. By calling Jesus the 'door', John is saying that he offers the way to salvation and 'abundant' life (cf. esp. vv. 9f. and 14.6).

Now Jesus says that *all* who came before him were 'thieves and bandits' (v. 8). How can Jesus describe all his predecessors in this way? Surely he cannot mean the Old Testament prophets? Most scholars assume that the allusion must be either to false messianic claimants, or to predecessors whose teaching fails to prepare the way for Jesus. Some see another reference to misguided religious teachers of Jesus' own day, e.g. those inevitable scapegoats, the Pharisees, or the leading priests (notorious for their worldliness and corruption). Behind all this lies the Old Testament background where unsatisfactory religious leaders and rulers are described as false shepherds (cf. esp. Ezek. 34).

Even allowing for Semitic exaggeration, the polemical thrust and exclusive claims of John 10.1–10 make it uncomfortable reading – and an odd choice for the Easter season. Perhaps the most positive approach is to read on. There, beyond our prescribed portion, we find the beautiful analogy of Jesus as 'the good shepherd', who sacrifices his life for the sheep (v. 11). There, Jesus speaks of 'taking up' his life again in resurrection (v. 18). But even in the continuation we cannot escape the polemical implications of the 'hireling' (v. 12), and John's sad underlying theme of Jewish misunderstanding and opposition. RE

The Fifth Sunday of Easter

Genesis 8.1–19 or Acts 7.55–60; 1 Peter 2.2–10; John 14.1–14

Genesis 8.1–19

The continuation of the flood story needs only a small amount of explanation compared with the readings of the preceding and following Sundays. The closing of the fountains of the deep and the windows of heaven indicates that God has reimposed order upon the creation, and has restrained its destructive forces. The mention of the birds sent out provides the closest parallel between the biblical version and the *Epic of Gilgamesh* (in J. B. Pritchard, *Ancient Near Eastern Texts relating to the Old Testament*, New Jersey: Princeton, 1955, pp. 94–5):

> I sent forth and set free a dove.
> The dove went forth but came back . . .
> Then I sent forth and set free a swallow.
> The swallow went forth, but came back . . .
> Then I sent forth and set free a raven.
> The raven went forth and, seeing that the waters had diminished,
> He eats, circles, caws, and turns not round.

The biblical story, however, clearly exhibits the presence of two sources at this point. Verses 6–12 are usually assigned to the 'J' source (which uses the divine name YHWH). In this source the ark is said to have had a window (v. 6) but no such feature is mentioned in the instructions to build the ark in Gen. 6.11–21, which is usually ascribed to the 'P' (priestly) source. Another indication of the two sources is the fact that in vv. 6–12 Noah discovers by sending out the birds that the earth has dried up. In vv. 13–18 Noah discovers this fact by looking out of the ark himself.

The fact that the flood story was present in the two sources that were combined to make up the story as we have it is an indication of how important the story was to the Old Testament writers. It enabled them to give expression to what they wanted to say about the themes of human evil, divine grace and the future of creation. JR

Acts 7.55–60

The first reading for the previous three Sundays had centred on Peter's Pentecost sermon and on the effects that that proclamation of the kerygma had on the apostle's hearers. The present lection deals with effects on its auditors of another sermon delivered by a different preacher. While the results of Stephen's message are quite different from those of Peter's, the contrast is intentional and probing. The proclamation of the gospel may win many hearts to an allegiance to Jesus Christ, but it also has the potential to arouse the deepest hostility on the part of others.

Stephen's lengthy sermon (Acts 7.2–53) is basically a recitation of the saving activity of God in the life of Israel, with emphasis on the manner in which God fulfilled the divine promises again and again. Yet also brought clearly into focus in Stephen's message is the continued intransigence of the people in the face of God's gracious overtures. The people rejected the prophet Moses (vv. 35–39), and they denied their dependence on God by worshipping idols crafted by their own hands (vv. 40–41). The flash point of Stephen's sermon is reached when he accuses his hearers of being of the same obstinate and rebellious stock as Moses' generation (vv. 51–53). Just as they denied the prophet Moses, so they have denied the latter and greater prophet, Jesus, whose office Moses has foretold (v. 37).

The narrative of Stephen's murder, today's lection, is terse and violent. The contrast the lectionary draws between the attitude of Peter's hearers and that of Stephen's audience is sharpened by the details of the text itself. Stephen's executioners are infuriated (v. 54) and deaf to all reason (v. 57), exhibiting the kind of rabid violence that thirsts only for blood. On the other hand, Stephen's vision is of beauty and joy (v. 55) and his spirit forgiving (v. 60), his prayer for mercy on his attackers being reminiscent of that of Jesus on the cross (Luke 23.34). The manner in which Luke has set these polar attitudes is striking, in that the mind of the reader is concentrated, first, on the hatred of the murderers (v. 54), then on Stephen's holiness (v. 55), then back to the killers (v. 57), and so on.

During the account of Stephen's stoning, the stage is set for the next major section in Acts by the mention of Saul/Paul (v. 58; cf. 8.1), the soon-to-be missionary apostle who at this time is still in the camp of the persecutors of the Church. (See the Acts reading for the Sixth Sunday of Easter.)

The celebration of Easter and its aftermath almost always concentrates on the victory that Christ has won over the forces of sin and death, and that is as it should be. 'Where, O death, is your victory?' (1 Cor. 15.55), Paul asks near the end of his extended invitation to the Corinthian Christians to celebrate the resurrection. His mood is almost taunting, as if he *dares* death so much as to raise its ugly head in response. But death is not dead yet, neither is evil or pain. They may be doomed, but they are still very pervasive realities, with which men and women must deal daily. And as if to remind Christians of the persistence of the enemy, Luke balances the positive response of Peter's hearers in Acts 2 – a response that leads to the explosive growth of the Church – with the negative reaction of Stephen's auditors, one that leads to the disciple's death. Not all good works result in benefits to those who do them. Not all fidelity to the truth of God brings immediate blessing on those who are faithful. Commitment to the Messiah of God may just as easily result in pain as in joy, in death – as it does here for Stephen – as in life.

Yet while acknowledging the continuing reality of evil, the text makes it quite clear that those who are really dead are not Stephen, but the disciple's killers. His pain may be the most immediate, but his joy is ultimate and final, while their twisted and hate-poisoned hearts show no inclination to be open to any good news of what God has done and is doing. And so the Easter victory is genuine and enduring, but in important respects it is a victory whose final consummation is still held in anticipation.

What medieval theologians referred to as the 'beatific vision' is, in certain important ways, the crux of the passage (v. 56). The words call to mind Jesus' baptism in the Jordan (Luke 3.21–22 and parallels), a feature of the text that is possibly quite deliberate and by which Luke intends to stress Stephen's 'rite of passage' – not from life to death, as it must have appeared to the murderers, but from life to life. Whereas Jesus' baptism and accompanying experience of the Holy Spirit marked the beginning of a new phase in his faithfulness to God, Stephen's vision identifies his full entrance into the kingdom and the consummation (for him!) of the Easter hope. It is this sense of the sureness of God's promises (detailed in Stephen's sermon) and of the certainty of the victory of God over all those ancient wrongs that distort human life and rob it of its joy – it is this sense and only this sense that can effect a joy so serene that it prays for the well-being of those who wish to do it to death. BG

1 Peter 2.2–10

This passage usually appears in discussions of the priesthood of all believers, or the spiritual priesthood. Within the context of First Peter, however, as John Elliott has demonstrated, this passage serves to introduce the notion of the 'household of God', which v. 5 signals with the unusual expression 'spiritual house', or 'spiritual household' (*A Home for the Homeless*; Philadelphia: Fortress Press, 1981, 23, 75). The household code of 2.18—3.7 underscores the importance of this motif, as does the use of the 'household of God' in 4.17. Recurring language that describes believers as 'newly born' or 'reborn' and that seeks the unity of believers within the community further enhances this motif.

Chapter 2.4–5 introduces the household language, which vv. 6–10 develop through a variety of biblical quotations and editorial comments. Indeed, the profusion of biblical quotations and allusions in vv. 6–10 seems bewildering apart from the underlying theme of the unity of believers in a single household. Understanding Jesus as the living stone, believers are also to see themselves as living stones, whom God builds into a single, spiritual house (vv. 4–6). Again, like Jesus, these stones will be rejected by unbelievers, by the world at large, but will be affirmed by God (vv. 7–8). The various descriptions of vv. 9–10 serve to reinforce this notion that the community of believers is *one* community. Together it constitutes 'a chosen race, a royal priesthood, a holy nation, God's own people'. These expressions, like that of the 'household', underscore the collective nature of the community.

The imagery in this passage may seem exotic, and perhaps even exclusivistic ('a chosen race, a royal priesthood'), until the author's specific pastoral goals become clear. First, the insistence on the unity of believers in *one* body – household, race, priesthood, nation – serves to create and maintain a social identity. If recent research is correct in its understanding that the audience of this letter consists of persons who are displaced and dispossessed, not only spiritually or religiously but socially, economically and politically, then what the author does here asserts that in Christ, God creates a new place for those who have none. The language of the household erects boundaries that provide place, purpose and community for those who 'have tasted that the Lord is good' (v. 3).

Second, the passage links this particular community with Jesus Christ. Commentators have often ignored the concrete social dimensions of this passage, but correcting that misreading should not lead to the conclusion that the social dimension constitutes the whole of the passage. This 'spiritual house' is not a social club, which exists solely for the needs of its members. It is, rather, a household of which the head is God and the cornerstone Jesus Christ. As much as believers belong to one another within this household, they also belong to God. God builds the house (v. 5), God lays the cornerstone (v. 6), the house is known (and accepted or rejected) by its cornerstone (vv. 7–8). By virtue of God's own mercy and nothing else, this household has come into being (vv. 9–10).

Third, as a result of their identification with one another and as members of God's household, believers within this new household have a new standing. No longer outcasts, marginalized by their social condition, believers may be described in powerful and positive terms. Like the prototypical 'living stone', Jesus, believers are 'chosen and precious in God's sight' (v. 4). The language of v. 9 exalts the community and implies its privileges before God. Even if the household was once 'not a people' and 'had not received mercy' (v. 10), it now can rightly claim to be the people of God's own possession.

Given the historical setting in which the author of 1 Peter wrote, the language of this passage serves an important pastoral need. That need continues in every Christian generation, for the Church constantly requires the recollection that God created it to be a single household, taking its identity from Jesus Christ and set apart from the world. Given the intractable human temptation to convert a gift into a possession, however, Christians have too often read passages such as this one to mean that *their* standing before God came as a result of their own goodness and permitted them to exclude others from membership in the same household. The text grants no such licence for exclusivity or condescension. The householder, God, has sole authority over admission at the doorway. BG

John 14.1–14

This familiar section of Jesus' farewell speech in John's Gospel offers at least three significant themes for preaching. The nature of the topics enables the preacher to think of separate sermons, and the context allows for this. At the same time, the themes are connected by a common logic and are not simply isolated theological reflections. If nothing else, the setting in which Jesus talks to the disciples about their life following his death offers a unifying thread.

First, Jesus promises the disciples a permanent existence lived in fellowship with him. Admittedly, 14.2–3 are notoriously difficult verses. The language describes Jesus' departure to the Father's house, then Jesus' return, at which time he gathers his disciples to take them to a permanent dwelling place (not unlike 1 Thess. 4.13–18). Commentators fret about this apocalyptic scenario, because the rest of the farewell discourse speaks of Jesus' coming in terms of his fellowship with the disciples in this life and not a departure to another realm (e.g. 14.23). Does the realized eschatology of the rest of the farewell discourse (and most of the entire Gospel) neutralize or reinterpret this mention of preparing a place and a future parousia?

The picturesque language of 14.2–3 unambiguously speaks of a location ('a place', 'my Father's house', 'many dwelling places') and expresses movement – a here and a there, a going and a coming – making it difficult to reduce these verses to purely realized or spiritualized eschatology. John makes no obvious effort to harmonize this apocalyptic scenario with the realized eschatology. A clue, however, to their connection may be found in the Greek word translated 'dwelling places' (14.2). It is the noun of the characteristically Johannine verb 'abide'. The 'abiding' in Christ that now marks the Christian experience (15.1–11) reaches its culmination in the permanent abiding place, which Jesus had prepared. What distinguishes such a 'place' is the security of the divine presence ('that where I am, there you may be also'). It remains appropriate, therefore, to hear in John 14 a word of promise regarding an established and unfading fellowship with Jesus, even beyond death.

Second, the language about going to prepare dwelling places in the Father's house raises the issue of the journey and leads to the affirmation that Jesus is the exclusive way to the Father. The question of Thomas (14.5) and the request of Philip (v. 8) evoke the strong statements of v. 6 and vv. 9–11. The knowledge of Jesus *is* the knowledge of the Father; the seeing of Jesus *is* the seeing of the Father. Nothing is more characteristic of John than this.

What often creates uneasiness among many interpreters is the exclusiveness of Jesus' revelation of the Father. 'No one comes to the Father except through me' (14.6). Does this imply that only those who deliberately embrace the Christian faith can be related to God or be saved? The usual way to deal with the issue is to ask at what or at whom the statement might have been aimed in the evangelist's day, and either to leave it there or to find a modern analogy. The problem with this approach is the uncertainty as to whether the statement is polemical in the first place, and if so, who the target is.

Another approach is to recognize that this exclusive Christology and soteriology are integral to the Johannine community's understanding of itself. Its distinctiveness lies not in its sense of moral superiority over its environment or in the influential position it can assume in the culture, but in its confession of and commitment to Jesus as the only way to the Father. The question to ask is: Could this dimension of John's perspective in any way be instructive to the modern Church as it struggles with its identity? The modern Christian community has so bought into the world's economics, its psychology and its standards of morality that visitors from outer space would have a difficult time discerning the difference between the social and political culture of the day, with its civil religion, and the Church. Maybe the real issue is not whether people outside the Church are saved, but whether people inside the Church have any sense of their distinctiveness. Could the confessions of the Johannine church help the contemporary Church begin to reclaim its unique identity?

Third, Jesus makes the pledge to the disciples (repeatedly) that their prayers will be answered (14.13–14; 15.7, 16; 16.23–24). The text makes clear, however, that this pledge is not a willy-nilly commitment to give to overly indulgent children whatever their hearts fancy. Prayers are to be made 'in [Jesus'] name' (14.13–14), that is, they are to be made out of the disciples' relationship established with and by Jesus. The answering of the requests does not serve those who pray, but is to the end 'that the Father may be glorified in the Son'. These are prayers offered on behalf of the community and the community's mission. They undergird the 'greater works' that the church is to perform.

Perhaps it does not need to be said, but the promise of a permanent fellowship with Jesus, the confession of Jesus as the only way to the Father, and the pledge that the community's prayers will be answered are all made to comfort troubled hearts. The opening verse (14.1) sets the tone and direction for the entire passage. CC

The Sixth Sunday of Easter

Genesis 8.20—9.17 or Acts 17.22–31; 1 Peter 3.13–22; John 14.15–21

Genesis 8.20—9.17

With Gen. 9.2–4 we reach the world of human experience, a world in which humans can now eat not only things that grow (see Gen. 1.30) but all other creatures, minus their blood. The distinction between clean and unclean creatures is not yet given to Israel, although the distinction is anachronistically introduced at the beginning of the passage (8.20).

Two matters call for especial comment: the reason for God promising never again to destroy the creatures of earth (8.21) and the significance of the rainbow (9.13). On the face of it the logic of 8.21 is odd. God promises never again to destroy the earth's living creatures 'for the inclination of the human heart is evil from its youth'. However, given that the perversity of the human heart was the cause of the flood and the destruction that it caused in the first place, it seems odd that this same perversity is given as the reason for God promising *not* to destroy living creatures in the future! The NEB translation 'however evil his inclinations may be' is an attempt to soften the difficulty. The odd logic is best taken as a declaration of God's grace. There are two ways of dealing with human perversity. One way is to destroy the human race and the rest of creation with it. The other way is to wean the human race from perversity to the love of peace and justice. But this cannot be done in the benign, vegetarian world of Gen. 1.30. It can only be done in the new, and compromised creation of Gen. 9.2–3.

The rainbow of 9.13 has become a universal symbol of peace; but is this its function in Gen. 9? The bow in the Old Testament is a sign of war; the broken bow is the sign of peace (cf. Ps. 46.9: he [God] breaks the bow, and shatters the spear). Because of this, it has been suggested that the bow in Gen. 9 is not a promise of peace but a warning to the human race that God will not be indifferent to human behaviour if it threatens to destroy the earth. God will not again bring a flood; but this does not mean that he will do nothing to preserve his creation.

It must be admitted that this interpretation seems to go against the concluding words of the passage, that the bow and the clouds will remind God of his covenant – a covenant, let it be noted, not just with humanity but with all living creatures. The bow can probably remain, then, as a promise not only of peace, but as an example of the way in which Old Testament narratives can exert powerful influence upon today's world. JR

Acts 17.22–31

The series of texts from Acts relating to the proclamation of the gospel on the part of the early Church is continued in this passage, an account of Paul's sermon to the assembly of Athenian philosophers. Stylistic and conceptual differences between this sermon and Paul's letters have resulted in a protracted discussion among commentators as to the authenticity of this text, that is, whether it is the sort of message Paul is likely to have composed, even in view of the distinctive nature of his audience. However that debate may be decided, it remains clear that this is a formulation of the Christian message on the part of some important spokesperson for the early Church, be that individual Paul, Luke, or whoever. Furthermore, its most distinctive element involves not some alternative understanding of the essential Christian message, but an accommodation of method to the prevailing interests among the community of Greek philosophers, principally the Stoics.

There is a smooth progression of thought in the passage, which suggests either that a period of time was involved in its composition, thus allowing the author opportunity to rewrite and polish the material, or that the sermon is the product of a mind that was accustomed to arguing in logical and coherent fashion. The initial section, Acts 17.22–23, acknowledges the religious (and not just philosophical) orientation of the audience. Most notable in this regard is Paul's reference to the altar dedicated 'To an unknown god', but that citation is anticipated by the preceding reference to the 'extremely religious' views of the assembled philosophers. The reality, of course, was that, although few Greek thinkers – including the Stoics – actually denied the traditional objects of religious devotion, these deities were often relegated to the sidelines of philosophical inquiry as being all but irrelevant. Thus, while the characterization given to Paul's audience in vv. 22–23 is not incorrect, it probably employs a certain hyperbole. One thinks of our own society, in which belief in God always ranks high in the polls, but appears to be less important in the living of daily life.

The second section, vv. 24–28, is introduced by the final sentence of v. 23, which says in effect, 'I am now going to tell you about the God of whom you are only vaguely aware.' There are several qualities to this God, according to Paul. First, this God is the creator of the cosmos. Second, this God so transcends human life that (unlike certain of the Greek deities) this Deity is independent of any need for human support. Third, this Deity is the Lord of all life, not only as creator, but also as the giver, shaper and sustainer of human existence. Fourth, the human dependence on this Deity has resulted in a universal quest for God (the implication being that the Greeks' altar is evidence of this quest), a God who is nearer to us than we sometimes suppose. The conclusion to this rather elaborate syllogism is: as humans, we relate to this Deity as children to a parent, a fact that some Greek thinkers have already acknowledged. 'In him we live and move and have our being' (v. 28) is perhaps (but not certainly) a quotation from the sixth-century BC writer Epimenides of Crete (to whom is also attributed the quotation in Titus 1.12). 'For we too are his offspring' is from the pen of Aratus of Soli (in Cilicia, the native region of Paul), who was active in the third century BC. In the introduction to his popular poem on astronomy and meteorology entitled *Phaenomena*, Aratus, who often reflected Stoic influences, wrote: 'Everywhere we all need Zeus, for we are also his offspring.'

As the final sentence of the first section introduces the second section, so the final sentence of the second section introduces the third (vv. 29–31). 'Since we are God's offspring . . .' certain things may be deduced. First, we cannot make God into some idolatrous form, in light of the fact that God has made us. Furthermore, while there may have existed a season in which God turned a blind eye to the ignorance of human-kind, that period is no more. It is at this point that the message becomes specifically Christian: God now demands repentance (v. 30), because the time of judgement is at hand, a righteous time presided over by a 'man' whom God has designated (v. 31a). The event that symbolizes the truth of this present and coming reality is the resurrec-tion of this 'man' from the dead, a resurrection brought about by God (v. 31b).

The skill of the writer of this text is demonstrated by the manner in which, having worked within Greek philosophical and literary contexts through the brief sermon, he turns to unreservedly Christian statements for the conclusion to the passage. And although the name of Jesus never appears, it is quite clear that Jesus is the centre-piece of the preacher's thought and that the Easter event is, in his view, the central fact of human history. The postscript to the sermon (vv. 32–33), although not included in the lection, leaves no doubt about that.

Jesus Christ and his resurrection, the primary event of human life, to Jew and to Greek, to man and to woman (note v. 34), to ancient and to modern! Thus, Acts 17.22–31, while dressed in Greek attire, is the same essential proclamation as Acts 10.34–43 and 2.14a, 22–32, 36–41, the other texts from Acts on which the lectionary has, to date, focused during this Easter season. BG

I Peter 3.13–22

Christ has ascended into heaven, but his followers continue to live in the world, and it is a world that is often hostile and suspicious. Peter gives his readers practical guidance on how to live in this situation. They have every right to expect that if they behave well, they will have nothing to fear: and good behaviour is necessary not just for their own protection but so that their faith may not be brought into dis-repute (4.15). There is a general confidence here in the ability of the non-Christian world to recognize goodness and to respond to it. Christians have no monopoly on morality and justice: that is why it is possible and proper for them to obey lawful secular authority (2.17). Conscience, a term more reminiscent of Stoic philosophy than distinctively Christian morality, is a general guide. However, the conscience of society is not an infallible safeguard. Christians may find themselves suffering precisely for doing what they see to be right. Here their guide for behaviour must be the model of Christ. The author has already appealed to this in his specific advice to the Christian slaves of unjust masters (2.18–25). The imitation of Christ has a long history as a basis of Christian morality, but in both passages in this epistle it is clear that the story of Christ is not just an example to be followed, but a transforming, saving event that makes a new way of living possible. So the advice on practical living is followed by an almost credal statement of the death, resurrection and ascension of Christ, as the means of dealing with human sin and of establishing a new relationship with God, appropriated through baptism.

The somewhat stylized statement of faith may well represent a form familiar to the readers, but allusions that they would no doubt have understood are unclear to us. Who are the 'spirits in prison' to whom Christ is said to have preached, when did he preach to them, and what is the connection with 'the days of Noah'? The reference may be to the period between death and resurrection, in which Christ 'descended into hell' and proclaimed the gospel to the dead from the time of the flood onwards; this may be echoed later at 4.6, and is how it is understood in the apocryphal Gospel of Peter (10.39). Alternatively, the spirits in prison might be seen as the powers of the underworld, maybe identified with the giants of the pre-flood period (Gen. 6.4) so that the passage serves as the foundation for the idea of the 'Harrowing of Hell' as portrayed in icons and medieval mystery plays. Again, Christ's proclamation might be located not in the time between death and resurrection, but in the sequence of both, seen as a victory over the demonic forces in the world (as v. 22 and Col. 2.15, 1 Tim. 3.16). The analogy between baptism and the flood is also unclear, since the waters of the flood themselves were hardly 'saving'. Noah and his companions, however, came through the waters of death to salvation and a new life; there may be a suggestion here in Peter of the Pauline interpretation of baptism as an incorporation into the death and resurrection of Christ, being 'buried with him in baptism' (Rom. 6.4). The mythological language provides a happy hunting ground for commentators, but the relation of the doctrinal statement to the practical advice remains clear: the risen and ascended Christ is the Lord of the Church, empowering it to face the world. SL

John 14.15–21

The passage set for today's gospel comes from the first 'farewell discourse', which the Johannine Jesus delivers to his disciples at his last meal before his death. The purpose of the discourses is to prepare them for his departure, and to encourage them in the face of the difficulties that lie ahead. These discourses would have had special relevance to the Johannine community, if (as many scholars believe) its members were feeling isolated, or even persecuted, in their estrangement from the synagogue (cf. 15.18; 16.2; 17.14).

The short extract chosen for our reading should be read in the light of the whole chapter, and its immediate literary context. It belongs to a section (14.12–24) highlighting a number of favourite Johannine themes: the importance of belief (or faith), obedience and love; Jesus' unity with the Father and their mutual love; Jesus' 'works' (in the sense of creative activity), and his love for those who 'keep his word'. It also contains promises which will be fulfilled at the resurrection, and in the future life of the Church.

In v. 16 Jesus promises to ask the Father to send his disciples 'another' advocate (Greek: *parakletos*). The word 'paraclete', familiar to us from traditional Christian hymns, occurs in the New Testament only in the Johannine writings: it appears four times in the farewell discourses (14.16, 26; 15.26; 16.7), where it is applied to the Holy Spirit, and once in 1 John (2.1), where it is used of Jesus in his role of intercessor (cf. 'another' in John 14.16). Meaning literally 'one called alongside', *parakletos* has been variously translated as 'advocate' (assuming a legal metaphor), counsellor, consoler, comforter (linking the noun with *parakaleo* in the sense of 'encourage', 'exhort'), or more generally 'helper', or even 'companion' (so Brodie). In John's Gospel the primary role of the Spirit-paraclete seems to be as teacher, who will lead the disciples into truth (cf. 14.26; 16.12–15). The Spirit-paraclete stands in opposition to 'the world' (14.17; 16.8–11); we are reminded of the dualism of 1 John, where the Spirit of truth is contrasted with the spirit of error (4.6).

Jesus also promises not to leave his followers bereft, but to 'come' to them. This promise was fulfilled on Easter Day when he returned to them (John 20.19), and in his appearance a week later (20.26). Most scholars see also further fulfilment in Jesus' abiding presence with the Church through the Holy Spirit. We should note that John does not follow the Lucan schema of a dramatic outpouring of the Spirit at Pentecost. Jesus 'breathes' the Spirit on (or into) the disciples on Easter Day, and gives them his peace, as promised (cf. 14.27). RE

Ascension Day

Daniel 7.9–14 or Acts 1.1–11; Ephesians 1.15–23; Luke 24.44–53

Daniel 7.9–14

The prescribed passage is the climax of the vision, written in Aramaic, in which the seer sees four beasts emerging from the sea (a symbol of chaos). Each beast, representing an empire, is more terrible than the one that precedes it, and on the head of the fourth beast there appears a little horn that displaces three horns, and which has eyes and a mouth.

With the beginning of the set passage, the scene switches from the source of the chaos and the destruction wrought by the beasts that emerge from it to a judgement scene on earth. The plural 'thrones' implies that there will be a panel of judges; but the dominating feature is the Ancient One (Aramaic, 'One ancient of days' i.e. years). The figure of white clothing and pure wool hair is meant to denote eternity and wisdom, and certainly not senility. The wheels of the throne are reminiscent of those of Ezek. 1, and the fire symbolizes purity and holiness. The fact that the beasts are only partially destroyed, even if their dominion is taken away, is an attempt to account for the persistence of evil in the world even after the judgement.

The climax is reached in v. 13 with the coming on the clouds of heaven of the 'one like a human being' (Aramaic, 'like a son of a human'). That this figure is in some sense 'heavenly' is indicated by his coming on the clouds of heaven, and by the qualifier 'like'. He is thus best thought of as an angelic figure. However, in the explanation of the vision in vv. 19–27, the dominion is given to 'the people of the holy ones of the Most High' (v. 27) in language almost identical with that of v. 14. These 'holy ones' are evidently those Israelites who have been persecuted and martyred by the little horn, usually taken to be Antiochus IV (175–164 BC) who banned Judaism from 168/7 to 164.

How can the persecuted ones be the same as the 'one like a human being'? This is the language of vision and symbols in which precision may not always be possible. The angelic figure may be a personification or may be a kind of heavenly guardian of the persecuted ones.

The fundamental message of the vision, however, is that the evil personified by the beasts, and embodied partly in the actions of desperate rulers, is ultimately subject to divine judgement. It is overcome not by greater, similar force, but by faithfulness to goodness and truth, which may lead to persecution and death. The dominion that is therefore given to the 'one like a human being' or the holy ones, is not based upon human ideas of power, but the experience of those who have drunk deeply from the well of suffering. JR

Acts 1.1–11

In the Lucan narrative of God's saving activity in Jesus Christ (the Gospel) and in the Holy Spirit (Acts), the story of Jesus' ascension marks the end of Jesus' post-resurrection appearances to his disciples and the prelude to the sending of the Spirit, thereby marking a transition point from Easter to Pentecost. In the liturgical tradition of the Church, Ascension is all of that and more, for it also has become a festival of the exaltation of the risen Christ.

The Acts lection for this day consists of two main components. The first (Acts 1.1–5) serves not only as an introduction to the entire book of Acts and thus to the work of the Holy Spirit in the life of the young Church, but also – in a more immediate sense – as an introduction to the Ascension miracle. The second part (vv. 6–11) is the account of the miracle itself. In both these sections, however, the primary emphasis is on the coming of the Holy Spirit.

Verses 1–5, after a brief statement of purpose (vv. 1–2) which parallels Luke 1.1–4, set forth a terse summary of the events of the 40 days following Easter, a time when Jesus 'presented himself alive to [the disciples] by many convincing proofs' (v. 3). It is perhaps assumed by Luke that 'Theophilus' has heard of these appearances of the risen Christ, since no effort is expended to provide the details of these encounters, other than what is offered in Luke 24. Following Jesus' order to the band of his faithful followers to remain in Jerusalem (Acts 1.4), he delivers the promise of God, namely, that God's Spirit is soon to be made evident in fresh ways. This coming of the Spirit is explained in baptismal terms: whereas water was the baptismal medium of old, 'you will be baptized with the Holy Spirit not many days from now' (v. 5).

The second part of our text (vv. 6–11) repeats this emphasis on the coming of the Spirit, but in a different context. Here this gracious and decisive gift of God's Spirit is compared to the political hopes the disciples had vested in the Messiah. Their question about the restoration of the kingdom to Israel (v. 6) betrays that not even the events of Easter and the succeeding 40 days had disabused them of a comfortable stereotype, that is, that God's Messiah would reinstitute the political fortunes of the old Davidic monarchy. Jesus deflects their question (v. 7) and refocuses their attention on the marvellous display of God's power and love that they are soon to see. It is not the restoration of the kingdom of Israel that will energize you, Jesus says in effect. Rather, 'You will receive power when the Holy Spirit has come upon you' (v. 8a). Thus vv. 5 and 8 lift before the reader an announcement from God that is not to be overlooked: the age of the Spirit is about to dawn.

Then Jesus is elevated beyond the limits of their physical senses, and 'two men in white robes' (compare Luke 24.4) gently chide the disciples for vacant gazing, even as they promise Jesus' second coming (Acts 1.9–11).

While the liturgical tradition of the Church has tended to make the ascension of Jesus into a festival to his glory and power, the emphasis in the biblical tradition is elsewhere. Not only is the ascension rarely mentioned in the New Testament (compare Luke 24.51 and Mark 16.19), but the interest in Acts 1 appears to be less in what is happening to Jesus than in what is about to happen in the lives of the earliest Christians. Twice in this brief passage the declaration is made that the Holy Spirit is about to infuse the life of the Church in new ways. Not that the Spirit was unknown before this. The 'Spirit of God' was the phrase that from very early times had been applied to special expressions of God's guiding and redemptive presence in human life (note, for example, 1 Sam. 11.6, and compare it to 1 Sam. 16.14). But the import of Acts 1.5 and 8 is that a new dimension to the Spirit's work is about to become evident. It is as different from what has gone before as the Spirit is different from the ordinary water of baptism. It is as different from what has gone before as the transcendent kingdom of God (v. 3) is different from the political kingdom of David and his descendants.

Just how the Spirit finds expression the disciples are not told. That is a matter of suspense, which will not be resolved until Pentecost (Acts 2). In the interim, they (and the disciples in every age) are to 'be my witness in Jerusalem, in all Judea and Samaria, and to the ends of the earth' (1.8). It will become clear only later that in this very activity of witnessing they will provide the channels for the Spirit's power and grace.

So in the New Testament perspective, Ascension is an interim time, a period – not unlike Advent – between promise and fulfilment. The disciples of Christ are called to live faithful and obedient lives and to remember that the wonder of God's love and presence revealed so radically in the cross and the open tomb still has in store fresh surprises of joy. The disciples of Christ are called to witness, little realizing how the Spirit lurks to transform all that they do into magnificent occasions for the outpouring of God's love. In this manner Ascension points to Pentecost and to all the marvellous ways of the Holy Spirit of God. BG

Ephesians 1.15–23

Like the earlier part of this opening chapter of Ephesians (1.3–14), in the original these verses are, grammatically, a single sentence. Both are statements of high rhetorical complexity and, to the modern ear, liable to be moving or even mesmerizing (rather than soberly illuminating) in their effect. The passage is such a baffling combination of Pauline phraseology and loftier-than-Pauline style that the suggestion is made that, in whole or at least in part, Ephesians is made up of liturgical forms – the prayers or hymns of Pauline Christians. The Jewish 'blessing' form of vv. 3–14 fits such a theory particularly well (though it is also found at the start of letters, even semi-artificial, literary ones).

Related to this is the still unsettled question of authorship. It can be maintained that the differences from Paul's genuine letters (long sentences, same words in different senses) are explicable on grounds of difference of purpose: this is less Paul the ethical pastor and teacher than Paul the preacher and worshipper; but the fact that Ephesians is little short of a catena of phrases from the genuine letters makes many see it as the work of a Pauline inheritor (like the Pastoral Epistles).

For our purposes the question is important chiefly as the ideas come up for consideration. Perhaps most interesting is the teaching in vv. 22–23, where Christ, very plainly in heaven (v. 20), is head of the Church, seen as his body, and now no longer in its various local manifestations but as universal in the fullest and most lofty sense. That is, there is both linkage and differentiation between Ephesians and undoubted Paul. In the more intense 'body of Christ' teaching of 1 Cor. 12, the Church and Christ are more thoroughly identified and fused: he and his people are a single entity, they in him. For all the high-flown language, the distinction here drawn makes the language of Ephesians look like a second-generation development, whereby the Church, of course dependent on Christ, nevertheless can be distinguished in its own right as a phenomenon in this world, while Christ reigns from above. It is close to the doctrine of Luke in Acts (for all its extravagance of expression), where the Church proceeds under the awesomely heavenly (and so now in effect distant?) Jesus.

Again like Luke, the writer distinguishes between the resurrection and ascension of Christ – helping, unwittingly, to warrant the Christian calendar of later years. Earlier, you could not sensibly make a distinction.

Nevertheless, Christians must themselves pray for heavenly insight: 'wisdom' and 'revelation' and 'enlightened' (vv. 17f.) are vibrant words in the piety of the time. And the cosmic perspective, as elsewhere, leans heavily on common early Christian proof-texts, Pss. 110.1 and 8.4, already part of Paul's stock-in-trade. Finally, 'fullness', part of an obscure final phrase, is again less innocent than it may seem: it was the sort of word probably to make the susceptible spine tingle, pointing the hearer to what we would see as proto-Gnostic connections, and lifting hearts to heaven. L H

Luke 24.44–53

The final verses of the Gospel of Luke are characteristic of the evangelist's picture of things and especially of his beliefs about the person and role of Jesus. On the one hand, he works with a division of history into the time of Israel, known in the Scriptures, the time of Jesus, and then the time of the Spirit-powered mission of the Church; but on the other hand, he is careful to show how the three phases interact, with the second and third 'emerging' from what preceded. So, though the Jerusalem temple had gone by the time of writing and though Jesus had foreseen its end, there is no gloating over this in Luke. Rather, he looks back to it almost fondly as the focal point of events surrounding Jesus' birth and upbringing and has shown Jesus grieving at the prospect of its fall; and here, at the end, it remains the holy place to which the disciples return to praise God at the close of resurrection day (and the motif will continue in Acts). Thus Jesus is in continuity with God's whole providential work and is, of course, its fore-ordained climax. Notice that to the formal 'law and prophets', Luke adds 'and the psalms' as giving the divine testimony to Jesus: it is a good addition for, in Luke as elsewhere, very many of the scriptural allusions and quotations come from the Psalter: it was a prime source of christological reflection and vehicle of communal self-understanding. This may be, in part at least, because scrolls of the psalms were more readily available than copies of some other parts of the old Scriptures; but many passages offered themselves, as it were on a plate, for Christian interpretation. The reference here to fulfilment is the second in the chapter: see also v. 27, in the Emmaus story. For Luke, the risen Jesus is at pains to root his work in sacred prophecy.

The passage also looks forward to the Church's mission, in effect to Luke's second volume, the book of Acts, where the horizon is no less than 'all nations', as indeed it has been since the beginning of the Gospel: see, for example, Simeon's words in 2.32 and the extension (by comparison with Mark) of the quotation from Isa. 40 in 3.4–6 to include the words, 'and all flesh shall see the salvation of God'.

Is Jesus' withdrawal in v. 51 a first shot at an account of the ascension, later rewritten and reframed, when Luke turned to write Acts? Or had he already planned his second volume, and is the idea here that Jesus withdrew at the end of this day, then manifested himself for the sacred period of 40 days (compare the temptation in ch. 4 and Israel's wilderness period) before his final bodily departure? It depends whether you think Luke had his whole narrative in view from the start – and there are many indications that he had. As generally in Luke, the ending is thoroughly up-beat and full of confidence in the Jesus-given future. LH

The Seventh Sunday of Easter

(Sunday after Ascension Day)

Ezekiel 36.24–28 or Acts 1.6–14; 1 Peter 4.12–14; 5.6–11; John 17.1–11

Ezekiel 36.24–28

This promise of the restoration of the people after the Babylonian exile tackles a fascinating problem in a way that raises further questions. Given that, from the moment of their deliverance from slavery in Egypt, the Israelites showed themselves to be selfish and distrustful of God's actions on their behalf (see especially the reading for the Third Sunday of Lent), the crucial question becomes 'How can the people of God live truly according to this calling?'

God's promise is that he will cleanse his people, replace the heart of stone with one of flesh, and put a new spirit within them. Whether the translation 'make you follow my statutes' is right, is a question that must be addressed. As it stands, it suggests a degree of compulsion that will rob the people of freedom and, in any case, make the statutes and ordinances of God redundant. This is a reason for taking the Hebrew, which is literally 'I will do (or make) that you walk in my statutes' to mean that God will create the ideal conditions for his people to follow his statutes, not that he will turn them into compliant robots.

The theme of creating the right conditions to make possible the service of God is important, because in restored Israel after the exile, as in today's world, the right conditions never existed. This is also true for any Christian interpretation of the passage which sees it as a prophecy of the giving of the Holy Spirit after the resurrection. It cannot be said of the churches that they are any nearer to exhibiting the ideal nature of the people of God than was the case with ancient Israel, in spite of the churches' claim to have the Holy Spirit. The question 'How can the people of God live truly according to his calling?' remains unresolved within the constraints of the world as we know it. JR

Acts 1.6–14

It is important to read this passage in the light of the concluding verses of Luke's Gospel (see pp. 146–7); for Luke now resumes, with repetitions of theme and wording, what he wrote there. The reason is not merely literary (volume two picking up where volume one had ended). There is also a theological point. Just as Luke is keen that Jesus' ministry should be seen, not as a novelty, but as stemming from the life and the prophetic Scriptures of Israel, so he emphasizes that the Church flows from the life of Jesus. It is no maverick, unauthorized society making a haphazard way through the cities of Palestine, then many parts of the

Empire, including Rome itself. Rather, it has credentials like those of Jesus himself and lives only under his instructions and, as will soon appear, the Spirit's empowerment. God remains at work and all is his doing.

Just as the use of Scripture and the 'old Israel' ethos (and language) of Luke 1—2 act as a bridge between phases one and two, so the apostles are the bridge between phases two and three, ensuring that there is no disjunction. Luke is the only evangelist to make significant use of the word 'apostles' to refer to Jesus' core-followers, preparing the way for the mission in Acts. But at the same time their role is adjusted. Here already they begin to be not simply witnesses and missioners, but in effect the governing council of the Church – see ch. 15 especially: even perhaps quasi-patriarchs of a new Israel. In this depiction, we see one of Luke's most fruitful legacies to subsequent Christian imagination and ecclesiology. Thus, just after this passage, with Acts hardly begun, the situation arising from Judas' death is regularized and his seat is filled by the hitherto unknown Matthias. The precise historicity of this view of things is not supported by the more contemporary Paul and shows a new dimension of church-consciousness by Luke's day.

The return of Jesus, prophesied already in the Gospel, is assured by the two angelic figures (cf. Luke 24.4). Mary, who dominated the opening of Luke's narrative, makes a final appearance here; and James the brother of Jesus, implied no doubt in Luke 8.19–21 and soon (though obscurely in view of the Twelve) to be central in the Church's leadership (ch. 15), steps modestly on to the stage, still unnamed. LH

1 Peter 4.12–14; 5.6–11

In this passage, 1 Peter's preoccupation with the suffering of Christians comes to its conclusion. The letter makes frequent reference to the suffering of the faithful and its prototype in the suffering of Christ (1.6; 2.18–25; 3.8—4.6). Although the exact nature of the suffering remains hidden from modern readers, it clearly includes verbal abuse and harassment (2.12; 3.15). By means of the motifs of the new birth and the household of God, the author works to draw together a community that can withstand suffering inflicted by external forces. The occasional reminder that believers should be subject to suffering only for a good cause and never as a result of actual wrongdoing (4.15) serves to recall the weakness that can enter the community from within its own ranks.

The language of this lection reveals that the sufferings of believers derive from real and powerful sources. First Peter 4.12 conjures up a 'fiery ordeal' that comes to test the faithful. Chapter 5.8b dramatically portrays the devil – 'like a roaring lion' – as the adversary of the faithful, which 'prowls around, looking for someone to devour'. In this striking personification, evil emerges as the enemy that actively and intentionally seeks to destroy those who belong to God. By contrast with contemporary tendencies to abstract or even to deny the existence of evil by reducing it to social or political or psychological factors, this writer knows that evil wills itself to happen, that evil engages in battle with God and with God's own creatures.

Alongside this acknowledgement that believers suffer and this vivid portrait of the cause of suffering, 1 Peter places Christian confidence in God. Believers may rejoice, not just in spite of but *in* their suffering, 'because the spirit of glory, which is the Spirit of God, is resting on you' (4.14). The humiliation of believers is a prelude to God's exaltation of them 'in due time' (5.6). God will care for Christians and take on their anxieties (5.7). The temporary suffering of Christians will find its end when God will 'restore, support, strengthen, and establish' them.

This emphasis on God's future reward for the sufferings of the present smacks of what is often referred to as 'pie in the sky by and by'. For those who will endure the present, putting up with the humiliation and suffering to which believers are subject, God holds out the promise of a future reward. One difficulty with this position is that it calls for certain groups to endure the status quo without confronting and overturning it. Another difficulty is that it views the present as meaningless, reducing human physical life to a mere threshold for 'real life' with God after death.

Such attitudes undeniably exist among Christians, some of them based no doubt on texts such as this one. The text itself, however, at least *implies* that the present has meaning in and of itself. The author does not exhort the audience to exit the world by denying the reality of physical suffering or by passively acquiescing to the circumstances. Instead, the author depicts an active and realistic response. First, believers humble themselves before God. An admonition to humility only *seems* to invoke the 'pie in the sky' attitude mentioned above. To humble oneself before God, 'the mighty hand of God', is to insist that God will finally triumph, even over the undeniable power of the devil. Out of this confidence in God comes a related admonition: 'Cast all your anxiety on him, because he cares for you' (5.7). God's strength is accompanied by a compassion that enables God to take on the cares and concerns of God's people.

The second kind of response believers can make to evil and suffering is to resist it: 'Discipline yourselves, keep alert . . . Resist him . . .' (5.8–9). In a sense, the whole of 1 Peter concerns the making of protective boundaries around a community made up of believers who have no clear social or political identity. These marginalized persons, part of a new household that God has created in Christ, together inhabit a new home whose walls are invisible to the naked, untransformed eye. Language about discipline, alertness and resistance invokes the need for such actions if the new household is to be maintained. Only the household that stays ready can face the intruder with confidence. (Here the 'intruder' is identified entirely with evil, never with yet another marginalized human being who might simply be led to join with the household.)

A final – and seemingly bizarre – response to evil is rejoicing. Suffering puts Christians in direct contact with the life of Christ, who suffered on their behalf. That connection, together with the expectation that Christ's glory will finally be revealed (4.13) prompts believers to the apparent absurdity of rejoicing even in the face of suffering. To the world outside God's household, of course, such laughter in the face of torment will go by the name of madness or weakness or cowardice.

Apart from an understanding that Christ's own suffering was salvific, the 'normal' rules hold, and suffering signifies failure and loss. Christians, however, know both the reality of evil and, somewhere down the road, its ultimate defeat. BG

John 17.1–11

In all the Gospels, but especially in Luke and John, Jesus appears as a person of prayer. Today's gospel reading comes from the longest prayer attributed to him, often called his 'high-priestly prayer' or 'prayer of consecration', because in it he consecrates (NRSV: 'sanctifies') himself and his followers, and intercedes for them. This prayer forms the climax of the farewell discourses (John 14—16). It falls into three parts: 17.1–5 – Jesus prays for himself; 17.6–19 – he prays for his disciples; and 17.20–24 – he prays for those who will believe through them. A brief conclusion (vv. 25f.) sums up Jesus' work.

The style of the prayer is hieratic, abstract and didactic. It probably stems from a late stage in the Gospel's composition, balancing the prologue in some aspects of its thought. We have reference to Jesus' pre-existence (17.5; cf. 1.1); to his role as One who makes God known (17.6; cf. 1.18, and the *logos* image); and to the life which Jesus brings (17.2; cf. 1.4). The prayer shares with the prologue the themes of 'glory' (17.1, 5, 24; cf. 1.14) and of Jesus' unity with the Father (17.11, 26; cf. 1.1). But the thought goes beyond the prologue as it anticipates Jesus' passion, the completion of the work God has given him, and his return to the Father (17.4, 11; cf. 19.30; 20.17). The prayer begins with a reference to Jesus' 'hour' (cf. 2.4, etc.); then Jesus prays that God may 'glorify' him, so that he may glorify God. When we speak of 'glory' (Greek: *doxa*), we normally think of honour, power and splendour, such as are enjoyed by God. We find *doxa* used in this sense in this prayer (e.g. 17.5, 22; cf. 2.11; 11.4, 40); but for John Jesus' 'glorification' involves also suffering and humiliation (e.g. 12.16, 23). Jesus' death is an integral part of the process of his exaltation and return to the glorious presence of God.

At first sight an extract from Jesus' passiontide prayer might seem an odd choice of reading for the Sunday after Ascension; but John has a curious attitude to time. Jesus speaks of having been 'glorified' at the moment Judas goes out to betray him (13.31); he refers to his ascension as if it has already occurred early in his ministry (3.13); he says that he is 'no longer in the world' when he is ostensibly praying with the disciples at the Last Supper (17.11). One has a strong sense that it is already the exalted Christ who speaks in this prayer. A case can be made for this whole prayer being precisely about Jesus' ascent to the Father (so Dodd; Brodie). Yet it is also about the disciples and future believers. It is Jesus' prayer that they may 'ascend' with him (17.24), to share his and the Father's unity and glory. RE

Day of Pentecost

Acts 2.1–21 or Numbers 11.24–30; I Corinthians 12.3b–13; John 20.19–23 or John 7.37–39

Acts 2.1–21

New life – sudden, unmerited, irresistible new life! That is the reality the Pentecost narrative in Acts 2 broadcasts, and the text transmits the story in the most expansive way imaginable. All the stops on this great literary organ are employed: a heavenly sound like a rushing wind, descending fire, patterns of transformed speech, and the like. It is as if not even the most lavish use of human language is capable of capturing the experiences of the day, and that is undoubtedly one of the emotions the text wishes to convey.

It is not accidental, of course, that the birth of the Church, this great 'harvest' of souls, should occur on this important festival. The Feast of Pentecost, or Weeks, as it is known in the Old Testament, marked the end of the celebration of the spring harvest, a liturgical cycle that began at Passover and during which devout Israelite families praised God for God's grace and bounty. It also was the beginning of a period, lasting until the autumnal Festival of Booths (or Tabernacles), in which the first fruits of the field were sacrificed to Yahweh. And among at least some Jews the Feast of Weeks was a time of covenant renewal, as the following text from the Book of Jubilees (*c.* 150 BC) makes clear:

> Therefore, it is ordained and written in the heavenly tablets that they should observe the feast of Shebuot (Weeks) in this month, once per year, in order to renew the covenant in all (respects), year by year. (*Jub.* 1.17; trans. O. S. Wintermute in James H. Charlesworth, ed., *The Old Testament Pseudepigrapha*; Garden City, NY: Doubleday & Co., 1985, vol. 2, p. 67.)

Pentecost/Weeks is thus a pregnant moment in the life of the people of God and in the relationship between that people and God. Or to put the matter more graphically, but also more accurately, Pentecost is the moment when gestation ceases and birthing occurs. Thus, it is both an end and a beginning, the leaving behind of that which is past, the launching forth into that which is only now beginning to be. Pentecost therefore is not a time of completion. It is moving forward into new dimensions of being, whose basic forms are clear, but whose fulfilment has yet to be realized.

Those who follow the cycle of lectionary texts (or, for that matter, those who simply read the book of Acts) have been prepared for this moment. Twice, in connection with Jesus' ascension, the coming of the Spirit has been promised: 'You will receive power when the Holy Spirit has come upon you' (Acts 1.8; compare 1.5). That promise is now realized in a manner far surpassing the expectations of even the most faithful disciples. New life for the Church! New life for individuals within the church! New life through the Spirit of God! That is the meaning of Pentecost.

No one present is excluded from this display of God's grace. Unlike other important moments in the history of God's mighty acts of salvation – the transfiguration (Mark 9.2–13), for example, where only the inner few are witnesses to the work of God's Spirit – everyone is included at Pentecost. The tongues of fire rest upon 'each' (Acts 2.3) of the disciples, and a moment later the crowd comes surging forward because 'each one' (v. 6) has heard the disciples speaking in his or her native tongue. In order that not even the least astute reader may miss the inclusiveness of the moment, the list of place names that begins in v. 9 traces a wide sweep through the world of the Greco-Roman Diaspora. That which happens at Pentecost is thus no inner mystical experience, but an outpouring of God's energy that touches every life present.

Yet not everyone responded to the winds and fires of new life, at least not in positive ways. Some mocked (v. 13) and, in their unwillingness to believe the freshness of God's initiatives, reacted with stale words (compare 1 Sam. 1.14) as they confused Spirit-induced joy with alcohol-induced inebriation. Perhaps it was the very extravagant expression of the Spirit's presence that drove them to conclude: 'This cannot be what it seems to be!' Yet what it seemed to be is precisely what it was. God's Spirit unleashed! New life – sudden, unmerited, irresistible new life! We may hope that those who mocked were among those who, on hearing Peter's sermon, were 'cut to the heart' (v. 37).

Peter's sermon begins – and this day's lection ends – with a quotation (vv. 17–21) from the prophet Joel (Joel 2.28–32a), and nothing could be more symptomatic of the nature of Pentecost than the transmutation of this text. That which in the prophet's discourse appears prominently as a forecast of destruction and death has become on Peter's tongue a declaration of new life. For Joel the signs of the outpouring of the Spirit are a prelude to disaster (see especially Joel 2.32b, c) but for Peter these wonders have been fulfilled in Jesus Christ, himself the greatest of God's wonders (Acts 2.22), and their purpose, *Christ's* purpose, is nothing less than the redemption of humankind. Again the Spirit has invaded human life in ways that shatter old expectations. It is not death that is the aim of the Spirit's visitation, but new life – sudden, unmerited, irresistible new life! 'Everyone who calls on the name of the Lord shall be saved' (v. 21). BG

Numbers 11.24–30

Numbers 11 is an odd narrative, in that the problem that stands at its heart is not the problem that endowment with the Spirit of God remedies. The story begins with a complaint of the people in the wilderness about their food. Manna is evidently too boring a diet, and the people remember with nostalgia the culinary delights of their time of slavery in Egypt. The irony of slaves enjoying a rich diet should not be overlooked. At the end of the chapter the craving for meat is satisfied by the provision of quails (birds whose Latin name is *coturnix coturnix*) and by divine punishment of the ungrateful former slaves. The material that intervenes hardly fits this scenario.

Moses complains to God that he cannot bear alone the burden of leading the people, a complaint similar to the story in Exod. 18 of Moses being persuaded to appoint other judges to help him deal with the people. God promises in Num. 11.16–17 that he will ease Moses' burden by putting some of Moses' spirit upon elders who can then help. What this has to do with the miraculous feeding of the complaining people by sending quails into their camp is hard to see.

The passage set as the reading deals with the carrying out of the promises to give some of Moses' spirit to elders, in this case 70. The proof that the transfer has been carried out is that those affected 'prophesy'. This is to be understood along the lines of 1 Sam. 10.9–13, a frenzy of ecstatic utterance and behaviour that was not necessarily edifying in itself, but which identified people as belonging to a particular group or sect. Nowhere in the narrative is it indicated that those endowed with the spirit subsequently assisted Moses either to judge or to feed the people.

The heart of the story is the endowment of Eldad and Medad, two otherwise unknown Israelites, with the spirit. It is tempting to see, but impossible to identify, the struggle of groups for legitimacy behind the story. Eldad and Medad then symbolize 'outsiders' who, contrary to what 'official channels' expected or encouraged, were clearly designated as ones approved by God. Moses' support for them and his sublime prayer 'would that all the Lord's people were prophets' need to be read, in the first instance, in the context of prophesying as frenzied, ecstatic activity. The groups that displayed these external symptoms were, in the stories of Samuel and Kings, groups fanatically loyal to the God of Israel, and prepared to take drastic action in support of their faith. In the context of Numbers, Moses' wish is for a people wholly committed to God, although the story clearly looks different, if read through Christian eyes. JR

I Corinthians 12.3b–13

When Christians recall the gift of the Holy Spirit to the early Church, Luke's account of the events of Pentecost inevitably comes to centre stage. The dramatic story should not, however, create the impression that the gift of the Spirit to the Church was a one-time-only event. Because the outpouring of the Holy Spirit at Pentecost is associated with the beginning of the Church's life in Jerusalem, it may be tempting to conclude that the Spirit functions somewhat as God's initial 'capital investment' in the Church; whatever happens after the initial investment depends on the labour of the Church itself. The Pauline reading for this Sunday can help to correct any notion that the gift of the Spirit is such an unrepeatable act.

This lection is part of an extended discussion of problems related to worship, and that fact needs to be taken into account. Beginning in 1 Cor. 11.2, with the discussion of the appropriate appearance for women who participate in worship, and running through the end of ch. 14, Paul addresses a variety of issues concerning *corporate* worship. What Paul says about the Spirit within this context, therefore, pertains to the corporate life of the community of believers, as the 'body' metaphor of this passage illustrates. Indeed, Paul seldom refers to the Holy Spirit as a way of talking about God's action in relation to the private faith of individual believers.

In the context of the Corinthian Church, Paul's reference to 'spiritual gifts' is already a mild act of pastoral confrontation. At least some of the Corinthians appear to have excelled in wisdom and have been speaking in tongues, activities they understood to reflect *their own* spiritual superiority and authority. By casting this discussion in terms of the Spirit's role, Paul makes a powerful theological claim that whatever their accomplishments, the Corinthians have only the Spirit (not themselves) to thank. These 'spiritual gifts' range from the exotic and dramatic (speaking in tongues, working miracles) to the less dramatic (interpretation). They begin with the gift of faith itself, the confession that Jesus is Lord (1 Cor. 12.3). Throughout Paul's comments runs again and again the reminder that these gifts, whatever they are, come from the Spirit alone. Because they are gifts, not achievements, they reflect on the Giver rather than on the recipient.

Apart from this underlying insistence that all spiritual gifts are indeed gifts, two inseparable issues dominate the passage: the variety of spiritual gifts and their place in the upbuilding of the one Christian community. While it may seem obvious that there is a diversity of gifts, that diversity regularly causes great trouble in the Church's life. At Corinth, the diversity threatened to become a hierarchy, in which the more dramatic gifts reigned over those that seemed to be more ordinary. Paul attacks this problem by means of several general observations about diversity. First, as noted earlier, he insists that each of the spiritual gifts comes from the same God (vv. 4–6). He then elaborates on the diversity by itemizing some of the gifts, especially those relevant for the worship setting (vv. 8–10). Within this listing, however, he repeats the phrase 'to one is given' or 'to another', thereby drawing attention to the fact that no individual receives every spiritual gift. Verse 11 makes the point explicit: 'All these are activated by one and the same Spirit, who allots to *each one individually* just as the Spirit chooses' (emphasis added). The one Spirit of God grants all these diverse and multiple gifts, but the Spirit grants them to individuals according to the Spirit's own plan.

Alongside this emphasis on the diverse distribution of gifts and, indeed, completely inextricable from it, stands Paul's insistence that the diversity exists solely for the upbuilding of the one Christian community. This concern enters the passage in v. 7, with the comment that 'to each is given the manifestation of the Spirit for the common good'. The 'common good' is a central issue in 1 Corinthians, where the pluralism of viewpoints seems strikingly akin to modern individualism and even relativism. Paul insists, over against the notion that individuals or small groups are free to employ their gifts as they please, that the spiritual gifts exist to serve the good of the whole community. In 1 Cor. 14 Paul explores the exact implications of this principle, insisting that speaking in tongues and prophesying without interpretation does not aid the community.

Following the itemization of various gifts, the issue of the common good emerges again in 1 Cor. 12.12–13 in the form of the image of the one body. Because believers, however different their gifts and even their social origins, are part of the one body, their gifts must be exercised within and for that one body. To think otherwise is to imagine that the hand can act independently of the arm!

The tension in this passage between the diversity and the unity of believers is well worn, but ever in need of proclamation. Whether discussing gifts related to worship or gifts related to education, service or fellowship, the concern for diversity and the concern for unity must be held together. To call for unity without acknowledging the fact, even the grace, of diversity is to confuse unity with uniformity. To celebrate diversity without seeking unity is to misunderstand what goal diversity serves. BG

John 20.19–23

Today's gospel from John has already been read as part of the longer passage set for the Second Sunday of Easter (see comments there). At first it might seem surprising to find it prescribed also for Pentecost. It serves here to offer a different perspective on the coming of the Spirit from that of Luke.

Historians of the early Church have long puzzled over why Christianity emerged as a new religion with such speed and vigour. One could argue that the time was 'ripe' in terms of the situation in the Roman Empire, with its excellent communications and comparative peace (though wars were never far away). One could argue that, for converts from paganism, Christianity filled an emotional void left by the formalities of the state religion, and offered an ethical content absent from the more exotic 'mystery religions'. One could argue that, for Jewish converts, it offered an alternative to the temple cult, destroyed for ever in the fall of Jerusalem to the Romans in AD 70. But all these 'rational' causes can only partially explain Christianity's phenomenal rise.

The New Testament authors have no doubt that the reason why Christianity spread was because God's Spirit was powerfully at work among believers. Luke expresses this idea in his dramatic account of the Spirit's outpouring at the Jewish Feast of Pentecost, when the disciples were transformed, inspired and gifted by God for the work of mission (Acts 2). This is seen as a fulfilment both of Joel's prophecy (Joel 2.28–32) and of the Baptist's proclamation that One coming after him would baptize with the Spirit (Luke 3.16), a promise repeated by Jesus himself after his resurrection (Luke 24.49; Acts 1.4f.). In Acts, this initial gift of the Spirit is followed by further dramatic outpourings at key points in the narrative (e.g. Acts 4.31; 10.44). Paul is equally aware of the Spirit's work in the life of the early Church, associating the Spirit with a wide range of gifts (see esp. 1 Cor. 12.4–11). In Ephesians, the spiritual gifts associated with ministry are directly attributed to the ascended Christ (4.4–13).

In John, the Spirit comes (as in Luke) to fulfil John the Baptist's prediction (1.33) and, even more, in fulfilment of Jesus' own words and actions. Sometimes the Spirit is alluded to through metaphor and symbolic language (e.g. 3.5–8; 7.37–39), sometimes through direct promises of the Spirit of truth, the paraclete (e.g. 14.16f.,

25; 16.13–15). In John, the Spirit is given to the assembled disciples on Easter Day. One should not disguise the fact that there are tensions between Luke's and John's narratives. (Luke is the only New Testament source for the idea that the Spirit came precisely 50 days after Easter.) What matters is not the *chronology* of the gift of the Spirit, but its *reality*. RE

John 7.37–39

A major theme of John's Gospel is how Jesus fulfils and supersedes (for Christians) the hopes and ideals underlying Jewish feasts. Today we find Jesus at the Feast of Tabernacles (Hebrew: *sukkoth*, lit. 'huts'), an autumn harvest festival, for which all male Jews were required to travel to Jerusalem. Tabernacles commemorated God's goodness in sustaining his people through their wilderness years when they lived in temporary dwellings. It was the feast at which Solomon was believed to have dedicated the temple and in post-exilic Judaism it took on eschatological and messianic expectations.

According to John, Jesus originally said that he was not going up to the festival, but later went up 'privately' (7.8–10). This may be to dissociate Jesus from the actual Jewish celebration. However, on its last day he appears publicly to offer water to all who are thirsty (7.37). The image of 'water' has a rich background in Jewish thought. Apart from purification, it may represent the quenching of physical and spiritual thirst, renewal of life, wisdom, the Law, even salvation. Through Moses, God provides his people with water from the rock (Num. 20.11; Ps. 78.15f.); God invites all who thirst to come to the waters (Isa. 55.1; cf. Jer. 17.13). When Jesus summons the thirsty, he is doing what God does. His words would have special significance at Tabernacles, whose rites (according to rabbinic sources) involved pouring out water from the Pool of Siloam before the temple as a symbol of fruitfulness (autumn rains were vital for Jewish agriculture).

In the prophets especially, 'water' has eschatological associations. Isaiah 12.3 (a text recited at Tabernacles) promises that 'on that day' God's people will 'draw with joy from the wells of salvation'. Ezekiel has a vision of water issuing from the temple (47.1–12; cf. Rev. 22.1f.). Zechariah prophesies that on the 'day of the Lord' living waters will flow out of Jerusalem (14.8; note the reference to Tabernacles, v. 16). Joel speaks of a fountain coming forth 'on that day' from the house of the Lord (3.18). John has already identified Jesus with the temple in respect of his body (2.19–22). He now suggests that he is replacing it as a source of eschatological salvation.

There are problems over the punctuation of vv. 37f. (contrast RSV; NRSV). In spite of the wealth of Old Testament background, no text corresponds exactly to the words quoted, and it is unclear whether the phrase 'out of his heart' (lit. 'cavity' or 'belly') refers to Jesus, as giver of living water (cf. 19.34) or to believers (cf. 4.10–14). On either interpretation Jesus is the ultimate source of the 'water'.

In 7.39 this water is identified with the Spirit (cf. Isa. 44.3, where 'water' and 'spirit' appear in parallel: 'I will pour water on the thirsty land ... I will pour my Spirit upon your descendants'). In some Jewish sources the water drawn at Tabernacles is identi-fied with the Holy Spirit, enabling God's people to enjoy salvation. For John, the promise of 7.37–39 is fulfilled on Easter Day. RE

Trinity Sunday

Genesis 1.1—2.4a or Isaiah 40.12–17, 27–31; 2 Corinthians 13.11–13; Matthew 28.16–20

Genesis 1.1—2.4a

Virtually every translation of the Bible, traditional or contemporary, begins with the words 'In the beginning'. For the ancient Israelites, like many other peoples all over the world, a story of origins, of creation, was of great importance. As we read through this account, we shall see that there were in fact eight acts of creation, but they are divided into six days, followed by a time of rest, so perhaps the material was deliberately organized so as to form a week-long festival. It is extraordinary that there are still those who try to discover literal, historical truth here. Light before the creation of the sun is not easy to envisage (compare v. 3 with v. 16). To become bogged down in such literal readings is to fall into the danger of distorting the basic message of the text. What we have is an imaginative picture of the world, not anything shaped by precise scientific discovery.

Conventional Old Testament criticism has seen in this picture of creation the source 'P', standing for 'priestly'. That same source is thought to have been responsible for some of the (to the modern reader) dry-as-dust lists and ritual requirements of Leviticus and Numbers. It is important to put that material in context. Here we are reminded of the universality of God's concerns. Most of the rest of the Old Testament will deal with the affairs of one particular community, Israel, and God's relations with that community. Here, however, we are reminded of the context within which those relations should be seen: God is pictured as creator of the whole world, not just of Israel, not just of humanity, but of every living creature.

The Christian record with regard to the environment has not always been a good one. Some have claimed that the picture of human beings having dominion over all other creatures (v. 26) has been one of the primary causes of the environmental crisis that affects our modern world. Until quite recently it has been taken for granted in virtually every Christian theological tradition that creation in effect equals humanity. This account, by contrast, placed at the very beginning of our Bible, stresses that 'we are all in this together'. We may note also that whereas the main biblical tradition takes for granted that humans may eat flesh-meat, here in v. 30 a vegetarian existence is pictured as part of the ideal world.

One other message for an over-stressed world may be important. At the end of the labours of creation 'God rested from all the work that he had done'. Thirty or forty years ago we were being assured that technological development would offer us all a life of leisure. Little sign of it yet! The importance of rest, of re-creation, is a matter we must not forget. R C

Isaiah 40.12–17, 27–31

The prophet's consummate skills as poet, theologian and pastor shine in this passage. It has to be remembered that he is speaking to those in despair, his fellow-country people in exile who have lost everything, and for whom day drags on after day with no hope. The pastor in him directs their attention, not to their own condition, but to God.

In a series of fine rhetorical questions he appeals to the greatness, majesty and order of God's creation which, as the sole God, he accomplished alone. He 'marked out' the heavens (v. 23, cf. Gen. 1.6–8) but *no one* (the force of the questions 'Who . . . ?') has 'marked out' (the same Hebrew verb) his Spirit (v. 13). No one can set limits to God or channel him into the small confines of their own beliefs or expectation. The God who can help individuals in distress is no cosy, household god of the community of faith only, but the creator of the universe and lord of all history.

He needs none to advise him (vv. 13–14) especially in showing him the path of 'justice', a noun derived from the verb 'to judge', which comes to mean a way of life based on God's judgements, the way which reflects God's essential 'rightness'. Hence the irony, and futility of the cry of those who say 'my *justice* is disregarded by my God' (v. 27). His ways are always right, however mysterious they may seem from limited perspectives.

The great oppressive powers of that day are dismissed contemptuously in vv. 15–17. The menace of the hostile and evil nations are no more than 'emptiness' before him. It is the same Hebrew word used of the 'chaos' that characterized the state of the universe before God brought the order and beauty of his creation from it (Gen. 1.2). This same God is the one who can be trusted to triumph over all the forces of 'chaos' in history.

The thought of the incomparable greatness of God might lead to despair. 'How can he possibly be interested in the fate of each individual?' The very opposite is true. It is because of his illimitable greatness and power that he can fully meet the needs of his children. The power and knowledge shown in creation are also available for them (v. 28). Indeed, this truth is brought out by a play on words. 'He does not *faint* or *grow weary* (v. 28) and so those who "wait" for him shall run and not *be weary* and walk and not *faint*', the last being not an anticlimax since human beings spend more time 'walking' through the common round of life than 'running' in its rarer, exalted moments.

Far from becoming worn out they shall 'grow, or renew, wings like an eagle', able to soar to those vantage points of faith and vision in which all life's problems fall into perspective, lit by the love of such a God. R M

2 Corinthians 13.11–13

An initial reading of the closing section of 2 Corinthians, especially 13.5–13, may cause us to wonder what has become of Paul's emphasis on God's grace. The exhortation with which this section begins, 'Examine yourselves to see whether you are living in the faith', can be read in a moralistic fashion, meaning that believers must prove their faith through their actions. The lection proper, vv. 11–13, reinforces this impression, for here it appears that God's presence with the community depends on their way of living out the gospel. Only a closer examination of the large context and the text itself will show that the text cuts in a different direction.

Second Corinthians 10—13, which may well be a fragment from a letter distinct from the letter (or letters) represented in chs. 1—9, addresses the nature of apostolic authority. Far from compiling an abstract thesis about such matters, Paul writes here a heated response to what is apparently severe criticism. Some 'super-apostles' (see 2 Cor. 11.5; 12.11) have questioned Paul's authority, charging that he does not display the signs of an apostle. Paul's biting response consists of his own apostolic boasting, not a boasting in his great miracles and visions, but in his suffering (11.21–29), in visions that are *not* to be described (12.1–6), and in his bodily affliction, which God declines to heal (12.7–10). Underlying this bitter irony is the theological claim that faith in Jesus Christ measures weakness and strength by criteria other than those used by the 'super-apostles'. Throughout 2 Cor. 10—13, Paul refers time and again to varying assessments of what makes for weakness and strength (10.1; 11.21; 11.29–30; 12.9), culminating in 13.3–4, where he speaks of Christ's crucifixion in weakness and resurrected life in power. When we turn to 2 Cor. 13.5–13 (NRSV), the admonition to 'examine *yourselves*' (emphasis added) takes on a different meaning. Because so much of what precedes has to do with the way in which Paul and his co-workers are being evaluated, what 13.5 does is to turn the tables: 'Examine yourselves [rather than examining us].' This interpretation finds confirmation not just from the context, but also in the fact that, in the Greek, the pronoun translated 'yourselves' stands first in the sentence: '*Yourselves* examine!'

The chapter continues to focus on the relationship between the Corinthians and the apostles. Verse 6 expresses the hope that the Corinthians will not determine that the apostles are 'unexamined', and v. 7 the hope that the Corinthians will pass the test, *even* if that means that the apostles themselves will have failed. Paul can even affirm that he is pleased when the Corinthians are strong and the apostles weak.

What is at stake here is not, of course, simply a social relationship. Paul desperately wants an improved relationship with the Corinthians, and he wants them again to acknowledge his authority, but that authority is not an end in itself. Instead, the relationship among believers has a christological warrant (see v. 5b); it is based directly on God's action in Jesus Christ. Believers do not belong to themselves, that they may do as they wish; believers belong to Christ, and the relationships among believers must reflect the One to whom they belong.

Belonging to Christ exerts an absolute claim over the life of the believer. The act of God in Jesus Christ (what we often call the 'indicative') and the called response of human beings (the 'imperative') are integrally related for Paul. God's gracious and unconditional gift is simultaneously a calling to 'what is right' (13.7). Doing 'what is right' also evidences itself in a life of peace and love within the community, as is clear in the closing lines of the letter, the lection proper (vv. 11–13). Prominent in these admonitions is the plea that the Corinthians attend to Paul's words ('listen to my appeal') and that they restore harmony within the community ('agree with one another, live in peace').

Because of its threefold nature the benediction in v. 13 is associated with Trinity Sunday, but the order (Christ, God, Spirit) distinguishes this benediction from that of later trinitarian formulas. Neither does this benediction focus on the relationships among the three members of the Trinity. The questions about the nature of the Trinity, over which the Church later struggled (and still struggles), were not a pressing concern for Paul, and attempts to find a doctrine of the Trinity in Paul's letters are exceedingly hazardous.

As important as it is to offer instruction about the Trinity, then, this passage may be of little direct use in that instruction. Here, the focus is not on the Trinity but on its gifts to human beings, the gifts of grace and love and fellowship. These very gifts are the ones that ensure that believers are not required to prove their faith, for their faith itself comes as God's grace. BG

Matthew 28.16–20

This familiar conclusion to the Gospel of Matthew is loaded with significance for the Church. In it many elements that have appeared and reappeared throughout the narrative are brought to a head, and the reader's attention is drawn to the import of the story of Jesus and what is to be done in response.

It is easy to identify with the 11 disciples. At the sight of the risen Jesus, they worshipped, just as they had done when he walked on the water (Matt. 14.33) and as the women had done when Jesus met them (28.9). But their worship was mingled with doubt. The sight of him did not remove all the uncertainties and questions. The Eleven wavered between adoration and indecision, between prayer and puzzlement. What is striking, however, is that the disciples are not excluded because of their questions. In fact, it is precisely to these followers, who are worshipping *and* doubting, that the great commission is given.

Jesus is the protagonist in this final scene, and it is to his words to the disciples that we must attend. First, *Jesus announces the premise on which the great commission rests.* Behind the imperative stands the divine authority. Jesus has the right to command the Eleven to 'make disciples' because 'all authority in heaven and on earth' has been given to him. It is not a surprising word for the reader, who has heard repeatedly through the narrative of Jesus' authority (7.29; 9.6, 8; 11.27; 21.23–27) and is reminded of it once again.

Though not surprising, this statement of authority is nevertheless a welcomed word when coupled with the commission. The word 'authority' carries not only the notion of warrant, but also the notion of power. To be sure, the disciples are given the credentials for their mission, but more, they are promised the potency to carry it out. They are invited to take part in an activity by a Commissioner whose power they have seen in action, a power exceeding their wildest dreams. The mission to which they are called, then, is not jeopardized by their weaknesses or limited by their uncertainties.

Second, *Jesus confronts the disciples with an awesome commission.* They are to 'make disciples of all nations'. (The 'go' is actually in Greek a participle and therefore subordinate to the imperative 'make disciples'.) Though earlier in the ministry of Jesus the charge was to avoid the Gentiles and Samaritans and to go only 'to the lost sheep of the house of Israel' (10.6), now, in light of the death and resurrection, the scope of the mission is universalized. Without rejecting Israel's pride of place, the *góyim* are included among those to be made disciples.

Two significant activities are mentioned as ingredients of the commission.

(a) 'Baptizing' highlights the priestly function, which introduces people to life in God's reign. The triadic formula no doubt accounts for the selection of this passage as the gospel lesson for Trinity Sunday. It goes without saying that the formula is not to be interpreted as if it came from the creeds of the fourth and fifth centuries, and yet its presence here should not be ignored. The 'in the name of' (occurring five times in Matthew and nowhere else in the other Synoptic Gospels) signifies 'with reference to' and implies a new belonging. Beyond repentance, those who are baptized confess that they now belong to the Father, Son and Holy Spirit. A relationship is established that marks them as a peculiar people. But this confession implies, too, that the baptized are claimed by no less than the triune God. Disciples remember baptism as a certification of this mutual commitment. It sustains them in times of puzzlement and confusion.

(b) 'Teaching them to obey everything that I have commanded you' adds a further dimension in the calling of the nations. The 11 are commissioned not only to instruct the baptized about what Jesus has said about the kingdom of God, to transmit his interpretations of the law, but also to teach them to *obey* Jesus. The didactic task is only completed when the nations in fact perform the teaching of Jesus.

This stress on teaching and obeying Jesus' words protects the Christian message from being reduced either to cheap grace or to a private faith. The intent is to nurture a community that does not take God's goodness lightly, but lives out in the world the discipleship to which it is called.

Third, *Jesus promises the divine presence to the Church as it responds to the Commission.* At the beginning of Matthew's narrative readers are told that Jesus' name is Emmanuel, God is with us (1.23). Along the way, they overhear the promise to the disciples that when they gather for worship, Jesus will be present (18.20). And now, at the end of the story, they read of this commitment of Jesus to accompany his disciples.

This means, on the one hand, that the Church must always beware of claiming too much for itself. It always baptizes, teaches, serves, speaks, makes disciples of the nations in the awareness of the presence of the risen Jesus. Its authority remains a derived authority, dependent on the One who possesses all authority. On the other hand, the Church after Easter is not abandoned. Though sent 'like sheep into the midst of wolves' (10.16), it can count on the attendance of the crucified and living Christ, even in its darkest hours. cc

Corpus Christi/Thanksgiving for Holy Communion

Genesis 14.18–20; I Corinthians 11.23–26; John 6.51–58

Genesis 14.18–20

Chapter 14 has long been regarded as an erratic block in the Genesis story. It seems to describe a situation in which the leading rulers of the known world all converged on the area of the Dead Sea. In the story Abraham is introduced at a late stage and is envisaged as a warrior, with an extensive retinue, engaged in battles with large-scale enemy coalitions. This is a very different picture from the family story of surrounding chapters. The older source-critics were quite unable to assign this chapter to any of their preferred sources. Most modern scholars regard the chapter as a late addition to the main Genesis material, perhaps aimed at drawing out Abraham's connection with Jerusalem (assuming that 'Salem' here is a short form of Jerusalem), but no consensus has been reached.

Within this larger context the verses of our reading pose their own problems. Many have taken them to be an entirely separate unit, unconnected with the remainder of the chapter. Nothing is known of Melchizedek in historical terms; he is presented here both as king and as 'priest of El Elyon' ('God Most High'). This became a name applied to Yahweh, especially in the Psalms (cf. Pss. 7.17; 91.1). Whether this was the name of an originally Canaanite deity or simply one mode of describing Israel's own God remains unclear.

Melchizedek became an important symbolic figure within later traditions. He is mentioned at Ps. 110.4 as the typical priest, and is also mentioned in the Dead Sea Scrolls. The theme of Melchizedek as the true priest is taken further in the Epistle to the Hebrews, where Jesus is credited with priestly status 'according to the order of Melchizedek' (Heb. 6.20), and the links between Melchizedek and Jesus are imaginatively developed in the following chapter.

In Christian liturgical tradition these verses have played another important part, because the 'bread and wine' (v. 18) have been seen as prefiguring the eucharistic elements. Overall, one may say that this is one of those passages that will prove frustrating for those who wish to have a clear historical account, of the kind that can be backed up by reliable supporting evidence. By contrast it will be a delight for those who treasure literary allusions and traditions and are not greatly concerned about historical details. RC

I Corinthians 11.23–26

See Maundy Thursday pp. 106–7.

John 6.51–58

With its frequent use of material things as signs and symbols of the spiritual, John's Gospel has been seen as the 'most sacramental' of all. On the other hand, some scholars deny that its author even knew the sacraments, or suppose him to be anti-sacramental. It is true that John gives no account of Jesus' baptism (some would say that he suppresses it), and that he omits 'the institution of the Eucharist' from the Last Supper; but other parts of his narrative seem to reflect on the sacramental life of the Church.

One such passage is set for today's Gospel. It comes at the end of the 'bread of life discourse', following Jesus' miraculous feeding of a large crowd. John has already interpreted the miracle as a sign that Jesus is the prophet like Moses (6.14; cf. Deut. 18.15–18), as a feeding of the people far surpassing the manna (6.26–32; cf. Exod. 16.4, 15), and as showing Jesus not just as *giver* of living bread, but as the bread itself (6.32–35, 41, 48). This 'bread' is freely available to all who come in faith to him (6.35, 40, 47). Believers *have* 'eternal life', i.e. they experience the joy of God's presence associated with the age to come (6.51a–b).

At 6.51c the interpretation takes a new turn. The 'bread' is interpreted as Jesus' flesh, given for the life of the world. Now, only those who 'eat' Jesus' flesh and 'drink' his blood have life in them. A sacramental allusion seems inescapable. But how does this relate to the idea expressed earlier, that it is those who have faith who receive eternal life? Some scholars find the tension so great that they attribute vv. 51c–58 to an 'ecclesiastical redactor'. Others see these verses as the climax of the whole of 6.1–58.

The main thought seems to be that the Lord's Supper or Holy Communion is a means of sustaining and feeding the faithful (v. 55). Through it we assimilate into ourselves Christ's very self; we become one with him as he abides in us and we in him (v. 56). We already have eternal life, and Jesus will raise us up on the last day (v. 54). Note that these verses do not speak of Jesus' sacramental *body*, but rather of his *flesh* (Greek: *sarx*, the word used of the incarnation in 1.14). Conceivably this passage was added (whether by the evangelist or another) to correct people with problems over a 'fleshly' understanding of the incarnation or Eucharist (cf. the views attributed by Ignatius to the 'docetists'). Observe the strong introductory words, 'Truly, truly, I say to you . . .' (v. 53), and the divisive effect of this teaching. It is a shame, however, to read vv. 51c–58 merely as polemic, and certainly wrong to interpret them too rigidly. Seen in the context of the bread of life discourse, they offer an understanding of the Eucharist as an important part of a wider pattern by which Jesus Christ, the Word of God, nurtures and sustains his people. RE

Proper 3

(Sunday between 22 and 28 May inclusive, if after Trinity Sunday)

Isaiah 49.8–16a; I Corinthians 4.1–5; Matthew 6.24–34

Isaiah 49.8–16a

It is unfortunate that the reading begins at verse 8 rather than verse 7 because the addressee is not then indicated and an important contrast is lost. In fact, the passage is addressed to 'one deeply despised, abhorred by the nations, the slave of rulers' (7a), i.e. the Israelite community in exile in Babylon; a group that has lost its self-respect as well as that of its captors. To this demoralized community God says, that he has answered and helped them. The Hebrew verbs are grammatically in the perfect, and thus rendered by past tenses in English. From the exiled community's point of view these acts of deliverance still lie in the future, albeit backed by the guarantee of God's promises.

The words do not just apply to the exiled community, promising release to them only, however. What God intends to do for the exiles will have repercussions for people far away (verse 12), people from north and west and from Syene, the name for the Jewish colony at Elephantine in southern Egypt, known today as Aswan on the Nile. Is the promise only for dispersed Israelites, or does it include Gentiles? It can be argued from the phrase 'covenant of the people' and the latter part of verse 6 ('I will give you as a light to the nations, that my salvation may reach to the end of the earth') that the release of the exiles will at the very least benefit other nations by witnessing to God's mercy and power.

The description of the journey of the freed exiles in verses 9b–11 draws upon images of passing through the wilderness. The provision of food, water and protection in an unfriendly environment hints at miraculous actions on the part of God who will be among his people. The events will have cosmic significance, as indicated by the summons to heaven, earth and mountains to rejoice at what God has determined to do (verse 13).

For Zion, the earthly Jerusalem that symbolizes the whole people, this is all too good to be true, and at odds with the desolate state of its current existence. The idea of God's closeness to his people that was earlier expressed by God providing for the people in the wilderness is now expressed by the female image of an indestructible bond forged between a mother and her child. The most important factor is not what the community thinks about itself, but that its destiny lies in the hands of a God who will never give up on it. However, if it is true that God will accomplish the redemption of the world through a dispirited and disillusioned community, does this have anything to say to the churches today? Is a change of perspective needed, from that of concern with survival to that of cosmic expectation? There are not a few parallels between the churches today and the exiled community that believed that God had forsaken it. JR

1 Corinthians 4.1–5

'Servants of Christ and stewards of God's mysteries' – such language may seem exalted and exotic when read as a part of Scripture, but the terms themselves are ordinary, household terms. Moving from his earlier comparisons of apostolic workers with farmers (1 Cor. 3.5–9) and with builders (3.10–15), Paul now compares himself and his colleagues with household workers. A servant (*hypēretēs*) is an assistant who might serve in a variety of contexts; a steward (*oikonomos*) is one who has oversight of a household and is directly accountable to the owner for actions taken. In other words, the apostolic workers are identified less with any power or privileges they might have than with their responsibilities. That is the case throughout Paul's letters, since the terms applied to Paul and his co-workers – slaves (*douloi*), apostles (*apostoloi*) – regularly suggest that they work at the request (or demand!) of and for the will of another.

From 1 Cor. 4.6, it seems clear that Paul has in mind at least Apollos and himself when he employs the first person plural ('us'). Nevertheless, the point he is after applies to all Christians, not only to a limited number. All believers are responsible for their actions; all labour as 'servants of Christ and stewards of God's mysteries', even if their tasks vary. The passage applies both to apostolic workers and to the members of their congregations.

The introduction of the terms 'servant' and 'steward' leads, not to a discussion of the role of the apostolic worker, but to an enlarged discussion of judgement (cf. 3.10–17). That this is Paul's intent seems clear, because the comment in 4.2 is so obvious as to be gratuitous. Making a point that stewards are required to be trustworthy is a little like insisting that pilots should be impervious to airsickness! The comment serves largely to introduce the issue of judgement, which dominates vv. 3–5.

Since judgement is a topic that appears infrequently in other Pauline letters but frequently in this section of 1 Corinthians, it is important to consider why that is the case. Corinthian Christians, at least as we may infer from Paul's letters, understood themselves to be beyond judgement. By virtue of their superior wisdom and their charismatic gifts, at least *some* Corinthians regarded their new life in Christ as a life of near perfection. As Henry Joel Cadbury described them, the Corinthians were 'overconverted'. Their own achievements not only placed the Corinthians beyond judgement but enabled them to classify and judge one another, and perhaps even Paul and his fellow workers as well.

Paul responds to the Corinthian 'overconversion' in several ways, one of which is by insisting that judgement does indeed lie ahead. When the time of the Lord's return comes (4.5; cf. 3.13), the work of every person will be submitted for inspection. Just as stewards must account to their masters for the way in which property has been handled, so all will give an account before God. The details of such an accounting and its consequences Paul leaves unstated, but he insists on its inevitability. Neither Paul nor the Corinthians nor any other believer has arrived at a point where God's discernment and assessment are unnecessary.

That judgement does belong to God and to God *alone* becomes clear in the passage. Neither the judgement of the Corinthians nor that of any human body impresses Paul (4.3a). He can even assert that he does not bother with judging himself (v. 3b), for 'it is the Lord who judges me'. Just as it is only God who establishes what is wise and what is foolish (1 Cor. 1.18–25), so it is only God whose criteria for evaluation and judgement have any true merit.

In the middle of this passage, Paul inserts the brief comment, 'I am not aware of anything against myself.' Over against a conventional portrait of Paul as plagued by guilt and remorse over his persecution of the Church, he here and elsewhere (see Phil. 3.6) asserts confidence that his conscience is, in fact, clear.

Although Paul's comments about judgement here have the apostolic workers in view, they speak equally well to all Christians, first-century and contemporary. For those Christians who find even the term 'judgement' to be distasteful, Paul's comments stand as a powerful reminder that all human beings are God's servants and stand responsible to God for their behaviour. No one escapes that accountability. For those Christians who, on the other hand, savour the prospect of judgement because they have already made judgements of their own, Paul's insistence it is God who judges may cause the tongue to pause mid-accusation. Paul's not-too-subtle point is that God requires no help or recommendations about the judgements of others.

Matthew 6.24–34

See Second Sunday Before Lent, p. 71.

Proper 4

(Sunday between 29 May and 4 June inclusive, if after Trinity Sunday)

Genesis 6.9–22; 8.14–19 or Deuteronomy 11.18–21, 26–28;
Romans 1.16–17; 3.22b–28 (29–31); Matthew 7.21–29

Genesis 6.9–22; 8.14–19

Gods in many religious traditions are unpredictable beings, and this is certainly true from time to time of the God of the Bible. Here we have a picture of the creator God dismayed because his creation had become 'corrupt'. In what ways, we are not told, though speculation has run riot down the ages. It certainly seems to be something more serious than the excessive noise which irritated the gods in the equivalent Babylonian story. The curious little episode in 6.1–4 has suggested to many that some form of sexual wrongdoing was involved, but however that may be, an important point to recognize is the way in which some form of moral wrongdoing led to the breakdown of the natural order. This is an insight of which religious traditions have too often lost sight. So God decided to 'make an end' of every human being and of the very earth itself. In the Christian tradition God's decisions are irrevocable, but the Old Testament has many stories in which God changes his mind.

Certainly the extent of destruction is soon modified in this story. In fact, if we read the whole of Gen. 6—8 we shall discover that the destruction is described very briefly, and much more attention is given to those who are to survive. The theme of an 'ark' as a vessel bringing salvation is very pervasive: the best-known of all aircraft carriers was called the *Ark Royal*, and Thomas Kinneally's prize-winning story of those saved from the Holocaust was *Schindler's Ark*. In Noah's ark every kind of created being is to be kept alive, two of each kind in this reading, but elsewhere (7.2) 'seven pairs of all clean animals'. The story has a number of minor inconsistencies of this kind, which may suggest that it was put together from different sources, but the overall impact is scarcely affected.

Our passage omits the charming details of Noah sending out raven and dove as the flood subsides, in order to look to the future. As in the creation story, we are reminded of God's concern for 'every living thing'. It is interesting that the various animals are pictured 'by families' (8.19). This is not a technical zoological qualification, but rather a recognition that all have their appropriate place in the hierarchy of creation. From this point on the overall story will concentrate on humanity, and before long upon one family within humanity. But the context provided by the creation story and by the flood, which can be seen as a kind of 're-creation', is that God's concern is with every created being. RC

Deuteronomy 11.18–21, 26–28

The command in this passage to bind 'these words' on the hands and the forehead and to write them on the doorposts (cf. also Deut. 6.4–9) has led to the practice in Judaism of wearing phylacteries at times of prayer and of putting *mezuzot* on doorways, a practice that continues to this day. A 'phylactery' (from the Greek *phylakteron*, 'amulet'; and *phylax*, 'guard') is a small, square leather box containing Deut. 6.4–9, 11.13–21 and Exod. 13.1–10, 11–16; while *mezuzot*, from Hebrew *mezuzah* 'doorpost', contain Deut. 6.4–9 and 11.13–21. Thus, the command that comes in this passage and elsewhere is taken literally as well as very seriously, even though the origin of phylacteries and *mezuzot* may derive from a more general belief in the ancient Near East that sacred words used in this way gave protection against misfortune.

The words 'heart' and 'soul' in Hebrew do not have the same connotation as in English. The 'heart' is the seat of a person's intellectual faculties in Hebrew, while the 'soul' is the seat of emotional and spiritual faculties. 'Heart' and 'soul' taken together denote a person's total life, physical, mental and spiritual. This is in contrast to our modern, secularizing, tendency to regard religion primarily as a matter of the mind.

A demand made on the total life of people is the bridge to the passage's concluding words. They are based upon treaty formulae that were common in the ancient Near East. A king would demand complete loyalty from a subject people, and promise them good things if they remained loyal. If they broke the treaty, they were warned of the dire consequences that would follow.

Bearing this background in mind helps to soften a problem that will confront modern readers, namely, that there is an element of threat in the conditions presented to the people, a threat that will extract reluctant conformity rather than whole-hearted obedience. The difference between vassal treaties and God's covenant is that the former were imposed upon subject people and meant to benefit the stronger party. God's covenant is the expression of divine love for largely undeserving people. It is designed for the benefit of that people, and especially its most vulnerable members. Even so, to disregard it totally is to choose a path that will inevitably lead to disaster. JR

Romans 1.16–17; 3.22b–28 (29–31)

A text such as this one, well known from the history of Christian thought and well worn in the pulpit, poses a difficult challenge for the preacher. How is it possible to break through the heavy cushion of familiarity to hear once again a fresh word from this text? One strategy is to pay close attention to the role this particular text plays within the conversation of the letter itself, looking for the cutting edge of the text.

Romans 3.22b–31 brings to a climax the point Paul introduces in 1.16–17, that the gospel is God's power for salvation to all people, Jew first and also Greek; the gospel reveals God's righteousness. In the very next verse (1.18) Paul parallels that revelation with the revelation of God's wrath. That statement initiates a discussion of the universality of human sin (1.18—3.20). All human beings have rebelled against God *as God*, by denying their own creatureliness. The forms of this rebellion have varied, but the result is the same. This line of argument comes to a head in 3.22–23: 'For there is no distinction, since all have sinned and fall short of the glory of God.' But 3.21–28 also returns to the revelation of God's righteousness, announced in 1.16–17 and here dominating the conversation: 'But now, apart from law, the righteousness of God has been disclosed.' (Even if the 3.22a is not part of the lection proper, it cannot be omitted from consideration here.)

But what does Paul mean by the 'the righteousness of God'? God's righteousness is not simply a quality comparable to God's goodness or God's immutability. Although God's righteousness is never severed from God, God's righteousness is a gift graciously bestowed on human beings. To glimpse Paul's meaning here we need to use active verbs, for God's righteousness is a way of talking about God's actions of reclaiming the world for God (to paraphrase Ernst Käsemann).

While God's righteousness is not a new thing, at the present time (vv. 21, 26) that righteousness has acted in a new way – 'through faith/faithfulness of Jesus Christ'. This somewhat more literal translation of *pistis Iēsou Christou* than that found in the NRSV demonstrates the ambiguity of v. 22. Most contemporary translations take v. 22 to mean that the righteousness of God is 'through faith in Jesus Christ' (NRSV), but a growing number of exegetes argue that the translation should be 'through the faith/faithfulness of Jesus Christ'. That is, it is Jesus' faithful act of obedience that reveals God's righteousness, which encompasses all people.

This interpretation of the 'faith of Jesus Christ' (*pistis Iēsou Christou*) helps to unravel v. 25, which may be translated: 'whom God put forward as a redemption through faith/faithfulness in his blood'. Here faith is once again the faithful obedience of Jesus Christ, which extends to the shedding of blood. What is striking about Paul's reference to Jesus in this text is that he links the revelation of God's righteousness directly to Jesus' death – not to his teachings, his exemplary life, or even his resurrection.

Of course, even if 'faith of Jesus Christ' means the faithful obedience of Jesus rather than the believer's faith *in* Jesus, the text still refers to human faith. Verse 22 refers to those who believe and v. 26 to those who live out of Jesus' faithfulness. This does not mean, however, that human beings now achieve their salvation by means of their faith. Not only would that claim make faith a matter of boasting (vv. 27–28), a work, but such a reading makes the text into a statement centred on the consequences of God's righteousness for human beings.

This is a difficult point for most Protestants to grasp, since we customarily read Romans through the filter of Luther's question, 'How can I find a loving God?' When read in that way, this passage yields the answer, 'You must have faith, and you will find a loving God.' But the focus of the text, as we see when we trace the argument from 1.16 on, is not on the human quest for a gracious and loving God. Instead, Paul's focus is on the radical act of God in reclaiming *all* humankind.

What Paul says about God here is precisely the cutting edge of this text, for Paul insists that God has, in Jesus Christ, shown grace and mercy to all human beings, each and every one of whom rebels against God. In the following chapter, Paul will refer to God as the one who justifies not the good or even the repentant, but the 'ungodly'. This, of course, sounds an unacceptable, even threatening, note to those of us who want to earn God's love. It sounds an even more unwelcome note when we want to be assured that God has forgiven us, but not those whom we identify as sinful. Paul's words place many of us in the role of the elder brother in the parable of the prodigal son; we may be glad to see our brother, but we want what we assume to be rightfully ours. Once again, we want to dictate terms to God, and this is precisely where Romans calls us up short. BG

Matthew 7.21–29

It is disturbing to read the Gospel of Matthew. Its anticipation of the coming judgement and its sharp words of warning to one group or another who live hypocritically or lawlessly create an uneasiness. They become particularly unsettling words when the group being judged is clearly a group of insiders, active followers, who might be expected to be commended for their piety or for their extraordinary accomplishments. Readers are repeatedly forced to ask questions about themselves.

Such is the case with the concluding words of the Sermon on the Mount. The text speaks of those who confess the highest christology ('Lord, Lord'), who utter profound prophecies, who demonstrate control over demonic powers, who even work miracles, but who fail to do 'the will of my Father in heaven'. With the devastating words 'I never knew you', such workers of lawlessness will be rejected.

Three observations about Matt. 7.21–23. First, the description of the group condemned has to be taken at face value. They *really do* affirm the basic creed of the Church ('Jesus is Lord'); they *really do* preach powerful sermons; they *really do* extraordinary deeds of exorcisms and healing – and all in Jesus' name! By all rights, they are not only in the Church – they are its leaders. They have accomplished amazing feats as a part of their involvement. They are clearly not the Jewish leadership against which harsh judgements are later brought (23.1–36), nor can they be dismissed too quickly as the bad guys, the outsiders. The words of the text leave the reader perplexed and a bit disturbed that such religiously active people can be so decisively renounced by Jesus, and their accomplishments labelled as lawless. It is clear that judgement begins with the people of God, not with the remote corners of the world where the gospel has never been heard. Hardly a balm for the reader's anxiety!

Second, the judge, who pronounces such a harsh verdict, is Jesus himself (7.23). The one who eats with tax collectors and sinners (9.10–11), who frets over Jerusalem as a mother hen cares for her brood (23.37), and who comes to save the people from their sins (1.21) utters the condemning words. Judgement and grace are not separated in Matthew's narrative, as if one comes from an angry God and the other from a loving Jesus. Rather, judgement and grace are both dimensions of God's movement toward the world. Jesus, the Saviour-Judge, graciously claims people for a life of obedience and relentlessly will not let them presume on the divine generosity. The words of judgement in the text are aimed at those who take that generosity lightly, who want acceptance without change, forgiveness without repentance, grace without discipleship.

Third, the problem with those judged is their failure to do God's will. Their downfall derives not from a faulty theology or an inadequate church life, but from the avoidance of the divine demands. The shocking reality in the text is that these are religiously active people. They have prophesied, exorcised demons and worked miracles. Only, the life of faith is not measured in terms of religious activity (which can be equated with lawlessness), but in terms of obedience and faithfulness.

But how is one to know God's will? The simple parable in 7.24–27 about the two builders takes the reader a step further. The wise builder who constructs his house on a solid foundation is described as one who hears and does 'these words of mine'. The divine will is opened up by the teaching of Jesus, who in three chapters of the Sermon on the Mount has turned out to be the authoritative interpreter of the Law (5.21–48).

But it is not simply a matter of hearing Jesus' words, of knowing God's will. What separates the wise from the foolish builder is the *doing* of 'these words of mine'. The words are not there to be toyed with or debated over or played off one against the other. They are to be obeyed. Or to put it another way, Jesus' words are not really 'heard' until they begin to work within the hearer to transform life and direct behaviour. Only in the changed action of the hearer is it clear that a proper 'hearing' has taken place.

The Sermon is concluded with the report that 'the crowds were astounded at his teaching, for he taught them as one having authority, and not as their scribes'. The scribes could only assume a form of derived authority. 'Rabbi X said such and such. And on the basis of this, I say this further word.' But here was one who needed to cite no precedent, who confronted people with the very presence of God. Jesus' words conveyed an unmediated reality. They announced decisions beyond which there was no appeal.

Furthermore, Jesus' words have the power to accomplish something. He spoke and things happened. 'Your sins are forgiven you.' 'Take up your bed and walk.' 'Stretch out your hand.' The linguistic analysts label it 'performative discourse'. It is language that does not merely describe or command, but that creates and re-creates – and with such an unheard-of ultimacy. In reality, to hear Jesus' words is to be grasped and reshaped by them, to be activated to obey them, to be set by them on a journey of discipleship. Thus, in these unsettling passages of Matthew's story are words of power and hope, speech that effects change, language that mediates the very presence of God. CC

Proper 5

(Sunday between 5 and 11 June inclusive, if after Trinity Sunday)

Genesis 12.1–9 or Hosea 5.15—6.6; Romans 4.13–25; Matthew 9.9–13, 18–26

Genesis 12.1–9

The picture of humanity offered in the opening chapters of Genesis has been universal. Right down to the story of the Tower of Babel (11.1–9) we hear of 'the whole earth'. But that story ends with a picture of 'scattering' and 'confusion', and from now on the focus will be very much concerned with one family: that of Terah's son Abram.

Abram is pictured as a migrant. Starting from 'Ur of the Chaldees' (11.31), he is pictured as travelling via Haran, probably on the Upper Euphrates, to the land of Canaan. In addition to the familiar story of Israel's origins in the exodus from Egypt, we have here another story: that those origins were to be sought in Mesopotamia, in modern-day Iran and Iraq. Perhaps the exile of many of the leading citizens to Babylon in the sixth century BC gave rise to this story; we hear virtually nothing of Abraham and the traditions associated with him in texts from before that date. Certainly the comment in v. 6, speaking of a time when 'the Canaanites were in the land' suggests that the story comes from a much later period.

But whatever the historical problems, the theological significance of these verses is beyond dispute. It arises first from the specific nature of God's promise here. Instead of reflecting on the whole of humanity, our passage focuses upon Abram and his family. A delicate balance was observed by the ancient author, and it needs also to be kept in mind by the modern reader. The blessing is not only upon Abram and his descendants, who are to become a 'great nation'; through him all the other 'families of the earth' are to be blessed. Most religions, Judaism and Christianity not excepted, have been much better at opposing others than at being a means of blessing to them.

The theme of vv. 4–9 is one that has exercised all three religions that honour Abraham (Judaism, Christianity and Islam) ever since. God is pictured as taking him, his family and his possessions, on a kind of tour, setting out the area that is to become their possession. The boundaries envisaged here are more modest than those laid down elsewhere in the Old Testament, but this is pictured as the possession of the 'offspring' of Abraham, a promise that continues to cause deep division, particularly between Judaism and Islam. Whatever the contemporary understanding, much of the remainder of the Abraham story, and in a sense of Genesis as a whole, will be concerned with this theme: first, the birth of the appropriate offspring for Abraham, and then the establishment of the appropriate successor. RC

Hosea 5.15—6.6

This passage is part of a larger section that probably goes from 5.8 to 7.16, and which has a particular setting in Israelite history. In 734/3, the Assyrian King Tiglath-Pileser III invaded Syria and Palestine. Pekah, king of the northern kingdom, Israel, allied himself to Rezon, king of Damascus, an event possibly alluded to in Hosea 5.11, and both kings unsuccessfully pressurized Ahaz of Judah to join them (cf. Isa. 7.1–2). The alliance failed, Damascus and Israel fell to the Assyrians, and Pekah was assassinated by Hoshea (2 Kings 15.30). Ahaz turned for help to Tiglath-Pileser and became his vassal.

In Hosea 5.14 God declares that, at this juncture, he will intervene in judgement against the northern and southern kingdoms, Israel and Judah. The opening words of our passage 'I will return again to my place' continue the imaginery of the preceding verse, in which God likens himself to a lion. The returning to his place is thus the lion going back to his lair after he has destroyed his prey. There he will stay until the people come to their senses, and seek God's face.

Verses 6.1–3 have been commonly regarded as a form of confession used liturgically in the people's worship. This is not necessarily so; the words could just as well be those of the prophet speaking to or on behalf of the people. However, the content is more important than the form, and contains the confident assertion that the God who has torn will heal. Verse 2 has attracted attention because it is the only possible candidate in the Old Testament for the New Testament belief that Christ's rising on the third day was 'according to the scriptures'. Here in Hosea it does not refer to resurrection but is a poetic way of saying that God will surely restore his people, given their present plight.

The closing section (vv. 4–6), God's response to his people's confession, has a touch of exasperation about it, and may even involve questioning the sincerity of the confession. Previous experience indicates the passing nature of the people's repentance; it lasts no longer than a morning cloud or early dew. It thinks that God is best served through the sacrificial cult, and that as long as formal religion is maintained, all will be well. What God actually desires is steadfast love, a term that many have taken to mean loyalty to God's covenant, and knowledge of God. This latter, unusual, phrase is probably best understood in the light of steadfast or loyal covenant love. Knowledge of God is knowledge of the content of the covenant, of the reasons for its existence, and the nature of the God that it reveals. JR

Romans 4.13–25

(See Second Sunday of Lent, pp. 84–5, for comments on vv. 13–17.)

Paul is determined to show that the inheritance promised to Abraham's seed is a promise for all who believe, both Jew and Gentile, a theme which runs like a refrain through much of his letter to the Romans. If the promise is only 'to those who are of the law' (the New American Standard Version's rendering of *hoi ek nomou* in v. 16) then Paul's gospel, he reckons, is empty and void; if the promise given to Abraham is for the Jewish people alone then salvation for the Gentiles could only come by their entering the law-defined identity of Israel. But Abraham, Paul is clear, is the 'father of us all', those of the law and those who share Abraham's faith, the father of both Jews and Gentiles.

Following a formulaic statement about God 'who gives life to the dead and calls into being the things that are not', Paul turns his thoughts to the fact that Abraham and his wife Sarah were as good as dead by the time God's promise was fulfilled in the birth of their son Isaac (the Greek in v. 19 literally refers to the deadness of Sarah's womb). Despite the impossibility seemingly inherent in their physical condition, Abraham was unwavering in his faith in God's promise and ability to fulfil his word (at least according to Paul: Gen 17.17 may suggest otherwise!). This steadfast faith was 'reckoned to him as righteousness' (v. 22; Gen. 15.6). Paul has already explained that this idea of righteousness being 'reckoned' to someone reflects its character as gift and not as wage (Rom. 4.3–5). And here he declares that the words 'it was reckoned to him' were written not just for Abraham's sake but for all believers who follow the pattern of his unwavering faith in the God who brings life from the dead. All such believers are made righteous through faith as the gift of God. There is a clear thematic link running through from v. 17 to vv. 24–25. Abraham entrusted himself to the God who brings life from the dead, and such was indeed in effect what took place, since both Abraham and Sarah were as good as dead when the promised new life was given to them. Likewise, Christians place their faith in this life-giving God, who raised Jesus from death. This leads Paul into the final acclamation, probably an established Christian formulation, concerning the death and resurrection of Christ. This is the first mention of Christ's resurrection since the opening comments in Rom. 1.3–4, and signals a further stage in Paul's extended argument: having considered the 'justification' which comes about through the death of Christ (see Rom. 3.21–26) and shown, by the example of Abraham, that this gift is for all who have faith, Paul now turns more to the new life which is lived 'in Christ' and which, he will later explain (7.6; 8.4f.), is empowered by the Spirit. DH

Matthew 9.9–13, 18–26

In Mark, the tax collector is called Levi son of Alphaeus, and he is not one of the Twelve. Why the earlier evangelist felt it necessary to provide this additional call story for him is unclear, perhaps to symbolize, through this Jewish 'outcast', the eventual opening of the gospel to *Gentile* 'sinners', by the efforts of irregular apostles like Paul. Matthew regularizes the situation by renaming the tax collector as one of the twelve apostles and giving rise, almost by accident, to the theory that Matthew was himself the author of this book. His other change to Mark is a typical appeal to Scripture (v. 13) to support the generous inclusiveness of the gospel.

Hosea 6.6, 'I desire mercy, not sacrifice' became a favourite text among Jews after the fall of the temple, for it showed that one could do the Lord's will, even if sacrifice was no longer possible. But atoning acts of 'mercy' (defined as public prayer, fasting and almsgiving, see Matt. 6.1–18) would not have included forgiveness for blatant law-breakers. However, Jesus, and Matthew no less, believed that not all sin was culpable disobedience; some arose from a sickness of the soul that required the gentle hand of a physician (v. 12). Jesus' joyful table-fellowship, anticipating the Kingdom to come, is contrasted in the next paragraph (omitted from today's reading) with the pious fasting-practice of other groups.

We continue instead with an abbreviated version of two incidents that appear quite a bit later in Mark (5.22–43). In the new arrangement, the theme of spiritual healing from moral uncleanness is complemented by that of physical healing of the ritually unclean, the haemorrhaging woman and the corpse of a dead child. But many of the subtleties of the Marcan narrative have been lost in this précis. There the little girl is very ill (not as here already dead) which creates an atmosphere of urgency and frustration at the delay in reaching her bedside. Her father is an official of the synagogue, but Matthew cannot bring himself to admit that faith could be found in an associate of that institution and calls him simply a ruler. Mark's ironic contrasts between two theories of healing – the almost electric power emanating from the healer, and the power of faith in the person healed – and between forcing the woman out into the open, and yet accommodating Jairus' need for discretion given his official position, are lost in Matthew. And finally, the secrecy theme, so emphatically asserted at Mark 5.43, is simply eliminated by Matthew's concluding comment on the spread of Jesus' reputation.

The main point, however, remains. This great physician is not infected by the dinner-company he keeps nor by the sick who touch him or whom he touches. On the contrary, it is his holiness that is infectious. JM

Proper 6

(Sunday between 12 and 18 June inclusive, if after Trinity Sunday)

Genesis 18.1–15 (21.1–7) or Exodus 19.2–8a; Romans 5.1–8; Matthew 9.35—10.8 (9–23)

Genesis 18.1–15 (21.1–7)

The stories relating to Abraham are essentially a series of separate units, held together by two recurring themes: the land where he was to settle, and the birth of an heir. Earlier, Abraham had been pictured as a wanderer moving from place to place; here he is a settled inhabitant, at the 'oaks of Mamre' near Hebron, the traditional burial-place of Abraham which is still held in reverence by modern Jews and Muslims.

Abraham is said to be visited by 'the Lord' (v. 1). Then quite unexpectedly, verse 2 refers to 'three men'. Christian theology of an earlier period saw in this a prefiguring of the Trinity; more recently and more prosaically scholars have seen the variation as indicative of more than one source. In fact no wholly satisfactory solution to the problem of the variation between one and three, which continues throughout the story, has ever been established.

It will in any case soon become clear that the concern of the visitation is the provision of an heir. Before that topic is raised, however, there are certain proprieties to be observed: proper hospitality is a recurring biblical theme. The preparations described in vv. 6–8 would in fact have taken several hours, but the story is told with such economy that we are tempted to envisage a fast-food setting. The narrator's concern is to stress that due hospitality was observed.

Previous chapters have described the birth of Ishmael to Hagar, taken by Abraham as a sexual partner at his wife's suggestion (ch. 16). But now a different resolution is proposed. Despite her great age Abraham's wife Sarah is to bear a child. This theme – of the birth of a child to a woman whose circumstances should apparently have prevented her from becoming pregnant – is a characteristic biblical one, continued in the New Testament in the story of the birth of John the Baptist. The same motif, differently expressed, underlies the story of the birth of Jesus to a mother who was virgin. The various biblical story-tellers clearly use this as a way of emphasizing God's power in overcoming all human limitations.

In our present episode the announcement of impending birth is almost overshadowed by the wordplay centring on the verb 'to laugh' (vv. 12–15). Such wordplay is characteristic of Hebrew story-telling, but it has an additional function here, in that the verb 'to laugh' is very similar to the name 'Isaac', and so we are prepared for the account of the birth of the son to Sarah, and his naming as 'Isaac' in ch. 21. RC

Exodus 19.2–8a

The portrait of the people delivered from slavery in Egypt in this passage differs, on the face of it, from what has preceded it in the narrative. Previous narratives have told of an ungrateful, complaining people, a people questioning whether God is really with them (Exod. 17.7), and regretting having left Egypt (Exod. 17.3). The divine view of things is that they have been borne on eagles' wings; and the response of the people in v. 8, 'Everything that the Lord has spoken we will do' is remarkable from the narrative point of view, because the content of the covenant and the laws which are to be obeyed have not yet been communicated to them!

This fact, and the order in which the verbs come in Exod. 24.7, have given rise to the charming story in the *Mechilta* (an early Jewish interpretation of Exodus) that when God was looking for a nation to adopt, he approached a number of different peoples, all of which first wanted to know what the laws were that they would have to obey. They were put off by commandments such as 'do not steal', and therefore declined to accept God's invitation. Israel, on the other hand, when approached by God, laid down no prior conditions. 'We will obey, we will hear' they said, i.e. their willingness to obey preceded their knowledge of what it was that they should obey.

The purpose of God's election is that the chosen people should be a 'priestly kingdom' and a 'holy nation'. 'Priestly kingdom' or kingdom of priests, implies that Israel will have a special role in mediating between God and other nations. The election of Israel is therefore the conferment of privilege only in the sense that it is a privileged role of service on behalf of God towards others. Part of the exercise of this priesthood will involve being a holy nation.

There are at least two ways in which being a holy nation can be understood. One way is that of withdrawal, of avoidance of contact with anything and anyone that might be regarded as contaminating. The difficulty with this is that it makes contact with those for whose benefit the priestly role is being exercised, problematic. The other way of holiness lies in direct engagement with, not withdrawal from, that which is degrading. Generalizing, one can say that, in the Old Testament stories, it was only the prophets who recognized that the second way of holiness was the only way in which the people could be a priestly kingdom. JR

Romans 5.1–8

See Third Sunday of Lent, pp. 87–8.

Matthew 9.35—10.8 (9–23)

Matthew has made a number of changes to the order of incidents in the Galilean ministry as compared with Mark's version, in a way that implies that he saw them less as accurate chronicle and more as 'typical scenes' that could, if appropriate, be arranged differently. In particular, the mission of the Twelve is brought forward and made to depend on Jesus' preaching on the kingdom in the Sermon on the

Mount, chs. 5 to 7, and the examples of his works of healing, collected together in chs. 8 and 9. Thus, the Twelve have witnessed in detail the pattern that they are now meant to follow in their own mission. Accordingly, Mark's heavy emphasis on exorcism (6.7) is lightened to include other kinds of healing and preaching.

In two other respects Matthew makes distinctive changes to his source: the scope of the mission is limited to Israel exclusively (10.5, 23) and the work will involve not just the possibility of failure but of hostility to the point of violent persecution (10.17–22). It is clear from 28.16–20 that Matthew was fully committed to the post-Easter mission to non-Jews, Samaritans and Gentiles (an account of which is given in the Acts of the Apostles). So, the restriction imposed here must be a temporary measure. Its purpose was to show that Israel was given the privilege of 'first refusal' of the offer of salvation by her Shepherd-King and his agents. The rejection of the Christian gospel by most Jews, increasingly evident in Matthew's own day, is thus shown to be deliberate and culpable (cf. e.g. 21.32, 41). Matthew, again reflecting the contemporary experience of his community, has moved Mark's prophecy of eschatological persecution (Mark 13.9–13) to this earlier position, in order to underline that it is an ever-present threat. The more the Christ-movement became dominated by Gentile adherents, the more Christian Jews like those in Matthew's church were liable to harassment and accusations of disloyalty to a tradition that was finding its sole focus of identity, after the fall of the temple, in the strict observance of Torah.

The preacher today needs to be aware of these specific circumstances that provoked Matthew's Gospel, particularly with regard to the delicate issue of evangelistic activities targeted towards the Jewish people. The emphasis should fall instead on the positive aspects of the Gospel's understanding of Christian mission: its huge opportunities, 'the harvest is plentiful, the labourers few' (an idealized inversion of the economic realities in first-century Galilee, see 20.6); the way it responds freely to grace freely received (v. 8); its heroic trust in divine providence (v. 9) and its fundamental aim to bring about peace and reconciliation (v. 13). JM

Proper 7

(Sunday between 19 and 25 June inclusive, if after Trinity Sunday)

Genesis 21.8–21 or Jeremiah 20.7–13; Romans 6.1b–11; Matthew 10.24–39

Genesis 21.8–21

The first verses of this chapter describe the fulfilment of the promise made earlier, that Sarah would bear a child despite her advanced years. (It is probably only the latest strand in the Genesis tradition, that known as 'P' because of its probable priestly origin and concern for exact details, that has Sarah as old as 90 when she became a mother, but all traditions are agreed that she was well past the normal age of childbearing. Even here there is some inconsistency, for ch. 20 had told of the attractiveness of Sarah to a foreign ruler, Abimelech.)

However these problems are resolved, the story now goes on to tell of another very real tension. Abraham already has a son: Ishmael, the child of Hagar. Sarah is jealous, and finds an excuse to have the two of them sent away. This much is clear; not at all clear is the nature of Ishmael's offence. In v. 9. the text simply says that he was playing, *metsaheq,* a wordplay with the name of Isaac, *yitshaq.* Speculation has run riot from ancient times as to the nature of his offence, but it must remain speculation. In any case Sarah demands that Hagar and Ishmael be expelled. Abraham is reluctant but finally agrees. This is one of those stories whose point depends on the 'omniscient narrator'. We are told (v. 12) that God encouraged the expulsion of Hagar and Ishmael, but it is simply taken for granted that God could make his will known, and that the message was a genuine one. It is a problem which arises in acute form in ch. 22.

And so Hagar is driven out with her son. The datings given elsewhere (17.25) make Ishmael at least a teenager by this time, but for the purposes of this story he becomes a child again, whom his mother could carry (v. 18), and indeed treat as if he were a defenceless infant (v. 15). The main biblical tradition takes a negative view of Hagar (cf. Gal. 4.24–25), but a number of modern writers have been much more sympathetic, regarding her as a victim of the whims of male domination, both in this story and in the account of her being required to offer her sexual services to Abraham in ch. 16. This is a valuable insight, though it is necessary also to bear in mind that her plight here was due to Sarah's jealousy. The references to Hagar also stress that she was Egyptian (v. 9), another negative indication for the biblical writers. We are reminded of the levels of sexual and ethnic tension which underlie so touching a story. Basic to them all, however, is the conviction that even if Hagar is an alien, rejected by her human master and mistress, God is still with her (vv. 16–19). RC

Jeremiah 20.7–13

This passage is part of the climax of what have sometimes been called the 'confessions of Jeremiah' – poignant and deeply personal utterances of the prophet in the first person singular. That the present passage, with the possible exception of vv. 11–12, represents the actual words of Jeremiah is broadly the conclusion of critical scholarship, although opinions are divided about when, or exactly why, Jeremiah let forth this outburst.

The opening words accuse God of having deceived the prophet, and attempts to soften this on the grounds that God could not be deceitful nor be thought capable of deceit, should be resisted. In fact, the Hebrew words used would justify a paraphrase that said that God treated Jeremiah as a man might behave who first befriended and then raped a young woman. By becoming a prophet of God, Jeremiah has become a laughing stock, and he hates intensely the fact that he is never taken seriously. Verse 8 is not easy to translate, and while the view that 'violence and destruction' is the content of his message is respectable, these words may also refer to Jeremiah's inner turmoil. He finds himself in an impossible situation in which he either speaks and is mocked, or is silent and deeply troubled within himself, because he does not or cannot speak out what he knows to be necessary. A further complication comes in v. 10, where mocking turns to active measures to silence Jeremiah, measures that probably entail providing evidence to the authorities that he is a traitor. The sudden change of tone in vv. 11–13, which also breaks the continuity with vv. 14–18, has led to the view that they are an interpolation.

Does God entice people, overwhelm them and make them a laughing stock and put their lives in danger? If this language is regarded as poetic, or just the way things seem to Jeremiah, it has to be said, on the other side, that these sentiments are not unique in the Old Testament. Moses is made to complain about his burden in leading the people (Exod. 17.4; Num. 11.11–15) and there are psalms in which it is clear that the psalmist's integrity provokes division and active hostility (eg. Pss. 38, 55, 56).

These, and similar passages, take us deep into the mystery of God, his dealings with evil, and the cost of discipleship that may be exacted from humans committed to, and caught up in God's purposes. The life and death of Jesus are assurances, within Christian tradition, that God does not lead his faithful servants further than he is prepared to go himself, and that beyond suffering lies resurrection. JR

Romans 6.1b–11

In Rom. 3.21—5.21, Paul had developed the theme of God's gracious gift of righteousness. Human beings, who are universally under the power of sin, are also the object of God's actions in Jesus Christ, actions that reveal the extent of God's grace. The claim that righteousness comes to humanity as a genuinely 'free gift', to use a contemporary redundancy, inevitably prompts some questions. Surely some in Paul's Roman audience found these remarks offensive, for they blur the cherished distinction between 'good' people, who are thought to have 'earned' God's favour, and those who are understood not to be good, to have 'earned' God's displeasure. If none of Paul's contemporaries accused him of espousing 'cheap grace', that is only because the phrase was not yet familiar. The facetious question he himself imagines someone asking in 6.1b reflects the response that Christians have made throughout the centuries to the radical notion of grace: 'Does that mean that it doesn't matter what I do?'

The answer to that question carries Paul throughout Rom. 6, but it begins with the emphatic 'By no means!' of 6.2. Paul's response has two major foci: the believer's union with Jesus Christ, and the believer's freedom from sin. At first glance, Paul's reference to baptism in 6.3 appears to be abrupt. Not only has he not spoken of baptism earlier in the latter, but this is the only place in which Romans refers to baptism. The reference here is essential, however, since Paul sees baptism as incorporating believers 'into Christ' (see Gal. 3.27) and bringing about the union with Christ that serves as the basis for Paul's comments in vv. 3–11.

Because baptism connects the believer's life with that of Jesus, it also connects the believer with Jesus' death. 'Do you not know that all of us who have been baptized into Christ Jesus were baptized into his death?' (v. 3). However, the death of a believer is not physical; it is instead a death to the 'old self' (v. 6), a death to sin (v. 11). Just as death can no longer have power over Christ, so sin no longer has power over the life of the believer. As is often the case in Paul's letters, the imagery here is physical in nature. The believer, by virtue of baptism, is *moved* from one arena of power to another. Baptism brings about a real and concrete change of location, so that the believer is no longer in the arena that belongs to sin. For that reason, to say that one can be in the arena of grace, the arena of Jesus Christ, and at the same time in the arena of sin is for Paul an impossibility. Paul operates with a theological version of the physical law that the same object cannot occupy two places at once.

Baptism not only incorporates the believer in the death of Christ but also in Christ's resurrection. Here Paul chooses his language with very great care, perhaps because at least some believers at Corinth had concluded that their baptism meant that they had already been resurrected. The first half of v. 5 ('For if we have been united with him in a death like his') leads one to expect that the second half will affirm that 'we have also been united with him in a resurrection like his'. Since the death of the believer is not a physical death, Paul might also refer to a kind of resurrection that has already taken place in the life of the believer. He carefully avoids making that statement, however, by anticipating the resurrection of the believer at some future time. Nevertheless, baptism already inaugurates a new or renewed life (vv. 4, 11). If believers are not yet resurrected, they are already 'alive to God in Christ Jesus' (v. 11). Having been removed from the arena of sin, the power of sin, believers now inhabit the arena that belongs to God.

Within the context of the believer's dying and rising with Christ, Paul refers to slavery and freedom. The one who is crucified in baptism is no longer enslaved to sin but has been given freedom from sin (v. 7). Perhaps because of modern preoccupation with and understanding of freedom as a kind of licence to do whatever one wishes, it is easy to read Paul's discussion of freedom as simply a freedom *from* the power of sin. But looking at the text that follows today's lection, we see that Paul's comments on freedom in 6.15–23 make it clear that Paul has in mind both freedom *from* the power of sin and freedom *for* obedience (see, for example, v. 17). In fact, v. 22 refers to Christians as having been 'freed from sin and enslaved to God'. The notion of enslavement, even enslavement to God, falls harshly on modern ears, but Paul does not operate with a generalized notion of freedom, in which human beings achieve a kind of independence from all powers and authorities. For Paul, humankind is always and inevitably enslaved to something or someone. The decisive question is not whether one is enslaved, but what form that slavery will take. The appropriate answer, in Paul's view, is that slavery to God stems from creation itself. God as the creator and redeemer of humankind rightly claims that humankind for God. At the same time, that profound enslavement means a profound liberation for genuine life and for service. BG

Matthew 10.24–39

Matthew has expanded the sermon on mission with a sequence of sayings, the gist of which is 'Do not let verbal abuse cow you into silence (vv. 24–27), do not be afraid of physical abuse, even to the point of martyrdom (vv. 28–33), and do not let even family ties stand in the way' (vv. 34–39). The passage begins by quoting a traditional proverb against insubordination. In antiquity, slaves could try to get the better of their masters especially, as was sometimes the case, if they were more intelligent and better educated, just as pupils regularly try to outshine their teachers. Matthew twists the proverb ironically (contrast Luke 6.40): 'If they have abused the master of the house, the household servants can only expect the same treatment.' The accusation against Jesus that he was the devil incarnate, Beelzebul (meaning literally, 'lord of the house'), has already figured at Matt. 9.34 and will surface again at 12.24, 27; no doubt it represents contemporary abuse suffered by Matthew's community. The saying in vv. 26–27 is similar to Mark 4.22 and almost identical with Luke 12.2 but interpreted differently in each case. Mark takes it to refer to the ultimately revelatory purpose of Jesus' riddling parables; Luke of the public disclosure of guilty secrets whispered in the dark; but for Matthew it is a call to fearless promulgation of the message of Jesus.

With regard to the next saying (v. 28) there is some dispute among interpreters as to whether 'the one who has power to destroy both body and soul in hell' is God or the devil. The gap between these views is not as wide as it might first appear. If the one with the power to destroy body and soul in the fires of hell is the Evil One from whom one is to pray for deliverance (6.13), then it is only at the bidding of the Lord of heaven that he could carry out a sentence to which he is doomed himself (25.41). The fatherly providence of God was illustrated at 6.25 in his care even for birds (Luke specifies ravens). Here the same image reappears in a darker colouring: sparrows are cheap (even cheaper in Luke 12.6) but the life of his saints is infinitely precious to God. The one whom the missionary risks life and limb to confess on earth will be their defender and advocate in heaven (v. 33).

Division within families as a result of leaving the synagogue and joining the Church (see already 10.21) is represented graphically as the sword which Jesus has come to wield (cf. Eph. 6.17). True peace (cf. Matt. 5.9) is not the cowardice of silent acquiescence, but the courage that abandons everything to the service of self-denying love (v. 39; see further the doublet of this saying at Matt. 16.24–25, Proper 17). JM

14

Proper 8

(Sunday between 26 June and 2 July inclusive)

Genesis 22.1–14 or Jeremiah 28.5–9; Romans 6.12–23; Matthew 10.40–42

Genesis 22.1–14

This is the story of the *aqedah*, the 'binding' of Isaac, and at several levels it is one of the most powerful passages within the whole Bible. In one sense it is, or should be, a cause of profound difficulty. What would the present-day media make of a story of a father who set out to kill his son on the grounds that he had been commanded by God to do so? Religious believers in both the Jewish and the Christian tradition seem sometimes not to realize how utterly offensive this story would be in 'real-life' terms. It is a story told to illustrate a particular set of beliefs, and must be treated as such.

Let us first consider the character of the story. Perhaps the first thing to strike us is the extraordinary economy with which it is told. No mention is made of Sarah, Isaac's mother; no picture is given of any agonizing self-doubt on the part of Abraham. He hears a call which he takes to be from God, and without a word and without delay ('early in the morning') he obeys. He realizes that the 'young men' must suspect nothing of what is to take place, and so he deliberately misleads them ('we will come back to you'), as of course he also misleads his son ('God will provide the lamb'). Isaac is old enough and strong enough to carry the wood of the burnt offering to a place 'far away', yet he does nothing to resist his father's murderous intentions.

In these ways the story retains its intensely dramatic qualities. But it is clearly not handed down simply as a story; it has a message to convey, of an immensely difficult kind. It is a demand that God's perceived requirements must be given an absolute priority over and above the normal demands of other human beings, even of one's own family. There is a sense, of course, in which the Christian story of the death of Jesus as being part of God's plan offers a parallel, but the tension is there eased because there were human agents who crucified Jesus. Here the potential killer is the young man's own father, who has been told that the victim is to be the one through whom his own line is to continue. (We recall that Abraham has sent away his other son, Ishmael, in the previous chapter, and we have no suspicion yet that Abraham is to have several more children [Gen. 25.1–2].) Here is a word picture that envisages that God's demands take such precedence that it would be wrong to 'withhold your son, your only son' if that was the sacrifice demanded.

Later tradition has made much of this story. Apart from the Christian parallel already noted, the link between the otherwise unknown 'land of Moriah' and the site of the Jerusalem temple is hinted at later in the Old Testament (2 Chron. 3.1), and has played an important part in the traditions of both Judaism and Islam. The present-day visitor to Jerusalem is still likely to be assured that the 'rock' that gives its name to the Dome of the Rock is the place where Abraham all but sacrificed his son: Muslims believe that the son was probably Ishmael. RC

Jeremiah 28.5–9

This passage is an extract from a longer story in which Jeremiah confronts another prophet, Hananiah. The year given in 28.1 is 597 BC, and it follows the first Babylonian capture of Jerusalem that same year, the exiling of King Jehoiachin and the removal of the temple vessels to Babylon. Jeremiah had been told by God to make a yoke and to wear it on his neck as a sign that nations should serve Nebuchadnezzar, the king of Babylon (Jeremiah 27.1–15). In his speech in ch. 27 Jeremiah also accuses the prophets who are saying that it will not be necessary to serve the king of Babylon, of being false prophets.

In the words that immediately precede the set passage, the prophet Hananiah proclaims that he has broken the yoke of the king of Babylon and that within two years the exiled king, the other exiles and the temple vessels will be returned to Jerusalem. Later in the story, Hananiah breaks the yoke that Jeremiah is wearing, in an act of prophetic symbolism (vv. 10–11).

The passage set records Jeremiah's response to Hananiah's confident prediction that everything will be restored in two years' time. The first question that has to be answered is whether Jeremiah's words 'may the Lord do so' are ironic or sincere. It is not easy to decide, but it can be presumed that Jeremiah was not in favour of bad news for its own sake, especially as his own pessimistic message caused people to mock him (cf. Jer. 20.7). Further, nowhere in this passage does he accuse Hananiah of being a false prophet. That comes later, some time after the present action (cf. vv. 12–17).

The passage thus presents us with two prophets, both of whom sincerely believe that they have a true word from God. In defence of his words, Jeremiah appeals to the past experience of prophets, to the fact that there has traditionally been a message of judgement exercised through war, famine and pestilence. He does not appear to rule out the possibility that Hananiah may be right and that he himself may be wrong. He simply asserts that the genuineness of the prophet who prophesies peace will be known by results.

The message of this passage, that the words of the true prophets come true, is necessarily disappointing, and of no help to believers today who may encounter modern-day prophets and their forecasts. The phenomenon of prophets giving contradictory messages was also disturbing in Old Testament times. Perhaps it was modesty that prevented Jeremiah from proposing a more convincing criterion for distinguishing true and false prophets, namely, that of personal gain or loss. Whatever may be said of Hananiah, it is indisputable that it cost Jeremiah personal anguish, and abuse and threats against his person, to speak what he did in the name of God. JR

Romans 6.12–23

When charting the sometimes troubled waters of Paul's argumentation, preachers and teachers often take their bearings from his use of opposites. Already in Romans, Paul has juxtaposed the figure of Adam with that of Christ (ch. 5). In Rom. 8, he will juxtapose life in the Spirit with life in the flesh. In this lection, three such pairs come into play: sin versus righteousness (or sin versus God), freedom versus slavery, and wages versus gifts.

As Paul sets in opposition sin and righteousness (or sin and God), he continues the argument from the earlier part of the chapter (see the discussion on Proper 7) about Christian freedom from sin. Readers who persist in the notion that sin means failing to do something 'good' or the commission of something 'bad' will find themselves utterly bewildered by Paul's talk about presenting oneself 'to sin' (v. 13) and the dominion of sin (v. 14). Sin cannot, at least in the Pauline letters, be equated with transgression or trespass.

By sharp contrast, Paul understands sin as a realm of power, more than capable of ensnaring and enslaving human beings. As is clear when he anthropomorphizes sin in Rom. 6—7, Paul views sin as virtually a personal power, set up in competition with the power of God. To speak of sin's exercising 'dominion in your mortal bodies' (v. 12), of being 'slaves of sin' (v. 17), is to understand sin as a force of vast proportions. To speak of being freed from sin, then, does not conjure up an individual's moral victory over the inclination to do bad things. Freedom from sin, instead, is being liberated from a real and dangerous force.

The large canvas on which Paul paints Rom. 6 contains portraits of two competing powers, God and sin. Human beings exist in a relationship of freedom and enslavement to those powers. With the second pair of opposites, this dynamic comes into view. Human beings are slaves of either God or sin, and human beings are free from either God (or the demands of righteousness, which stem from God) or sin. Verses 17 and 18 set out this assumption, as Paul gives thanks for the move of Roman Christians from slavery to sin toward obedience 'from the heart to the form of teaching to which you were entrusted', having become 'slaves of righteousness'.

With the legacy of a century of depth psychology, contemporary readers may rush to protest Paul's thought here. His assumption that one is *either* under the power of sin or free from sin, *either* obedient to righteousness or disobedient, strikes modern sensibilities as wildly naive. Again, it is necessary to recall that Paul has his eye on a competition of what we might call superpowers, God and sin. The topic here is not spiritual growth or personal development, but the power of the gospel of Jesus Christ over against the power of sin.

What is at stake for human beings comes into view with the third pair of opposites, which enters the lection only at the very end. If it is true, as Paul assumes, that every human being is free from something and every human being is enslaved to something, then one might ask whether it actually matters whether one is freed from sin. No absolute freedom lies around the corner. No autonomous life has been promised. With the third pair of opposites, however, Paul makes it quite clear that this is not a matter of indifference.

'For the wages of sin is death, but the free gift of God is eternal life in Christ Jesus our Lord' (v. 23). A first reading of this statement might anticipate that Paul would juxtapose the 'wages' of sin with the 'wages' of God. Instead, this clinching assertion actually transforms the language of 'wage' into 'gift'. Sin does pay out a wage to its slaves, but the wage is death itself. God, however, pays no wages. Instead, God grants the gift of life. That is to say, no one earns anything from this obedience.

For many contemporary readers, Paul's use of slavery language will constitute a profound offence. Particularly in contexts where systems of human slavery lie in the not sufficiently distant past, every use of the terminology risks anger and pain. Although the workings of the slave systems of Greece and Rome were different from those known in more recent times, they constituted a real and present factor in the regions of Paul's mission (as his letter to Philemon makes clear). It is presumably because Paul knows what slavery is that he elects such a forceful way of insisting that all human beings are, rightfully, slaves of God who made them.

Equally offensive to modern sensibilities will be Paul's insistence that God pays no wages (v. 23). Even if no one utters a protest or enters into dispute with the text, readers of Paul again and again manage to diminish the force of his argument here. The perennial desire to believe that obedience to God somehow achieves salvation or deserves the reward of eternal life successfully silences the text. And yet it stands: eternal life is God's free gift! BG

Matthew 10.40–42

For three Sundays the lectionary has directed us to Jesus' missionary charge to the Twelve in Matt. 9—10. Unlike Luke, Matthew makes no mention of the actual mission itself, whether the Twelve ever went or what their mission experience was. The effect of the omission is to highlight the speech as a direct address to the readers. The audience is left not so much with a historical report of what occurred in the ministry of Jesus as with a description of its own ministry. Many of the features of the charge fit better a later period in the first century (see 10.17–23). The warnings and promises of the text, then, are warnings and promises to those long after the time of the Twelve who find themselves commissioned by 10.7–8 and who discover that the announcement of the dawn of a new age is forever risky business.

The final paragraph (10.40–42) should not in fact be separated from the rest of the speech. In a sense it responds to the sharp words of vv. 34–39 and the recognition that the gospel can and does split families, setting one member over against another. These were no less harsh words in the first century than they are today. What is offered, however, is a more binding relationship than even the natural family.

In the carrying out of their mission, the disciples are rejected by some but received by others. In the welcoming process, a connection is forged between hosts ('whoever welcomes you'), disciples, Jesus ('me'), and God ('the one who sent me'). By means of the principle of identification, the four parties are joined in a profound solidarity.

A new family is created of those who faithfully carry out the mission and those who openly receive the mission, and a fellowship is established that includes the divine presence. The message is not unlike that of Matt. 12.46–50, where Jesus relativizes the natural family relations and establishes a new family bound together by a common commitment to do God's will.

The new family does not *automatically* emerge to replace the support of the old family ties. It is born in the context of mission. The community 'on the road' is the community needing to be welcomed and needing to receive a cup of cold water. They are the ones bonded together with the divine presence.

But attention in the text is focused not only on those bearing the message but also on those who receive the messengers. In connection with them, the word 'reward' is used three times in today's paragraph. We are not told the nature of the reward. Maybe hospitality to God's messengers carries its own reward; maybe the new fellowship that emerges is the reward. In any case, the notion of reward suggests that the act of welcoming does not go unnoticed by God. God is intimately involved in the mission, both in sustaining the messengers (10.31) and in rewarding those showing hospitality. cc

15

Proper 9

(Sunday between 3 and 9 July inclusive)

Genesis 24.34–38, 42–49, 58–67 or Zechariah 9.9–12; Romans 7.15–25a;
Matthew 11.16–19, 25–30

Genesis 24.34–38, 42–49, 58–67

The constraints of length in church services, and perhaps a general diminution in our span of attention, mean that it is impossible to read the whole of Gen. 24 in the normal course, but those who have opportunity to do so should certainly be encouraged to read and savour the whole chapter. Its repetitions and its gentle unfolding of the charming plot make it one of the narrative high points of the Bible. If anyone can still recall the 1662 Book of Common Prayer Marriage Service, it may be remembered that Isaac and Rebekah were there held up as the model couple for those newly married to obey (though Gen. 27 will show the attentive reader that everything was not always ideal in that household).

The story as a whole is an example of what has been described as a 'type-scene' of a kind found with minor variations in different parts of the Bible. The hero (or, as here, his representative), away from his homeland, meets one or more young women drawing water at a well. His credentials are established either by a divine message (as here) or by some act of heroism (as, for example, Moses, in Exod. 2). Hospitality is offered, and the upshot is the marriage of the hero and one of the young women who had been drawing water. Such a story is told of Jacob in Gen. 29, of Moses, and of Jesus in John 4, though with important variations: most obviously, that story has no marriage theme.

Here the concern for an appropriate marriage is an important issue. Throughout the Old Testament, as in many religious traditions to this day, it is an issue of central significance that marriages should be between appropriate partners. The claim that a particular community is a specially chosen one means that there is a threat if its members 'marry out', and thereby weaken the cohesion of the community. Some parts of the Old Testament address that issue in a very unattractive way (e.g. the harsh condemnation of mixed marriages in Ezra and Nehemiah); here the same issue is addressed, though in a much more positive way. It is possible that this story comes from a time not far removed from that of Ezra and Nehemiah; details such as the domestication of the camel, taken for granted throughout the narrative (e.g. vv. 61–64) suggest that the story reached its final shape at a date much later than the events it purports to describe. We are reminded once again of the tradition that the community of the Second Temple, or 'post-exilic', period, claimed to have come, like Abraham, from Mesopotamia. RC

Zechariah 9.9–12

Zechariah 9.9 is probably the best-known verse in the book of Zechariah on account of it being cited in Matt. 21.5 and John 12.15 in connection with Jesus' triumphal entry into Jerusalem. Who the speaker is depends on whether the Hebrew 'I will cut off' or the Greek 'He will cut off' (so NRSV) is read at the beginning of v. 10. If the Hebrew is followed, the speaker is God; if the Greek, it is a prophet or, possibly, a chorus. This decision also affects the understanding of the role of the coming king. The Hebrew 'I' implies that it is God who will make wars to cease, thus establishing a peaceful world over which the king will then rule. The Greek 'he' means that the king will first defeat all enemies and then preside over the peace. Which of these views is correct further depends on the translation of the words rendered as 'triumphant and victorious' by the NRSV in v. 9. The first word, *tsaddiq* means 'just' or 'righteous' and is rendered in this way by the AV, RV and NIV. The second word, literally 'saved', is rendered as 'having salvation' by AV and RV.

It is difficult to decide which line to follow and best to be aware of the two possibilities. What is clear from the passage is that at a time when Jerusalem has no king, a future king is promised, the language undoubtedly drawing upon hints in the Old Testament about coronation rituals (see 1 Kings 1.33, where Solomon is made to ride on David's mule). However, what is envisaged is not just a king for Jerusalem, nor a renewal or enlargement of David's empire. The authority of the king will extend 'to the ends of the earth', and its purpose will be to put into effect the peace and justice that only God can bestow.

Verses 11–12 are joined to the two preceding verses by the second person feminine singular personal pronoun 'you', referring to 'daughter of Jerusalem' (v. 9). 'The blood of my covenant with you' (Hebrew: the blood of your [feminine singular] covenant) may be an allusion to the covenant ceremony recorded in Exod. 24.3–8, or to Israelites who laid down their lives fighting on behalf of the covenant people; or the reference may be to the sufferings of the covenant community in the exile. In any case, the point is that God is faithful to the people of the covenant made with him, and will set their prisoners free and deliver the people from their enemies. JR

Romans 7.15–25a

If preaching from texts that are unfamiliar and alien to congregations has its difficulties, preaching from highly familiar passages such as this one offers its own challenges. A survey of the great variety of interpretations of this passage, both scholarly and popular, would reveal that it functions for readers much like a Rorschach test: readers see in it what they bring to it. The reasons for this vast array of interpretations lie ready to hand. On the one hand, the passage itself contains a number of problems that make for conflicting readings of it: the identity of the speaker (the 'I') of the passage, Paul's varying uses of the term 'law', the relationship between the passage and the larger context. On the other hand, the passage stimulates a powerful sense of identification among many readers, and that sense of identification prompts interpretations that are highly individualistic.

Given this situation, clarity about Paul's intention will probably remain elusive. Is Paul speaking autobiographically, or is the 'I' here the equivalent of 'one', as seems to be the case in 1 Cor. 13? Does he refer to the period of his life prior to his own conversion, the time of his conversion, his life as a Christian, the time in human history before the coming of Jesus Christ? In all likelihood the answers to these questions will remain obscure, although the context makes it unlikely that the 'I' refers simply to Paul's own personal experience. Even if he includes himself within the 'I', he refers to the experience of humankind.

Whatever the concrete autobiographical or historical details of the situation Paul has in mind, the passage stems from his prior remarks about the relationship between the Law and sin. Given Paul's comments about the Law earlier in this letter, readers or hearers of Paul's letter might conclude that the Law itself is sinful (7.4). Paul strenuously objects to this possible conclusion, but he does concede that sin uses the Law. Sin is capable of 'seizing an opportunity in the commandment' (7.8, 11). Even if the Law is 'holy and just and good', sin is nevertheless able to employ that Law to bring about its own evil ends.

Taking that observation as a starting point, Paul's primary concern in vv. 14–15 comes into view (though the actual lection text does not begin until v. 15). If sin can use God's Law, twisting even God's Law so that it leads to death, then sin's power can surely prevail over any human being, even one whose intentions and motives are good. If sin can use the Law, which is spiritual, sin can even more readily invade the human being (7.14). The conflict Paul described in vv. 15–20 is a fundamental human conflict between willing and doing. Despite every good intention, every healthy resolution, every excellent desire, human beings find that they do not follow through on those plans: 'I can will what is right, but I cannot do it.' This state results, in Paul's analysis, not from some defect of character or some psychological burden, but from the omnipresence of sin ('sin that dwells within me', v. 20).

This description pertains not simply to all humanity, in that all have failed to acknowledge the existence and power of God (see e.g. Rom. 1.21), but especially to those who desire the good. Paul has in view here the religious person, the responsible member of the human community, the one who wants to be a contributing member of society. Despite every attempt to accomplish good for others and for self, the efforts of the religious person come to nothing. Ernst Käsemann succinctly summarized Paul's point in this passage: 'What a person wants is salvation. What he creates is disaster' (*Commentary on Romans*; Grand Rapids: Wm. B. Eerdmans Publishing Co., 1980, p. 203). Sin's power is such that it corrupts even the best instincts of the most faithful and religious person.

In contemporary Christianity, proclaiming this passage as a profound psychological insight would be relatively innocuous and even comforting ('How marvellous that Paul understood our problems!'). Acknowledging the power of sin to corrupt human life, even religious human life, will prove to be more difficult – even offensive. Few faithful Christians relish the thought that their resolve to be good people nevertheless leads them into sin. To complicate matters further, as has often been pointed out, the topic of sin is itself offensive. Failures and shortcomings may be attributed to psychological problems or social contexts, but seldom if ever to the power of sin. Nevertheless, Romans relentlessly insists, not only in this passage but throughout the letter, that sin powerfully invades and controls human existence.

What is the remedy for this problem, if not more human resolve to do good, more human will? God has acted in Jesus Christ to free humanity from the power of sin. For those who are in Christ, there is 'no condemnation' (8.1). No human initiative, no matter how good or forceful, can overcome the power of sin, but only God, who has already acted in Jesus Christ. That initiative of God's enables human beings to live free of the paralysing conflict Paul describes in Rom. 7, because they are confident that God has already acted to deliver them. They know that God can take their motives and actions, however flawed, and turn them into service of the good. BG

Matthew 11.16–19, 25–30

The opening parable rounds off the preceding section (11.2–15), which has explained the relation between Jesus and John the Baptist. Both the forerunner and the one to come will share the same fate as the prophets (v. 12f.); both are criticized, but for different reasons, the one as a crazy ascetic, the other as a self-indulgent libertine. Such silly accusations cancel each other out: they are typical of children squabbling in the marketplace because they cannot agree whether to play funerals (with John, and mourn over their sins) or to play weddings (with Jesus, and celebrate the dawning kingdom). Both, of course, are necessary and complementary, for wisdom is justified by deeds not words (v. 19).

After the intervening verses, which continue to denounce unresponsive Israel (vv. 20–24), the wisdom theme is taken one stage further. In this 'cry of jubilation', Jesus gives thanks for those who are childlike in the other sense – sincere and honest, not 'too clever by half' like the scribes. To such is imparted the insight that Jesus is the perfect child of God ('like Father like Son'), uniquely able to reveal him to others. The lofty christology here should be compared with that of Paul (e.g. 2 Cor. 4.6) and John (1.1–18; 17.1–5). Just as Jewish spirituality feeds on the study of Scripture as a book of divine wisdom, so Matthew's Jewish-Christian spirituality feeds on communion with the one in whom Wisdom is at last embodied in human form (see Ecclus 24.19–22 and especially 51.23–27).

Luke (see 10.21–22) does not include the final appeal to those who are 'heavy laden', but it is particularly important for Matthew. Christian discipleship is not a watered-down version of Judaism; the demand for righteousness (cf. 5.20) is even greater (contrast 23.4). But anyone who is willing to go back to school with Wisdom will find that contemplation of the beauty of goodness can turn a heavy demand into an easy yoke and a light burden, one that produces inward and lasting peace. Matthew 11.28–30, with its benign encouragement and Christ-centred vision, is the other side of Matthew's strict and stern face.

This passage is pivotal for understanding the Gospel as a whole. It parallels and anticipates its climax (28.16–20). Thus, 'All things have been handed over to me' cf. 'All authority has been given to me' (28.18); 'Come to me' cf. 'Go, therefore'; 'and learn from me' cf. 'and make disciples' (28.19). For Matthew, the gospel of salvation through the death and resurrection of Christ cannot be separated from patient learning and faithful obedience to the wisdom of Jesus. JM

16

Proper 10

(Sunday between 10 and 16 July inclusive)

Genesis 25.19–34 or Isaiah 55.10–13; Romans 8.1–11; Matthew 13.1–9, 18–23

Genesis 25.19–34

The concern for the succession to Abraham runs through much of Genesis. Abraham's own death had been described earlier in this chapter (25.8–11), and now the question arises: Who will succeed his son Isaac? Isaac himself is a curiously shadowy figure, pictured as a victim (ch. 22), or a potential bridegroom who has his wife chosen for him (ch. 24), or as a pathetic old man (ch. 27). Whereas the story of Isaac's birth had featured Abraham rather than Sarah, here Rebekah is much more the centre of attention.

Two themes characteristic of biblical succession stories emerge: the expected mother's barrenness (v. 21), and then when that is overcome, the birth of twins, seen as potential rivals. This rivalry between Esau and Jacob dominates the latter part of this chapter, and emerges again in the well-known story in ch. 27. It begins before the babies are even born; the motif of the younger child being dominant runs through Genesis from the story of Cain and Abel (ch. 4) onwards.

The two children are given names which reflect a love of wordplay, with Esau being characterized as 'red' (a wordplay not explained until v. 30), and Jacob's name being linked with a story involving the grasping of his brother's heel (*'eqeb*).

Rivalry between them continues as they grow up, and now another element is introduced: Esau is given another name, Edom, and thus comes to be regarded as the ancestor of the Edomites, a people who were Israel's neighbours. A not very attractive feature of the Abraham stories is the way in which discreditable origins are attributed to neighbouring people; 19.30–38 tells an insulting story about the origins of Moab and Ammon. Esau is here pictured as rejecting his birthright, the privilege of the older brother, and this contempt for the proprieties becomes a cause for God's 'hatred' in later biblical tradition: Mal. 1.2–5, where it is possible that rivalry between Judah and Edom continues, and twice in the New Testament, where the story is given wide-ranging application (Rom. 9.13; Heb. 12.16–17).

One other point should perhaps be made about these stories, which is applicable still more to the deception of Isaac in ch. 27. They cannot be made the basis for ethics. They reflect the delight of a people who regarded themselves as the underdogs (symbolized by being the younger), in the cunning their ancestor had shown in gaining the prize – and thereby establishing that he was the one favoured by God – despite all disadvantages. RC

Isaiah 55.10–13

These verses bring to a conclusion that part of Isaiah that began with ch. 40, and the idea of the active word of God forms a narrative arch between 40.8 and 55.11. Whether the Israelites knew that rain and snow return to the atmosphere in the form of vapour is unlikely. The Old Testament view of these things is that God has storehouses of snow and hail (cf. Job 38.22) and that water is kept in the heavens in waterskins (Job 38.37). Presumably these were not thought of as unlimited supplies; rather, such things as rain and snow were divine messengers that were sent to do specific tasks before returning to report to God. God's word is then to be seen in these terms.

What is God's word and how does it return to him? The prophets employed a mode of speaking that has been called the 'messenger formula', which was used when kings sent messages to each other. The king would speak his message in the presence of an ambassador, and the latter would then travel to the court of the king for whom the message was intended, and repeat the message verbatim. When prophets used the formula 'thus says the Lord' they were implying that they were uttering a message that they had heard God speak. This may help us to make sense of the mechanics of vv. 10–11. Their main point is that all the words that have been spoken in chs. 40—55 will be fulfilled as surely as rain and snow help plants to grow.

The final verses (12–13) envisage the return of exiles from Babylon to Jerusalem towards the end of the sixth century BC. The ending of exile has been the main preoccupation of these chapters since 40.2. It has been recognized, however, that the prophet thought of the ending of exile and the return as an event that would transform the created order. Already in 40.3–5 a 'coming' of God is envisaged that will fill valleys and remove mountains, and in 55.12–13 it is promised the earth will no longer produce thorns and briars. The language about mountains and hills bursting into song is similar to that in Ps. 98.8, where it is God's coming to judge the world that is being celebrated.

God's promises in Isa. 40—55 were fulfilled in the sense that the power of Babylon was broken and the exiles were free to return home. The transformation of the created order did not take place, and subsequent prophecy had to wrestle with the fact that life in the restored community often fell well below the hope that the return had excited. JB

Romans 8.1–11

Certain portions of Rom. 8 are among the most familiar parts of Paul's letters. Verses 31–39 appear often in funeral liturgies, where they serve as an appropriate reminder of the faithfulness of God to God's people. Less happily, v. 28 has a tendency to appear when Christians attempt to make sense of tragic events. Three consecutive readings covering all of this chapter give the preacher an opportunity to show the way in which these passages serve a larger argument.

This first lection begins by recalling some major themes of the earlier sections of

Romans. Accustomed to written texts, we forget that the earliest audience for this letter would have *heard* it read. Without the printing press, much less the techniques of photocopying, Christians could not rely on individual copies of texts. Paul had to provide ways in which listeners could follow what he was saying. Thus, the chapter begins by recalling God's action in Jesus Christ, an action that means that there is no condemnation for those who are in Christ Jesus. God has done what human beings could not do because of their sinful state (see Rom. 3.21–31).

Even as Paul reviews what he has said earlier in the letter, he also introduces some new terms that will play a prominent role in this discussion. He talks about two kinds of people, those who 'live according to the flesh' and those who 'live according to the Spirit'. The words 'flesh' and 'Spirit' may cause us to think that Paul is talking about two different parts of a human being – the flesh, the stuff that covers up your bones and the spirit, an unseen part that has to do with feeling and perceiving.

In this particular text, however, when he talks about living 'according to the flesh' and living 'according to the Spirit' Paul juxtaposes not two parts of the person but *two ways of living*. As in Rom. 6 and elsewhere, Paul describes the Christian situation by means of opposing powers or arenas of power. In Rom. 8.1–17 he opposes the Spirit of God to flesh. People either walk 'according to the flesh' or 'according to the Spirit'. If their minds are 'set . . . on the flesh', they are set on 'death'. Believers are not 'in the flesh', but 'in the Spirit'. Notice that one cannot be in both arenas at the same time; neither can both Spirit and flesh influence a person. These are mutually exclusive categories.

Despite the first impression this flesh-Spirit opposition leaves, Paul is not simply invoking a moral dualism between the flesh as evil and the Spirit as good. The dualism reflected in this passage is cosmic or transcendent rather than moral, since the realm of the flesh refers to the realm ruled by sin, while the realm of the Spirit refers to the realm ruled by God. In this passage, Paul employs the terms 'flesh' and 'Spirit' in a metonymy, a figure of speech in which one feature of an entity serves to refer to the entire entity (e.g. 'counting heads' for counting persons, 'the hand of God' for God). 'Flesh' then refers to the rule of sin, in which human flesh, while in itself neutral rather than evil, is held hostage and is subject to corruption (along with the rest of creation). 'Spirit', by contrast, refers to the realm ruled by God, in which the Spirit of God exerts its powerful role.

'Liv[ing] according to the flesh', then, does not necessarily mean living a life of gluttony, or indolence, or vanity. It means living in a way that is shaped by, controlled by, the values and standards of the world in rebellion against God. What Paul refers to here is not a list of bad behaviours but what we would call a 'mindset' – a mindset that daily makes its way in the world apart from its creator. Paul contrasts this way of living with living 'according to the Spirit'. Paul's comments about this manner of living are a bit elusive. Here he simply says that living according to the Spirit is to have one's mind set on the Spirit; it is life and peace.

Having read this contrast between living in the Spirit and living in the flesh, the immediate response of many will be to look at ourselves and around at our neighbours: Who stands where? We are pleased to find ourselves living in the Spirit, although we may have some concerns about various of our friends and neighbours. And we begin to congratulate ourselves on our good judgement. Or we may simply conclude that Paul wants us to choose: the proverbial fork in the road is before us. Which path will we select?

Reading v. 11 should correct this response: 'If the Spirit of him who raised Jesus from the dead dwells in you, he who raised Jesus from the dead will give life to your mortal bodies also through his Spirit that dwells in you.' By a simple reassertion of the Easter event, Paul teaches us a most important lesson. First, the Spirit does not belong to human beings. The Spirit is always God's Spirit, never a human possession. Second, God *gives* the Spirit. If even Jesus did not raise himself from the dead but was raised by the Spirit of God, then human beings cannot earn the Spirit. We cannot choose or obtain the Spirit. The Spirit is always and forever a gift of the one sovereign and powerful God. BG

Matthew 13.1–9, 18–23

The third great discourse in Matthew's Gospel consists entirely of parables of the kingdom, collected from Mark (the sower, and the mustard seed), traditions shared with Luke (the leaven, the treasure and the pearl) and his own special sources (the wheat and the weeds). They put equal emphasis on two main themes: mission (looking back to ch. 10) and judgement (looking forward to chs. 24—25).

In the section omitted from this reading (vv. 10–17), Matthew expands and slightly changes Mark's explanation for Jesus teaching in this way. He adds an explicit citation from Isa. 6.9–10 to show that the Messiah, longed for by prophets and the righteous (v. 17), was bound to teach in parables when he came (cf. also 13.35 from Ps. 78.2). But while Mark had implied that the crowds' failure to understand the parables was a foreordained and temporary condition, soon to be shared by the disciples themselves (cf. e.g. Mark. 6.52; 8.17), for Matthew incomprehension of the obvious truth of the message is a moral fault (see v. 19) of which the disciples are not guilty (13.51).

The parable of the sower is allegorized with reference to different kinds of reaction to the preaching of the gospel. The language and the situation described fit closely the actual experience of the early Church. Flat rejection and almost satanic hostility on the part of some; short-lived enthusiasm from others that melts away as they count the cost of discipleship – the risk of harassment and violence and the demand on the purse to support poorer members of the community. But alongside these types of failure, success is also promised. Mark had described this as (4.9) 'thirtyfold, sixtyfold, a hundredfold', symbolizing the extraordinary and rapid expansion of the mission to the Gentiles. Matthew has reversed the order for some reason, perhaps because he is thinking more of the different levels of (moral) fruitfulness on the part of individual members of the community, some of whom are 100 per cent perfect (cf. 19.11, 21) while others need to be encouraged to try harder.

The scholarly consensus is that Jesus' parables were unlikely to have been intended as allegories that could be understood only after such decoding. They were probably more immediately accessible to his hearers. If so, the strange emphasis on the (surely avoidable) loss of valuable seed corn in this story requires some explanation. On the assumption that Jesus told this parable in some form and that it should be interpreted naturalistically with all traces of secondary meaning discarded, then it would become a story about a farmer of rare incompetence, who nevertheless brings in a bumper crop, thus confronting the audience with a challenge similar to that at Matt. 20.15.'Do you begrudge the unmerited generosity of God?' JM

17

Proper 11

(Sunday between 17 and 23 July inclusive)

*Genesis 28.10–19a or Wisdom of Solomon 12.13, 16–19 or Isaiah 44.6–8; Romans 8.12–25;
Matthew 13.24–30, 36–43*

Genesis 28.10–19a

The stories relating to Abraham are essentially separate episodes, though concerned
with connected themes. The main body of material relating to Jacob in Gen. 28—
35, however, is more closely integrated. Its basic concern is the relation between
Jacob and those around him, especially his twin brother Esau and his uncle Laban.
Jacob was pictured as the forefather of the later nation Israel, a name which he was
himself to be given, and so relations between Israel and its neighbours were an
important concern.

The setting of the present passage is Jacob's flight from Esau to seek hospitality
(and, hopefully, a wife) from Laban's family, pictured as living at Haran in Mesopotamia. The accounts of both his outward journey (this episode) and his return (ch.
32) offer descriptions of an important encounter with the divine. Departure from
and entry into the holy land represent important rites of passage.

Here, then, we have an account of a theophany, a manifestation of God to his
worshipper, with a particular message. Stories of this kind are frequently used by
the biblical writers to picture encounters with the divine; we may think of Moses at
the burning bush (Exod. 3) and Isaiah's vision (Isa. 6), as well of course as the
accounts of Jesus' transfiguration (Mark 9) and Paul's 'Damascus Road' experience
(Acts 9) in the New Testament. The appropriate response is one of godly fear and
awe, and both of these are found here (v. 17). A slightly unusual feature of this
story is that the name of the place where it happened is provided: Bethel, which
continued to be an important holy place in Israel, often as a rival to Jerusalem (1
Kings 12.29–35). Tensions between different religious claims were a feature of
ancient Israel, as they continue to be in much of the modern world.

Tension is inherent, too, in the promise made in the theophany. On the one hand
it can be seen as a restatement and a development of the promise made to Abraham
at 12.1–3, and that brings out the universal aspect of God's commitment (vv. 14–
15). On the other hand there is a strongly local basis, linked to the particular holy
place. The expression 'Jacob's ladder', based on v. 12, has become traditional, but
it is easier to envisage it as a stairway or ramp (cf. NRSV footnote); the holy place
was similar to the famous ziggurats excavated in Mesopotamia (modern-day
Iraq). RC

Wisdom of Solomon 12.13, 16–19

These verses come in the third part of a long theological discourse in Wisdom 11.15—12.27. The theme of this discourse is the balance between the power of God and his mercy. In 11.15—12.1 that balance is strongly present. The God who created the universe has such power that he can easily create wild beasts, the very sight of which will slay the wicked. At the same time, God loves all that exists (11.24) and therefore tempers his power with mercy. An exception is the Canaanites who lived in the land prior to the arrival of the Israelites (12.3–11). Such was their wickedness in the holy land that God allowed the Israelites, a people more worthy to possess it, to destroy them. Yet even this process was gradual, and gave the Canaanites the opportunity of repentance.

The third section begins (12.12) with a rhetorical question that implies that no one is in a position to question how God runs the world. This is followed by the assertion, with which the selected passage begins, that God does not have to justify his actions to any other god, since no such entity exists. Neither is there anything that is in a position to accuse God of being inconsistent. If God chooses, he can show mercy; where it is necessary he can display his power and judgement.

The main message of the passage is that mercy should not be taken as a sign of weakness. It comes from God's strength; and if people are to be the followers of God, they must use whatever strength or power that they have in the same way. 'Through such works you have taught your people that the righteous must be kind' (v. 19). JR

Isaiah 44.6–8

These verses are a noble expression of the incomparability of God, and form a striking contrast with the following section of the chapter (vv. 9–20) which describes in a mocking way how men fashion idols and worship objects that are no more powerful than their maker. The difference between God and the gods is that only the former can declare in advance what is about to happen; and in the specific context of Isaiah 44.28—45.3 the declaration which God gives to his prophet concerns the triumphant progress of the Persian king Cyrus, who is explicitly mentioned there. Impressive though the buildings, culture and temples of Babylon may be, they are merely human achievements, and they will fall to the victor whom God is empowering, so that Israel can be freed from the Babylonian yoke.

The power of the passage lies in its adversarial style. Other gods are challenged to prove that they, too, can declare in advance what is to happen. The Israelites form a kind of jury ('you are my witnesses'! v. 8). When they bring in their verdict it will have to be in favour of Israel's king and redeemer, the first and the last. JR

Romans 8.12–25

See Second Sunday Before Lent, pp. 70–1.

Matthew 13.24–30, 36–43

The parable of the wheat and the tares (or 'darnel', a weed indistinguishable from wheat in the early stages of its growth) is only found in Matthew and in several respects it is particularly characteristic of the evangelist's outlook. Whereas the sower parable earlier in the chapter allows that certain environmental factors may affect the productivity of the seed, this story points to the intrinsic goodness or evil of different kinds of seed. Like the angel interpreter of 2 Esd. (4.26–37), Matthew seems to believe that humanity can be divided into good and bad types, the former sown by God, the latter by his enemy, the devil (v. 38). This apocalyptic dualism is designed to draw the battle lines more sharply, and so to put the final judgement beyond dispute (cf. Rev. 22.11–12).

Matthew, however, pulls back from an entirely sectarian divide between good and evil, between 'us' and 'them', by admitting that even the Church can be infiltrated by the spawn of Satan. Premature attempts to differentiate between them might disturb the growth of those who have the potential to become saints. Both therefore are to be allowed to grow together until the harvest (v. 30). In practical terms Matthew is not entirely consistent on this issue. If some noxious weed (cf. 18.17) can be sufficiently isolated from the rest of the community, then he can be plucked out cleanly by excommunication. But the remainder is an unknown quantity. Church people have a tendency to think of themselves as safely 'on the inside': Matthew's rhetoric poses a salutary challenge to this sort of complacency.

The prompt for this special Matthean composition may have been the obscure parable of the seed growing secretly (Mark 4.26–29), which he has otherwise omitted. There the farmer does nothing but sleep at night and spend all day leaning on his gate watching the corn grow. Matthew may have tried to 'discover' some reason for this inexplicable inactivity. While the farmer was asleep, perhaps an enemy came and sowed weeds in his field and that would explain why he was unable to do anything about it, while awake. In the allegorical explanation, the good seed represents the 'sons of the kingdom' (v. 38); earlier (at 8.12) the same phrase had been used to describe Jews who are destined to be excluded from the messianic banquet. This ambivalence is probably deliberate, and it further qualifies the predestinarian tendency of the parable. For there are some who ought to belong but who have excluded themselves, just as there are others who ought not to belong, but who will be weeded out only when the time is ripe. JM

18

Proper 12

(Sunday between 24 and 30 July inclusive)

Genesis 29.15–28 or 1 Kings 3.5–12; Romans 8.26–39; Matthew 13.31–33, 44–52

Genesis 29.15–28

The comic elements in the story of Jacob deserve more attention than they usually receive from commentators. In ch. 31 the joke will be at the expense of Laban, who schemes cunningly, but is outwitted by Jacob. But the story-teller was not averse to showing how the great trickster Jacob could himself be tricked, and the present episode illustrates this vividly.

The preceding verses of this chapter have told of Jacob's encounter with the beautiful Rachel, at the well where she was feeding the sheep, and we know from previous acquaintance with this motif (Isaac's servant and Rebekah in ch. 24) that a wedding may be expected. But a complication arises; Laban has *two* daughters. We already know of Jacob's meeting with Rachel, but she has an older sister, Leah. She is described only with reference to her eyes, and it is not at all certain what the Hebrew description means. NRSV 'lovely' takes it as a compliment, but the thrust of the story makes it more likely that some such rendering as REB 'dull-eyed' is nearer the mark.

At all events, Jacob asks for, and is apparently given, permission to marry Rachel. (In the earlier story Rebekah's agreement had been sought; the sisters are not consulted here.) In the event Jacob is tricked; Leah has been substituted for Rachel! This is a dramatic device used by the story-teller; we need not enquire into the details of marriage customs, the use of veils and the like. For the moment Laban has outwitted his guest Jacob. But of course the young man's infatuation with Rachel makes him ready to go on working for Laban for another seven years. The story-teller is not concerned about bigamy; indeed Jacob is provided with a third female companion. Zilpah is described in v. 24 as 'Leah's maid', but 30.1–13 will make it clear that both she and Rachel's maid Bilhah are intended to provide sexual services for Jacob. It is very much a man's world that is portrayed; here as elsewhere in the Old Testament men who could afford to do so are pictured as having more than one wife – indeed, in the case of King David, a veritable harem. It is not only the disregard for women's feelings that warns us that the biblical picture of marriage is not one that can be easily taken over in the modern world. RC

1 Kings 3.5–12

Instructions given by gods to people facing difficult decisions are a common theme in the literature of the ancient Near East, and although there is no exact parallel to the story of Solomon's request for wisdom, the account falls into this general genre. Further, in the ideology of kingship in the ancient Near East, the endowment of wisdom was the virtue that was most highly valued in the king. The present narrative, whose origins have been sought in a 'history of Solomon' composed towards the end of the reign of Hezekiah (727–698 BC), therefore presents the king as representing the highest ideals of kingship.

Why the incident should be set in Gibeon is unclear. Gibeon was undoubtedly a large and important sanctuary five miles north of Jerusalem that was eclipsed by Jerusalem when the latter became the capital of Judah. Accordingly, some commentators have seen the origin of the narrative in a cult legend preserved at Gibeon. Those who see the hand of the deuteronomistic editors in the present form of the story argue that Solomon's sacrificial activity is placed at Gibeon (1 Kings 3.3–4) because the Jerusalem temple had yet to be built.

A striking feature of the passage is that Solomon's reply to God in response to the offer 'what should I give you?' has much more to do with his succession to the throne than a request for wisdom. It has been plausibly argued that the purpose of this language about the succession is to counteract the impression given in 1 Kings 1 that the succession to David's throne was a hasty and improvised contest between two rivals. Here, its divine origin is emphasized, and the idea that the new king is but a little child (Solomon may have been around 20 at the time, so the phrase may be a way of expressing humility) expresses the idea that his appointment as king cannot depend on any merit of his own.

One of the ironies of the biblical account of Solomon's reign is that his fabled wisdom does not appear to have enabled him to rule his people particularly wisely. He may have been able to impress other monarchs such as the Queen of Sheba, but after his death, the people of the northern kingdom said to his son, Rehoboam, 'your father made our yoke heavy' (1 Kings 12.4). Further, during Solomon's reign a prophet foretold the division of his kingdom after his death, because of Solomon's love of other gods (1 Kings 11.29–33). It is therefore not enough to be granted wisdom. The exercise of it demands constant care and attention. JR

Romans 8.26–39

The conclusion of Rom. 8 begins with an astonishing assertion of weakness and concludes with an even more astonishing claim about the future. Far from having escaped the world, believers do not even know how to pray as they should. The language of v. 26 leaves it unclear exactly what Paul means by 'We do not know how to pray as we ought'. Although often taken as a reference to the subjective stance of those who pray (e.g. who do not know what words to use or how to express their petitions), little elsewhere in early Christian writings indicates a feeling of inadequacy in prayer. Paul may have in mind a more theological weakness in Christian prayer; that is, even believers do not know what the will of God is that they should be seeking in their prayer.

Verse 27 reinforces this reading of the passage, recalling that God knows what is in the mind of the Spirit and that the Spirit intercedes according to God's will. Despite the weakness of humankind and its sense of isolation from God and longing for God, what Paul conveys here is a deep interconnectedness between God, God's Spirit and God's creatures.

In vv. 28–30 Paul turns from this direct consideration of the suffering, longing and weakness of humanity to explicit and powerful words of comfort. The first statement of comfort has often emerged from interpreters' hands as a word of law or a litmus test of faith: 'We know that all things work together for good for those who love God, who are called according to his purpose.' However, to say that everything works together for good means, *in this context*, that the longing of creation, the activity of the Spirit, even humanity's inarticulate cries do not exist apart from God's will. God is able to use even those things which reflect the depth of human weakness and turn them for the good.

The lines that follow reinforce this seemingly outrageous claim: God foreknew, God predestined, God called, God justified, God glorified (vv. 29–30). The point here is not to figure out who belongs within the circle of the justified and who does not. As is generally the case in Romans, Paul has in view the action of God and only very subordinately its implications about human standing. The insistence here, then, is not that some people are predestined to be among God's family and others are not. Instead, Paul insists that *God* is the one who designs, desires and brings about the good. Everything that God has put in place has been for the salvation of humankind. No human act can secure this salvation, and no human act can jeopardize this salvation. It belongs to God alone.

The opening question to the third section of the lection signals that what follows is to be important (cf. e.g. 3.9; 4.1; 6.1). The words that immediately follow this question tip Paul's hand by revealing that the paragraph itself will say: 'If God is for us ...' For Paul, the 'if' does not indicate that he has a question about God's allegiance. Instead, 'if' signals the presupposition from which other questions are to be answered. God *is* on humanity's side.

The dominant question throughout the passage is, 'Who?' First it appears in the form of 'Who is against us?' If God has already given up his only Son on behalf of God's people, will God not also give them everything else? This form of logic strikes modern ears as strange, since God might conclude that the gift of the Son was sufficient and more. Paul is using a method of reasoning that was well established in his day, in which it was regarded as logical to reason from something greater to something lesser.

The second 'who' question comes in v. 33: 'Who will bring any charge against God's elect?' and is followed immediately by a restatement: 'It is God who justifies. Who is to condemn?' The language recalls that of a courtroom, and Paul pauses to suggest one who might be imagined as prosecutor: Jesus Christ. But since Jesus died and was raised and, indeed, intercedes for God's people, Jesus will certainly not prosecute God's own.

The third 'who' question comes in v. 35: 'Who will separate us from the love of Christ?' This question moves away from the courtroom scene of vv. 33–34, and so it may seem formally different from the ones that have preceded. In a sense, however, this question not only restates the preceding questions, but pulls them together. This indeed is the underlying question: Who or what can effect a separation between God and humankind?

Having arrived at the heart of the matter, Paul offers a sustained and emphatic response. First, he asks yet another question about what can separate humankind from God, and then he provides a list of threatening events or experiences that have in common the fact that human beings themselves can and do bring them about. Second, Paul quotes a psalm to interpret these experiences as happening for the sake of Christ. Finally, not content to let the audience deduce his answer from the questions he has asked, Paul asserts emphatically: 'No, in all these things we are more than conquerors through him who loved us.' Now the horizon expands dramatically. Not only are human actions unable to bring about separation from the love of Christ, but even those powers that go beyond the merely human (death itself, angels, powers that rule this world) cannot separate humanity from Christ's love. BG

Matthew 13.31–33, 44–52

In the Gospel of Mark, the story of the sower in ch. 4 occupies a key role, with numerous echoes in other parts of the book. In Matthew, ch. 13 seems to have comparable connections elsewhere, though in different ways. It is – as is readily recognized by the concluding formula (v. 53) that is, with small variations, common to all five of them – the third of Matthew's great blocks of teaching by Jesus, perhaps echoing Judaism's five books of the Law. Two of them start virtually from scratch (chs. 5— 7 and ch. 18), while the others are, in various manners, developments of Marcan passages; and ch. 13 is of course in this category. But the parables that make it up relate in theme to the subject matter of two of the other discourses: some of them relate to mission, like ch. 10, the others to the final judgement, like chs. 24—25 (cf. on Proper 10). This chapter is then a kind of keystone among the five discourses; after all, as Matthew tells us, following Mark, Jesus' way of teaching simply was parabolic (v. 34).

In our present passage, we have examples from each category. In the former, there are the mustard seed (vv. 31–32), based essentially on Mark's version in 4.30–32, and the leaven, with a parallel in Luke 13.20–21, and then the two uniquely Matthean parables of the treasure (v. 44) and the pearl (vv. 45–46). All these speak of the incalculable necessity and value of the spread of the good news of the kingdom. It is worth anything and everything to secure its achievement.

But the dragnet in vv. 47–50 shares with the tares (see Proper 11: its interpretation fills the verses omitted here) the characteristic Matthean message of threat, judgement and punishment. Our lection also omits the equally typical quoting of Ps. 78.2, where, as is his practice, Matthew backs this feature of Jesus' activity with a scriptural passage which uses the key word *parabolē*.

The last two verses are also Matthean. Here we find the disciples acting as the best of people, understanding what their teacher has told them (contrast Mark 6.52; 8.14–

17). And in the final verse, we have what may well be the precious, cryptic signature of the evangelist himself, who shows himself, from start to finish, having all the interpretative skills in handling scriptural texts of one trained as a scribe – but who has now gloriously transferred his allegiance to the 'kingdom of heaven', the cause that Jesus has come to propagate and fulfil, as the Messiah of God. It sums up in a single statement the whole self-awareness and programme of this writer as he works to present his sense of Jesus, and it is to this end that he has been trained. LH

Proper 13

(Sunday between 31 July and 6 August inclusive)

Genesis 32.22–31 or Isaiah 55.1–5; Romans 9.1–5; Matthew 14.13–21

Genesis 32.22–31

Jacob's marital adventures in the East are over; he is returning to his homeland. Just as there had been a divine encounter on the outward journey (ch. 28), so on his return he is confronted with 'a man', who is quickly shown in the story to be no ordinary human being. We were told in Gen. 1 that human beings were made in the image of God, so it is not surprising that on more than one occasion in Genesis divine appearances take human form (cf. Abraham's visitor(s) in ch. 18).

The powerful description of the present encounter can be read at many different levels. There are what are known as 'aetiological' elements, that is to say, explanations of such matters as unusual place names ('Peniel' = 'face of God') or eating habits (the verse following our reading, 32, refers to this). More important, the story functions in several different ways as a 'rite of passage'. It begins with Jacob 'left', bereft of 'everything that he had' – wives, children and possessions. Jacob is then pictured as being required to make the crossing which was the only means of access to the holy land. That land was occupied by his brother Esau, whom he fears will be hostile; can it be that the blessing was after all intended for him? Jacob receives a new name, 'Israel'; both in the Bible and in many human situations the giving of a new name is an important symbol of a changed status. (In a Christian context the giving of a name in baptism is the most obvious example.) The name given here is a clear pointer to the identity of the community of Israel which will be the main concern of the Old Testament and, in another sense, of the New. Another 'passage' underlying the story is that it all takes place as night becomes day; God's help is regularly pictured as coming 'in the morning' (e.g. Ps. 30.5).

Basic also to the story is the presentation of fundamental human experiences in terms of a struggle with the divine. This is an element played down in some Christian traditions, which emphasize submission to God's will, but the portrayal of Jesus in the New Testament several times pictures his relation with God in terms of struggle (e.g. in the passion narratives). Jacob's persistence is finally rewarded, 'I have seen God face to face and yet my life is preserved'. We have moved a long way from the cunning and treacherous Jacob of the earlier part of his story. RC

Isaiah 55.1–5

It may be obvious to modern Western readers that public resources of water should be freely available to all thirsty people. This is not obvious in the Middle East where water is scarce, and where traditional sources of water may be jealously guarded and defended. The invitation to everyone who is thirsty to come to the water must therefore be seen in this light. The thirsty are also likely to be the hungry, and they, people without money, are invited to buy and eat. The invitation then spirals higher to embrace wine and milk, which are not priced.

The sequel, in which people are chided for spending money on what is not bread, makes it clear that water, food, wine and milk are not to be taken literally in this passage, although this point should not be developed in the direction of supposing that only 'spiritual' and not practical things are being spoken of. There probably is a contrast between at least two types of religion implied in these words. There is religion that involves payment and gives little in return (which was probably how the prophet thought of idolatry) and religion that depends upon the gracious and free gift of the God of Israel. Yet, as the paradox of buying food when one has no money implies, the gifts of God are not free, the cost being borne by him.

The second part of the passage moves to practicalities, and at the same time brings more surprises. God promises to make an everlasting covenant with his people, based upon his love for David. Yet its scope is not restricted to Israel. David was not a leader of the people (singular) but a leader of peoples. There are echoes here of royal ideology found, in certain psalms such as Ps. 2.8 'ask of me, and I will make the nations your heritage'; but whereas this royal ideology may have the sense of Israelite rule and thus domination over other nations, the emphasis in the present passage is different. The nations will gladly accept any invitation to be included in the covenant; indeed Israel may be knocked over in the rush to join (cf. v. 5)! This will be because of the graciousness of God made apparent in what he does for Israel, but his purpose will be to show that that graciousness is intended for everyone. JR

Romans 9.1–5

In Romans 9 Paul turns to the 'problem' of Israel: if God has now acted in Christ to save all who have faith, both Jew and Gentile, without partiality, and if converts to Christ are children of Abraham, sons and heirs of God, then what has become of God's covenant people, the Jews, and what has become of God's promises to them?

These questions are by no means academic for Paul, and recent scholarship on Romans has almost unanimously overturned the judgement of an earlier generation which saw Rom. 9—11 as something of a digression, less than central to the letter as a whole. No, this issue is pressing and important for Paul, and the cause of heartfelt anguish. Whatever the hyperbole in vv. 1–3, Paul's seriousness should not be under-estimated. And if we are suspicious that he protests his anguish too much, virtually swearing an oath in Christ's name that he is speaking the truth, we should remember that Paul was accused of abandoning God's law, of turning his back on his ancestral customs and people (Acts 21.21). Romans may in part represent Paul's attempt to correct slanderous and inaccurate views of him (cf. Rom. 3.8), in advance of visiting a congregation he has not previously met.

Paul is clear that the Israelites are his brothers and sisters (*adelphoi*), his kinsfolk 'according to the flesh' (in distinction from those who are now his siblings 'in Christ', in whom Paul no longer views people 'according to the flesh': 2 Cor. 5.16). To them belong all the privileges and responsibilities of God's own people and from them came the Messiah. Throughout the varied and difficult arguments of the following chapters Paul wrestles to hold together his convictions that God has acted in Christ to save both Jew and Gentile and that Israel's gifts and calling are irrevocable. He sees in the announcement of the gospel to the Gentiles a part of the grand divine plan which will in turn lead to the salvation of 'all Israel' (Rom. 11.26) and ultimately of all people (Rom. 11.32). In the end, though he confesses it as a 'mystery', Paul cannot believe that God will abandon his people the Jews. While it is a struggle for Paul to make sense of all this, at least he struggles with the tension, refusing to resolve it by abandoning his conviction about God's stead-fastness towards Israel. Unfortunately, many of Paul's Christian interpreters, enmeshed in very different historical situations, resolved it – with pernicious conse-quences – by declaring that the Church had simply replaced Israel.

Verse 5, as well as containing the important, if obvious, affirmation that Jesus was a Jew – an 'obvious' affirmation all too often lost sight of in Christian history and in images of blond-haired, blue-eyed Jesuses – also contains a notoriously ambiguous final phrase with implications for understanding Paul's christology. Does Paul mean to say that *Christ* is 'over all, God blessed for ever' or should we render the final phrase as a separate sentence (so e.g. RSV), a typically Jewish blessing of God, but not an acclamation of Christ as God (which would be unique in Paul's undis-puted letters)? The commentaries on Romans present the arguments on both sides, while comparing biblical translations reveals the translators' dilemma! DH

Matthew 14.13–21

The feeding of the five thousand occurs in all four canonical Gospels, probably not just because some kind of reminiscence of such an occasion, however it is to be explained, was firmly rooted in the tradition, but also because, more importantly, this story is so rich in symbolic meaning.

Matthew connects Jesus' withdrawal 'to a lonely place' directly with the news of the martyrdom of John the Baptist (v. 13); presumably he wanted to grieve in private for the death of the great prophet. Mark's account of the story of John's death had not implied that it took place at precisely this chronological point in Jesus' ministry; instead he connected the feeding story with the return of the disciples from mission (Mark 6.30), and their need for a little rest, and at the same time thereby providing a clue to its interpretation: the abundant left-overs become a symbol of the promise of a greater mission to the nations (cf. Mark 7.24). Since Matthew's reordering of Mark has located the mission much earlier, this feeding miracle stands more by itself, with a slightly different character and function. Matthew has made other alterations to Mark: Jesus' compassion for the crowd is rendered concrete by the mention of acts of healing (v. 14), and the sarcasm of the disciples at the suggestion that they should feed such a multitude (Mark 6.37) is discreetly removed. The number of those fed is specified as 5,000 men (with healthy appetites) 'quite apart from the women and children' (v. 21, who together no doubt ate as much again!).

There is a rich symbolism in this story. First, it recapitulates the experience of Israel in the Sinai desert, fed by God with the manna from heaven (Exod. 16, cf. John 6.31–32, explicitly); later Jewish tradition added fish as a relish. The point here is that Jesus is the new Moses who brings redemption from slavery and want. Second, it recalls the miracles of Elijah (see 1 Kings 17.8–16) and Elisha (see 2 Kings 4.2–4, and especially 4.42–44). The latter had fed 100 men with 20 loaves; Jesus, the greater successor of the returned Elijah betters that a thousandfold. Third, the incident foreshadows the Christian Eucharist, especially in its emphasis on Jesus' prayer of thanksgiving (v. 19): 'he looked up to heaven and blessed and broke the bread', cf. Matt. 26.26. This moves the emphasis away from the provision of ordinary sustenance to the greater miracle of faith in the sacrifice of Christ. Finally, the motif of sheer abundance anticipates the messianic banquet (8.11, cf. 2 Baruch 29.5, 'The earth will also yield fruits ten thousand fold'). For people who were always undernourished, and often near starvation, the prospect of total satisfaction and inexhaustible supply was heaven itself, in a way that well-fed modern Westerners can scarcely appreciate. JM

Proper 14

(Sunday between 7 and 13 August inclusive)

Genesis 37.1–4, 12–28 or 1 Kings 19.9–18; Romans 10.5–15; Matthew 14.22–33

Genesis 37.1–4, 12–28

The last part of Genesis centres around the fortunes of Joseph, one of the twelve sons of Jacob, who was specially favoured because he was the long-delayed child of his beloved wife Rachel (30.22–24). We saw that the Abraham story consisted largely of separate, unrelated elements. Jacob's travels were described with particular themes in mind, though each episode was largely self-standing. Now, by contrast, the literary structure becomes much more sophisticated. The dealings between Joseph and his brothers in this reading will reverberate through the rest of the book, so that in its very last episode (50.15–21) the wrong done in this chapter is still in mind. Opinions will differ sharply about the historical plausibility of the events here described; no one can doubt the literary skill that they display. Those with opportunity to do so should certainly be encouraged to read the whole of this chapter and then chs. 39—50 during the time that three brief sections are used as the liturgical reading.

The story begins with the famous coat: traditionally 'coat of many colours', more recently 'the amazing Technicolor dream-coat'. The 'long robe with sleeves' seems dowdy by comparison, but the exact meaning of the description is uncertain. Some will feel that Joseph's wearing such a fine garment as he goes off to search for his hostile brothers (v. 23) points to a weakness in his character; was he perhaps over-confident in his manifest destiny? At times throughout his story he appears as an insufferable prig.

The overall thrust of the last part of the story is clear enough: Joseph is sold to traders going to Egypt. So too is the motif of one brother being less harshly disposed. Some of the details are less clear. Was the 'friendly' brother Reuben or Judah? Was Joseph's confinement in the pit the effective putting him to death, or was it a less extreme punishment from which he might be rescued (v. 22)? Were the traders Ishmaelites or Midianites? It used to be customary among scholars to detect two sources interwoven together here; some attempts have more recently been made to see only one hand at work, the tensions in the narrative serving to heighten the suspense. In any case the overall effect is clear. Whereas we might have supposed that the promises to Abraham meant that the land had been given to his descendants as a permanent possession, now we are alerted to the fact that first one, and eventually all, of the founding family, are to find their way to Egypt, the context in which another story of the people's origin is to be set. RC

I Kings 19.9–18

This passage is part of a longer narrative which begins with Elijah's victorious contest with the prophets of Baal on Mount Carmel. There is considerable irony in the fact that, having proved to all and sundry that the God of Israel is superior to Baal, Elijah flees from the land for his life when threaten by Baal's devotee, Queen Jezebel. Elijah, indeed, becomes sulky and introspective (a reaction against his great success?) and finally reaches Mount Horeb, which is an alternative name for Mount Sinai.

Readers may be forgiven for thinking that Elijah's justification for his flight, given twice in this passage (vv. 10, 14) is somewhat exaggerated. He is the only one servant of God left and he must accordingly preserve his life. This is a far cry from what happened after he routed the prophets of Baal (cf. 18.36–40). The complaint, incidentally, that the people have thrown down God's altars, shows that the narrative is not aware of the command in Deuteronomy that there should be only *one* altar where sacrifice should be offered (cf. Deut. 12.13–14).

The theophany, or manifestation of the divine presence, that Elijah now experiences invokes phenomena that are usually associated with God's presence. Earthquake and fire are present on Mount Sinai when Moses brings the people to its foot prior to receiving the law (Exod. 19.18). A wind capable of splitting mountains and breaking rocks in pieces must be mighty indeed, and it recalls the effects of God's voice in Ps. 29. However, God is not 'in' any of these awesome phenomena, but seems to come to the prophet in or as a faint murmuring sound (v. 12). The rendering 'sound of sheer silence' in the NRSV conveys little or no sense.

The reason for the presence of God in a murmur rather than a storm is that God's purposes in Israel will not be achieved by spectacular physical phenomena, but by people carrying out God's will. All that Elijah's spectacular victory on Mount Carmel achieved was Jezebel's anger and Elijah's abject flight. Now, Elijah is to lay down long-term plans not only for the future of kingship in Israel but also for the future of kingship in Syria, Israel's enemy. In addition, Elijah is to ensure proper succession to his own leadership as a prophet. This is because there are far more faithful Israelites than Elijah ever realized. Neither his, nor anyone else's, judgement of the state of affairs at a time of deep depression is likely to be anywhere near the truth. JR

Romans 10.5–15

Of all the lectionary readings taken from Romans, this one may deserve to be labelled as the most challenging for the preacher. To begin with, the reading seems to have no concrete setting at all. It appears in the middle of what is already a digression about how it is that Israel 'did not succeed in fulfilling that law' (Rom. 9.31). As a whole, of course, Rom. 9—11 considers whether Israel's rejection of Jesus as Messiah compromises God's faithfulness to God's promises. In 9.31—10.21, Paul departs from that larger topic to give an account of Israel's situation. The present lection comes within that digression but, as it stands, nothing in the lection concretely refers to Israel, making it easy to speak in abstract and vague terms that ignore the context. On the other hand, explaining the context could involve the preacher in a lengthy excursus.

Even without these problems of context, the passage presents an array of difficulties. Is Paul contrasting the 'righteousness that comes from the law' with the 'righteousness that comes from faith', as most commentators insist? Or is he engaging in a scriptural argument to demonstrate that the two are in fact the same? Does he draw on pre-existing Christian tradition, on Jewish interpretive practices, or on Jewish wisdom reflection? A review of the standard commentaries will show just how contested is virtually every inch of this exegetical turf.

How might the preacher approach this passage without becoming sidetracked by either these internal exegetical questions or the complicated relationship between this passage and its context? One approach might be to attend here to the way in which Paul engages in a lively reading of Scripture. (For an extremely suggestive discussion of Paul's exegesis, see Richard Hays, *Echoes of Scripture in the Letters of Paul*; New Haven, Conn.: Yale University Press, 1989.) Although a recital of the technical discussion about Paul's use of Scripture here would be deadly, stepping back from that debate to notice Paul's profound engagement with Scripture might be very illuminating. The passage opens with a quotation from Lev. 18.5, and then takes up lines from Deut. 30.11–14, which Paul reads through the lens of Christian proclamation; it is Christ who is in heaven and Christ who comes up from death. Deuteronomy 30.14 becomes, for Paul, a summation of what it means to confess faith in Jesus Christ with the mouth and with the heart. Quotations from Isa. 28.16 and Joel 2.32 reinforce Paul's ongoing argument about the gospel's inclusion of all, both Jew and Greek.

Even the most cursory study shows that Paul blatantly ignores the historical context of these passages. That, of course, is to be expected; he follows the exegetical conventions of the first century rather than the twenty-first. What is more important, however, is that here we see Paul's sense of engagement with Scripture. He is not so much reading Scripture here and interpreting it (an action by Paul on a passive object), or even turning to it as an authoritative source of information, as he is in lively and enlivening conversation with it. He seeks language in Scripture that will enable him to address the needs of the present.

Another possibility for preaching from this passage is to focus on its articulation of continuity between God's actions in the past and those in the present. This issue certainly is directly connected with the way in which Paul reads Scripture, for he sees in Scripture evidence that, even in Israel's past, what God wanted was 'the righteousness that comes from faith' (10.6). To say that Deuteronomy refers to Christ (vv. 6–7) is, historically speaking, absurd and can promote a supersessionist mentality. What Paul is after, however, is a way of asserting that God's dealings with Israel have remained faithful and fair. After all, one way of responding to the anguish of Rom. 9.1–5 is to say that God is the guilty party, that God has proven to be fickle (see the denial of this claim as early as 9.6 and throughout Rom. 9—11).

Yet another aspect of this passage that might lend itself to preaching occurs in vv. 11–13, with its insistence on the universal availability of God's salvation. When Paul quotes from Isa. 28.16 in v. 11, he inserts 'no one', making way for the inclusive claims of vv. 12 and 13. There is 'no distinction between Jew and Greek', God is 'Lord of all' and generous 'to all', and 'everyone' who calls on God will be saved. This prominent theme from the early chapters of Romans returns as Paul recalls that God's salvation knows no boundaries. Just as all stand condemned of sin, so all may live within God's salvation.

The final verses of this lection (vv. 14–15) are intimately connected with the passage that follows (through 10.21), about Israel's unwillingness to hear the word that has been preached. Read in connection with vv. 5–13 and apart from the conclusion of the chapter, they add little to the passage. Nevertheless, they constitute a powerful reminder to preachers about the importance of their task. With the plethora of expectations and responsibilities most pastors carry, it is altogether too easy to demote preaching into one more routine task of the week. Paul's words here, surely a reflection of his own sense of vocation (see also Rom. 15.14–21), forcefully recall for contemporary preachers the place of Christian proclamation in the mission of God and God's Church. BG

Matthew 14.22–33

The eerie incident of the walking on the water in all the Gospels that include it (Luke's being the only exception) forms the sequel to the miracle of the loaves, so they were probably linked together very early on in the tradition. This pairing is significant. Both stories echo exodus themes; the manna in the wilderness (Exod. 16.15) and the escape dry-shod over water (Exod. 14.29, the Red Sea; Josh. 3.17, the River Jordan). The point would have been to show that incidents in the ministry of Jesus fulfilled the classic redemption narrative of Israel and showed Jesus to be a 'new Moses'. Indeed, he is one greater even than Moses who, like the Lord of heaven, tramples the waves of the sea (Job 9.8).

Yet there are also marked differences between the two stories. Whereas the feeding was a compassionate and 'hidden' act of power, provoking no reaction from the crowds, the walking is an overt display of the miraculous intended to test the disciples' faith, and in Matthew's retelling leads them to worship him expressly as Son of God (v. 33); Mark, by contrast, concludes his account by merely noting the disciples' amazement and lack of understanding (Mark 6.51f.).

Matthew regularly softens Mark's negative portrayal of the disciples; but his account of Peter's failure to imitate Christ reintroduces a note of criticism. Apparently, the Church's leadership is not necessarily exempt from timidity and inadequate faith: the rock who is Peter may sink like a stone (16.18, cf. 26.69f.). This peculiarly Matthean appendix provides a further implication, which is significant for interpreting the preceding story: the ability to walk on water is not the exclusive property of the Son of God. So perhaps we will need to look elsewhere, i.e. to Scripture and to Jesus' authoritative teaching, for more definitive proof of his Messiahship.

For the modern reader, there is a rather uncomfortable similarity between the walking on the water and the comic-book fantasy of Superman, lending a helping hand to mere mortals who may, momentarily, share in his free-floating omnipotence. The atmosphere even of this gospel story is very different. The reason Jesus stays behind is to pray alone to God (v. 23) on whom entirely he depends; for he himself walks by faith (v. 31), a faith that will be tested in the end almost to breaking point on the cross. The deepest meaning of this story is that the one who so often appears to be absent in the storms of ordinary life is yet in truth always present (28.20). JM

Proper 15

(Sunday between 14 and 20 August inclusive)

Genesis 45.1–15 or Isaiah 56.1, 6–8; Romans 11.1–2a, 29–32; Matthew 15.(10–20), 21–28

Genesis 45.1–15

This is in many ways the climax of the story of Joseph in Egypt. Despite the unpromising circumstances of his arrival there he has prospered and has become the pharaoh's right-hand man. (It is interesting to note that whereas in Exodus the pharaoh is pictured as a vain and ineffective despot, here the portrayal is much more sympathetic. Speculation in either case as to who the actual historical ruler may have been is not very rewarding; they are both literary products.) Back in Canaan, meanwhile, Jacob and his remaining family, now augmented by another brother, Benjamin, are suffering the effects of famine. A visit to Egypt in search of provisions brought them under suspicion and one brother, Simeon, was left as a hostage. Only if they bring with them Jacob's youngest son Benjamin will Simeon be released and more provisions made available. Benjamin is allowed to accompany his brothers on the next journey despite his father's misgivings, but the drama is heightened when Joseph orders him to be arrested on a trumped-up charge. Will the brothers abandon him to his fate, as they had done with Joseph himself years before? Ch. 44 had ended with a declaration of loyalty by Judah, to his father and to his young brother.

Joseph is persuaded that the brothers' attitude had changed, and our reading is the happy reconciliation. Joseph is not modest in setting out his own position ('father to Pharaoh', v. 8, is not a title that Egyptians would have recognized), but the main points are that the immediate crisis of famine is averted, and the long-term reunion of the family can now be envisaged. For the moment there is no talk of return to Canaan; from this story we might suppose that the extended family is to settle in Egypt permanently. We know, however, that this episode in the story is part of a larger whole. It is being told as a preliminary to the account of the exodus; indeed it may have been composed deliberately to reconcile two traditions of the people's origins, one speaking of migration from Mesopotamia, the other of exodus from Egypt. Whatever we decide about that, this episode deserves to be taken at its immediate level, of a reconciliation seen by believers as the direct result of God's planning (vv. 7–8a). RC

Isaiah 56.1, 6–8

The community centred upon Jerusalem that rebuilt the temple around 515 BC and restored the religious life of the people, was one split by deep divisions, if Isa. 56—

66 is anything to go by. There were those who seem to have questioned whether there was any need for the temple to be rebuilt at all (Isa. 66.1–4) while others were sharply critical of some of the religious observances (Isa. 58.1–9).

The present passage, with its inexplicable omission of vv. 2–5, is evidently concerned with the problem of non-Jews belonging to the chosen people and participating fully in its temple worship. Its sentiments are only understandable if there were people in the Jerusalem community at the end of the sixth century BC who maintained that non-Jews could not belong to the Jewish community.

We can only speculate about who these non-Jews were who had joined or who wanted to 'join themselves to the Lord' (v. 6). They may have been non-Jews who had moved into Palestine during the exile, from southern Trans-jordan, or they may have been Babylonians who had been involved in the administration of Judah during the period 597 to 548. It is less likely that they were Babylonians who deliberately journeyed back to Jerusalem because they wanted to embrace faith in the God of Israel.

On the face of it, that there were such people should have been a cause for satisfaction if not joy. After all, Isa. 45.2 contains a call to 'all the ends of the earth' to turn to God and to be saved. Foreigners, however, cause problems in all societies in all ages. If they are too successful they arouse resentment; if they perform below the average they are blamed for a society's troubles. We may also detect in the passage disputes about the layout and accessibility of the rebuilt temple. Unfortunately, we know nothing about its layout; but the temple that Herod the Great enlarged and rebuilt at the close of the first century BC certainly allowed access to certain parts only to Israelite males. The passage certainly promises to non-Jews who observe the sabbaths and hold fast to the covenant that they will be able to join fully in the worship of the temple, and that their sacrifices will be acceptable. We do not know how the dispute over non-Jews was resolved at the end of the sixth century. Sixty years later, Ezra and Nehemiah made a determined, and apparently successful, attempt to exclude the non-Jewish wives of Israelites from the community (Ezra 9.1–4; 10.1–15; Neh. 13.1–3, 23–29). The implications of the passage for today's churches with regard to their attitude to all 'outsiders', especially those of African and Asian ethnic origins, should not be difficult to discern. JR

Romans 11.1–2a, 29–32

The key question of Rom. 9—11 is here concisely expressed: 'Has God rejected his people?' As with his other rhetorical questions concerning God's faithfulness and justice, here too the question receives Paul's forthright negation: 'by no means!' (cf. Rom. 3.4, 6; 9.14; 11.11). Paul himself is evidence to the contrary, for he is a Jew. He quotes Ps. 94.14, which affirms that God will not reject his people, changing the future tense of the Septuagint to the aorist (God 'has not rejected') and adding the clause 'whom he foreknew'. This may be meant in the restrictive sense of those individuals from among the people whom God knew to be truly his, or in the wider sense, more probable here, of God's previous election of his people as a whole. The lectionary reading now jumps to v. 29, thus omitting the substance of Paul's argument and leaving his references to 'you' and 'they' in vv. 30–31 without an explanatory context. Before we can understand these closing verses, therefore, we need some sense of how Paul proceeds from v. 2a to v. 29. He first mentions the idea of the 'remnant' (cf. also 9.6–13, 27): as in the time of Elijah, so now there is a 'remnant' of Israel, chosen by grace. But the hardening and consequent stumbling that Paul sees as the condition of the remainder of the Jews is not a permanent state of affairs (11.11). Their stumbling is for a purpose; it has meant that salvation has come to the Gentiles. And if such a blessing came from such misfortune, how much greater the blessings to come from their 'full inclusion' (11.12, 15) – the end goal towards which Paul sees God's purposes moving. Paul warns his Gentile hearers against any arrogant presumption that they have taken Israel's place. Indeed they have been grafted onto the root of Israel, like wild olive branches joined to a cultivated stock (11.17–24), but their place is by no means unshakeable (v. 21) and the natural branches can well be grafted back in, if they come to have faith (vv. 23–24). Israel's temporary hardening serves the purpose of salvation for the Gentiles (v. 25), but in the end 'all Israel' will be saved (v. 26).

This is the context in which Paul affirms that 'the gifts and the calling of God are irrevocable' (v. 29), and his view of the saving purposes of God is reiterated in vv. 30–31: Israel's disobedience has led to mercy for the Gentiles, which will in turn lead to mercy for Israel. The essence of God's gracious plan is summed up in v. 32: the purpose of consigning all humanity to disobedience is in order that God may show mercy to all. This mysterious yet marvellous plan leads Paul to break out into praise (vv. 33–36). The details of Paul's logic are not easy to penetrate, and one must certainly question his notion that Israel will come to faith when provoked to jealousy by the mercy shown to the Gentiles. Two thousand years of (often bloody) history might well lead to the conclusion that Paul was simply mistaken. But perhaps what is important is the broader vision which he struggles to articulate, a vision of a God whose purpose is to show mercy to all, and who will by no means abandon his people Israel. D H

Matthew 15.(10–20), 21–28

The Pharisees and scribes, who have not figured in the preceding two chapters, come back with a vengeance in ch. 15. They start with the complaint that Jesus' followers do not observe the *halakah* (the oral laws) on purity and hand-washing (15.2, 20). But this concern for the niceties is hypocrisy, a smokescreen for evading the plain sense of the written law of Moses (v. 5).

The theme of purity continues with Jesus' puzzling saying to the crowd that begins this reading (v. 10). It is unlikely that he intended to overthrow all the laws on unclean foods (but contrast Mark 7.19): what he must have meant was that purity of the heart (cf. 5.8) was simply a higher priority; but his words were ambiguous enough to cause the Pharisees offence (v. 12). The disciples, who have obviously been picking up criticisms like this from Jewish outsiders, are told to take no notice and have nothing more to do with such blind guides (v. 14, cf. 23.16).

The Pharisees get a bad press in the Gospels, probably unfairly. Their later hostility towards the Church coloured the way they were portrayed. Many of them, after all, would have agreed with the principle that it is the evil inclination in the human heart that produces the most heinous crimes, and Jesus himself may well have been sympathetic to the Pharisaic movement (cf. e.g. Matt. 22.23–33). The lectionary provides the option of omitting this rather bitter, and to us obscure, anti-Jewish controversy.

There follows the encounter with the Canaanite woman (Mark calls her a Syrophoenician) from the coastal region of Tyre and Sidon to the north of Galilee. Though a Gentile, she knows how to address a Jewish teacher respectfully ('Son of David', v. 20). He ignores her and the disciples try to shoo her away. These are all additions to Mark that underline Matthew's restriction of Jesus' mission to Israel alone (v. 24, cf. Matt. 10.5–6, 23). But the woman's faith (not just her smart rejoinder, as in Mark 7.29) pays off, and she secures the healing of her daughter as a special exception. The pro-Jewish sentiment of this passage is in stark contrast to the anti-Jewish tone before; the point is perhaps to hold the two in balance, for 'in Christ there is neither Jew nor Greek' (Gal. 3.28).

It is often asked whether Jesus himself could have referred to Gentiles so offensively as 'dogs', as scavengers hanging round the table of the children of Israel. That is not impossible; after all, as fully human (according to Christian doctrine) his outlook and sympathies would necessarily be conditioned by his own Jewishness. But more likely perhaps, we are overhearing here an echo of the struggles of conscience within the early Church, on the legitimacy of preaching a law-free gospel to the non-Jew (cf. Gal. 2.15–21). Whichever way, the reader of this Gospel is invited to join Jesus and with him cross the barriers of race and culture. JM

Proper 16

(Sunday between 21 and 27 August inclusive)

Exodus 1.8—2.10 or Isaiah 51.1–6; Romans 12.1–8; Matthew 16.13–20

Exodus 1.8—2.10

(For notes on 2.1–10 see Mothering Sunday, p. 93.)

The 'pharaoh of the oppression' as the Egyptian king of this passage is often called, may have been Seti I (1291–1278) whose reign saw the undertaking of vast building projects. However, the present passage is far removed from being a historical account from these times, and it is a narrative full of other kinds of interest.

Two contradictory themes are present in the narrative: the use of the Hebrews to undertake building work and the Egyptian attempt to restrict the growth of the population of the Hebrews. Although the narrative of 1.9–14 is not unaware of the paradox, it will be obvious that the way to maintain a large pool of slave labour is not to try to reduce its size. A second anomaly is that if one is going to reduce a population by killing its children, it is much more effective to do this by killing baby girls rather than baby boys. However, the killing of baby boys is necessary to the narrative as the prelude to the hiding of Moses in the bullrushes, so that he is found, and brought up by the pharaoh's daughter.

The most interesting part of the story concerns the two (!) midwives who serve a population whose size is so worrying to the Egyptians. This part of the narrative is far removed from actual reality. The pharaoh was a god-like figure surrounded by an impenetrable bureaucracy. It is most unlikely that he would have summoned and conversed with the two midwives. Nevertheless, the narrative is extremely interesting. The two midwives have been ordered to do something that is morally wrong: to kill Hebrew boys at birth. At great risk to themselves they fear (i.e. obey) God and do not carry out the king's instructions. If they were Egyptian – their names are Hebrew, but a case can be made for taking them to be Egyptians in the story – they were deliberately disobeying the orders of their ruler that they considered to be wrong. In the interrogation to which they are subjected, they clearly lie when they claim that they never get to Hebrew women in time to assist the births and kill the babies. The narrative accepts that this lying is justified, seeing that it is intended to prevent a greater evil.

The story is thus evidence that sophisticated moral thinking went on in ancient Israel. The passage clearly indicates that it is more important to obey one's own conviction of what is right and wrong than to obey the orders of the ruler or the state, and that lying can be justified if it prevents a greater evil. The resourcefulness of women and their ability to outwit those in power is also emphasized; and if the midwives really are Egyptians in the story, the text indicates that not all Egyptians in the narrative are bad (and cf. the pharaoh's daughter in 2.5–10) and that the ability to perceive and to do what is right even at great personal risk is not restricted to the chosen people. JR

Isaiah 51.1–6

This passage is a rich tapestry of themes from the Old Testament woven together in a striking pattern. It is addressed either to Israel in exile as a small minority among the Babylonians or to a group of faithful people among the exiles. Either way, it is a small minority that is addressed and the point is made that God's plan for his people once began with only two individuals, Abraham and Sarah. From these two came a much larger nation (v. 2). What God did in the past, he can do again in the present and near future.

The mention of Sarah is the only occurrence of her name outside Genesis, and suggests familiarity with the Genesis tradition, either written or oral. The mention of Eden in v. 3 further reinforces this, and takes the thought back to the creation stories, except that a re-creation of Zion is envisaged, so that it becomes like the garden of Eden.

With the second strophe beginning 'Listen to me' (there are three such strophes in the complete section) there is an allusion to the giving of the law on Mount Sinai, except that it will be given not just to Israel but to all nations. (Later Jewish tradition suggested that the law was available to all nations at Sinai but that only Israel responded.) The reference to God's 'arm' could be an allusion to the exodus (Exod. 6.6) but applied to all nations.

The final verse brings a surprising and unexpected transformation of the Genesis tradition. The created order is temporary. It will wear out like a garment and its inhabitants will likewise cease to exist. Only God will remain as a reality, but along with him will be those who have been embraced by his salvation. What began with Abraham and Sarah, and what will shortly begin again with Israel in exile, will have implications for the created order – and beyond. JR

Romans 12.1–8

Paul's appeal is based specifically on the immediately preceding verses (11.32–36), where he has expressed his wonder at the mercies of God, and more generally on the extended presentation of God's saving work in Rom. 1—11. This is the basis for his exhortation that his readers offer their bodies as a sacrifice to God (and not, therefore, as slaves to sin; cf. Rom. 6.12–14 etc.). This service (*latreia*) Paul describes as *logikē* – which generally means that which is reasonable or rational, but may mean that which is metaphorical or spiritual (cf. 1 Pet. 2.2). Echoing oppositions earlier in the letter between slavery to sin, living according to the flesh and belonging to God, living according to the Spirit, he contrasts the notion of conformity 'to this age' with that of a mind transformed and focused towards the discernment and practice of the will of God. 'This age' is a common Jewish designation for the current era, often contrasted with 'the age to come'; Paul never uses this latter phrase, though the idea of the two ages seems to underlie his thinking. Christians, as they are renewed by the Spirit, live as members of the age to come, and so turn away from the values and practices of 'the present evil age' (Gal. 1.4).

This introduction sets the scene for the ethical teaching to follow in the closing chapters of the letter. Paul begins by urging his readers not to think too highly of themselves, though his idea that people should consider themselves 'according to the measure of faith' perhaps leaves it open for some to rank themselves above others on the grounds of their 'measure of faith'. Paul's main concern, however, seems to be to foster a sense of community solidarity, for he proceeds to the affirmation that all are members of one body, an image of the Church Paul developed in 1 Cor. 12.12–27 and which was widely used in Paul's time as an image of society. As in the more extended discussion in 1 Corinthians, here too Paul uses the body image to encourage both unity and diversity in the Church. There is – or should be – an essential oneness, but also, as with any functioning body, a diversity of functions among the members. These varied activities are described as *charismata* – gifts of grace – given by God to each person, who should use their *charisma* fully for the good of the community. It is interesting that the gifts Paul mentions here include fewer 'supernatural' gifts than are listed in 1 Cor. 12.8–10 and that here in Romans they are not explicitly attributed to the Spirit (contrast 1 Cor. 12.4–11). The gifts listed in Romans include those that involve the proclamation of God's word (prophecy, teaching), ministry or service (*diakonia*), and more practical activities such as encouraging, sharing, leading and doing acts of mercy. Perhaps Paul was aware of differences between the congregations to which he wrote – the Corinthian church seems to have been marked by an interest in 'supernatural' gifts, especially speaking in tongues – and was prepared, within limits, to accept these differences in congregational character and style. DH

Matthew 16.13–20

The confession of Peter is a turning point in the gospel story. The disciples have seen and heard the words and works that point conclusively to Jesus' authority as Messiah. They have struggled, though not so much as in Mark's Gospel, with their fears and inadequate faith. But now, with Peter as spokesman, they turn conviction into explicit confession. Others may believe that Jesus is no more than a successor to John the Baptist (cf. 14.2) or Elijah sent back from heaven (cf. 11.13) or a prophet of old – Matthew specifies Jeremiah, because he, like Jesus, had prophesied the destruction of the (first) temple and had lived a life of celibacy and suffering. But such estimates fall short of Jesus' true significance, for as Christ he is 'Son of the living God', a Matthean addition that underlines the distinctively Christian reworking of the Christ title.

Whereas Mark has Jesus immediately silence Peter (8.30) and rebuke his failure to understand that the Son of man must suffer (8.33), Matthew delays these motifs (cf. vv. 20, 21–23) and first warmly congratulates him for getting the right answer (vv. 17–19). As a Jewish-Christian, Matthew has no hesitation in calling Jesus Son of David and true King of Israel; for he can pay no higher compliment. He is also clear that the abundant evidence for these claims has been knowingly and perversely ignored by his fellow-Jews, and that their rejection of their own Messiah is a colossal and dreadful tragedy.

Using his Jewish name, Simon son of Jonah (contrast John 21.15; John and Jonah are easily confused), Jesus commends his insight as God-given and renames him 'Peter the Rock', in virtue of his faith. Correct understanding of the person of Christ is for Matthew, as it was for Paul (1 Cor. 3.11), the foundation of the new community. The word 'church' is used only here and at Matt. 18.17 in the Gospels, and in two different senses: in the latter it is the local congregation, but here it has a universal, indeed cosmic significance (cf. Eph. 1.22f.). The 'gates of Sheol' (a Semitic metaphor, meaning 'the powers of death') will not be able to withstand the message of the gospel of life (cf. Matt. 27.51–56). The Church is entrusted with the keys of the kingdom (contrast Matt. 23.13) and can determine which laws are still binding in the new dispensation, and which can be set aside. In a certain sense, Matthew is reinstating here a reformed version of the scribal office within the Christian community (cf. 13.52; 23.34). But even so, he remains cautious about titles of dignity ('rabbi' and 'father') and a concept of hierarchical power that fails to reflect the humility of the Servant-Messiah (see 23.8–12). JM

Proper 17

(Sunday between 28 August and 3 September inclusive)

Exodus 3.1–15 or Jeremiah 15.15–21; Romans 12.9–21; Matthew 16.21–28

Exodus 3.1–15

The story of the call of Moses extends over chs. 3 and 4 of Exodus and takes the form of the call of a prophet. A manifestation of divine presence, perhaps mediated through natural phenomena (a dawn or sunset illuminating a bush?) leads to a divine commission, which the one called seeks initially to avoid (cf. Isa. 6.1–13, Jer. 1.4–10). In the present passage, the beginning of Moses' attempt to decline the commission begins with vv. 13–15.

We know too little about the historical Moses to be able to say whether he actually experienced a burning bush at his call. He would have lived at least 400 years before these traditions began to receive written form and it is most likely that he has become an ideal, or representative figure after the manner of a prophet. That, however, does not in any way diminish the importance of the narratives in which he appears. The stories about him have absorbed the accumulated experience of many generations.

Much attention naturally focuses upon vv. 13–15, the revelation of the divine name YHWH, which occurs nearly 7,000 times in the Old Testament. Recent attempts to discover the origin of the name have concentrated upon Egyptian references to 'Yhw in *shasu* land'. The *shasu* were tribal peoples living in areas including that between the Egyptian delta and Gaza, and 'Yhw in *shasu* land' may associate a God Yhw with a mountain or region where the *shasu* lived. The Old Testament connection of Moses with both Egypt and Midian (southern Trans-jordan) may refer back to this.

Whatever the origin of the name YHWH, it is derived from the Hebrew verb 'to be' (*Hyh* or *Hwh*) according to the present passage and it is translated variously as 'I am who I am', or 'I am what I am' or 'I will be what I will be'. It has been pointed out that whereas some of the gods of the surrounding nations were personifications of natural phenomena – Baal was the god of the storm clouds and Shamash the sun god – YHWH cannot be connected with any force of nature. He is above nature and is the source of all that exists.

It is important to go further, however. The present passage connects the name YHWH with the exodus, with God's observing the misery of his people and hearing their cry for help. YHWH is not simply the 'ground of being'. He is known because he has acted in compassion to free his people from slavery. The important question is not whether God exists, but what kind of God he is. The biblical answer is that he is a God who sets his people free, that they may ultimately be the means by which he sets all the nations free. JR

Jeremiah 15.15–21

This is one of the so-called 'confessions of Jeremiah', a passage in which there is an intense and personal dialogue between the prophet and God. The opening verse (v. 15) is a plea to God to vindicate the prophet, because the insults and threats that he endures are suffered for the sake of God. Can, or should, God be untouched or indifferent to what his servants suffer in his name? The prophet further backs up his claim for God's manifest support by mentioning his call as a prophet, and how this has affected his social relationships and his inner life. The statement about eating God's words (v. 16) is strongly reminiscent of the call of Ezekiel (Ezek. 3.1–2), where that prophet eats a scroll that tastes as sweet as honey. The joy mentioned in the present passage may therefore refer to an initial or continuing joy in God's service which has to be reckoned alongside the pain and anguish. Being called by God has involved Jeremiah in his social and inner experiences, however, not in joy but in isolation and suffering. The conviction that he must for ever proclaim the bad news of imminent judgement is like a pain which cannot be dulled and a wound that never heals. This leads Jeremiah to accuse God of misleading him, of turning his initial joy to profound disillusionment.

The opening words of the divine response (v. 19), in the second person singular, are difficult. In what sense is it necessary for Jeremiah to turn back to God? Is it considered that his complaint to God is a sign of disloyalty of which he must now repent? If so, this passage is different from Job or those psalms where individuals pour out their complaints to God, and it becomes a charter for those who maintain that we must never question God's ways. One solution is to regard the words 'if you turn back' as addressed to the people as a whole, but this is hardly convincing. It is true that v. 19 is highly poetic, with wordplay upon the Hebrew verb 'to turn' – a phenomen easily observed in the English. The easiest solution is to understand 'if you turn back' to mean 'if you continue to be a prophet'. God reassures Jeremiah that the people will have to respond to him because he says what is true (precious) even if they continue to oppose him.

In the event, there certainly were those in Jerusalem who supported Jeremiah (e.g. Jer. 26.16, 24) and who heeded his message. Today's passage is one of the most profound insights into the mystery of being caught up in the divine pain that is involved in human redemption. JR

Romans 12.9–21

This passage of ethical instruction mostly comprises short, pithy sayings, indebted in parts to the Old Testament and occasionally, perhaps, to the sayings of Jesus. There are also notable parallels between Paul's teaching here and that found in 1 Thess. 4.9–12; 5.15–18; 1 Pet. 3.8–9; 4.7–10 and Heb. 13.1–2, suggesting that this moral teaching was part of a basic stock of early Christian material.

The first section (vv. 9–13) is primarily concerned with relations among believers. Fundamental to early Christian teaching was the appeal to love one another with a love like that between brothers and sisters (no mention here of love for those 'outside', though they are to be blessed and not cursed – see v. 14). Paul's readers are urged to maintain their commitment, to sustain their zeal in serving the Lord, even in suffering. Their Christian love is also to find expression beyond the limits of their local congregation: they are to contribute to the needs of the saints (as a number of churches did in the collection Paul organized for poor Christians in Jerusalem: see 1 Cor. 16.1–4; 2 Cor. 8—9; Rom. 15.25–28) and to offer hospitality to strangers, another virtue widely practised in early Christianity (cf. Heb. 13.2).

From v. 14 onwards the focus is more upon relations with those outside the Christian community, a focus which continues through the opening verses of ch. 13 (13.1–7). The exhortation to 'bless those who persecute you' may echo a saying from the Sermon on the Mount (Matt. 5.44), though there people are urged to *love* their enemies. Verse 15 may echo Sirach 7.34: 'Do not avoid those who weep, but mourn with those who mourn.' In v. 16 Paul returns to the theme of 12.3, urging Christians not to be haughty or high-minded, but to show equal concern for one another, getting on 'with those who are lowly' (or, perhaps, 'with humble things/tasks' – either translation is possible). Paul then turns back to the theme of response to evil or persecution (v. 17), urging his readers to resist the temptation to return evil for evil and instead to keep to what is acknowledged by all as 'good' (cf. the close parallel in 1 Thess. 5.15; also Lev. 19.18. The idea that it is a better thing to suffer evil than to inflict it was also expressed by Plato, among others). Drawing on various Old Testament texts, he explains that his readers' restraint is not intended to remove all thought of recompense for evil, but rather to leave room for God's wrath (v. 19; cf. Prov. 20.22; Deut. 32.35). Instruction for the Roman Christians is drawn from Prov. 25.21–22: they are called to respond to their enemies with generosity and not violence, thus conquering evil with good (cf. also Matt. 5.39). Unfortunately the meaning of the intriguing phrase 'for in doing this you will heap burning coals on their heads' is not entirely clear: it may mean that meeting evil with good will bring shame on one's enemies, or will lead them to repentance, or that it will increase their guilt and thus their eventual punishment by God. DH

Matthew 16.21–28

Matthew follows and modifies Mark 8.31—9.1. The factor that most obviously leads to his modifications is his decision to improve the depiction of Peter. This is in line with Matthew's general dissatisfaction with (failure to see any point in?) Mark's common negative depiction of the Twelve who, like us all, stand in need of the benefits that Jesus alone can give. For Matthew, they are rather, despite inadequacies (and, in the case of Judas, appalling wickedness), the embryonic and model leaders of the Church and its mission. This is true of Peter above all, as the inserted verses, 17–19, make plain.

However, Matthew has a problem. If he will follow Mark, what can he do about Peter's rejection of Jesus' prophecy of his coming condemnation and death (here, v. 21)? And, even more, about Jesus' devastating identification of Peter with Satan when he rejects (brusquely in Mark) that prophecy? Luke simply dropped the satanic naming, thus avoiding difficulty. Matthew was more faithful to Mark, but he did modify Peter's rebuke, making it almost a courtier's polite disclaimer (v. 22). The lectionary 'helps' by dividing the passage at v. 20, but it leaves the Marcan original as a single reading, 8.27–38.

The crucial teaching that follows, on the cross-marked character of the Christian life, is taken from Mark, and Matthew only adds (v. 27) his characteristic point about the equitable character of the coming judgement facing all (cf. ch. 25 and the fate of Judas in 27.3–10). It vies with a gospel message (good news indeed) that insists on the abundant saving grace of God to sinners, all of us being in that same boat. Yet the Marcan message of Jesus continues to shine through.

The final verse (again typically) works with a picture of Jesus as king, as God's viceregent, in the future denouement, and already latently. We should contrast this verse with Mark 9.1, speaking of the kingdom, which Matthew here personalizes in terms of the Son of man. Matthew did the same with the cry of the crowds at the entry of Jesus into Jerusalem: compare Matt. 21.15 with Mark 11.10. And the image is impressed upon us in Matt. 25.31–46. So Matthew inaugurated the imagery that came to dominate Christian liturgy and art at all levels; though in fact the idea of Jesus' kingdom, albeit temporary, appears first in 1 Cor. 15.22–28. In Mark, Jesus points unequivocally to the kingdom *of God*, and only his enemies call him king (15.2, 26) using the very word, though 14.62 admits Messiahship – but, as in Mark's version of our present passage, only and firmly in the context of death, insisting on paradox. In Mark it was left unclear when he thought Jesus' prophecy in 9.1 would be fulfilled: was it, in a cryptic way, at the passion, or did it lie still in the future? Matthew gave us his answer: see 28.16–20. LH

Proper 18

(Sunday between 4 and 10 September inclusive)

Exodus 12.1–14 or Ezekiel 33.7–11; Romans 13.8–14; Matthew 18.15–20

Exodus 12.1–14

(See Maundy Thursday, p. 105.)

Ezekiel 33.7–11

This passage substantially repeats 3.17–21, except that the preceding verses in ch. 33 expand the material in ch. 3 by way of an example from daily life. The example is that of a sentinel (NRSV's gender-free equivalent of the more familiar 'watchman') who sees an enemy approaching and who warns the people by blowing a trumpet. Obviously, any watchman who failed the people in this way would be held responsible for the disaster that consequently overtook them. As applied to the prophet, the easiest way to take the comparison is to regard it as the prophet's vindication of his ministry. Confronted by those who object to the prophetic message of coming judgement, the prophet replies that he is like a watchman who has seen an approaching enemy and is issuing a warning in order to alert the people. If he fails to deliver his message, he is as culpable as the watchman who fails to sound the trumpet.

This interpretation has the merit of alleviating what is otherwise problematic in the text. Is it fair that the prophet should be held responsible for the actions of other people? Ezekiel, after all, is a prophet who lays great stress upon personal responsibility (cf. Ezek. 18). Why should he be blamed if people choose to persist in doing evil? The answer is that although God is not indifferent to evil and will punish it, neither does he enjoy meting out punishment. 'I have no pleasure in the death of the wicked' (v. 11). God is not simply an austere God of justice who indifferently upholds a moral universe. His justice is shot through with compassion and with the desire to deal with the wicked by winning them over to love what is good. This is one reason why he calls and commissions prophets – prophets whose testimony to a God of justice and compassion has been preserved and come down to us in the Bible for today. JR

Romans 13.8–14

After his much discussed and controversial teaching urging submission to the governing authorities (13.1–7) Paul turns back to instruction focused mainly on relations between members of the Christian congregations. Again their obligation to love one another is stressed (cf. 12.10); this is an overriding and all-encompassing obligation which in itself fulfils the law (v. 10). For all his insistence that no one will be saved by the works of the law, and his negative statements on the impact of the law (e.g. Rom. 3.20; 1 Cor. 15.56; Gal. 3.10–14), Paul believes that Christians should fulfil it (cf. Rom. 8.4; Gal. 5.14). All the commandments, he explains, are summed up in the command to love one's neighbour, not itself one of the ten commandments but found in Lev. 19.18. Love, then, for Paul, is the fulfilment of the law. Here we see clearly the influence of the Old Testament, Paul's Bible, on his ethical teaching: there are disagreements as to how far Paul abandons aspects of the Jewish law in practice, but that it continues to form his moral convictions can hardly be denied. Nor should Paul's idea that the heart of the law may be encapsulated in a single saying be regarded as a peculiarly Christian viewpoint: there is a wonderful story in the Babylonian Talmud (Shabbath 31a) about a Gentile who said to the famous rabbis Shammai and Hillel, 'Make me a proselyte, on condition that you teach me the whole Torah [the Jewish law] while I stand on one foot.' Rabbi Shammai chased him off with a stick, but Hillel said to him: 'Whatever is hateful to you, do not do to your neighbour. That is the whole Torah, the rest is commentary; go and learn it.'

While the Jewish Scriptures provide a good deal of the substance in Paul's ethical teaching, Christian motivations are also evident. In vv. 11–13 the idea that the end, the day of the Lord, is drawing nearer provides a basis for the encouragement to live a moral life. Christians should live as people of the 'day', whose good deeds can be seen in the light, unlike evil deeds which are done behind the cover of darkness. (For the typically sectarian contrast between day and night, light and dark, see also 1 Thess. 5.5.) The list of unseemly vices includes standard items (cf. Gal. 5.19–21; 1 Pet. 4.3) along with 'quarrelling and jealousy', which Paul specifically confronted at Corinth (1 Cor. 3.3). A distinctively Christian motivation for upright living appears in v. 14: the idea of 'putting on Christ'. This image, often associated with baptism (e.g. Gal. 3.27), reminds Christians that they have died to their old life and begun a new one, lived 'in Christ'. It follows, as Paul has already stressed in Romans (6.1–14; 8.5–13) that they should live in Christ, walk by the Spirit, and shun the sinful desires of the 'flesh' – the old self enslaved to sin (Rom. 6.6). DH

Matthew 18.15–20

Chapter 18 of Matthew is the fourth of the five main discourses, ending like the others with a standard formula (cf. 19.1). It is sometimes called the community rule, echoing the Dead Sea text of that name. Indeed this passage is very similar to the Qumran document, at least initially, with its three rules for settling community disputes cast in a casuistic (case-law) form. But it ends with material of a different kind, three oracle-type sayings, which are more common, along with aphorisms and parables, in Jesus' teaching elsewhere. The difference in style may indicate that the earlier part of this passage originated from the Church.

The purpose of these instructions is to limit the damage to unity caused by internal disputes among the members. If the disputing parties cannot reach a satisfactory reconciliation in private (v. 15), arbitrators are called in (v. 16; two or three witnesses, reflecting Jewish legal practice). Only if the offender remains obdurate should the church (i.e. the local assembly, contrast the universal sense of this word in its only other use in Matthew at 16.18) become involved. The exact nature of the offence at issue is not specified. It may be not so much that a particular sinful act has been committed, but that there is disagreement over whether a particular act is sinful or not. The formula for dismissal from membership of an offender – 'Let him be to you a Gentile and tax collector' – is on both counts very surprising. Tax collectors are not stigmatized elsewhere in the Gospel as beyond the pale; they are rather characterized as responsive hearers of the word. And while there are a few other hostile references to Gentiles (see 6.7, 32), a positive attitude towards Gentile mission emerges eventually from the narrative (28.17). Pharisaic narrow-mindedness, elsewhere critiqued, seems here to have infected the community's own perspective; it is a virus easily caught.

The power to legislate, expressed in the Jewish terminology of binding and loosing (i.e. applying a general prohibition to a particular action or allowing an exemption), is here invested in the community meeting together, rather than in its apostolic leadership (cf. 16.19). The church's disciplinary rulings are assured of divine endorsement ('bound in heaven').

The next saying emphasizes a positive corollary; ecclesial unity and harmony reinforce the effectiveness of intercessory prayer. The catechism on prayer in 6.5–15 has earlier stipulated two other conditions for effective intercession: brevity of expression (6.7) and prior mutual reconciliation (6.14). And again, human actions receive divine endorsement. A theological problem raised here is whether God's sovereign autonomy is not compromised by attributing power to the initiative of human beings.

The final saying may have been borrowed from the contemporary Jewish proverb (Mishnah *Aboth* 3.2): 'If two sit together to discuss the Law, the *Shekinah* rests between them.' If so, it has been thoroughly christologized: it is meeting in the name of Christ, not studying Torah in the synagogue, that guarantees the presence of the true 'glory' of God (which is Jesus himself). The 'I' who speaks here is clearly not the Jesus of history but the spiritual risen Christ (28.20) present in the church gathered for worship. JM

Proper 19

(Sunday between 11 and 17 September inclusive)

Exodus 14.19–31 or Exodus 15.1b–11, 21b or Genesis 50.15–21; Romans 14.1–12;
Matthew 8.21–35

Exodus 14.19–31

(See Second Sunday of Easter, p. 118.)

Exodus 15.1b—11, 21b

This extract from the 'Song of the Sea' in Exodus 15 is bound to present considerable difficulties to many readers. Although its date and genre are matters of profound disagreement among scholars, it is indisputable that it gave, and has continued to give, liturgical expression to joy at God's overthrow of Israel's enemies. Such sentiments fall below the religion of the Old Testament at its best and foster the kind of nationalistic and vindictive sentiments that have been turned against the Jews themselves over the centuries, culminating in the atrocities of the twentieth century.

Feminist scholars have pointed out that v. 21b was sung by Miriam (this information in vv. 20–21a is absent from the abstract) whereas vv. 1b–18 are attributed to Moses (again, in information omitted from the abstract). They have suggested that, given the close similarity of the words of 1b and 21b, the song was originally sung by Miriam and the women, and that the attribution of the song to Moses is an instance of the silencing of women's voices in the Old Testament. Interestingly, v. 21b has been regarded as the original core of the song and possibly the oldest liturgical reference in the Old Testament to the exodus. The feminist suggestions, however, make women responsible for a poem that gloats over the divine punishment of the Egyptians, a sentiment that will probably not be universally welcomed in women's movements.

If the passage is to be redeemed it will have to be by way of idealization; by seeing the Egyptians as representing the forces of evil and their punishment by God as representing the hope of a better world. It will have to be read and appreciated not in a spirit of moral superiority, but of humble acknowledgement of all human involvement in the world's evil. The words 'Who is like you, O Lord among the gods, Who is like you, majestic in holiness, awesome in splendour, majestic in holiness' (v. 11) will then take on a different meaning from that in their context, but a meaning that can be honestly used in today's world. JR

Genesis 50.15–21

These verses function both as a happy ending and as a reminder that the story is far from over. First, as a happy ending. Much of Gen. 12—50 has been concerned with rivalry and tensions within families: Abraham and Lot; Isaac and Ishmael; Jacob and Esau; Jacob and his uncle Laban; the different sons of Jacob by his different wives. From ch. 37 on, in particular, the driving force behind the story has been provided by the jealous rivalry between Joseph and his brothers. (Strictly they were only his half-brothers, but that point is not emphasized in the biblical account.) Now with the death of Jacob the brothers are fearful that Joseph's welcome was only to keep a united front while the old man was still alive. (Such a situation reminds us that though in some respects the biblical characters seem very alien to the modern West, certain all too familiar tensions recur again and again.) Joseph is at pains to assure the others that he has no evil intentions; all had been part of the divine plan, and he 'reassured them'. The tension built up since ch. 37 is released.

But of course in another way this little episode is not an ending at all. It is a pity that the reading stops where it does, for the following verses make clear that the story is far from over. The brothers, and we the readers, are to look forward to a return to the land from which they had descended to Egypt (v. 24). A similar kind of ambiguity is found at the beginning of Exodus, where sometimes it is made clear that the events described are a continuation of an earlier narrative, but sometimes it appears as an entirely new story. The older kind of source-criticism (J, E, D and P) stressed the element of continuity, with each of the narrative sources in particular running right through from Genesis onward. Perhaps a more satisfactory way of looking at the material in the Pentateuch is to see it as a series of related but largely separate blocks of material, with each episode effectively self-contained. The end of the Joseph story and of the book of Genesis marks the end of one such episode. RC

Romans 14.1–12

Quarrels regarding religious practice plague every Christian generation, perhaps every congregation. In Rom. 14.1—15.13, Paul addresses some specific quarrels and articulates a theological framework for dealing with them. Whether these specific quarrels are characteristic of the church at Rome remains unclear, for Paul does not explicitly say that he knows about such issues being a problem in Rome. The issues themselves could have existed in many early congregations, especially in those that involved both Jews and Gentiles. The quarrels have to do with diet and with special days, although again the specifics are unclear. Some believe that their faith allows them to eat anything, while others (perhaps from concern about contact with food that would be impure according to kosher laws, or eating meat sacrificed to pagan idols) eat only vegetables (14.2). Some observe special days, while others regard all days as the same (14.5).

Despite the remoteness of these specific debates from contemporary Christian practice, many pastors will recognize and identify with the dilemma Paul faces here. How can quarrels be adjudicated without destroying the fabric of the community? What is most striking about Paul's response is that he does not attempt to decide the specific issues of food laws or feast days. He issues no call for an orthopraxis by which believers may be assessed or evaluated. Instead, he makes several important theological observations and trusts that they will lead toward reconciliation. In other words, in this instance the health of the believing community takes precedence over 'right' belief or 'right' observance.

The central conviction Paul brings to bear in this conflict appears first in vv. 3–4 and again in vv. 6–9: 'Who are you to pass judgement on servants of another? It is before their own lord that they stand or fall' (v. 4). Consistent with the argument of the letter as a whole, Paul asserts that Christians belong to God. God created them, and in the Christ-event God has reclaimed them. That relationship takes precedence over all others, without exception. For this reason, the specific religious practices or nonpractices of any individual stem from that person's standing as a servant of God. The one who eats everything without scruple does so to the honour of God; the one who abstains from everything acts likewise. What matters is the integrity of the relationship with God, not the specific religious practices.

In addition to recalling that Christians belong to God rather than, first of all, to one another, Paul urges that people be 'fully convinced in their own minds' (v. 5). Further on in this chapter he will articulate the unusual judgement that people who act contrary to their own consciences are condemned (v. 23), underscoring again the importance of conviction. To act contrary to conscience is indeed a dangerous thing. Whatever decision is reached about specific religious practices, the decision needs to have behind it the integrity of genuine reflection rather than the doubt and confusion that grow out of haste or group pressure.

A third aspect of Paul's instruction in this passage is his injunction against judgement: 'Why do you pass judgement on your brother or sister?' (v. 10). As is evident already in Rom. 9—11, Paul believes that only God has the right to judge human beings. Christians certainly may not judge one another, for all of them serve the same Lord (v. 4) and must recognize the right of that Lord. Since all human beings are accountable to God, there is no reason for Christians to usurp God's role (vv. 10–12).

To this point, it would appear that Paul is advocating a kind of individualism in this passage. Believers belong to God and are accountable only to God, not to one another. Believers must act out of their individual consciences and convictions. Believers will stand before divine, not human, judgement. A fourth feature of this text places that pluralism firmly within a community context. The entire section of the letter begins with 'Welcome those who are weak in faith', and that 'welcome' recurs importantly in 15.7. What Paul seeks in this passage is not merely the tolerance of diversity, a grudging acceptance of the inevitability of differences. Instead, he articulates an active welcome for those with conflicting views and practices. If Christ welcomed all people (15.7), then Christians must find a way to welcome one another and to respect the integrity of one another.

We would be quite mistaken to take this passage as an endorsement of any and all behaviours, for Paul elsewhere insists on certain limits. For example, the needs of the larger community dictate what one does in worship (1 Cor. 11). Similarly, sexual practice is not a matter of indifference, but must reflect the fact that human beings belong to God both spiritually and physically. What Paul has in view in Rom. 14—15 is perhaps close to contemporary disputes about forms of baptism or celebration of the Eucharist. What one group regards as permissible another will see as prohibited and another as required. These debates will always characterize the life of the Church, as one or another emphasis comes to the foreground, but the debates should not prevent a common understanding of the Lordship of God and the servanthood of believers. BG

Matthew 18.21–35

The Bible repeatedly tells us that we ought to forgive those who have injured us. We know that. It is ingrained in our minds from the Lord's Prayer and from passages such as the one listed for this Sunday. Congregations are full of people who know they should forgive, who intellectually recognize that there is some positive value in letting go of cherished hurts, but who find it well-nigh impossible to do so. Being cheated on by a spouse or double-crossed by a business partner are experiences that engender shame and rage, that leave the injured party feeling defective, defeated and never quite good enough. To be told that one *ought* to forgive and let go of the pain simply does not effect a change; in fact, it may aggravate the situation by heaping a load of guilt on to an already enraged and shamed person.

In such a setting, we seek to read and interpret the two pieces of our lesson from Matt. 18. The first piece is a brief exchange between Peter and Jesus about the extent and nature of forgiveness (vv. 21–22). 'Seventy-seven times' is Jesus' way of telling Peter that forgiveness is not a commodity to be reckoned on a calculator. Not only is it limitless, but it cannot even be quantified. The language of numbers is inappropriate when one contemplates forgiveness. (This is illustrated in the parable that follows, with the absurdity of the indebtedness of the first servant.)

The second piece of the reading includes the vivid parable of the king who forgives one servant an impossible amount of indebtedness, but that servant is then unable to forgive a fellow servant a reasonable debt. At first blush, the parable evokes considerable consternation. Why does the first servant, having been treated so generously by the king, immediately act so ruthlessly towards his fellow servant? He seems an unrealistically heartless ogre. No one would do that. The king is certainly justified in his harsh retaliation – torture and imprisonment.

But when we sit with the parable awhile and reflect on the difficulty of genuine forgiveness, it takes on a different tone. Does the concluding verse (18.35) mean that if I do not forgive those who injure me, God will withhold forgiveness? Is divine forgiveness conditional on my letting go of grudges and hurts? That seems to be the conclusion here as well as elsewhere in Matthew (6.12, 14–15) – though it is not necessarily so.

Look again at the parable. The most obvious point is that human forgiveness is rooted in divine forgiveness. The king forgives the servant an incalculable amount of indebtedness. Ten thousand talents represents more than the wages of a day labourer for 150,000 years! There is simply no way to measure the extent of God's generosity when it comes to forgiving. 'Seventy-seven times' doesn't say it, and neither does 'ten thousand talents'.

But what happens to the first servant? There is a remarkable gap in the parable. On hearing of his release from the obligation, the servant shows no appropriate response – no rejoicing, no gratitude, no celebrating with wife and children who are spared imprisonment, no reflection about the meaning of freedom. We hear only that on the way out he refuses the pleas of a colleague. The 'gap' in the parable has to be taken seriously. The first servant clearly has not 'discovered' forgiveness. We already see something of the problem in his initial plea to the king. Though in debt beyond any conceivable capacity to pay, he nevertheless makes his case on a quid pro quo basis. 'I will pay you everything' (18.26). He imagines he is dealing with the king on the basis of justice. What he receives but never grasps is the king's mercy.

Forgiveness has to do with something very different from distributive justice. The parable wants us to know that. The first servant still thinks of indebtedness/forgiveness as a power game. He has not come to view himself in a new light as a truly 'gifted' person, the recipient of mercy rather than justice. He is not able, therefore, to see himself in the same situation as the second servant, and is not able to show mercy as mercy has been shown. The final verse (18.35) makes it clear that forgiveness is a matter of the 'heart', a transformation of the inner disposition of the recipient, something the first servant has not discovered.

How, then, does the passage address seriously injured persons, persons battling with shame and alienation? It portrays in a dramatic story the incredible kindness of God, who surprises people not by dealing with them on the scale of justice, even though they seek it, but by showing mercy. It invites readers to view themselves as forgiven debtors – no more, no less – living with and among fellow debtors. The difference between the debtors is only slight. To be forgiven means to give up the power game of playing innocent versus guilty, and to join a fellowship of forgiven sinners. CC

Proper 20

(Sunday between 18 and 24 September inclusive)

Exodus 16.2–15 or Jonah 3.10—4.11; Philippians 1.21–30; Matthew 20.1–16

Exodus 16.2–15

This passage is one of several in Exodus and Numbers that deal with the complaints of the Israelites in the wilderness and divine intervention to satisfy their needs. They have their origin in natural phenomena that occured in the wilderness. Quails (*coturnix coturnix*) arrived in northern Sinai in August-September in great numbers from the Sudan and Ethiopia and, exhausted from their journey, could be easily hunted and gathered. Manna is a secretion from a flowering tree such as the tamarisk bush, assisted by the sting and secretion of a tree louse.

This 'natural food', well known to anyone used to living in the wilderness, has become the basis of accounts of miraculous feeding of the Israelites; but it should be noted that the narratives have also become object-lessons that must have figured in religious instruction.

This is most obvious in vv. 4–8. The sabbath has not yet been instituted (cf. Exod. 20.8), but the Israelites are instructed to gather twice as much on the sixth day as they normally gather, the implication being that they will then not need to gather any manna on the seventh (sabbath) day. Later in the chapter, there is an explicit command to the people not to gather any manna on the seventh (sabbath) day (v. 23) and the Israelites discover that if they keep manna overnight on days one to five it will go bad, but that if they gather twice as much on the sixth day to be used on the seventh, it will keep. Israelites who ignored the instruction about gathering twice as much on the sixth day and who went looking for manna on the seventh day are disappointed (vv. 27–30).

Another charming feature of the story (not included in today's reading) in vv. 17–18 is that however much people gathered it amounted to the same: those who gathered much had nothing over, and those who gathered little had no shortage (v. 18). This is not a charter for laziness, but a way of saying that God met each person's needs completely, and independently of the human competitiveness that would undoubtedly result in some getting more, at the expense of those who gathered less.

This passage, then, shows God graciously responding to the people's complaints. Later episodes show how the people redeemed from slavery began to try God's patience. JR

Jonah 3.10—4.11

Jonah is a book full of ironies. It centres upon a prophet who, although he believes in the God of heaven, who made the sea and the dry land (Jonah 1.9), believes that he can escape from God and his commission. A further irony is that when he eventually arrives in Nineveh and announces God's impending judgement, the people of Nineveh repent and proclaim a fast. The irony is twofold. First, Nineveh is the capital of the hated Assyrian people, a people responsible for destroying the northern kingdom, Israel, and for taking its people into exile (2 Kings 17). How can such a response be expected from such a quarter? Second, the prompt repentance of Nineveh contrasts with the unwillingness or inability of the people of God to hear the warnings of their prophets. A complaint in Jeremiah is that 'I have sent to you all my servants the prophets, sending them persistently, saying, "Turn now everyone of you from your evil way…" But you did not incline your ear or obey me' (Jer. 35.15).

Jonah seems to have anticipated that things would turn out oddly, that God would end up by showing mercy and not judgement (Jonah 4.2), and this deeply upsets him. Here, he resembles those religious people who like to feel that they alone belong to the elect or the true church, while everyone else is damned. He resembles those who are distressed by the thought that other members of their family, or their neighbours, or criminals, could truly turn to God. Such a reaction, which is human and natural, betrays an inner insecurity, a desire to possess God for one's own benefit, so that others become unwelcome competitors. In this regard, Jonah also personifies the people of Israel and many manifestations of the Christian Church. His request for God to take away his life (v. 3) is the reaction of a sulking child.

Nevertheless, Jonah still seems to have some hope that God will destroy Nineveh and thus act in accordance with his forecast of impending doom. He makes himself a booth and sits down to watch developments. God now teaches Jonah a lesson via the bush, that gives him welcome protection from the sun. Its withering distresses Jonah for the purely selfish reason that it no longer affords him protection. Using an argument from the lesser to the greater, God points out to Jonah that if the prophet cares about the bush, why should not God care about Nineveh? Two striking features here are the description of the Ninevites as people 'who do not know their right hand from their left' (v. 11) and God's concern about the animals in the city. Thus does the passage spell out in even greater depth the implications of God being merciful and gracious (v. 2), a truth that is so difficult for Jonah to come to terms with. JR

Philippians 1.21–30

This is the first of four consecutive epistle readings taken from Paul's letter to Christians at Philippi, a letter that poignantly reflects on Paul's imprisonment and his intimate relationship with this church. Following the thanksgiving (1.3–11), which expresses Paul's confidence in the partnership of Philippian Christians, he turns to the difficulty posed by his imprisonment. If later generations of Christians see in Paul's imprisonment an indication of his faithfulness, that apparently was not the case with at least some of his contemporaries. Perhaps he encountered the notion that prison meant failure for the Church, or that 'real apostles' would not find themselves subjected to such humiliation. It is easy to imagine that some Christians would be shocked at the sight of an imprisoned apostle (see, for example, the attitudes Paul attacks in 2 Cor. 10–13).

Paul's own interpretation of his imprisonment differs dramatically from this negative assessment, as Philippians readily demonstrates. Prison has not hindered, but spread, the gospel, since those around him plainly see that Paul's imprisonment is 'for Christ' (Phil. 1.12–13). The fact of Paul's imprisonment has made other Christians bold in their own preaching of the gospel (v. 14). Paul himself will not be shamed by these events, but rather through him the gospel will be exalted (v. 20).

In addition to the need to explain his imprisonment, Paul recognizes that the Philippians have a natural concern about his physical safety. Although Paul seems to anticipate his eventual release (v. 19), he cannot know what the outcome of his imprisonment will be ('whether by life or death', v. 20). For that reason, he attempts in our passage (vv. 21–30) to show the benefits of either outcome and to encourage the Philippians in what may well be a time of doubt and anxiety.

Paul's stay in prison may lead to his death or it may yield his eventual release. Neither of these outcomes does he regard as failure or loss: 'For to me, living is Christ and dying is gain' (v. 21). He could as easily have reversed the two parts of this sentence and written that 'living is gain and dying is Christ'. Dying, he writes in v. 23, in fact means a departure and the opportunity to 'be with Christ'. Dying, then, does not signal the end, but rather the culmination of a Christian's hopes in the triumph of Jesus Christ. While death is not to be sought, its arrival is also not to be dreaded. Living in the flesh, on the other hand, also 'is Christ'. Even the finite life available to flesh nevertheless permits a profound connection with Christ (see e.g. Gal. 2.20). Continued life in the flesh also means an opportunity for extended labour as an apostle.

Throughout vv. 21–23 Paul juxtaposes the two possibilities that lie before him: to live versus to die, departing to be with Christ versus remaining in the flesh. He even discusses these two possibilities as if the choice is his own, although that probably reflects the need to assure the Philippians that events have not overcome him. With v. 24 the even-handed consideration of these two options comes to an end: 'to remain in the flesh is more necessary for you'. Here Paul's vocation comes to the foreground. He has been called as an apostle and labours under a tremendous compulsion to proclaim the gospel in new locales *and* to care for the churches he has already established. He cannot abdicate that commitment in favour of an escape from the world, no matter how attractive that escape might be. The vocation comes first.

As Paul reflects on his own situation and the possibilities that confront him, he also addresses the situation of the Philippians. By expressing confidence about his own future, he exhorts the Philippians to have confidence as well. Moreover, his references to the 'progress and joy in faith' (v. 25) of the Philippians functions rhetorically to impress the Philippians with the need to live up to Paul's expectations. Like the parent who praises the good behaviour of a child, Paul probably expects that his comments about the Philippians here and elsewhere in the letter will in fact lead to further progress and deeper faith.

The connection between Paul's situation and that of the Philippians becomes explicit in v. 26 with the reference to a future visit of Paul to Philippi, and in v. 27, which marks a transition from consideration of Paul's imprisonment to the situation of the Philippians. Whatever happens to Paul, he wants to be assured that they are secure in their faith. He admonishes them to 'live your life in a manner worthy of the gospel of Christ'. This brief instruction contains the outlines of Paul's understanding of a Christian ethic. The gospel is freely given to human beings; their appropriate response is to live in accordance with that gospel.

The remainder of the passage announces themes that will carry throughout the letter. The Philippians should be 'standing firm in one spirit, striving side by side with one mind for the faith of the gospel'. Paul's repetition here of 'one spirit' and 'one mind' provides a glimpse into his concern for the unity of the Church. That unity appropriately reflects the mind of Christ and secures the Church against its opponents and the suffering it too may be forced to endure (vv. 28–30). It also would reassure an imprisoned Paul that his own work would survive his death. BG

Matthew 20.1–16

There is no more cherished word in the Christian's vocabulary than 'grace'. Simply put, it describes the mercy of God demonstrated in countless ways to undeserving people. It is not surprising that polls show 'Amazing Grace' to be the favourite hymn of many. But just because of its popularity, the notion of grace often loses its cutting edge. It gets acculturated, divorced from the character of a righteous God, resulting in saccharine permissiveness. When that happens, nothing jolts and jars the sentimentality quite like a reading of the parable of the labourers in the vineyard (Matt. 20.1–16). In a vivid and even abrasive story, the radical and offensive nature of grace is depicted, inevitably leaving the reader with the questions: was the owner really fair? Don't the labourers who worked all day have a legitimate beef?

One word of warning: this is a parable that needs very little explanation or interpretation. Its impact is so forceful, so direct, so engaging that the preacher has to worry about staying out of the way of the parable's confrontation with the congregation. The trick is to let the story have its own way, and then perhaps to help hearers understand their response to the story.

Two dimensions of the context set the parable in proper perspective. First, the audience is primarily the disciples (19.23, 27; 20.17). The passage is a part of their instruction as they make the move from Galilee to Jerusalem (19.1; 20.18). The parable is not in the first instance addressed to the crowds or even to seekers, but to insiders, those who know, at least in a measure, about divine grace. Second, the story is bracketed by two reversal sayings (19.30; 20.16), sayings that in themselves carry enormous threat for persons who identify themselves as insiders, as the privileged who enjoy a special place with Jesus (see 20.20–28). The parable in effect depicts what it means that the first shall be last and the last first.

As for the parable itself, the radical and offensive character of grace is evident in two sets of relationships. First is the relationship between the owner of the vineyard and the labourers who work all day. The precise telling of the story leaves us with a final scene in which the labourers who work the entire day stand by and watch as the manager pays the other labourers a full day's wages. The first group's anticipation of a bigger wage mounts as they see the generosity shown to the others. When they receive 'only' the agreed-upon wages, understandably they grumble against the land-owner.

We need to linger a bit over the apparent unfairness of the owner. Imagine what would happen if the world really functioned this way! What if the 'equal pay for equal work' principle were not operative? Why, people would sleep late and come to the labour pool only in the late afternoon if they knew they would get paid for the whole day! The owner's action upsets the whole arrangement of societal order, by no means an evil arrangement since it institutionalizes an important principle of justice.

Divine grace, of course, does not rest on the merit system. But because it doesn't, we insiders are prone to grumble. We wonder if grace does not undermine the whole reason for being good, for observing standards, for keeping rules, for living justly. We second-guess a God who breaches the system and equalizes the pay like this. We could support the owner's generosity if the groups of workers that came after noon had merely been delayed, if the truck that brought them to the fields had broken down. But the owner's actions are not the sign of a little generosity to an unfortunate few. They call for a totally different way of viewing God.

But the second set of relationships in the parable gets us even deeper into the offensive character of grace – the relationship between the labourers who work all day and the labourers who come late. The former group express their gripe by saying, 'These last worked only one hour, and you have made them equal to us' (20.12). They are envious of the generosity shown the others. Presumably had *they* been the recipients of the owner's gracious method of book-keeping, they would have been overjoyed. What they cannot take is the beneficence that puts these latecomers on a par with them. The grumblers are not really against grace; they are against grace shown to others and what that implies.

It is an old story. Jonah sat on the brow of the hill outside of Nineveh and pouted when God spared the city. The elder brother thought his father a doting old fool when his father invited him to join the celebrating at the prodigal's return. The Pharisee at prayer thanks God that he is not like the sinful publican. Divine grace is a great equalizer which rips away presumed privilege and puts all recipients on a par. That's hard to stomach when we have burdened ourselves with a merit system and want to see some reward for our labours. That's hard to stomach when we discover those guilty of wrongs we have long opposed (for example, racism, sexism, colonialism, and the like) are brothers and sisters to whom the divine gener-osity has been shown. Grace no longer seems so sentimental. cc

Proper 21

(Sunday between 25 September and 1 October inclusive)

Exodus 17.1–7 or Ezekiel 18.1–4, 25–32; Philippians 2.1–13; Matthew 21.23–32

Exodus 17.1–7

(See Third Sunday of Lent, p. 87.)

Ezekiel 18.1–4, 25–32

The selection of particular verses from Ezekiel 18 and the use of a gender-free translation (NRSV) in the lectionary has a considerable effect on the impact that this passage makes on hearers/readers. The chapter has classically been regarded as one which stresses individual responsibility above all, on account of its language. Thus v. 26 reads in the RSV, accurately representing the Hebrew, 'When a righteous man turns away from his righteousness and commits iniquity, he shall die for it'. This is distorted in the NRSV's attempt to avoid the word 'man'. The omitted verses, especially 5 to 18, convey, if not irony, a series of cases that are seemingly deliberately overstated. Thus vv. 10–12 give us a picture of a wicked man that is so unrealistic as to be almost laughable: 'If he has a son who is violent, a shedder of blood, who eats upon the mountains, defiles his neighbour's wife, oppresses the poor and needy, commits robbery, does not restore the pledge, lifts up his eyes to the idols, commits abomination, takes advance or accrued interest; shall he then live? He shall not.' The pictures of the righteous as absolute paragons of virtue (vv. 5–9, 14–17) are similarly unrealistic.

This seeming exaggeration may, however, be the clue to a correct understanding of the passage. If it is right to attribute it to Ezekiel in exile in Babylon between 597 BC when the first exile took place (see 2 Kings 24.8–17) and 587 BC when the Babylonians destroyed Jerusalem and the temple, the prophet is meeting the complaint summed up in the proverb of v. 2 that the exiles are suffering not because of their own wrongdoings but because of those of their parents. The prophet's reply is directed not towards individuals among the generation of the exiles, but to the generation as a whole. The portraits of the good and bad character in vv. 5–20 are portraits not of individuals (how could they be?) but of generations in which there will be found individuals, some of whom commit and some of whom abstain from some of the vices and virtues listed in the chapter.

The difficulty with trying to account for misfortune in terms of divine punishment is that it overlooks the righteous who suffer and the wicked who prosper, as the Old Testament is well aware (cf. Ps. 73). This mismatch does not entail, however, that one should give up believing that the distinction between right and wrong is important.

The proverb quoted by the exiles in Babylon was an attempt on their part to evade their moral responsibility by accusing God of presiding over an immoral universe. In reply, the prophet asserts that, however things may appear, the ways of God are ultimately not unfair and that there is no alternative to people recognizing their wickedness and seeking God's forgiveness. It would be a mistake to suppose that Ezekiel's response to a particular problem is a complete solution to the complex matter of the relationship between corporate and individual responsibility, and the cases that disprove any neat solution. JR

Philippians 2.1–13

(See Palm Sunday, p. 103.)

Matthew 21.23–32

For the next few Sundays, the gospel lessons from Matthew relate encounters of conflict between Jesus and the Jewish religious authorities – chief priests and elders of the people, Pharisees, Herodians and Sadducees. The situation of the text obviously reflects historical engagements, both within the ministry of Jesus and within the circumstances of Matthew's community. But our communities and contexts are different, and there are hazards in making the leap from ancient settings to modern ones, especially since these texts in Matthew carry a strong polemic couched in sharp invectives. How do we preach on these passages today?

Two comments about the interpretive move. First, the uniqueness of the ancient contexts prohibits us from generalizing about the Jewish religious authorities. Their picture throughout Matthew's narrative may be something of a caricature, and the modern interpreter must be on guard not to carry over from the passages, directly or subtly, an anti-Jewish sentiment. What was an intramural struggle in the biblical settings would not be so today. Second, the task is to isolate as discretely as possible the *issue* that sets the authorities over against Jesus, often an issue that has immediate relevance to modern audiences. At times there are even pointers within the text itself that tell us that the narrator envisions a wider application.

The brief parable of the two sons follows immediately on the heels of the discussion in the temple about Jesus' authority (Matt. 21.23–27). The religious leaders are put on the spot when Jesus raises the matter of John's baptism, and employ a face-saving tactic by refusing to answer. In turn, Jesus refuses to answer their initial question about the source of his authority. But there comes from Jesus to the authorities a rhetorical invitation to reflect on the upcoming story to be told ('What do you think?'), a story on which they are to be tested.

A father of two sons directs the first to go and work in the vineyard. He declines, but then changes his mind and goes. The second son is given the same directive, agrees to go, but then doesn't. The authorities are kept in the conversation by Jesus' simple question to them: 'Which of the two did the will of his father?' They really have only one option – to say 'the first'. While their previous face-saving tactic momentarily got them off the hook, there is no possible evasion now.

Before going on to Jesus' conclusion, we can note that the second son's response to the father ('I go, sir [*kyrie*]') may be one of those subtle pointers that suggest a broader application of the parable. The Greek word behind the 'sir' is reminiscent of Matt. 7.21, where Jesus says, 'Not everyone who says to me "Lord, Lord [*kyrie, kyrie*]", will enter the kingdom of heaven, but only the one who does the will of my Father in heaven.' The second son, who so graciously agrees to work but then fails to fulfil his commitments, recalls all those who declare loyalty and even profess a high christology, but who exhibit no consistency between words and deeds, between religious activity and obedience. The narrator retells Jesus' parable in such words that those within the Christian community cannot assume that it is directed only to the Jewish authorities and not to them. Doing the will of the Father is as much a Gentile problem as a Jewish one.

The authorities' acknowledgement that the first son is obedient, while the second son isn't, leads to Jesus' pointed application of the story. The tax collectors and prostitutes may not on the surface look much like God's people, especially when compared to the pious religious authorities, but they are identified with the first son, and the religious authorities with the second. The difference lies not in appearances, but in their respective responses to the message of John. The tax collectors and prostitutes believed the message of John, while the religious authorities were resistant.

The prominence of John (cf. 21.25–27) in a narrative written long after his death reminds us that his message lingers on. It is interesting that the text does not exclude the authorities; it does not finally shut the door in their faces. Rather they are invited to rehear John's message and to be open to the reversal it urges. It is the same message Jesus preached; 'Repent, for the kingdom of heaven has come near' (Matt. 3.2; 4.17). Through the text, modern-day religious authorities as well as those of Matthew's day are faced with the demand for a similar transformation in the light of God's coming reign, for the same reversal experienced by the first son, who initially rejects his father's directive but changes his mind and obeys. cc

Proper 22

(Sunday between 2 and 8 October inclusive)

Exodus 20.1–4, 7–9, 12–20 or Isaiah 5.1–7; Philippians 3.4b–14; Matthew 21.33–46

Exodus 20.1–4, 7–9, 12–20

Recent research on the ten commandments has reached two conclusions: that the commandments are a literary distillation of laws from several social settings in ancient Israel, and that this distillation played an important role in shaping other parts of the Old Testament. This second point can be illustrated in several ways. First, there are two fairly similar versions of the ten commandments, the other version being in Deut. 5.6–21. Second, the ten commandments stand at the head, i.e. the most important position of, the so-called Book of the Covenant, the laws contained in Exodus 20—23. Third, a case can be made that Deut. chs. 12—26 largely follows the order of the ten commandments, and is a kind of elaboration and enlargement of them. Fourth, passages such as Lev. 19 and Ps. 50 are arguably based upon or allude to the ten commandments (see Seventh Sunday of Epiphany, p. 65).

The various backgrounds from which the ten commandments have been taken may be indicated by changes in the form of address. Verses 2–6 are a speech of God in the first person singular, vv. 7–12 talk about God in the third person while vv. 13–17 could be spoken either by God or a human representative. The second section, vv. 7–12, has been thought to represent the standpoint of the exile, with the particular emphasis on the sabbath, while the origin of vv. 13–17 has been sought in family law, the purpose of these verses being to protect the family and its property. The opening section is more difficult to place, presupposing as it does belief among the people in the existence of other gods and the attractions of idolatry. The general consensus of critical scholarship, however, is that in their present form, the ten commandments date from the exilic or post-exilic periods.

The fact that the ten commandments have been distilled from other laws and have then become the basis of further elaboration and expansion in the Old Testament indicates that they should not be regarded as a last word incapable of alteration. A reason given for observing the sabbath in Exod. 23.12 is that it will enable the ox and the ass to rest; and Lev. 19 adds further laws designed to protect the poor and needy. Christian tradition, too, has used the commandments creatively. The sabbath law, concerning Friday night to Saturday night, has been applied in various ways to Sunday; and Calvin's exposition of the ten commandments in the *Institutes of the Christian Religion* Book 2, Ch. 8 are a fine example of how their spirit can lead to more profound ethical reflection. JR

Isaiah 5.1–7

Because the autumn Feast of Booths was the occasion on which the grape harvest was celebrated, it has been suggested that the prophet sang his song to the people gathered together on this occasion. This may be correct, although there is no direct evidence that this was so. The song acts as a parable; that is, it invites the listeners to make, or agree with, a decision before the implications of that decision are spelled out.

The song begins with the singer acting on behalf of his male friend, describing the infinite care taken with preparing the best possible site for a vineyard, and planting the best possible vines. The hearers will be worried, if not shocked, to learn that the outcome was not choice grapes but wild grapes.

The owner of the vineyard now takes up the song. He asks the listeners, in effect, what they would do in the circumstances (vv. 3–4). He expects them to agree with him when he dismisses the case as hopeless. He will disown the vineyard, remove its protecting wall, no longer prune or hoe it, and will let it become overgrown. He will also tell the clouds that it will be a waste of precious water if they rain upon it.

We must assume that the listeners agree, or that the owner describes what they, also, would do. Verse 7 applies the parable. The vineyard is the house of Judah, and instead of producing justice (Hebrew *mishpat*) it has produced bloodshed (Hebrew *mispach*); instead of righteousness (*tsedaqah*) there has been a cry of the oppressed (*tseaqah*). By agreeing with the song, that the vineyard that produced wild grapes deserves to be left to turn into a wilderness, the listeners have been forced to agree that they deserve an analogous fate.

Within the narrative structure of Isa. 5 the song introduces a set of statements of judgement which spell out in greater detail the accusation that the chosen people have produced the opposite of what could be reasonably expected. Modern readers are entitled to ask, however, whether the action taken in regard to the unproductive vineyard was the only action possible; whether it might not have been worth trying again. Within the context of the original setting of the song, its message is clear: the people deserve and will get judgement because of their wickedness. On a longer term view, the good news is that God did not abandon his vineyard to become a wilderness, but that he gave it, and continues to give it, a further chance. JR

Philippians 3.4b–14

In the verses that immediately precede this reading, Paul issues a warning against 'the dogs', the 'evil workers', 'those who mutilate the flesh'. Scholars debate a number of details about the group Paul has in mind, but it appears that its adherents insist on circumcision for Gentile Christians and boast about their connections with Israel (see Phil. 3.2–4a).

This lection constitutes part of Paul's response to this group. He begins with the claim that he has more reason than they for 'confidence in the flesh' (v. 4). Verses 5–6 form a kind of curriculum vitae, beginning with aspects of Paul's life that were decided by virtue of his birth. He was 'circumcised on the eighth day, a member of the people of Israel, of the tribe of Benjamin, a Hebrew born of Hebrews' (v. 5). The second half of the list includes matters over which Paul did have a choice: 'as to the law, a Pharisee; as to zeal, a persecutor of the church; as to righteousness under the law, blameless' (vv. 5–6). He himself made decisions to pursue and maintain these behaviours.

The picture these phrases create contradicts the general impression many people have, in large part a legacy of Augustine and Luther, that the 'pre-Christian' Paul was riddled with guilt over his inability to live as the law demanded. On the contrary, Paul presents himself as an accomplished Jew who had been deeply involved in the best part of his tradition and who defended that tradition zealously. (The reference to persecuting the Church does not necessarily contradict this picture, since Paul's persecution may well have been social and economic harassment, which he saw as part of protecting his people.)

The break between v. 6 and v. 7 is dramatic. Without ever even hinting at a vision or a light or a 'road to Damascus', Paul marks the change conventionally referred to as his 'conversion': 'whatever gains I had, these I have come to regard as loss because of Christ.' Again contrary to the general impression of Paul, he does not depict his call or conversion as the solution to a problem, the release from some deep moral or psychological or spiritual crisis. Quite the opposite! 'Because of Christ', all these accomplishments became for him simply 'loss'.

Verse 8 restates this assertion more strongly. It was the 'surpassing value of knowing Christ Jesus' that led to the radical transformation of Paul's values. He now regards them as 'rubbish'. At this point the NRSV is somewhat euphemistic in its translation; the monographic word 'dung' is much to be preferred. Even the best that Paul had accomplished he came to regard as nothing more than garbage because of the revelation of Jesus Christ.

What Paul means by 'knowing Christ Jesus' becomes more clear in the remainder of the lection. First, it means being 'in him' (v. 9), the connection with Christ and all believers that elsewhere Paul terms 'the body of Christ'. Second, it means leaving aside the righteousness of one's own accomplishments in favour of the righteousness that 'comes through faith in Christ' (v. 9). No longer can Paul speak or act or think as if his work is his own alone, or as if his work acquired for him standing before God. The righteousness Paul now seeks is God's own. That righteousness finally ends in the resurrection itself (v. 10).

Despite the significant change Paul has experienced, he is careful to acknowledge that he has not yet arrived at the goal. The goal itself appears to be of two sorts. First, he identifies 'the resurrection from the dead' as his goal; that is, he aims at being with Christ following his own death (see 1.23). The second goal is spiritual maturity, but that goal is somewhat obscured by the NRSV. Translated more literally, v. 12 opens with the words, 'Not that I have already received this or already been made mature.' Paul acknowledges that he has not yet achieved the goal he would set for himself.

He continues to pursue that goal 'because Christ Jesus has made me his own'. The

English translation here needs to be more forceful as in 'because I have been overtaken by Christ Jesus', Paul's understanding is that he was seized or captured by Christ, not that he initiated the relationship, or that he earned it somehow. Because of that seizure, which Paul now understands to have been a gift of grace, he continues to strive toward what lies ahead.

Paul's interpretation of his own conversion is highly suggestive for contemporary reflection on what it means to proclaim the gospel. Unlike many traditional approaches to evangelistic preaching, which offer the gospel as the answer to problems in people's lives, Paul understands the gospel to be just the opposite. It gave him no answers to problems, but instead it disturbed his answers and sent him in search of a new 'solution', a new understanding. More precisely, it thrust a new understanding on him, an understanding that required radical reassessment of past, present and future. BG

Matthew 21.33–46

The parable of the wicked tenants provides the interpretative key to the approaching passion. Matthew has placed it between two other parables, the two sons (vv. 28–32) and the marriage feast (22.1–14), which help to reinforce the message that the fault of the tenants was not just their maltreatment of the vineyard-owner's agents, but also their failure to produce the fruits of righteousness in due season (v. 41). So even on their own terms, quite apart from belief in Jesus as Messiah, they do not come up to scratch.

Isaiah's famous song of the vineyard (Isa. 5.1–7) is unmistakably evoked by the topographical details given in v. 33. But whereas Isaiah had blamed Israel as a whole for the sourness of its fruit, the gospel parable singles out her leaders for special responsibility. Mark has three servants sent separately, and treated ever more violently, the last being murdered; and then a wave of others, some maltreated, some killed. Matthew has bunched them into two groups, perhaps because he is thinking of the three great writing prophets in Hebrew Scripture (Isaiah, Jeremiah and Ezekiel) and their later successors (the Book of the Twelve). He specifies the stoning of the prophets as a particularly outrageous act of defiance against God (see 23.37). While Mark has the owner's son killed in the seclusion of the vineyard and his body tossed unceremoniously over the wall, Matthew recalling the historical circumstances of Jesus' death reverses the order of events (v. 39). The parable ends with a fearful message: this is the last straw – God's patience with his people is finally exhausted, and their judgement is inevitable (as it proved to be, in historical terms, in the fateful uprising against Rome AD 66–70).

But the Christian gospel requires some positive addendum. The death of the Son (in Hebrew, *ben*) is the rejection of the stone (Hebrew, *eben*) which, according to Ps. 118.22, will nevertheless become the foundation of the new Jerusalem. Thus, the risen Christ will gather to himself a new people (even a new 'nation', v. 43) who shall, Matthew is adamant, produce the fruits of true righteousness.

Verse 44 is relegated to a footnote in most modern translations. It is probably a harmonization to Luke 20.18, which derives in turn from the stone destined to destroy the might of pagan empire in Dan. 2 (see vv. 34, 44). But it is not inconsistent with Matthew's own view. According to him, belief in Jesus as the crucified Messiah was a stumbling block to many Jews (cf. 1 Cor. 1.23) and their rejection of that belief was the ground for their future punishment (cf. Matt. 22.7). In interpreting this bitter first-century polemic, the reader today will want to ask how the love of God in the self-giving of the cross (Rom. 5.8) and the grace and forgiveness of the risen Christ can be given a central place in the overall picture. JM

Proper 23

(Sunday between 9 and 15 October inclusive)

Exodus 32.1–14 or Isaiah 25.1–9; Philippians 4.1–9; Matthew 22.1–14

Exodus 32.1–14

A comparison of this passage with 1 Kings 12.25–33 makes it likely that, at one stage in the development of Israel's faith, Israelite sanctuaries contained bull images that served as the throne of the invisible YHWH. When Jeroboam I said of the golden calves in Bethel and Dan 'Here are your gods' (or, 'Here is your God') 'who brought you up out of the land of Egypt' (1 Kings 12.28) he was arguably appealing to Israel's traditional faith as opposed to Solomon's new-fangled temple designed and built by a foreign architect.

If this is correct, a long period has elapsed between the time when a golden calf was legitimately to be found in an Israelite sanctuary, and the story of the golden calf in Exod. 32. That period will have seen the bitter war waged by the prophets against the bull as a fertility symbol, as well as Josiah's attempt in 622 BC to reform the cult (2 Kings 23). What was once commonplace will have become a symbol for the worst kind of idolatry.

In the narrative structure of Exodus, this chapter is a turning point. Hitherto, the people have complained against God and Moses and demanded signs and wonders, including water made sweet (Exod. 15.22–25), the manna and quails (Exod. 16) and water from the rock (Exod. 17.1–7). In ch. 32, however, the ultimate apostasy occurs when the Israelites make a golden calf and worship it. This later leads to civil war (vv. 25–29) and to the destruction of the tablets of stone (vv. 19–20).

A notable feature of the narrative is the role of Moses in averting God's wrath, and of his refusal to let God destroy the people so that God can make a great nation out of Moses (v. 10). Moses reminds God of his promises to Abraham, Isaac and Israel (Jacob). While there are no doubt deep currents running here, which reflect disputes within the Jerusalem community in the post-exilic period, Moses' action can be taken at its face value at the surface of the narrative – as refusal to profit personally at the expense of others to whom promises had been made.

In the history of interpretation this incident has been used by the churches to justify the belief that not all of the Old Testament law is binding upon Christians. It has been argued that all the sacrificial laws follow Exod. 32 and were directed to faithless Israel and designed to prevent any further apostasy.

Thus they are of no concern to Christians, who need only to heed the Old Testament laws that precede Exod. 32. At a deeper level, the story is a contrast between two types of religion – that which demands that the divine be made immediate, visible and accessible, and that which waits upon a God who seems to tarry when human impatience demands action (v. 1). JR

Isaiah 25.1–9

Isaiah 25 is part of the so-called Isaiah apocalypse (chs. 24—27), a section that is among the latest parts of Isaiah to be written, and in which the idea of resurrection is hinted at (Isa. 26.19). The set passage falls into two parts: vv. 1–5 are in the form of a song or psalm of thanksgiving, while vv. 6–9 are a continuation of 24.23.

Dealing with the second part first, the apocalypse begins (in 24.1) with a sombre account of God's impending judgement on the earth. The link between moral order and the order of creation entails that the wickedness of earth's inhabitants is so great that all that sustains human life physically will no longer be available, with the result that civic life will completely break down. The judgement will be so complete that it will also embrace the stars of heaven, the kings of the earth and the sun and moon (24.21–23). This will be the prelude to God assuming kingship on Mount Zion.

Verses 6–9 describe the joyful outcome of this divine enthronement. In contrast to the devastation of the earth, God will invite all nations to take part in a banquet which celebrates his kingship (v. 6). The 'shroud' and the 'sheet' that he will destroy are probably those that are worn by people mourning the dead. They will become unnecessary objects because God will destroy death, that personification of the greatest power that confronts God, and which causes most perplexity to human attempts to make sense of the world. Tears will be wiped away from all faces (v. 8) and those who are invited to the celebration will hail it as the better world for which they have hoped and waited (v. 9).

Verses 1–5 interrupt the sequence of 24.23—25.6, and were probably inserted to help make the transition from the deep gloom of ch. 24 to the brilliant light of ch. 25. They are a song celebrating the demise of a city (v. 2); whether a particular one is meant or whether it is a city personifying the power of evil is not clear. The point is that the destruction of this city is an assurance to the poor and needy that God is ultimately on their side (v. 4). For the powerful and ruthless peoples of the world, the downfall of the city is a warning to them that they will not have the last word.

The verse about the sun and moon being abashed and ashamed (24.23) is possibly alluded to in Mark 13.24 prior to the coming of the Son of man on the clouds with great power and glory. The passage about the banquet on Mount Zion is reminiscent of the saying in Matt. 8.11, that many will come from east and west and eat with Abraham, Isaac and Jacob in the kingdom of heaven. The passage is thus extremely rich, not only in its own context, but with echoes into the New Testament. JR

Philippians 4.1–9

As one approaches this passage in its own right, it needs a resolute mind to detach oneself from the music of Henry Purcell and the dismissal in the Holy Communion liturgy of the Anglican Prayer Book. It is the classic New Testament passage about both joy and peace.

The proper names, however, counter the feeling of timelessness and give a sense of immediacy to the passage. More than that, Euodia and Syntyche are significant as examples of the prominent place occupied by women in the early days of Christianity, notably in Paul's mission, but also in, for example, the world of the Gospel of John. We have no feeling that they are in any way 'inferior' to male co-workers. With the exception of one or two particular cults, this is remarkable in the culture of the period, especially in view of the Jewish matrix of the Church: though even here, there are exceptions, notably in the synagogues of some cities in Asia Minor where women were particularly active in civic life.

'Peace' is the keynote of the passage, and it has the strong force of the Hebrew *shalom*. It stands for a total well-being of which God is the only true source, and it amounts to the same protective shield as the gift of salvation.

For 'the book of life' (v. 3), see Old Testament precedents in Exod. 32.32 and Ps. 139.16, and then, in a closer apocalyptic connection, Dan. 12.1 and Rev. 20.12–15. This is probably less a memorial book, beloved of town halls in present-day routine, than a record that will be used at the judgement and which will ensure the eternal safety of those destined for 'life'.

It is not easy to know how to take the final verse. Perhaps the two 'if' clauses are best seen as summing up the contents of the 'whatever' clauses. They characterize the desired contents of Christian behaviour. And the expected return of Christ (v. 5) dominates the context in which all – mission, church life, state of mind, moral endeavour – is to be taken. L H

Matthew 22.1–14

Most preachers, given the option of choosing either Matthew's or Luke's version of a parable of the banquet as the text for a sermon, would unquestionably choose Luke's. The story in Luke (14.15–24) is more straightforward, cleaner, without the violent and complicating features that characterize the allegorical retelling in Matthew. Luke's parable has a powerful quality of engaging the reader with the characters in the plot. The unusual details of Matthew's account, however, result in an unrealistic and unbelievable story.

The meal is a wedding feast hosted by a king. When the servants are sent to tell the invited guests to come, a strange thing occurs: they are made light of, mistreated and even killed (much as the servants were in the parable of the wicked tenants, Matt. 21.35–36), an odd way to treat servants who have come to perform a positive and helpful function. Understandably, the king reacts with rage, but then the story of the feast itself is interrupted long enough to allow the king time to marshal his troops, destroy the invited guests, and burn their city. The meal is held in abeyance until the violence is over. Then the story is taken up again: the second group of guests are invited off the streets, and the wedding hall is filled.

Apparently Matthew's parable is the result of applying a simpler version of the story of the banquet to the Jewish rejection of the Christian gospel. The servants calling the invited guests are preachers who have been abused and whose message has been rejected by Jewish leaders. The vengeance by the king seems to relate to the havoc wrought on the city of Jerusalem by the Romans in 70 AD (perhaps interpreted in the light of Isa. 5.24–25). The guests brought in from the streets are the Gentiles, who end up enjoying the wedding banquet. Just as the parable of the two sons reflects the Jewish rejection of the message of John (Matt. 21.28–32) and the parable of the wicked tenants reflects the Jewish rejection of Jesus, who comes in the line of the prophets (21.33–43), so the parable of the wedding banquet reflects the Jewish rejection of Christian messengers, who bring the invitation to the kingdom.

But just as in the two previous parables, the narrator will not let the audience bask complacently in the judgement pronounced on others. The jolt comes in the added scene – the guest found at the festivities without a wedding garment (22.11–14). Here again there are details in the story hard to fathom. Should a guest invited off the street be expected to have the appropriate clothes? What is implied when the guest is described as 'speechless' (22.12)? Is this evidence of guilt, or is he stunned into silence? Isn't 'the outer darkness', with its 'weeping and gnashing of teeth', a hard punishment for one who only lacks the proper attire?

In spite of its sharpness, the story works its purpose of challenging the smugness of the audience. The Jewish leaders or people are no longer in view, only the Christian hearers/readers. As in every period of the Church's history, Matthew's community is composed of 'both good and bad' (22.10). Sometimes the issue is whether the community should rid itself of the bad, pull up the weeds that have grown amid the wheat (13.24–30, 36–43). Here there seems to be no such issue, only the effort to confront the audience with the hapless and disquieting figure of the guest without a wedding garment. Judging others is no business of the audience; rather, they are to attend to themselves, their own preparedness to meet the King, their readiness in the face of judgement.

In this allegorical retelling of Matthew, what does the wedding garment signify? A host of answers have been given, going all the way back to patristic times, but in Matthew's context the wedding garment must symbolize '[doing] the will of my Father in heaven' (7.21), having 'a righteousness [that] exceeds that of the scribes and Pharisees' (5.20), producing 'the fruits of the kingdom' (21.43). All are expressions to identify the consistency between speech and life, words and deeds, that is appropriate for those who call Jesus 'Lord'. The garment represents authentic discipleship, and the parable prods the audience to self-criticism lest they find themselves among the bad, who are finally judged.

While the Lucan version of the parable of the banquet seems more to the point and is certainly more popular, Matthew's version presses an ancient issue about the quality of our lives: whether in the ordinary dimensions of our relationships we manifest a genuineness, a trustworthiness. The surprise surrounding the verdict of the king on the man without the wedding garment is reminiscent of the surprise shown by the two groups gathered before the final judgement when they hear words of commendation or judgement (25.37–39, 44). What matters is a life without pretence or guile, that takes seriously the grace given in Jesus Christ. CC

Proper 24

(Sunday between 16 and 22 October inclusive)

Exodus 33.12–23 or Isaiah 45.1–7; 1 Thessalonians 1.1–10; Matthew 22.15–22

Exodus 33.12–23

This passage cannot be understood apart from the whole of ch. 33; also, the setting of ch. 33 within the whole book of Exodus is relevant. Following the incident of the golden calf, God tells Moses to lead the people to the land promised to them. This good news is tempered by the bad news that God will not accompany the people (33.3). The people are so obstinate and complaining that God fears that he will destroy them if he accompanies them (33.5). Only an angel will go with the people on the remainder of their journey (33.2).

Moses now intercedes with God on behalf of the people, reminding God that the nation is his responsibility. If God does not accompany the people, in what respect will they be different from any other nation (v. 16)? God relents, and even consents to allowing Moses to see his glory – an important Old Testament term for the divine presence especially prominent in Ezekiel (Ezek. 11.22–33). In fact, we get an exposition of the name YHWH to complement that previously given at Exod. 3.15. There, the name was linked to the Hebrew verb 'to be', and concentrated upon God as the ground of being. Here, the emphasis is upon God's active qualities of graciousness and mercy. The scene with Moses standing in a cleft of the rock while God's glory passes by (v. 21) can be compared with the story of Elijah standing in a cave on the same mountain, while God passes by (1 Kings 19.11–13).

The passage raises many questions at both the critical and practical levels. Was the story originally an alternative account of the disclosure of the name YHWH to Moses? Are the stories of Moses and Elijah on the same mountain different variations of one tradition? At the practical level there is the problem of Moses having to persuade God to face up to his responsibilities as the one who has brought the Israelite nation into being. How much confidence can people have in such a God?

At a deeper level, the most fascinating argument used by Moses to get God to go with them to the promised land is the one that, otherwise, the Israelites will be no different from any other people (v. 16). But the people have already abundantly proved that they are no different from other nations! In spite of being freed from slavery they have continually complained, and have sealed their apostasy by making the golden calf. The ultimate paradox is that, because of the intercession of a mere human, God will accompany the people after all. One reason is that his nature is graciousness and mercy. The people will, then, be different from other nations, not at the level of human achievement, but because they are accompanied by a God who endures their selfishness, and because they have a leader (Moses) who is able to be selfless. JR

Isaiah 45.1–7

This is a remarkable passage because it calls Cyrus, a Persian monarch, God's anointed, i.e. his Messiah. Cyrus, whose Persian tribe was a vassal of the Medians, succeeded in defeating the kingdom of Lydia in 546 BC. He then turned his attention to the Babylonians and, having defeated them twice in battles along the Tigris River, entered Babylon with little resistance in 540 or 539 BC. A decree recorded on the Cyrus Cylinder (now in the British Museum) enabled exiled peoples to return to their lands and to restore the temples that the Babylonians had destroyed. This was the basis for the rebuilding of the Jerusalem temple in 515 BC and the reconstruction of the Jewish community there.

The prophecies of Second Isaiah in chs. 40—55 see the progress of Cyrus towards Babylon as God's work, directed towards freeing his people from exile. It is the proof that the God of Israel is in control of the world and its affairs, that he is incomparable (v. 5) and that nothing can withstand what he proposes (v. 7).

The form of the language, especially vv. 1–4, has been compared with coronation rituals as practised in the ancient Near East, and of which there are glimpses in the Old Testament Pss. 2 and 110 and Isa. 9.6–7. The rituals included giving a throne name to the king (cf. Isa. 9.6 and 45.4. 'I surname you') and promises of victory (cf. Pss. 2.8–9; 110.5–6; Isa. 45.1). If these allusions were apparent to the original hearers/readers, the passage would have been even more remarkable than it is. In the absence of a king of Jerusalem, God has anointed a foreign king to act as shepherd to his people (cf. Isa. 44.28) and to restore them for the sake of God's purposes.

Cyrus, presumably, remained ignorant of the God of Israel and the divine task that he was fulfilling. He was driven mainly by human ambition to extend his power. Yet this ambition was tempered with generosity, even if there were selfish reasons for him allowing captive peoples to return home and rebuild their temples. He no doubt hoped that the restored gods would be favourable to him. The statement that God creates light and darkness and weal and woe (v. 7) can best be understood to mean that, in the real world of imperfect humanity, the fulfilment of divine purposes will entail bad as well as good; Cyrus's victories were good news for the exiled Israelites. They were presumably not such good news for the armies and their soldiers that were defeated along the way. JR

I Thessalonians 1.1–10

First Thessalonians, probably the earliest of Paul's letters and therefore the earliest written evidence of Christianity, opens with an extended thanksgiving. The thanksgiving begins with 1.2 and continues perhaps as far as 2.16. In the lectionary reading for this week, 1 Thess. 1.1–10, Paul expresses his thanks to God regarding the reception of the gospel among the Thessalonians. What is striking about this passage, however, is that Paul depicts an evangelism that differs from the conventional image of a unilateral action by an evangelist on a receptive audience. Here evangelism involves the interaction of Paul and his co-workers with the Thessalonians, an interaction that leaves both sides changed, an interaction that results in the Thessalonians themselves becoming evangelists as well.

First, the Christian evangelists make the gospel known among the Thessalonians. Influenced by the public speeches Luke describes in the Acts of the Apostles, most readers will imagine Paul and his colleagues preaching on street corners or at other public places. Paul himself gives few clues as to what forms this early stage of evangelism took; he may have taken advantage of his trade to talk with people in workshops and in small, informal gatherings, rather than in larger, public settings.

Whatever the form of Paul's preaching, he indicates that 'our message of the gospel came to you not in word only, but also in power and in the Holy Spirit and with full conviction' (v. 5). Since the gospel itself is more than words, more than intellectual assertions to be affirmed, its reception also must take many forms. The reception of the gospel manifested itself also in the Thessalonians' imitation of Paul and his co-workers: 'And you became imitators of us and of the Lord, for in spite of persecution you received the word with joy inspired by the Holy Spirit' (v. 6). The Thessalonians' reception of the gospel extended well beyond intellectual assent. They took the Christian evangelists as their models, specifically as models of joy in the face of persecution.

Even this element in Paul's comments differs from some understandings of evangelism, for Paul clearly has in mind not simply an evangelism of preaching followed by a profession of faith. He understands that an adequate response to the gospel involves action as well as assent. More striking, however, is what Paul says about the way in which the evangelists themselves are influenced by this relationship. Not only did the Thessalonians change, but 'you know what kind of persons we proved to be among you for your sake' (v. 5). Paul and his co-workers found themselves to be different because of the relationship that was established. Evangelism involves a mutual exchange, involving both sides. For the sake of the Thessalonians, the evangelists themselves behaved differently. This notion is expanded in the early lines of 1 Thess. 2, where Paul describes himself as a nurse who cares for her own children and as a father with his children. Because of their deep involvement with people at Thessalonica, Paul and his colleagues find themselves vulnerable.

The result of this relationship between Paul and his colleagues and the Thessalonians is not simply the conversion of some people at Thessalonica. The Thessalonians themselves become ministers by virtue of the impact of their conversion on others. Paul writes that 'you became an example to all the believers in Macedonia and in Achaia' (1.7), signalling that other Christians find themselves influenced by the lives of the Thessalonians. They have in turn become models of the faith. Both those who are already Christians and those who are not have come to know about the faith by means of the Thessalonians: 'in every place your faith in God has become known, so that we have no need to speak about it' (v. 8). Even if we suspect Paul of considerable exaggeration here, the point he makes is nevertheless important. The new Christians at Thessalonica, although they are not formally designated as apostles or preachers, become both by virtue of the impact their conversion has on the lives of other people.

The conversion of these Gentiles to the Christian faith is summed up in vv. 9–10 in very traditional language: 'You turned to God from idols, to serve a living and true God, and to wait for his Son from heaven, whom he raised from the dead – Jesus, who rescues us from the wrath that is coming.' The first half of this statement draws on a conventional Jewish understanding of what conversion involves. Gentiles turn to the one God from their service of many gods, or better, Gentiles turn to the only real God from their service of false gods. The second half of the statement reflects Christian eschatological expectation, in that those who have joined with the Christian movement live in the knowledge of Jesus Christ's resurrection and in the expectation that he will return as part of God's final triumph over evil. Within the context of 1 Thessalonians, of course, this traditional language will serve a very specific purpose. Gentiles who have turned to the one God must live lives consistent with that understanding and must forgo practices that may have been acceptable in their earlier lives (see 4.1–8). They also live in full confidence that God will accomplish Jesus' return, although the time of that return is not subject to human prediction (4.13—5.11). BG

Matthew 22.15–22

The passage for the gospel reading for today has been a favourite one on the basis of which to address issues of Church and state. The statement 'Render therefore to Caesar the things that are Caesar's, and to God the things that are God's' (RSV) becomes a basis for discussing the extent to which the Church is or is not involved with the political process and what responsibilities Christians have to the state. The problem, however, is that the text does not answer very many questions, particularly for those who live in a democratic state. Furthermore, isolated from the rest of the biblical witness about Church and state, the passage lays itself open to a variety of interpretations and to sometimes radically different doctrines of Church and state. The incident certainly has its place in the broader perspective of both Testaments and as one of several texts to be considered, but alone it hardly provides a basis for a precise definition of Christians' obligations in the political arena.

There is more to the passage than simply Matt. 22.21b, and the other parts are critical to a serious grappling with its meaning. The text begins with the plot of the Pharisees, who try to rig the conversation with Jesus. They send some of their younger protégés, together with a few Herodians, first to flatter Jesus and then to put him on the spot. 'Is it lawful to pay taxes to the emperor, or not?' A yes-or-no question like this is bound to get him in trouble, they suppose. If Jesus says yes, then much of the crowd would be disillusioned with him, for there were many voices arguing that paying the Roman poll tax was an act of treason. Even handling the coinage with Caesar's image stamped on it was offensive to some. But if Jesus answers no to the question, then he is guilty of treason, and the Herodians are there in the audience to press their accusations against him.

At one level Jesus' response – asking for a coin, having the questioners tell him whose head is on it, declaring 'Give therefore to the emperor the things that are the emperor's, and to God the things that are God's' – is clearly evasive. He successfully escapes the trap laid for him. He does not answer the query directly, but throws the issue back on the audience, who will have to decide for themselves where to draw the line between the emperor's jurisdiction and God's jurisdiction. Even his questioners (who have already been exposed as 'hypocrites') are amazed at his brilliance and go away and leave him alone.

At another level, however, the vignette is much more than an example of Jesus' outwitting the opposition. When Jesus asks for a coin, he also asks, 'Whose head [*eikōn*, image] is this, and whose title?' The coin of course bears Caesar's *eikōn*, and belongs to Caesar. Humans, on the other hand, bear the *eikōn* of God. They may pay the infamous poll tax, but they do not belong to the emperor. They themselves belong to God. The declaration of that ultimate belonging has powerful implications.

Another way to put this is to say that the passage does not make God and Caesar to be equals, nor are they symbolic names for separate realms. If so, one could be led to the notion that the emperor has his realm in which ultimate allegiance can be demanded, and God is relegated to another realm. Quite the opposite is implied in the text. Humans bear God's image, and wherever they live and operate – whether in the social, economic, political or religious realm – they belong to God. Their primary loyalties do not switch when they move out of church and into the voting booth.

Read this way, the text does not solve the question of Church and state. It does not answer many lingering issues about Christians' obligations to the government – taxation, military conscription and the like – but it does set allegiances into an ultimate and penultimate order. The text is certainly not iconoclastic regarding governments. It gives space to political arrangements, but at the same time it conditions those arrangements by the reminder that not only we, but all God's children, bear the divine image and therefore belong to God. Furthermore, the text operates subversively in every context in which governments act as if citizens have no higher commitments than to the state. When the divine image is denied and persons are made by political circumstances to be less than human, then the text carries a revolutionary word, a word that has to be spoken to both oppressed and oppressor. cc

Proper 25

(Sunday between 23 and 30 October inclusive)

Deuteronomy 34.1–12 or Leviticus 19.1–2, 15–18; 1 Thessalonians 2.1–8; Matthew 22.34–46

Deuteronomy 34.1–12

This passage continues Deut. 32.48–52 where Moses is commanded to ascend Mount Nebo, warned of his coming death, and reminded that he will not be allowed to enter the land because he and Aaron did not maintain God's holiness at Meribah-Kadesh. That incident is recorded in Num. 20.2–13, and the fault of Moses and Aaron is apparently that they did not remonstrate sufficiently strongly with the Israelites who complained that there was no water to drink. Modern readers will be forgiven for thinking that Moses is badly treated by being barred from the promised land, especially as the reading for Proper 24 shows him interceding with a seemingly reluctant God not to give up on his people! The reason for this tradition may be that at one stage, the location of Moses' tomb in Trans-jordan was known (cf. 34.6), and that the question had to be answered as to why Moses had died so close to, but not in, the promised land.

Chapter 34 is a kind of epitaph, and allows Moses to exit in a blaze of glory in spite of not setting foot in Canaan. The viewing of the whole of the land from the top of Mount Nebo may be a legal act of taking possession of it. In reality, if the Mount Nebo visited by tourists today is the correct site of Pisgah, what Moses saw cannot be seen on a clear day, and clear days are rare! Nonetheless, Moses has viewed the land even if he has not trodden it, and his work is complete. His death at the age of 120 with unimpaired sight and unabated vigour is a way of describing a perfectly fulfilled life, although the biblical narrative elsewhere has not minimized his difficulties. These include his flight from Egypt when he killed an Egyptian (2.11–15), the many occasions on which he had to hear the complaints of the Israelites against their conditions in the wilderness, the divine anger against Israel that he had to deflect, opposition from his brother Aaron and his sister Miriam (Num. 12.1–2) and the rebellion of Korah, Dathan and Abiram (Num. 16.1–3). The two strands have to be held together – the eulogy in Deut. 34 and the other parts of the story – if justice is to be done to the character of Moses. To concentrate on the former is to get the false impression that being a unique leader was a glamorous task!

The mention of Joshua enables the overall narrative to continue into the book of Joshua. JR

Leviticus 19.1–2, 15–18

(See Seventh Sunday of Epiphany, p. 65.)

I Thessalonians 2.1–8

Today's passage from 1 Thessalonians continues Paul's recounting of the ministry he and his co-workers established with and among Christians at Thessalonica. Already Paul has written of the reception the Thessalonians gave to him, and now he turns to the nature of his own work with them. It is important to note that this letter, probably the earliest among the extant Pauline letters, does not begin with Paul's description of himself as an apostle. In fact, Paul uses only the names 'Paul, Silvanus and Timothy'. By contrast, his later letters will emphasize his calling as apostle (1 Cor. 1.1; 2 Cor. 1.1; Gal. 1.1; Rom. 1.1), sometimes at considerable length (see the openings of Galatians and Romans). In 1 Thessalonians, where he has not yet taken up this practice, he seems to describe the apostle's work in this passage rather than to identify it succinctly in the letter opening. Perhaps, indeed, Paul is here working out his understanding of what it means to be called 'apostles of Christ' (v. 7).

Paul's understanding of apostleship emerges here in three distinct but related characteristics. First, to be an apostle is to have the courage needed to proclaim the gospel: 'We had courage in our God to declare to you the gospel of God in spite of great opposition' (v. 2). The fact that Paul refers to opposition and that he prefaces this statement with comments about suffering and mistreatment at Philippi prompts the reader to think of courage as the willingness to act in the face of adversity. But any proclamation of the gospel requires courage, for the gospel inherently and inevitably causes offence to its hearers.

The courage required of apostles comes to them not from their own resources or their own discipline. The apostles have courage 'in our God', that is, they receive courage as a gift of the God who empowers and legitimates their task. Alongside this text might be placed the scene in Acts 4 in which the gathered Christian community in Jerusalem prays together for boldness to speak the gospel in the face of threatening officials (Acts 4.23–31). Without such boldness, without courage, the gospel is never proclaimed.

A second characteristic of the apostles is their integrity. Paul describes this integrity in 1 Thess. 2.3–6. The apostles acted without 'deceit or impure motives or trickery', without 'words of flattery' or with 'a pretext for greed', because their task was one of pleasing God rather than human beings. Unlike the unscrupulous salesperson who decides that a sale justifies any strategy or device, the genuine apostle knows that strategies reflect their goals. Strategies that simply attempt to move people, to win their consent or their support, are strategies that ultimately will fail. Because it is God who has authorized the apostles, they cannot select sales techniques that contradict that authorization. It is God who has approved of the apostles and entrusted them with the gospel itself (v. 4).

The third characteristic of the apostle has to do with the character of the relationship between the apostle and the convert. That relationship has already been referred to in 1.2–10 (Proper 24), but it emerges again here in striking imagery about the roles Paul and his co-workers adopted in relationship to the Thessalonians. They treated the Thessalonians as would a nurse who was charged with caring for her own children (v. 7). They exhorted the Thessalonians as a father would, treating each one individually (v. 11). A good case can be made that v. 7 should read 'But we were infants among you', rather than 'But we were gentle among you' (see the footnote in the NRSV). If that is the case, Paul uses in this brief passage three distinct and even conflicting images to convey the apostolic role. The apostle is as weak and unprotected as an infant; the apostle is as gentle as a mother with her infant; the apostle is as protective as a father.

What ties these three images together is the utter vulnerability they attach to the figure of the apostle. In this interpretation, the apostle is not a powerful and authoritative figure, whose message is conveyed by sheer personal charisma. Rather, the apostle is one who undertakes a profound relationship with others, risking humiliation and painful rejection, so that the truth of the gospel might be made known to others. Small wonder that Paul concludes the passage by recalling that they had determined to share 'not only the gospel of God but also our own selves' (v. 8).

Paul says little about the 'results' achieved by this apostolic strategy. The indications that come through have nothing to do with numbers of people converted or financial security acquired or influence achieved. He simply asserts that 'our coming to you was not in vain' (v. 1). That use of negation for emphasis (technically referred to as *litotes*) occurs elsewhere in the New Testament (see e.g. Rom. 1.16) and does not reflect a kind of false modesty. It is, however, important to notice that Paul measures the apostolic work by the integrity of response rather than by its size. BG

Matthew 22.34–46

Matthew, like Mark, supplies a sequence of controversy stories before the passion to explain in more detail the sort of objections to Jesus' teaching raised by the Jewish authorities that led to his trial. So far we have overheard conflicts about taxes: here we move on to the issues of Torah and Messiahship. They are interrelated issues and no doubt highly controversial still for Matthew's community: could Jesus have been the true Messiah, if his followers fail to observe the Law?

Whereas for Mark the discussion with the scribe who is 'not far from the kingdom' is a moment of relief from mounting hostility, in Matthew even this is turned into a test question from a Pharisaic lawyer, anxious to join the fray in place of the silenced Sadducees (v. 34). The question is made more precise, i.e. not which is the 'first' commandment (which could, after all, be the circumcision law of Gen. 17.10) but which is the 'great' or foremost commandment. As far as the duty of obedience is concerned, Judaism made no distinction between one commandment and another; indeed seemingly irrational commands like the law on phylacteries (cf. 23.5) were, for that reason, more purely a test of obedience. Some commandments were deemed lighter but others were heavier (cf. 23.23) and were the key principles on which the rest depend (v. 40). Perhaps the motive behind the hostile question was to get Jesus to say that some could be dispensed with altogether (as Matthew's community may have believed for its Gentile converts). But Jesus' answer here stays focused on what is central. The greatest commandment is to love God with one's whole heart, soul and strength. A Jewish teacher would expound this text as more than tautology for the sake of rhetorical emphasis: to love God was to obey Torah from the heart (i.e. the 'will'), to risk one's life (or 'soul') in defence of the faith and to put one's strength (i.e. property and resources) at the disposal of God's elect. Thus, love can appropriately be commanded because it is not an emotion but a programme of action. The second commandment (Lev. 19.18) is 'like' the first because it is inextricably linked to it: one cannot love the invisible God without also loving one's only too visible neighbour in need (whether fellow Jew (Luke 10.29), fellow Christian (1 John 4.20), or fellow human?).

In the next scene, Mark has Jesus take the offensive, addressing the crowds directly, but Matthew rewords this episode too as a controversy with opponents. First-century Jewish beliefs about the expected Messiah were quite varied: the connotations of the Son of David title were open to debate: military leader, miracle worker, temple builder, teacher of wisdom. Solomon, David's actual son, could be portrayed as any of these. The answer that is given here spells out the fundamental distinction between Christian and Jewish messianism. No earthly title or function can fully measure up to the unique Lordship of the risen Christ, 'seated at the right hand of God' (cf. 1 Cor. 15.25; Rom. 8.34; Acts 2.34f.; Heb. 8.1). JM

Bible Sunday

Nehemiah 8.1–4a, (5–6), 8–12; Colossians 3.12–17; Matthew 24.30–35

Nehemiah 8.1–4a, (5–6), 8–12

This passage should really begin at 7.73b, with its important information that the events described happened in the seventh month which was, or was to become, the new year, and which was also the month in which the Feast of Booths was celebrated (see 8.13–18). Such is the tangled relationship between the books of Ezra and Nehemiah that it is usually accepted that Neh. 8 once formed part of an Ezra memoir, and that it was removed by an editor into Nehemiah material in order to provide a climax to the work of Ezra and Nehemiah. It is further broadly agreed that the reference to Nehemiah at 8.9 is an addition to the original text, designed to make the two men contemporaries. This is, in fact, the only occurrence of the two names together.

Several matters regarding the selection of the verses and the translation need to be pointed out. The use of the word 'book' is misleading since books, in the sense in which we understand them, would not be invented for another 600 years. 'Opened the book' (v. 5) should be taken to mean 'unrolled the scroll'. Second, by omitting the list of names in v. 4b, the selection gives the false impression that Ezra was standing alone on the platform. Those 'who could hear with understanding' (vv. 2, 3) were children old enough to be included in the gathering. The date of this event is tied to complex critical questions about the books of Ezra and Nehemiah. A setting in the latter part of the fifth century BC is a reasonable compromise.

A public reading of the law before all the people gathered together has several overtones. It is similar to covenant ceremonies where the conditions of the covenant were rehearsed (cf. Deut. 31.9–13 where a septennial reading of the Law during the Feast of Booths is commanded) and it is also reminiscent of the way in which laws were promulgated much later in Scandinavian countries (and still today in the Isle of Man). Within the narrative structure of Ezra/Nehemiah, the reading of the Law, which was part of the Pentateuch as we know it, had the effect of re-creating the community as a people brought into being and sustained by the God of Israel. The laws that were read set out the groundwork for relations between members of the community, and between the community and God. A sense of purpose and unity was discovered. The reaction of weeping (v. 9) can be understood in two ways. It can be seen as tears of joy for a renewed sense of communal belonging; it can be seen as tears of penitence as the words of the Law disclose to the people what they had failed to do. At the end of the passage, it is joy that predominates. 'The law of the Lord is perfect, reviving the soul . . . the precepts of the Lord are right, rejoicing the heart' (Ps. 19.7–8). JR

Colossians 3.12–17

(See Mothering Sunday, p. 95.)

Matthew 24.30–35

Seated on the Mount of Olives (24.3) across from the temple, Jesus instructs his disciples privately about the future. His dark prophecies of the great tribulation to come echo the themes of Jewish apocalyptic, especially the book of Daniel (quoted at 24.15). The experiences of the earliest Christians are painfully reflected in this passage but it also provides them with an explanatory framework in terms of God's saving plan. They have to endure times of violent upheaval, poverty and disaster (v. 7), the persecution and martyrdom of some believers (v. 9), the desecration of the temple and the exile of the Judean church (vv. 15f.) and internal divisions caused by false prophecies about the timing of the end (v. 24). The purpose of all this suffering and disorder is to purify the faith of the elect and mark them out as those who can hope for ultimate deliverance. The end when it finally arrives, so Matthew claims, will be entirely unambiguous, unlike the political events of his day.

The 'sign' (or ensign, battle-flag) of the Son of man will appear in the sky (cf. 24.27) and all the warring tribes on earth will cease from mayhem and start to worry instead about their own fate (v. 30). (These are the only additions Matthew makes to the material he has taken almost verbatim from Mark.) The leaves on the fig tree (in spite of Matt. 21.18–19!) are the unmistakable harbinger of summer fruitfulness. The tension between the last two sayings ('This generation will not pass away'; cf. 'heaven and earth will pass away') may imply that the gospel writers already sensed the problem that Jesus' predictions of an imminent end within one generation had proved mistaken in the literal sense; and yet they preserved these words of his for the deeper truth they contained.

This passage has been chosen as the gospel for Bible Sunday presumably because it both reflects the seasonal theme of Advent, and also refers to Jesus' enduring words, implying an analogy with Scripture. What is the relation between these two themes? The effect of fixing the canon of Christian Scripture was not only to privilege apostolic testimony to the Christ-event above all later interpretations, but also to keep this pristine vision of the end constantly in the forefront of the Church's imagination. The ambiguities of ordinary living are thus bracketed by the past and the future, by the clarity of the revelation delivered once for all in Christ and the revelation ('apocalypse') still to come when the same Christ will be manifested as judge and saviour. JM

Dedication Festival

(The First Sunday in October or Last Sunday after Trinity)

I Kings 8.22–30 or Revelation 21.9–14; Hebrews 12.18–24; Matthew 21.12–16

I Kings 8.22–30

It is generally agreed that Solomon's prayer of dedication of the temple, in the form in which we have it, dates from during the exile, or possibly later. The reason for this is that there is no mention in the prayer of sacrifice, which was one of the main functions of the temple when it was in action. Instead, the temple has become a place *towards* which people pray, and the prayer implies that the Jews are in exile as well as in their own land. Thus vv. 46–53 explicitly mention the situation in which the Jews have been taken captive by an enemy and then pray in their land of exile towards the temple. Further, vv. 41–43 envisage foreigners 'not of your people Israel' (v. 41) coming from distant lands to pray towards the temple, a sentiment echoing the universalism of Isa. 40—66. In the book of Daniel the hero prays three times a day in his upper room, which has windows open toward Jerusalem (Dan. 6.10).

Regardless of its date, the passage is a noble meditation on the imminence and transcendence of God. 'Will God indeed dwell on the earth?' asks Solomon, and answers his own question in the words 'even heaven and the highest heaven cannot contain you' (v. 27). But this is too remote to satisfy many people, who need to focus their devotions. The temple is a focus for the divine presence; yet even here there is sophistication, for the prayer does not say that God dwells in the temple, but that God has said 'my name shall be there' (v. 29). There is thus location and identity, but God remains fully transcendent.

In our modern Western world, in which nature fills us with delight rather than the anxiety and terror which it produced until comparatively recently (and still produces in many parts of the world), it is often said that it is better to worship God out of doors rather than in church buildings. It is there that the first part of the reading becomes important. Nature is an ambiguous phenomenon, as destructive as it is beautiful. The noble sentiments in Solomon's prayer about the transcendence and immanence of God were not drawn from a contemplation of nature (and see v. 34!) but from the traditions of God's promises to his servants and the covenant that he had made with them (vv. 23–24). A building is not an end in itself; but it is, or should be, a place where the preservation and realization of the story of God's grace results in God's people being grasped by his majesty and his mercy. JR

Revelation 21.9–14

St Augustine drew the title of his great work, *The City of God*, from Ps. 87.3, but the inspiration and imagery that dominate his sense of the interaction between the Church and society came from the final chapters of the Revelation. Not that the empirical church was identified crudely with the heavenly city. Rather, the latter was defined as the community that is marked by 'the love of God right up to the contempt of self'. It was a question of love and allegiance, not mere membership.

This is not quite the seer's way of thinking in our passage. Even more than Augustine, his eye is on the destiny before us. For believers, God's people, it is to be seen in terms of a new Jerusalem, a heavenly city. This is not based on any picture-postcard view of 'the heavenly Jerusalem that now is', any more than is Paul's use of the idea in Gal. 4.25; and in any case the real Jerusalem was a battered ruin by the time Revelation was written. Rather, the symbol draws on the rich tradition of apocalyptic imagery, of course with deep roots in the corporate awareness of Israel, with Jerusalem as its politico-religious centre, and with the temple at its heart as the earthly 'location' of God's presence with his people. Now temple and city seem to be fused, and in any case the former is superseded by the reality of the Lord God Almighty and the Lamb, who 'are the temple' (v. 22).

This assured gift of the real presence of God and of Christ, filling the city, which is the home of the community of the redeemed, is put in the symbol of a perfect cube – not an architect's or town planner's brainwave, but a sign of utter completeness. The line of imagery, developed along futuristic lines for the ultimate hope of God's people, comes from Ezek. 40—48; in the aftermath of the traumatic Babylonian captivity, still deep in the psyche which the seer shares. Now it finds its Christian consummation in the Church, whose foundations are the recent flesh-and-blood figures of the apostles of Jesus. The reference to them in v. 14 goes a little way to bridging the gap between the common prosiness of the Dedication Festival at 'our church' and the intense poetic flights in these chapters of the Revelation. The preacher may steer the worshippers from the one level to the other. LH

Hebrews 12.18–24

The opening verses summarize the description of Sinai in Exod. 20, the place where God is present, but a frightening, dangerous and inaccessible presence. Even Moses, the only one who can go into the presence of God and bring back his message to the Israelites, is full of fear. This is the setting for the making of the old covenant between God and his people, and the giving of the ten commandments. By contrast the author of Hebrews invites his readers to Mount Sion, the heavenly Jerusalem. (The contrast between Sinai and Jerusalem is reminiscent of Paul's allegory in Gal. 4, though the purpose of the comparison is very different.) There is now access to God, and also to a great community with him. First are the angels, as if at a festival (the word suggests the great public celebrations of the gods in the hellenistic world). Then there is the assembly (*ekklēsia*, the word used for the

Church) of the firstborn enrolled in heaven: their identity is more uncertain. Hitherto Jesus has been called 'the firstborn' (1.6), but with brothers and sisters, and in Rom. 8.28, in Col. 1.18 and Rev. 1.5 he is the 'firstborn of the dead'; it is possible that the group of firstborn here in Hebrews are the Christian dead who have already followed him to heaven. The 'spirits of the just made perfect' are easier to identify: they are the saints of the Old Testament whose faith was celebrated in ch. 11 but who would not reach the city to which they looked forward 'without us' (vv. 10, 39–40).

The image is like the great west door of a gothic cathedral, the ranks of angels, saints and prophets welcoming into heaven the Church on earth. In the midst of them is God; he is still judge, but with Jesus not Moses as the mediator between him and his people. Moses in Exod. 24 sprinkled the blood of sacrificed oxen on the altar and the people. The author of Hebrews has already alluded to this in ch. 9 in the course of his explanation of the sacrifice of Jesus on the analogy of the Day of Atonement ritual: the blood of sacrifice that Jesus presents in the true Holy of Holies that is heaven, is his own. Here in another link in a chain of allusions, the sprinkled blood of the covenant at Sinai suggests to him the shed blood of Abel (Gen. 4). That blood called on God the judge to avenge it in punishment of the brother-slayer; Jesus is the brother whose blood gives forgiveness of sins (a comparison drawn in Edward Caswall's passiontide hymn, 'Glory be to Jesus', *NEH* 83). Finally, this access to God through Jesus is not a vision of the future but an experience of the present: the author twice uses the perfect tense, we 'have come' to where we are. SL

Matthew 21.12–16

Matthew provides a brief introduction to the incident in the temple, noting that all Jerusalem was quaking with messianic expectation after Jesus' triumphant entry (v. 10). Everyone was watching for him to perform some prophetic sign, and so he does, in fulfilment of Mal. 3.1–5: 'the Lord whom you seek will suddenly come to his temple ... for he is like a refiner's fire ... he will purify the sons of Levi.' The object of his reforming zeal turns out to be, not the ruling priests directly, but those whom they franchise to provide services to pilgrims. Pigeons were regularly offered in sacrifice as substitutes for larger animals; and they could only be purchased with the temple's own special currency, so there was more than one opportunity for sharp practice.

Jesus denounces them for making a den of robbers out of God's house of prayer, echoing Jer. 7.11 and Isa. 56.7 respectively. Matthew has omitted from the latter the phrase 'for all nations' (with its eye on wider inclusivity) which Mark had included; he also omits Mark's reference (Mark 11.16) to Jesus preventing goods being carried through the precinct, presumably as a short-cut to market in the centre of the city. Matthew's eye is on the sheer impiety of what Jesus saw. Although the evangelists saw great significance in the cleansing of the temple, completing as it did the mission of the martyred prophet, John the Baptist (Matt. 21.25, cf. 11.9f.), in itself the incident seems to have been a rather minor and short-lived protest: it did not lead, after all, to Jesus' immediate arrest. So Matthew adds what is for him a much clearer proof of Messiahship (cf. 11.4–6), namely the healing of the blind and the lame (v. 14) in the very temple itself. To the outrage of the authorities, these wonders are greeted by children with shouts of 'Hosanna to the Son of David', imitating the grown-ups (cf. 11.9) and defended by Jesus with a final proof from Scripture (Ps. 8.2). The testimony of the children is a nice touch; for they represent the pure of heart who simply accept the truth (cf. Matt. 11.25; 18.3); and 'little ones' is a favourite term in Matthew for true disciples (e.g. 10.42; 18.6).

Even with the temple now in ruins (Matt. 23.28), as Jesus had predicted (Matt. 24.1–2), Matthew does not gloat over its downfall. When its outward offerings of worship and sacrifice were accompanied by the spirit of forgiveness (Matt. 5.24), mercy (Matt. 9.13) and prayer (v. 13 and cf. Luke 18.10–14), this building had effectively symbolized the gracious covenant of God with Israel. Yet now a greater than the temple (Matt. 12.6) is to be found in the person of Christ himself. JM

All Saints' Day

(1 November)

Revelation 7.9–17; 1 John 3.1–3; Matthew 5.1–12

Revelation 7.9–17

Who are the great multitude seen in heaven? One answer is to contrast them with the 144,000 sealed from the tribes of Israel in the preceding verses: those were drawn from the Jews and these are from the Gentiles. Another way is to note the alternation of 'hearing' and 'seeing' in vv. 4 and 9, as in Rev. 5.5–6, where the seer 'hears' about a lion and 'sees' a lamb: they are not two but one. So the 144,000 and the great multitude may be one group: God's true chosen people, drawn alike from all the nations of the world. Perhaps more importantly, however, they are martyrs. In the seer's vision the martys have a special place: they have been seen already under the altar of heaven in ch. 6; and for them alone is the first resurrection of ch. 20. In a situation where Christians experience active persecution, or have cause to anticipate that it will come (which seems to be the case with the book of Revelation), it is natural that those who share with Christ in suffering and death, who have 'washed their robes . . . in the blood of the Lamb', are seen to have a special status as his closest followers or witnesses – and it seems to have been the author of Revelation who extended the meaning of the Greek word *martus*, 'witness', to mean specifically witness in death, as in 2.13. In the modern West it is more common for Christians to experience indifference than active hostility, and the role of the martyr may seem a matter of past history, but modern martyrs are rightly commemorated in the new statues at the west end of Westminster Abbey, and Christians continue to suffer for their faith, not least in the Asia Minor of the book of Revelation and in the Holy Land itself.

The vision of the great multitude is punctuated with song. Here the martyrs proclaim the salvation of God and the Lamb, and their acclamation is confirmed by the *Amen* of all the inhabitants of heaven: the songs of humanity and of heaven are joined. Outbursts of song are characteristic of the Apocalypse: sometimes they seem to echo the psalms, but more often to be new compositions. It is possible that they represent hymns used in the early Christian communities (e.g. Col. 3.16), but perhaps more probable that they are the free composition of the poet-seer himself. Certainly they express his high christology: salvation belongs both to God and to the Lamb; God is seated on the throne, but the Lamb is at the centre of the throne. SL

I John 3.1–3

In two respects, the First Letter of John here resolves matters on which there is some ambiguity (perhaps theologically deliberate) in the Fourth Gospel – the two writings doubtless coming from the same stable, though probably not the same author. First, on the question of how to view 'the world'. In the Gospel, there are both positive and negative passages: the world is God's creation and the object of his love, yet there is a chasm of hostility between it and those who are Christ's. Here it is plainer that the world is not only hostile but even unrecognizing and uncomprehending: it 'does not know us'. Only 2.2 and 4.14 strike a more positive note, and it remains prospective as far as realization is concerned. And as in the Gospel, what is true of believers had of course first been true of Jesus: 'it did not know him'. The dualism is stark, with no hint of any of the redeeming features (as we innocently say) that have been so clear to creation-minded, more recent Christians. The writer has no eye for them, but only for questions of loyalty, adherence, orientation of life. In this, he is broadly at one with the rest of the New Testament, and one can see how Gnosticism, with its radical negativity about the world, now and at any time, was waiting in the wings.

Second, on the question of the future: in the Gospel of John, though there are a few references to a future consummation of judgement and resurrection (5.24–27; 6.39 etc.), they seem to many readers almost anomalous, perhaps even the work of a final, out-of-tune editor; for the whole doctrine of the book lays weight on the all-sufficient present life in Christ, already bestowed by God through Christ and received by those who are his. Already they have moved from death to life (5.24), already they have crossed the rubicon of judgement (3.17–19), and already they have received the Spirit (20.22), perpetuating Christ's presence with them. But here there is also a fervent hope of God's future, understood as his self-revelation – whether in his own persona or via Christ is unclear and probably immaterial to the writer. The revelation and triumphant 'presence' of Christ at his return is of course the normal early Christian doctrine, but the Johannine mind scarcely distinguishes: 'he that has seen me has seen the Father' (John 14.9). This common faith of New Testament Christians reflects a sense of themselves as part of an unfinished God-given process. Despite the perspective of the Fourth Gospel, the present is too unsatisfactory to be all that there can be.

There is here, however, a further dimension to the hope. 'When he is revealed, we shall be like him, for we will see him as he is.' The hope of the vision of God is paralleled elsewhere in early Christian (and indeed Jewish) hope, e.g. Matt. 5.8. The idea of the transforming power of that vision takes us a step further. It is a powerful idea that to 'see' some object (or at any rate to 'see God') is to take on the character of that which is seen. This idea of 'resemblance' is no doubt suggested by the common theme, here as elsewhere, of believers as God's offspring: like father, like child (3.9; cf. Rom. 8.29). It is the root of the rich spiritual tradition of salvation as divinization – a stirring doctrine for all its pitfalls, so obvious to sober Western Christians. L H

Matthew 5.1–12

Matthew has arranged his Gospel in alternating sections of narrative and teaching. There are five sections of teaching, each ending with virtually the same formula that marks the transition from direct speech to narrative (see e.g. 7.28–29). The first of these speeches is the Sermon on the Mount (5.3—7.27), and today's gospel is the beginning of it.

In the previous narrative (chs. 1—4), Matthew has prepared his readers for this section of his book by comparing Jesus to Moses: both were threatened by wicked kings; both escaped, one out of Egypt and the other into Egypt; Moses received, and now Jesus commends and revises, the Law of God, on a mountain.

John the Baptist and Jesus have proclaimed the coming of the time when God will rule and the need for repentance (3.2; 4.17); so the first speech addresses the question that this raises: who is it that will enter this new age?

There are eight Beatitudes, marked out by an *inclusio* – the repetition of the promise: 'The kingdom of heaven is theirs' (5.3, 10). Each beatitude consists of two parts: the statement that certain people are blessed, and the promise of their reward. After the eighth beatitude, the form of the language changes, from third person plural ('Blessed are the ...') to the second person ('Blessed are you ...'); these eight sayings can be read as the 'text', or as a kind of prologue, for the rest of the Sermon, which then begins at 5.11.

The order of the eight sayings is different in some of the manuscripts and ancient versions from that which is found in most printed editions of the New Testament, and it is not certain which arrangement is original; there is much to be said for following the witnesses that place v. 5 before v. 4. If this is done, then the Beatitudes form four pairs: the poor and the meek; those who mourn and those who fast; the generous and the single-minded; the peace-makers and those who are persecuted.

The seven different promises in the second halves are in effect all one promise (just as the petitions in the Lord's Prayer are in effect one and the same), because each of them refers to entry into the kingdom of heaven, the time when God will rule on the earth (see 6.10). They are not alternative options, so that one cannot choose some and reject others, for example preferring comfort and mercy to seeing God. The future passive verbs (shall be comforted, filled, receive mercy, be called God's children) are all ways of describing God's actions in the coming end-time of fulfilment; he will comfort, fill, be merciful, and he will declare who are his children.

Similarly, the eight statements in the first halves of the Beatitudes refer to everyone who is to enter the coming age: all of them are poor, meek, mourning for the way things are in the world, longing for God to rule, abandoning status and privilege, peace-makers, and (inevitably) persecuted by those who do not want God to rule. Again, these are not alternatives.

A major theme that runs through the Beatitudes and the Sermon on the Mount, and indeed this Gospel as a whole, is: many who are first will be last, and the last first (19.30; 20.16). Discipleship means the acceptance of a life that is not what the majority choose. What is required of those whom God will bless is poverty and the giving up of any compensating 'religious' rewards in the present (see. 6.1–21; 23.1–33). The character of the follower is, of course, the same as that of the one whom we follow. JF

All Saints' Sunday

Isaiah 56.3–8 or 2 Esdras 2.42–48; Hebrews 12.18–24; Matthew 5.1–12

Isaiah 56.3–8

(See Proper 15, pp. 218–19.)

2 Esdras 2.42–48

2 Esdras (also known as 4 Ezra) is a composite work. Chs. 3—14 were written in Hebrew or Aramaic around 100 A D as a response to the destruction of the second Jerusalem temple by the Romans 30 years earlier. The Semitic original is lost and the chapters are known only in translation, in Latin, Syriac and Ethiopic to name only three languages. The Latin version contains additional material in the form of chs. 1—2 and 15—16 which are often referred to as 5 Ezra and 6 Ezra respectively.

Chapter 2, from which today's reading is taken, is a Christian addition, probably dating from the second century A D. We therefore have the phenomenon of the Old Testament (Apocrypha) reading being later than the New Testament readings!

A comparison of the reading with parts of the book of Revelation (cf. Rev. 7.9–14) indicates that Revelation is the probable source for the material in 2 Esd. 2. However, 2 Esd. 2 is more explicitly Christian than Revelation in the sense that it features a young man of taller stature than any other, who places crowns on the heads of the martyrs (v. 45). He is later identified (v. 47) as the Son of God. In this reading the focus is arguably mostly upon the tall young man. In Rev. 7.9–14 the focus is more upon the martyrs. JR

Hebrews 12.18–24

(See Dedication, pp. 267–8.)

Matthew 5.1–12

(See All Saints' Day, pp. 272.)

The Fourth Sunday Before Advent

Micah 3.5–12; I Thessalonians 2.9–13; Matthew 24.1–14

Micah 3.5–12

Micah is an interesting prophet, who was active in the second half of the eighth century BC and who, coming from the provinces of Judah, saw things from a perspective critical of Jerusalem. It is arguable that in ch. 2, he severely criticizes the forced militarization of his part of the country as Jerusalem prepared for the Assyrian invasions from around 715 BC.

The set passage contains some of the most bitter denunciations of Jerusalem and its rulers found anywhere in the Old Testament. Verses 5–8 target the professional prophets who, like modern 'spin doctors', were employed to put a fine gloss on events, but whose message could be influenced by personal gain (v. 5). They are told that their alleged sources of information will dry up, while only the true prophet will be empowered to tell the truth (v. 8).

Verses 9–12 are directed against the rulers of the people. While they invoke the traditional reassurances of Zion theology, that God is with them (cf. Ps. 46.7, 11) they in fact build Zion with blood (i.e. the lives of innocent people put to death) and Jerusalem with wrong (e.g. the oppression of the poor).

Micah's final word (v. 12) is that Jerusalem will be destroyed and never rebuilt. This is the implication of saying that the 'mountain of the house' (i.e. where the temple stands) will become a wooded height, for it will take years for the trees to establish themselves and reach maturity.

In one sense Micah was right and in another he was wrong. The temple was destroyed (over a century later) but it was rebuilt. However, the value of his words lies in their alternative view of things. If it is right that Micah was a contemporary of King Hezekiah (cf. Jer. 26.18–19) he fiercely criticized a monarch and period that are highly praised in 2 Kings 18–19. 'The Lord was with him [Hezekiah]; wherever he went he prospered' (2 Kings 18.7). This is a far cry from Zion being built with blood! It is a reminder that people at the centre of things, including the churches, may often see things less clearly than those working at the margins. Advent may be a time to pay especial attention to their voices. JR

I Thessalonians 2.9–13

This reading continues Paul's recollections, begun in 1 Thess. 1.2, of his earlier stay in Thessalonica. Paul writes, however, not simply to preserve a record of this experience or to reflect on it for himself. His recollections carry within them an exhortation to the Thessalonians to continue in the faith to which they have been called. Much as a teacher or parent uses praise for positive reinforcement, Paul uses memories of his visit with the Thessalonians to introduce issues about which he has some instruction to offer. The eschatological issue that comes to the foreground in ch. 4 already slips into the conversation here in 2.16 and in 2.19 (compare also 1.10). Paul also introduces here the question of the behaviour of these former Gentiles (2.12–13), an issue that will come to prominence in 4.1–12. The relationship between Paul and the Thessalonians allows Paul to assert a powerful claim over their behaviour. How can they act in ways that contradict the gospel if they are Paul's own 'crown of boasting'?

The passage opens with a further remembrance of the apostles' behaviour at Thessalonica. The apostles themselves worked 'night and day' in order to provide for their own needs and thereby not burden the Thessalonians. Their behaviour was 'pure, upright and blameless'. Drawing again on the familiar language of 2.1–8, Paul compares the apostles to fathers, who treat each of their children with care, 'urging and encouraging you and pleading that you lead a life worthy of God'. Despite this appeal to the relationship between the apostles and the Christians at Thessalonica, it is essential that the gospel be understood as God's word rather than a human word (v. 13). What the Thessalonians received was not simply a relationship with Paul and his colleagues, but the gospel of Jesus Christ.

Standing behind the transition from apostle to gospel in v. 13 is the complex relationship between the world that is proclaimed and the agent of that proclamation. As is clear elsewhere in Paul's letters, he understands full well the role of the apostle or preacher. People respond to the integrity of that individual, and the response of believers to the apostles is their sole ground of boasting. The gospel does not find a hearing apart from the human agent who makes it known. Nevertheless, the apostle is simply an agent of the gospel and not the gospel itself. What the apostles proclaim is never their own action but the action of God in Jesus Christ.

What the Thessalonians received is God's word, and that word is now at work not only in and through the apostles, but in and through the Thessalonians themselves (2.13). Paul has already referred to the way in which the Thessalonians have become a form of proclamation (1.2–10). In the present passage he gives as additional evidence the fact that they have become imitators of believers in Judea, in the sense that the Thessalonians have experienced persecution at the hands of their compatriots as have Judean Christians at the hands of the Jews. BG

Matthew 24.1–14

In Matthew's arrangement, this passage immediately follows the lament over Jerusalem (23.37–39), which has evoked Jesus' protective love for the Holy City (like a mother hen with her chicks) and denounced the obduracy that murdered the prophets and is about to do the same to their successor. So we know how to take what follows: Jesus' prediction of the destruction of the temple is not vindictive; it implies no disloyalty towards Israel's history or opposition to the sacrificial cult (cf. 5.24); it is just the inevitable and final consequence of rejecting the Lord's Anointed (cf. 21.41).

As the disciples left the temple in Mark, they acted the part of tourists, gawping at its massive stonework: Matthew, always concerned to improve their reputation, casts them more as tour-guides pointing out the different buildings. For this evangelist, Jesus' prediction of disaster had already been fulfilled (cf. 22.7), vindicating both his words and his claim.

The private seminar that follows is on a different topic, an event that is still in the future, the second coming of Christ. The Greek word for this, *parousia*, literally means 'presence', and often refers to the retinue of courtiers or guards that create a presence around a king or general. So it comes to mean an arrival in state. The Messiah came first in humility, his return will be in power and glory, accompanied by an army of angels (cf. 24.30–31) who will bring this age to its 'consummation' in a new world.

The extent of the interval between the fall of the temple and the *parousia* is left unspecified, but it has been long enough already for Matthew's community to start developing its traditions and institutions. It will be marked by increased external threat and suffering, but also by internal division. Those who will come saying 'I am the Christ' (contrast Mark 13.6: 'I am he') may sound like usurpers of Jesus' role, but they do so 'in his name', which points rather to deviants within the Church who raise false hopes of the nearness of the *parousia* (see 24.23–26). The end is after all 'not yet' (v. 6): this is just the beginning of the birth pangs (v. 8). The latter phrase may hold out a little glimmer of hope, that the tribulation will ultimately bear fruit.

Matthew has already used Mark's description of persecution (in his discourse on mission, 10.17–22) and so here contents himself with a brief summary (v. 9), and he begins to look beyond present Jewish harassment of the Church to what will come later: universal hatred, apostasy and heresy. Initial enthusiasm will wane (when has it not?), love will grow cold (v. 12), but perseverance will reap the reward of salvation (v. 13) and the task for the Church remains a positive one amid all this opposition, to preach the gospel of the kingdom to all the nations (v. 14, cf. 28.19). JM

The Third Sunday Before Advent

Wisdom of Solomon 6.12–16 or Wisdom of Solomon 6.17–20 or Amos 5.18–24;
I Thessalonians 4.13–18; Matthew 25.1–13

Wisdom of Solomon 6.12–16 or Wisdom of Solomon 6.17–20

Wisdom 6 falls into two parts. In vv. 1–11 kings, judges and rulers are condemned. Because they owe their authority to God he will hold them to account if they have abused their power. The greater the power and responsibility, the more severe the judgement will be (vv. 5–6). Humans may be impressed by degrees of rank and greatness: this is not so with God. This condemnation then leads into the two selected readings by way of an injunction to rulers to desire God's words.

The main thrust of vv. 12–16 is the reciprocal relationship between Wisdom and her devotees. In reply to the question 'do the devotees seek Wisdom or does she seek them?', the answer is both, but with the greater emphasis on Wisdom's search. She makes herself readily available to those who desire her. However early they rise in the morning, she will be waiting for them (v. 14). In addition, she actively goes about looking for people who will wish to be her devotees, making herself known to them whenever and wherever she can (v. 16). Indeed, the passage is replete with the language of wooing, with the female taking the initiative. In the context of the whole chapter, the passage is as much a warning as a promise. Because Wisdom is so active in seeking devotees, it follows that the kings and rulers who are condemned in vv. 1–11 were not likely candidates for Wisdom; or if they were, they deliberately spurned her advances.

Verses 17–20 contain a poem in which the argument proceeds by way of steps from one idea to another, this type of argument being known in Latin as *sorites*. To desire Wisdom is to want *instruction*, instruction is a concern for *love*, love is keeping *laws*, keeping laws assures *immortality*, immortality brings one near to God, and thus a desire for Wisdom (the starting point) leads to a kingdom. What is meant by kingdom in v. 20? The GNB paraphrase 'Wisdom can prepare you to rule a kingdom' captures the sense, and refers the passage back to vv. 1–11. The statement that 'keeping laws assures immortality' (v. 18) raises the question of the translation of *aphtharsia*. In addition to immortality it can mean 'sincerity' (see Eph. 6.24) and thus several translations have 'incorruptibility' (so NAB, NJB; AV has 'incorruption'), which is probably to be preferred. JR

Amos 5.18–24

This famous passage in Amos has traditionally been understood to radicalize and invert the idea of the 'day of the Lord'. The concept has been linked to 'holy war' in ancient Israel, according to which the 'day of the Lord' would be a day on which the Lord of hosts (i.e. heavenly and earthly armies) would defeat Israel's enemies and restore her prosperity. One can compare the 'day of Midian' (i.e. the day of the defeat of Midian) in Isa. 9.4. Recent commentators have confirmed this approach. Amos takes an idea from popular and official (court) religion and utilizes it for prophetic language, prefaced by the word 'Alas', which was often used to introduce words of mourning for the dead. The desired day will bring not victory but judgement. The enemy against which God will fight will be Israel herself, and there will be no escape (v. 19).

Verses 21–24 are a separate speech in which Amos criticizes Israel's sacrificial cult. The words need little comment; their intention does. Does Amos envisage a religion of Israel without a sacrificial cult? Does he argue that the maintenance of justice is more important than the cult (v. 24)? The likelihood is that Amos was saying that the cult was, and would be, ineffective not per se, but because of the lack of justice in Israel. It is an Old Testament equivalent of the New Testament teaching that God's forgiveness is ineffective if those forgiven cannot forgive others. Without concern for justice and the poor and needy (Amos 2.6–8) the cult becomes an exercise in selfishness, and a denial of God's laws. This is as true of modern-day Christian worship as it was of the cult and society that Amos spoke against. JR

I Thessalonians 4.13–18

No passage in Paul's writings brings home more forcefully the urgency with which the first generation of Christians envisaged the return of Jesus, seen, no doubt, as part and parcel (indeed, in their eyes, the centrepiece) of the end – the triumphant culmination of God's work for the world and for his people. As no such return took place, subsequent generations have modified this belief in a variety of ways, some merely slackening the urgency, others transposing it to other modes, such as interior devotion to God or the Church, or to society's unending need for the remedy of its desperate ills. Always, however, there have been some to revive the belief in the imminence of the great consummation – with supreme disregard of common sense and history's lesson. More specifically, Paul was having to deal with a question which, presumably, he had not seriously thought would arise: what will happen to those of our community who have died since they accepted the gospel you brought to us – and the Lord has not appeared? The situation compelled Paul to think out an answer and to write out, in this the first of his surviving letters, his description of how things would turn out. (He was to repeat the exercise, with a few refinements, in the light of resurrection belief, in 1 Cor. 15.)

That picture naturally presupposes the prevailing view of the universe: as, in modern terms, small and describable, with God to be found just beyond air, firmament and heavens (cf. 2 Cor. 12.2). On the basis of such a picture, Paul offers a 'logical' answer to the difficulty, laying out the sequence of events that he sees as occurring one day, shofar and all (v. 16). The 'staging' comes straight from the imagery of Jewish apocalyptic, itself indebted to temple liturgy. It is, in other words, an adaptation, in the light of Jesus as God's Messiah and heavenly Lord, of Paul's cultural inheritance. Paul believes his solution to be informed 'by the word of the Lord' (v. 15), a claim which he does not elaborate: does it refer to Jesus or to God, and whence or how? (Supposing it to be really what Jesus said, some see Mark 13 as offering a clue.) The substantial warrant, however, is the death and resurrection of Jesus (v. 14), which form the basis of the hope that Paul affirms. Verse 17 leaves matters, literally, in the air: does Paul envisage, like Rev. 21, 'a new heaven and a new earth'? We cannot tell.

The passage's most lasting legacy is surely at the beginning: we are not to grieve like those 'who have no hope'; life 'with the Lord' is assured and, however it is seen, is the pearl of great price, the supreme gift of God. Ideas about programmes and details have always come, in numerous forms, and they come and they go. Rather than say nothing, Paul was doing his level best to say something that would help, using the best tools available to him. LH

Matthew 25.1–13

'Keep awake' – a watchword of early Christian preaching (cf. 1 Cor. 16.13) – implies both a lively hope for the imminent return of Christ and a concern for moral vigilance amid the corruption of this passing age. In the previous chapter, Matthew has illustrated this theme with the parables of the watchful householder (parallel Mark 13.32–37) and the servants waiting for their master's return (parallel Luke 12.41–48). Here he begins to ring the changes on the theme with the parable of the ten maidens. The wedding that these village girls are staying up late to watch is not a particularly 'religious' ceremony, but a kind of ritualized abduction. By night the groom steals his bride away from her family home, accompanied by his dancing attendants, the 'sons of the canopy' (cf. 9.15). By lighting the way to the front door of the couple's new home, the girls hope to be invited in to enjoy the continuing celebrations inside. But some are poorly prepared for their role. It is not quite clear whether their folly is the failure to take reserves of oil in the event of a possible delay (cf. v. 5), or the more extreme, almost comic, stupidity of taking no oil with them at all. Refused help from their companions, they rush off into town to buy some, but the delay is fatal, and comedy turns to tragedy.

Matthew was an allegorizer of the parables of Jesus (see 13.36–43), so the following correspondences are probably intended: the girls represent Christian disciples waiting for the return of Christ; the delay allows them time to accumulate the oil of good works (see Matt. 5.16), for without it, their faith alone cannot save them (cf. v. 11; 7.20f.). The exclusion is the loss of eternal life. But if this interpretation is correct, why do all the girls doze off to sleep (v. 5), since the moral of the story is 'Keep awake' (v. 13)? Maybe the realism of the underlying illustration here pokes through the allegory, or maybe Matthew could be acknowledging that all contemporary believers can expect to die (i.e. fall asleep) before the *parousia* comes. Nevertheless, their good works are safely stored in the heavenly treasury (cf. 6.20) and when judgement day arrives they will rise up (v. 7) to receive their reward.

One needs to remind oneself that the point of this severe warning is not to predict the number and fate of the damned, but to encourage the saved to respond to grace (the Bridegroom!) with the genuine luminosity of goodness. JM

The Second Sunday Before Advent

Zephaniah 1.7, 12–18; 1 Thessalonians 5.1–11; Matthew 25.14–30

Zephaniah 1.7, 12–18

The prophetic transformation of the 'day of the Lord' by Amos in the second half of the eighth century BC (see the Third Sunday Before Advent, pp. 278–9) from a day of expected victory over Israel's enemies to a day of judgement of Israel, is continued around a century later by Zephaniah. The opening words of the reading (v. 7) probably allude to a coronation banquet accompanying the enthronement of a king. On his day, the God of Israel will invite guests to his banquet, at which they will enjoy a sacrificial meal. The irony of the word 'consecrated' is obscured in the reading by the inexplicable omission of vv. 8–9, which provide the guest list in terms of officials who dress in foreign attire and those who practise violence and fraud. The guests will have an unexpectedly unpleasant time!

The reading resumes with a condemnation of those who are indifferent about the ways of God, who say 'The Lord will not do good, nor will he do harm' (v. 12). These will discover that the Lord will do harm to them. The language about their homes and vineyards (v. 13) should be compared with Isa. 65.21–22, where opposite sentiments describe a time of peace.

The description of the day of the Lord in vv. 14–16 is the most explicit connection of this idea in the Old Testament with the theme of war, from which the idea is probably derived. However, in vv. 17–18 supernatural images take over from those of battle. A war of God against Israel becomes something that will consume the whole earth and all its inhabitants (v. 18). On the face of it, this is grossly unfair, especially as the Old Testament is elsewhere quick to point out that sensitivity to God's ways exists outside the chosen people even if not within it (cf. the book of Jonah). Allowance must be made for poetic exaggeration of course; but there is a certain implicit logic involved. If God has chosen a people to be a light to the nations and that people produces darkness, the destruction of the chosen people and the nations may have to be a prelude to a new beginning. At any rate, the passage warns against neutrality, against the view that God will do neither good nor harm. JR

1 Thessalonians 5.1–11

The previous week's reading, from 1 Thess. 4.13–18, concludes with an admonition that seems to bring to an end Paul's discussion of the anticipated return of Christ. The present reading, however, takes up the topic once again. Paul knows, either from some inquiry on the part of the Thessalonians or from experience elsewhere, that the promise of Christ's *parousia* always prompts the question of time. If Christ is to return, when will that be and how can people make sure that they are ready for him?

For most people, the *parousia* will be sudden and its conquences unavoidable. It will come 'like a thief in the night'. Just as a thief enters the houses of those who believe themselves to be secure, so the 'day of the Lord' will break in upon those who take for granted that the ways of the world will continue without challenge. When that day does come, it will be inescapable, just as are the pains of a woman in labour. She can find no rest, no escape from her agony.

Paul does not here explicitly say that no one knows when the day of the Lord will be, a theme that is sounded elsewhere in the New Testament (Matt. 24.36–44; Mark 13.32–37; Luke 21.34–36; Acts 1.6–7). Indeed, 1 Thess. 4.13–18 seems to suggest that Christ will return during the lives of at least some among Paul's generation of believers. Nevertheless, the implication of 5.1–3 is that no timetable may be drawn up or predictions offered.

If Christians have no schedule by which to await and prepare for Christ's return, the coming of that day should still not catch them by surprise: 'But you, beloved, are not in darkness for that day to surprise you like a thief' (5.4). Christians belong to the light, to the day, and should be constantly prepared for the return of Christ. The metaphors of v. 8, with their martial imagery of a breastplate and a helmet, emphasize the need for constant readiness. In other words, for the Christian the answer to the question 'When will the day of the Lord come?' is always 'Now!'

The dualism that Paul expresses here exists in a variety of early Jewish and Christian literature, as well as in literature from the larger Greco-Roman environment. Its presence often troubles contemporary readers, who may hear in it echoes of racist or anti-Semitic or other forms of a rhetoric of exclusion, by which one group vilifies another to justify itself. While Paul's language in this passage can be twisted into such a rhetoric, it is important to see that the dualism in this passage serves to admonish the Christian to live a life of watchfulness rather than to vilify the non-Christian. Paul's interest in the passage lies in the way Christians understand and respond to the hope of the return of Christ rather than threatening those outside the Christian circle.

The Christian watchfulness and wakefulness that Paul advocates will sound strangely outmoded for a generation of Christians that lives nearly 2,000 years removed from Paul's letter and knows that Christ has not yet returned! But the watchfulness to which Paul urges Christians is not merely a matter of time. It is also a matter of importance. To watch for the *parousia*, even 2,000 years after its promise, is to confess that God stands both at the beginning and at the end of human life and that humankind remains accountable to God for its behaviour.

With vv. 9–11 it becomes clear that the question of time is not, in Paul's judgement, the most important question. What is really at stake in this passage is not so much when Christ might return as what that promise means. Verses 9–11 answer that question: Christ's return means salvation. God's will is to bring about salvation through Jesus Christ (cf. 1.10), and part of that will is that 'whether we are awake or asleep we may live with him'. As in the previous discussion of the fate of those Christians who have already died (4.16–17), the most important point for Paul is that Christians ultimately will somehow live with Christ. When that life is fully accomplished, how it is to be accomplished, and what it will look like – the answers to these questions lie beyond human understanding. What is important is the confident hope that Christian life culminates in God.

The end of this lection repeats and expands on the exhortation that concludes ch. 4: 'Therefore encourage one another and build up each other, as indeed you are doing' (5.11). The 'therefore' signals that this exhortation is not an independent refrain, tacked on to the end of Paul's comments but not substantially related to them. Indeed, it is *because* of their confident expectation that the present life in Christ leads to another and unending life in Christ that Christians are able to encourage one another. They also are to 'build up each other'. More characteristic of 1 Corinthians than any of Paul's other letters (cf. 1 Cor. 8.1, 10; 10.23; 14.4, 17), 'up-building' in this context anticipates the exhortations that will follow in 1 Thess. 5.12–22. Upbuilding also involves the general need for Christians to understand themselves to be profoundly connected with one another, so that the needs of others within the community are understood to be one's own needs as well. BG

Matthew 25.14–30

In the first-century world, a talent was not a natural aptitude but a weight (just under 100 pounds), and thence a heavy silver coin worth about 6,000 denarii, or 20 years' pay for a day labourer. To possess even one was beyond the wildest dreams of a peasant; to have eight to play with in investments, like the central character here, puts him firmly in the upper classes (cf. Luke 19.12 'a nobleman'). The talents are allocated to the three slaves unevenly, 'according to their ability'; so they represent (allegorically, for sure) not the basic gift of Christian discipleship (which all share equally, as at Luke 19.13) but different functions and levels of responsibility in the Church. To be entrusted with spiritual gifts is to be offered the chance of a rich reward in heaven, but also, if they are not put to productive use, the risk of fearful punishments in hell (cf. Matt 18.6), involving the grinding of teeth in sheer agony (cf. 8.12; 13.42; 13.50; 22.13; 24.51 for this favourite expression of Matthew's). The motif of an unexpected delay and a sudden return in the previous parable of the ten girls is missing here; the emphasis falls instead on the need for faithfulness during an inevitably long absence (cf. v. 19) that reflects the disturbing delay in Jesus' return.

This allegorical message so overwhelms the underlying parable that we no longer even notice the sharp edge of social critique which the original must have had. The master is not only fabulously wealthy, he also has a reputation as a 'hard man' in business. His so-called good and faithful servants manage to double his capital; how, we are not told, but a hint may be given at v. 26, through buying up the land of struggling smallholders, who fall into debt between seedtime and harvest and are thereby reduced to the status of tenants. The 'wicked and lazy' slave who, understandably in such company, has lost his nerve, is told that he should have put his master's money in the bank, without even a flicker of regard for the strict prohibitions against usury in Torah (see Exod. 22.25; Deut. 23.19f.). This parable, like several others told by Jesus (e.g. the labourers in the vineyard, Matt. 20.1–16, and the wicked tenants, 21.33–41) accurately describes the oppressive and sordid realities of daily life in Palestine but then leaps exponentially into a vision of the age to come. Would that we had the same dedication to labour for the kingdom of the poor (cf. Matt. 5.3) as the slaves of Mammon (cf. Matt. 6.24) have in the present kingdom of the rich! JM

Christic the King

Ezekiel 34.11–16, 20–24; Ephesians 1.15–23; Matthew 25.31–46

Ezekiel 34.11–16, 20–24

Kingship and shepherding had been closely associated together for centuries before Ezekiel uttered these words of consolation and warning soon after receiving news of the fall of Jerusalem in 587 BC (Ezek. 33.21). The shepherd's crook is found among the symbols of kingship of the Egyptian pharaohs.

Ezek. 34 begins with a fierce condemnation of the shepherds of Israel. This could mean both successive dynasties of kings as well as the rulers in office before the fall of Jerusalem. The shepherds are accused of using their sheep to their own advantage, of eating the fat, using the wool for clothing and of slaughtering the fatlings (v. 3). At first sight this is odd. Surely, sheep exist ultimately for the benefit of their human owners; and perhaps these words of judgement were meant to arouse indignation, to provoke the rulers into saying that it was surely obvious that people that were governed existed for the benefit of the rulers, and not vice versa. That might be a reasonable response from shepherds and rulers alike; but in God's view of this the shepherds exist for the sake of the sheep. In order to make this point more strongly, it can be said that in Ezek. 34, the shepherds should not appear to derive any personal benefit at all from having sheep. Theirs should be entirely a ministry of giving and caring.

It is perhaps because the divine view of shepherding and thus of kingship is that it entails unrewarded giving, that ultimately only God himself can fulfil the function perfectly. This is the implication of vv. 1–16 in the context of ch. 34.

In vv. 20–24 the image changes. No longer are shepherds condemned, but the fat sheep that have pushed, butted and scattered the weaker sheep. Among the sheep this may be a natural mechanism that enables the stronger to survive at the expense of the weaker. Such a regime is unacceptable to God, however. All members of the flock are equally precious, and those who are strong have no natural right to lord it over those who are weaker. Whereas vv. 11–16 envisage that God will be shepherd, vv. 20–24 speak of David as shepherd. This is an anticipation of the restoration of the royal dynasty of David, but under new conditions. The condemned shepherds will have included Davidic kings. The restored monarchy will be in circumstances in which God ensures that no more of the abuses of the flock will be possible. JR

Ephesians 1.15–23

(See Ascension Day, pp. 145–6.)

Matthew 25.31–46

The so-called parable of the sheep and goats is really a visionary 'apocalypse' of the last judgement – its figurative element is minimal, a mere passing comparison between the action of the Son of man (or King v. 34) in separating the saved from the damned to a shepherd settling his mixed herd down for the night (v. 32). Whether it is intended to reinforce the same message as that conveyed by the two preceding parables (the ten girls and the talents) or whether it widens the scope to make a wholly new point about the judgement of non-Christians is a scholarly dispute that has long affected its interpretation.

Is this passage a warning to complacent members of Matthew's community that their salvation could be in doubt unless they act with charity towards their needy fellow Christians ('the least of these my brethren', v. 40) or anyone else (cf. 5.46f.)? Or does it offer the prospect of salvation (or its opposite) even to outsiders, on the grounds that good works involve an implicit acknowledgement of 'Christ incognito'? Or third, is it intended to encourage Christian missionaries with the assurance that people who offer them hospitality and assistance will be rewarded, but those who reject them will be punished (cf. 10. 40–42)?

There are difficulties with every view. If the passage is speaking only of good and bad Christians at the last judgement, then 'all the nations' in v. 32 will be something of an exaggeration (cf. 28.19), unless there are a host of uninvolved spectators in this scene. Furthermore, the list of acts of charity is hardly comprehensive, and the absence of reference, for example, to care for widows and orphans (cf. Jas. 1.27) would be odd. If the passage offers the full enjoyment of salvation (v. 34; and not just a more lenient judgement, as at 1 Enoch 72) on the basis simply of good works, then it is rather out of line with what the Gospel says elsewhere about the importance of repentance and faith. Finally, the third explanation, though it can account for the acts of kindness as those particularly needed by itinerant preachers (cf. 2 Cor. 11.23, 27, 30) and chimes in with Matthew's 'churchy' sense of Christians as Christ's brothers and sisters, the reward they win seems over-generous and there is little else we can point to in this part of the Gospel to support such a limited interpretation.

Whatever view is taken, the main point is christological: Christ the Judge identifies himself with those who suffer, and love for them is service to him.

The Feast of Christ the King was instituted by Pope Pius XI in 1925, and it reflects some of the same ambiguities as the Gospel text. The theme of the Kingship of the Christ may, as originally intended, be a counterblast against the rise of neo-paganism and fascism; but it can also fuel a kind of Christian triumphalism. One answer to this problem is to recall that Matthew's Gospel is just about to move towards its narrative climax, in the hunger and thirst, nakedness, loneliness and imprisonment of the King of the Jews who reigned from a cross (27.42). JM

Harvest Festival

Deuteronomy 8.7–18 or Deuteronomy 28.1–14; 2 Corinthians 9.6–15;
Luke 12.16–30 or Luke 17.11–19

Deuteronomy 8.7–18

Two lifestyles are contrasted in Deuteronomy ch. 8: a prosperous one that will accrue from living in the land with flowing springs, abundant trees and minerals from which iron and copper can be obtained; and the lifestyle of the wilderness in which the Israelites depended not upon the natural resources of the land but upon God's special provision, as in the giving of the manna (cf. Exod. 16). The Israelites are warned not to suppose that the prosperity that they will enjoy in Canaan is the result of their own efforts, with the result that they forget God.

The rhetoric of the chapter relies on a certain amount of idealization. Life for subsistence farmers in the hill country of Judah and of Samaria was not easy, and famines are mentioned in the stories of Abraham, Jacob and Ruth as well as in prophetic warnings. On the other hand, groups that lived in the wilderness lived largely off the natural vegetation and other resources of the area, and they did not have to construct terraces, organize ploughing, sowing and harvesting, or arrange for fields to lie fallow more frequently than once every seven years. On the face of it, Deut. 8 has reversed what was actually the case, namely, that settled life needed much more organization and application than the mobile life of the wilderness.

We may detect in the rhetoric something of an antagonism that was widespread in the ancient Near East between the wilderness and settled ways of life. The simplicity of the wilderness, its closeness to nature and the virtues of independence, courage and hospitality that it engendered were prized above what was seen to be the idle luxury, corruption and injustice of life in cities (cf. Isa. 3.16; 4.1; Amos 4.1; 6.4–7). The God of Israel was a God who had come from the wilderness (Ps. 68.7–8) and who had revealed his law in the wilderness. The problem addressed in Deut. 8 is therefore how the Israelites could maintain honesty, simplicity and justice in reliance upon God in an environment that bred, and had bred in Israel's history, a disregard for God, and that produced in its turn a disregard for fellow Israelites. JR

Deuteronomy 28.1–14

This section, which cannot be interpreted in isolation from the whole chapter, sets before the Israelites the choice of blessings that will follow obedience to God's laws. For modern readers this may sound immoral. Is service of God that is undertaken in order to enjoy blessings worth the name? It receives sharpened focus in the light of the grizzly nature of some of the threatened punishments, omitted from the reading. These punishments far exceed the promised blessings. The latter occupy vv. 3–14 and are followed by curses in vv. 16–19 that parallel exactly the blessings of vv. 3–6. At this point the similarities end. The seven verses (7–13) that describe blessings are overbalanced by 49 (20–68) that detail disasters.

A striking feature of vv. 20–44 is their similarity at some points with the vassal treaties of the Assyrian King Esarhaddon (681–669). Whether these, and some more general, thematic similarities prove that the writer of Deut. 28.20–44 actually used a version of the Assyrian vassal treaties is a matter of opinion. However, at the least they indicate that Deut. 28 is to be seen as a Hebrew version of a type of literature well known in the ancient Near East at one time. A plausible case can be made for the view that, during the seventh century, the kings of Judah had been required to agree to an Assyrian vassal treaty similar to that known from the vassal treaties of Esarhaddon, and that a similar form was employed in Deuteronomy in order to articulate Israel's need for exclusive loyalty to God.

The subject matter of the chapter needs little comment. The real problem of the material is its apparent attempt to coerce Israel's obedience by the threat of dire punishment. No entirely satisfactory answer can be given to this problem for modern readers, but several points can be made.

1. The use of the treaty formula inevitably highlights the coercion factor.
2. Within the context of Deuteronomy, with its stress on the humanitarian treatment of others, particularly the poor and disadvantaged, the coercion takes on a different significance. God, as opposed to an Assyrian overlord, does not desire blind loyalty so much as humane and sensitive dealings with fellow Israelites. God's threats of punishment are directed against a nation that ignores social justice.
3. Other parts of the Old Testament (e.g. Ps. 73, the book of Job) make it clear that there cannot be a simple correlation between obedience and blessing, and disloyalty and disaster. The Old Testament at its most realistic knows that the righteous may suffer and the wicked may prosper. Faith and obedience then become things done for their own sake; yet they need the confidence that the universe is ultimately a moral universe, and this is certainly what the deuteronomic scheme of blessings and curses is meant to uphold. JR

2 Corinthians 9.6–15

The passage is suffused with metaphors redolent of a traditional rural harvest festival. Its theme is, however, something entirely different from the usual main focus of the occasion, and the preacher will need skill to move happily from the surface imagery to the message. With care, he or she will find both connections and a basis for challenge.

Paul is concerned with reciprocity in the communal life of Christians. It is one of his favourite and most characteristic doctrines and here receives extended and profound treatment. For Paul, the Church is in no way an association of like-minded individuals, happening to share an interest or an allegiance. It is a wholly intertwined society where exchange is the name of the game. Moreover, it is 'given': like the family and the nation, and despite appearances of personal choice, it is bestowed – in this case, by God himself.

The reciprocity operates at two levels. First, between God and his people. He is the sole source of all their good: 'his indescribable gift' (v. 15). Then, there is the interchange among believers themselves, with the generosity of one redounding to the advantage of another. In the background is the doctrine expressed elsewhere (e.g. 1 Cor. 12) in the imagery of the body.

At the same time, the passage is much concerned, like 2 Cor. 8—9 as a whole, with Paul's campaign to raise funds for the church in Jerusalem, which arose partly because he had entered into the obligation to do so (Gal. 2.10) but more deeply out of a sacramental sense of obligation due from Gentile converts to their Jewish patrimony (Rom. 15.25–27). The high-flown language has what might seem a predestrian objective: to stimulate giving. But Paul would not see it so; in 8.9, he goes so far as to root his money-raising in the very core of the gospel, the sacrificial coming of Christ among us. 'Harvest' turns to 'stewardship' – and never did the latter get so far-reaching and sharp a theological grounding. L H

Luke 12.16–30

On the one hand, the first part of this passage concerns a standard theme of 'wisdom' teaching (cf. Ecclus. 11.17–19; Prov. 28.11; Jer. 9.23): riches are a snare and it is foolish to trust in them. On the other hand, in the case of Jesus, it received special emphasis, taking it to the limits: property must be abandoned by those who will follow him (Mark 10.17–31; Luke 18.18–30). It lost its full sharpness in the urban churches of the Pauline mission and later, by reason of the practicalities of long-term Christian community existence in an urban setting; but the moderate and traditional form it receives here in Luke retained validity.

The teaching against anxiety (vv. 22–30) strikes a different note (in Matthew's parallel, 6.25–33, it appears within the Sermon on the Mount). Here, it is not that wealth is futile but that worry about even basic provision is unnecessary. In the setting of modern (and indeed ancient) poverty, this can seem hopelessly 'out of touch' or callously frivolous. But the context is the rather heady atmosphere of the early days of Jesus' mission, when the kingdom was dawning and the end was near. Meanwhile, of course one must abandon oneself to the divine providence. Even by Luke's time of writing, the teaching must have begun to be subject to a measure of sophisticated treatment; perhaps it was part of Luke's tendency to warm his readers' souls by depicting the time of Jesus and the first apostles as a kind of golden age (cf. Acts 20.29f.). Taken literally, it can lead to pure quietism and the sort of idleness or reliance on the labour of others that robust early Protestantism found so repellent. At a deeper level, however, it meets the teaching in the earlier part of the passage: whatever one's outward economic circumstances (and there can be further discussion of the morality involved in their style and level), all are transient, and dependence on God, and trust in his bounteous love is to be the single, underlying direction of the heart. L H

Luke 17.11–19

The message is the duty, both morally and theologically rooted, of gratitude to God – wholly appropriate to the celebration of harvest; though the fruits of the earth are nowhere in view here. In context, the story exemplifies once more Jesus' positive discrimination in favour of outcasts of society: for 'leprosy' (whatever precisely was meant in the way of skin diseases) was accounted ritually unclean (Lev. 13) and a ground for exclusion from ordinary social intercourse – probably more for its abnormality than for medical reasons.

The gratitude of the single Samaritan further accentuates the theme of Jesus' indiscriminate welcome, and highlights the location of the positive response to him, anywhere but in mainstream Israel. The story has its eye on the future situation of the Christian mission, of which Luke was the narrator; and this concern leads Luke to a failure in realism, for no Samaritan could surely report to the Jerusalem priesthood to certify recovery (v. 14; cf. Mark 1.40–45, perhaps a prototype for this story). As often, Luke's Gospel shadows what is to come in his second volume.

In Acts 1.8, we read that Samaria, as schismatically Jewish, is an early stage in the foreseen spread of the Christian mission, out from Jerusalem to 'the ends of the earth'; and Acts 8 describes this development in some detail. It is presented as a major move, marked by an apostolic visit from Jerusalem (so that it has the aspect of a centuries-long breach now, in the Christian movement, repaired: Jesus' healing work goes on); marked too by the Spirit's ratifying and empowering gift. From the Gospel of John (ch. 4) too we have evidence of early Christian interest in and accommodation of Samaritans. This is the practical face of early Christian universalism.

But gratitude to God is the theme: he is the giver of all good, including reconciliation of the estranged back to the human race as a whole – a gift which merits its appropriate and necessary response. L H

Biblical Index